That Noble Cabinet

Also by Edward Miller:

PRINCE OF LIBRARIANS:
the Life and Times of Antonio Panizzi

That Noble Cabinet

A HISTORY OF THE BRITISH MUSEUM

by

EDWARD MILLER, F.R.Hist.S.

Foreword by Sir John Wolfenden

Ohio University Press
Athens, Ohio

Published in the United States
by Ohio University Press, 1974

Copyright © 1974 by Edward Miller
All rights reserved

Printed in Great Britain by
Cox & Wyman Limited
London, Fakenham and Reading

ISBN 8214–0139–4

To my wife

Contents

List of Illustrations

Acknowledgements

THE author wishes to express his gratitude to Sir John Wolfenden, CBE, Director of the British Museum, for kindly consenting to write a foreword to this history, and to Mr K. B. Gardner, Principal Keeper of Printed Books, for his encouragement and advice.

He would also like to express his deep appreciation of the help received from the staff of the Director's Office, of the Departments of Manuscripts and of Prints and Drawings and of the Map Room and, as always, from his wife.

Grateful thanks are due to Her Majesty the Queen for her gracious permission to quote from a letter of George IV to Sir Robert Peel; to the Keeper of Western Manuscripts, the Bodleian Library, Oxford, to quote from the Journal of Sir Frederic Madden; to Mrs R. M. Dickinson to quote from letters of her father, G. F. Barwick, and from other papers; to Dame Kathleen Kenyon, DBE, to quote from letters of her father Sir Frederic Kenyon; to Lord Peel to quote from the papers of Sir Robert Peel, and to the Trustees of the British Museum to make use of the Committee Minutes, the official papers of Sir Anthony Panizzi, J. W. Jones, and other papers now in their custody, and for permission to reproduce the illustrations used in this book.

Acknowledgements are also made to the following for permission to make use of published copyright material:

Messrs Ernest Benn, to quote from G. F. Barwick, *The Reading Room of the British Museum* and from E. Nesbit, *The Story of the Amulet*.

The British Academy, to quote from Sir F. Kenyon's memoir of Sir E. M. Thompson.

The Clarendon Press, Oxford, to quote from *The Diary of John Evelyn*, edited by E. S. de Beer.

The Diary of Elias Ashmole, edited by R. T. Gunther.

The Correspondence of Thomas Gray, edited by P. Toynbee and L. Whibley.

The Controller, H.M. Stationery Office, to quote from various Parliamentary Papers, from Hansard, and from other official publications.

Editions Gallimard to quote from *Memoires de Casanova*, Bibliothèque de la Pléiade.

Messrs. William Heinemann Ltd to quote from *The Greville Diary*, edited by P. W. Wilson, and from Evan Charteris, *The Life and Letters of Sir Edmund Gosse*.

The Keeper of Public Records to quote from *The Calendar of Treasury Papers*.

Messrs John Murray Ltd to quote from Gordon Waterfield, *Layard of Nineveh*.

Messrs Putnam & Co. to quote from S. Mayes, *The Great Belzoni*.

The Society for the Promotion of Hellenic Studies to quote from vol. 36 of the *Journal of Hellenic Studies*.

The Trustees of the British Museum (Natural History) to quote from *History of the Collections contained in the Natural History Departments* and from Warren R. Dawson, *The Banks Letters*.

Messrs A. P. Watt & Son and to Mr Peter Newbolt to quote from Sir Henry Newbolt's autobiography, *My World as in My Time*.

Yale University Press and Messrs Methuen Ltd to quote from the Yale edition of Horace Walpole's correspondence.

Finally the author would like to pay a special tribute to Mrs Brenda Onatade for her cheerful patience and skill in typing and retyping his manuscript, and to Miss P. Smyth for her invaluable assistance.

Foreword

EDWARD MILLER has spent a life-time working in the British Museum. He is 'a Museum man' through and through, erudite, knowledgeable and urbane. Above all, he has a deep-rooted affection for the place and for its history, buildings, collections and scholarly functions.

All these qualities he brings together in this book, transmitting his enthusiasm and bringing the reader right into the heart of the Museum's life. His encyclopedic knowledge and his first-hand day-to-day experience combine to make a book which must remain for years to come the standard history of the institution he has served with such distinction for so long.

It is an astonishing story that Mr Miller has to tell, from the travail of the first beginnings through two hundred years of collectors, donors and excavators to the imminent changes of the present day. From his detailed and closely documented narrative at least four conclusions may be drawn. The first and most striking fact is the astonishing range and variety of the Museum's collections, which the specialist scholar or researcher may not always appreciate in the close attention he gives to one particular element in the whole. The range was even wider in the days before the Natural History collections migrated to South Kensington; and it says much for Mr Miller's sense of proportion that he can synoptically survey the whole of this panorama.

Second is the apparently haphazard and accidental way in which the collections have grown. In fact this is almost inevitable. It is seldom possible to know in advance when new material is going to become available, by gift or through the saleroom or by discovery. So it is not easy to pursue a planned and deliberate policy of acquisition.

Third, as the story unfolds it becomes more and more clear how much the Museum, over the years, has owed to private benefactors. It is sometimes assumed that acquisitions usually, or even invariably, are financed from public funds. It is true that the annual purchase grant from the Treasury has been substantially increased in recent years. But it is also true that without the gifts which have come from generous individuals or such collective benefactors as the National Art Collections Fund or the City Companies, the resources available to the public would be immeasurably poorer than they are.

Fourth, and perhaps most important of all, is the devotion, down the years, which the members of the staff have shown to the life and work of the institution. They have not agreed with each other on every point, but not one of all those whose names appear in these pages could be accused of indifference or disloyalty.

Mr Miller also provides implicitly the answer to the question I am asked almost every day, 'Who is the British Museum for?' Another form of the question is disjunctive, or even antithetical, 'Is the British Museum for the scholar or for the general public?' As this book clearly shows, it is for both, and for many other categories of person too, who occupy places on the spectrum between the world famous scholar at one end and the rampageous schoolchild at the other. The Museum has been likened to a postgraduate university, to a hospital medical school, to a country house and (once) to Battersea Fun Fair. Whatever else it may or may not be, it is an institution which is visited for purposes of work or pleasure or both by annually increasing numbers of people from every part of the globe.

I have mentioned 'impending changes', and Mr Miller's last few pages describe the setting-up of the new British Library. It has always been a distinguishing characteristic of the British Museum that the collections and the books have been within a few yards of each other under the same roof and under the same administration. Before long this arrangement will end, the 'Library Departments' will pass to the care of the British Library Board and a new building will arise on the south side of Great Russell Street to house them. Ties of tradition and sentiment will eventually be broken. But some such solution has long been inevitable. An inflexible building on an island site cannot for ever meet rapidly growing demands for growth and convenience; and there is every reason to expect that the new Library and the old Museum will collaboratively add to the opportunities which the unitary institution has for so long provided for millions of visitors.

It is fitting that Mr Miller's book should appear now, as the record of a noble past and the harbinger of a distinguished future.

The British Museum, 1972   JOHN WOLFENDEN

Author's Note

IN this book I have attempted to tell the story of the British Museum from the formation of the great founding collections until the present day, when this now venerable institution stands on the threshold of fundamental and far-reaching changes, which will radically alter it forever.

For within a short space of time, the British Museum as it has been known for well over two hundred years will have ceased to exist and new organisations, based upon it, yet developing along very different lines, will come into being. It is to be hoped that these bodies, the need for which was foreseen over a century ago by such members of the staff as Antonio Panizzi, and which will form the new National Library of which so many have dreamed, will not lose touch with the traditions that have been built up through the years during which the Museum has grown from being a nine-days' wonder, a mere 'cabinet of rareities', into one of the greatest institutions of its kind in the world.

Hitherto the Museum has retained something of the spirit of the private house in which it was once lodged and of the intimacy and essential friendliness that that entails – and sometimes, of the bitter feeling that now and then breaks out within a family. We still have a housekeeper and housemaids and not just cleaners; we still carry house-keys; our names and ranks are recorded in a house-list, and we enter and leave the Museum by the Front Hall, as did our predecessors in the days of old Montagu House.

It is this spirit of continuity, which I have endeavoured to stress throughout this book. One generation gives place to another and yet the Museum lives on, ever changing, yet, in a sense, ever unchanged.

Many works have been written about the treasures of the Museum, concerning wonderful objects of all ages and from every land. Such treasures have here been touched upon only incidentally and then for the most part in relation to those, whether members of the staff or not, who secured them for the Museum and thus for posterity. The purpose has been to show how the Museum came into being, how it grew and developed or, indeed, at times merely stagnated, to tell of those who gave their lives to its service and of what changes have taken place during the course of its long and honourable story.

When I first came to the Museum, well over thirty years ago, it was still fundamentally the British Museum of the later nineteenth century. There were many on the staff who had begun their careers under such almost legendary figures as Richard Garnett or Augustus Franks, and who, in their own youth, had served under men whose memories went well back into the middle years of the last century, into that stormy period of Museum history when Panizzi and Madden had struggled for mastery. Now changes come at an ever-increasing rate and the whole aspect of the Museum is continually altering. No longer is it true, as it was until quite recently, that many in the Museum had had a father, an uncle or a grandfather in the Trustees' service and had spent or were prepared to spend a lifetime in the same service. Then all knew each other, at least by sight, and, for the most part, to speak to. Now faces come and go with bewildering frequency and one scarcely knows the members even of one's own department.

Yet changes must come and are of course necessary. The Museum has always been a living, growing thing and has often pioneered new developments, such as the introduction of electric light in public buildings. It is as foolish to regret as to forget the past. The new age needs the improved services, which recent technological developments have made possible and which a more discriminating public rightly demands.

This then is the story of the British Museum, from its comparatively humble beginnings to the pre-eminence which it now justifiably enjoys, its name now known to a vast number of people throughout the world, whether scholars or members of the public, as that of one of the greatest of museums and libraries, one in which I have been proud to have spent my life.

December 1972   E.M.

CHAPTER ONE

The Beginnings

MUSEUMS are no new thing, a product merely of artistically sterile ages, which, unable to create masterpieces of their own, painstakingly collect those of earlier and more virile periods. In one form or another they have graced almost every civilisation, whether as collections brought together to illuminate the past and to inspire the present or as jealously guarded sanctuaries within which were preserved the relics of departed saints or heroes, together with the offerings of the pious.

The Hellenic world had many temples and famous shrines, crowded with sculptures, paintings and rare and curious objects, which, like the great libraries of Pergamum and Alexandria, were frequented by artists and scholars from the Greek lands and beyond. Indeed, it was not only paintings and statues which could be seen. Many natural history specimens were kept in temples, either from their reputed connection with the gods or heroes or else as genuine 'curiosities'. Thus the skin of a female gorilla was brought back by Hanno, the Carthaginian explorer, from one of his African voyages and hung up in the temple of the goddess Astarte at Carthage.

Though no institution in the ancient world exactly corresponded in its scope and purpose to the modern museum,[1] in Rome the finest collections, both private and public, resembled something of that kind. With more and more of the civilised world being overrun by its armies, a thriving trade in both antique and modern works of art rapidly developed to satisfy the demands of the growing number who had wealth and leisure enough to satisfy their artistic cravings or snobbish instincts. At first by pillage, but soon as a highly organised and lucrative business, the treasures of the Hellenic East flowed steadily westwards.

The Emperors, and the rich who imitated them, devoted much time

1. The 'Museum', founded at Alexandria by Ptolemy Soter in about 280 BC, was similar in scope and purpose to a modern university research institute. Its aims were entirely literary and educational, and about a hundred students were engaged on various projects. After many vicissitudes, it seems to have been finally abandoned in about 400 AD.

and energy to forming magnificent collections of pictures, statues and jewellery. That created by Hadrian at his villa near Rome, for example, was a veritable open air museum. Libraries, too, flourished. The first public library within the City was said to have been founded by Asinius Pollio, in 39 BC during the last days of the Republic, in the Atrium Libertatis on the Aventine Hill.[1]

In the course of the following century, Augustus and his successors generously endowed great libraries at their own expense.[2] It became more and more widely recognised that both libraries and collections of statues and other objects of artistic importance should be made freely available to scholars and, indeed, to the general public. With the decay of the official state religion, the temples themselves became, to an ever increasing extent, virtual museums of fine and applied art, open to all comers. Never again, until the eighteenth century, would the ordinary man have such chances to see so freely great collections of masterpieces as the citizens of Imperial Rome.

With the downfall of the ancient world, all this vanished. Libraries it is true, survived, much reduced in size, in monasteries and cathedrals, but only very gradually did the idea of a museum, as a collection of beautiful objects, valued both for their own sake and for the lessons they taught, re-emerge from the chaos of the Middle Ages.

The first signs of such a thing appear in the 'treasuries' attached to every great ecclesiastical establishment. Enriched by the gifts of monarchs, these became storehouses of works of art, maintained and enlarged over the centuries, but, except on great public and religious occasions, they were seen by few. Nevertheless, it was in such places throughout Europe that much was preserved which otherwise might have been lost for ever.

With the passing of the Middle Ages, there came a renewed interest in the antique world and in its artistic achievements. Wealthy men once again formed collections, both for their own pleasure and for the edification of such artists and men of letters as they deigned to honour. Even in the later Middle Ages such connoisseurs were not unknown. In fifteenth-century France, for instance, the Duc de Berri was the en-

1. Gaius Asinius Pollio, 76 BC–5 AD, was a friend and follower of Julius Caesar and, subsequently, of Antony. During the reign of Augustus, he devoted himself to literary pursuits, in particular, to history and criticism. He wrote a history of the Civil Wars, now lost.

2. Augustus founded two libraries, one on the Porticus Octaviae, in the Campus Martius, the other on the Palatine. Both were closely connected with temples.

lightened owner of many incomparable treasures, including the famous *Très Riches Heures*, (now at the Musée Condé at Chantilly).

But it was above all in Italy that the idea of a museum once more flourished. At both Venice and Florence, remarkable collections were formed, notably that assembled by the Medici in Florence from the middle of the fifteenth century onwards. At Rome, the resplendent and cultivated Popes of the High Renaissance were not far behind. In 1471, Sixtus IV created a museum of antiquities on the Capitoline Hill, which included amongst its exhibits the famous bronze she-wolf of Rome. Early in the following century, the Belvedere Gardens were designed by Pope Julius II to house an open air museum of classical statuary. The other states of Italy were not to be outdone. At Sabbioneta, near Mantua, there yet stands the oldest existing building specifically erected as a museum. Built between 1580 and 1584 by a branch of the Gonzaga family, it is still used for its original purpose.

Ten years before this, Duke Francis I of Tuscany had begun to turn the building constructed in Florence by his father to house government offices into a museum and art gallery. Thus was founded the famous Uffizi Gallery. His successor, Cosimo I, formed a collection devoted mostly to specimens of natural history, both originals and casts. Minerals and gems of every description were included in it, together with numerous botanical and zoological drawings. In addition, there were many rare objects from the Americas and from the arts and crafts of primitive and savage men.

By the end of the sixteenth century, the great European collections, such as that of Ferdinand of Hapsburg at Innsbruck, might well contain classical Chinese paintings or bronzes from Benin, as well as such curiosities as the hand of a mermaid or the bones of giants drowned by Noah's flood.

It was soon the custom for many museums and galleries to be no longer the exclusive preserve of their owners, whether princes, or great noblemen, but to be made available to all members of, at least, the educated public. Intending travellers would be told what collections were worth visiting and during what hours it would be possible to view them. Some museums charged their visitors a modest entrance fee; others displayed near the entrance rules and regulations to govern the conduct of such as came to gaze upon their treasures.

A trade in both genuine and spurious antiques developed. Ships' captains were charged to bring back from their voyages any strange object that they might come across, and the digging up of relics of the past was everywhere pursued with sometimes misguided zeal. To satisfy the demands of both the learned and curious, basilisks, for instance – fabulous reptiles hatched from cock's eggs – were created by the judicious manipulation of a small ray, skilfully provided with the necessary wings, claws, fierce eyes, and forked tongue; mermaids put together from the head and shoulders of a monkey, neatly attached to the body of a fish or, perhaps, dead rats transformed into the likeness of young dragons. Amsterdam now became the centre of a more reputable trade in pictures, frequent exhibitions being held there at which prospective buyers might view the paintings and place their orders.

It was thus in northwestern Europe rather than, as hitherto, in Italy that, the great collections were being formed during the seventeenth century. In France, those founded by Cardinal Mazarin, a *collectioneur maniaque* if ever there was one, and his great successor, Colbert, were to constitute the basis of the future national museums. In England, Charles I brought together one of the outstanding collections of paintings of all time, containing not only masterpieces of the High Renaissance, but many contemporary paintings from the Netherlands and elsewhere. Its wanton sale and dispersal between 1650 and 1653 under the Commonwealth was a major tragedy, both for England and for the whole world of art.

Thomas Howard, 21st Earl of Arundel, was a collector of even wider tastes than his royal master. His superb collection of antique statues, gems, coins, vases, pictures and manuscripts, was the fruit of many journeys to Italy during a period of more than thirty years. Displayed at Arundel House in the Strand, it consisted of 37 statues, 128 busts, 250 inscribed marbles, such as altars, and many pictures, in particular a number by Holbein. The greater part of these were inherited by his grandson, Henry Howard, afterwards sixth Duke of Norfolk. At Evelyn's request, in 1667 he gave to the University of Oxford 'those celebrated & famous Inscriptions Greeke and Latine . . . whatever I found had inscriptions on them that were not Status'.[1]

At the same time, Howard presented to the Royal Society the Earl's library and such manuscripts as were not reserved for the College of Arms, to whom were sent all manuscripts relating to genealogy or kindred subjects.

Of the statues, some, for a while, were preserved at Tart Hall, a residence built by Nicholas Stone for the Countess Alathea, Arundel's widow, situated 'without the gate of St James' Park near Buckingham

1. Evelyn, *Diary*, edited by E. S. De Beer, vol. 3, pp. 495, 6.

House'.[1] These were sold in 1720 for £6,355. Dr Mead, the collector, bought there the famous head of Homer, which eventually came to the British Museum. Others were noticed by Stukeley in the collection of Sir Francis St John, at Thorpe near Peterborough. Many of the statues, however, especially the mutilated ones, had been carried off across the Thames by Boyder Cuper, the Earl's gardener, to ornament his notorious pleasure gardens at Lambeth.

Most of the pictures were sold by the seventh Duke in 1685 and 1691. The cameos and gems were taken away by his Duchess, on leaving him in 1685. Twenty years later she bequeathed them to her second husband, Sir John Germain, whose widow, in turn, bestowed them on Sir Charles Spencer and the Duke of Marlborough. The coins and medals, brought by the Earl of Winchelsea, were sold at his death in 1696.

Arundel was among the first to realise the importance of Asia Minor and of Greece as sources for the treasures of the Ancient world. His agents scoured the confines of the Ottoman Empire, as well as Italy, Germany and the Netherlands, to add more treasures to his collections. He even dreamed of bringing back to England the remains of the Mausoleum, the great tomb of King Mausolus erected at Halicarnassus in 353 BC, a feat which was finally accomplished two hundred years later.

After the death of the Earl in 1646, the collection, which had long remained at Arundel House in the Strand and there made available to scholars, suffered greatly from the indifference and neglect of his heirs and successors. John Evelyn describes vividly the state in which he found them: 'These precious Monuments, when I saw miserably neglected & scattered up & downe about the Gardens & other places of Arundell-house & how exceedingly the corrosive aire of London impaired them, I procured him [Henry Howard] to bestow on the Universite of Oxford'[2]. What was left of the library was eventually given to the infant Royal Society by Arundel's grandson in 1667, whilst the inscribed stones – the celebrated Arundelean Marbles – went to the University of Oxford. The statues were for the most part lost, broken up for rubble or otherwise disposed of. The antique gems and cameos passed into the family of the Duke of Marlborough and eventually little was left of this once incomparable collection. The manuscripts, however, were destined to form part of the national collections, being

1. Horace Walpole, *Anecdotes of Painting in England*, vol. 2, p. 153.
2. Evelyn, *Diary*, vol. 3, p. 495.

sold by the Royal Society to the British Museum in 1831 and 1832 for
the sum of £3,559.

Within a few years of Arundel's death, a further collection was
being formed on a far humbler scale, which was to survive to become the
nucleus of one of the great museums of Europe. This was the collection
of rarities put together by John Tradescant the elder, commonly known
as 'Tradescant's Ark'. Located at Lambeth, it was the first popular
museum in England and the first to be so called, *Museum Tradescantiarum*
in the title of a catalogue of it published in 1656.

The elder Tradescant, who died about 1637, was said to be of
Flemish or Dutch extraction, but this is considered doubtful, the name
being almost certainly of English origin. A skilful gardener, he had
travelled extensively throughout Europe including Russia and the
Aegean and in North Africa. After being gardener to the Duke of
Buckingham, he entered the royal service in about 1627 and it seems
to have been then that he set up his museum in his house at South
Lambeth. At his death, the 'Ark' passed to his son, John Tradescant the
younger, who with the aid of Elias Ashmole and other antiquaries,
greatly enlarged it. Having lost his only son, Tradescant decided to
leave the collection to Ashmole. On the former's death in 1662,
Ashmole, after considerable litigation, acquired both the 'Ark' and his
old friend's house at South Lambeth, a result so distressing to Tradescant's widow that she drowned herself in a pond. In 1677 Ashmole, then
aged sixty, offered the whole of the collections, both those of the
Tradescants and his own, to the Oxford University, on condition that
the authorities provide a special building, specifically designed to house
them. Unfortunately, before they could be transferred many of the
books and coins were destroyed by fire. In his diary Ashmole describes
what then happened: 'I began to put up my rarities in cases to send to
Oxford' and finally on 14 March 1683 'The last load of my Rarities
was sent to the barge this afternoon I relapsed into the gout.'[1] In 1683
the new museum was opened in a small house in Broad Street by the
Duke of York, later James II, with Dr Robert Plot as its first Keeper.
But it was not in provincial Oxford, but in the capital, London, that
the greatest museum of all was to be founded, a museum which, moreover, would eventually house one of the greatest collections of books in
the world.

Libraries in England had been strangely neglected. Despite her
great wealth and growing political and commercial ascendancy, she had

1. Ashmole, *Diary*, pp. 123, 4.

for long almost nothing to compare with the libraries of far lesser powers.

In Italy great libraries, both public and private, had flourished since the middle of the fifteenth century. In the semi-barbarous, parvenu kingdom of Prussia, a national library had been opened at Berlin by the Great Elector, Frederic William, in 1661 and then, almost at once, made public, whilst in Paris the Bibliothèque du Roi was one of the glories of civilised Europe. By the time of the Revolution it contained over 300,000 volumes, besides a great collection of medals and coins, which had been added to it during the seventeenth century. In 1735 it was finally opened to the public. Already its rival the Mazarin Library, only slightly smaller, had been opened in 1643 and once more in 1691.

Great libraries had long been established in Vienna, Munich and other cities throughout Europe, but in England, the position was far otherwise. Outside the ancient universities, the cathedral libraries, and the specialised collections of the Inns of Court and of the Royal Society, there was little opportunity for one not a member of a learned profession or the client of a wealthy patron to gain access to the books he needed. During the seventeenth century a few small public libraries had been founded, such as that opened at Norwich in 1608, at Bristol in 1615, or the library founded by Archbishop Tenison[1] at St Martin in the Fields in London in 1684, and which was, apart from the mainly theological libraries of Sion College and of Dr Williams, the sole public library in the capital for many years. For a poor and friendless youth, such as the young Samuel Johnson, there was little to do but haunt the shops of sympathetic booksellers.

Even at the end of the eighteenth century, Gibbon complained

1. Thomas Tenison (1663–1715), later Archbishop of Canterbury, founded a library for the use of the inhabitants of his parish of St Martin in the Fields. After his death, no funds were available to extend it and it became increasingly neglected. In February 1845, the Rev. Philip Hale, its librarian, complained to Sir Frederic Madden, Keeper of Manuscripts at the British Museum, that by then the parishioners had turned it into a mere newspaper library. He suggested that the library, or at least the manuscripts, might be incorporated with the Museum collections. When Madden and Josiah Forshall, the Secretary to the Trustees, inspected the Tenison Library, they found the manuscripts to be 'in a filthy, dirty condition'. According to Hale, the Tenison trustees were' for the most part only respectable tradesmen' and would willingly agree to the transfer. (*Madden Journal*, 8 and 17 February 1845.) The deal, however, seems to have fallen through, presumably owing to the Trustees' lack of interest in old manuscripts. In July 1861 the library was at last sold for the benefit of the school, which Tenison had likewise founded, for nearly £2,900.

bitterly of the lack of proper library facilities in London, though, by that time, the British Museum was well established. Museums, indeed, of a kind there were; cabinets of curiosities for the entertainment, rather than for the instruction of the public, as for example in the Chelsea coffee house run by John Salter. This, founded in 1695, was situated at what is now 18 Cheyne Walk and was a well-known London sight. Salter, whose nickname 'Don Saltero' was given him by one of the establishment's habitués, Admiral Sir John Munden, was said to be an old servant and compatriot of the physician and collector, Sir Hans Sloane, and his coffee house was filled with numerous objects, many of which came from his former master's collections. 'Mr Salter's collection of curiosities' was very popular and is referred to by such contemporaries as Steele, Swift and Benjamin Franklin. Steele in the *Tatler*, no. 34, is sarcastic as to the worth of Salter's exhibits. 'There is really nothing, but, under the specious Pretence for Learning and Antiquity, to impose upon the World'. This criticism is borne out by the *Catalogue of the Rarities to be seen at Don Saltero's Coffee House*, first issued in 1729, which went through numerous editions up to the end of the eighteenth century. It contains particulars of many odd and amusing 'curiosities' which the proprietor had collected 'for the Delight of the Publick', such as the Queen of Sheba's Fan and Cordial Bottle, Robinson Crusoe's and his Man Friday's shirt, the Four Evangelists cut on a cherry stone, a curious Ball of Fishbones found near Plymouth, and Pontius Pilate's Wife's Chambermaid's Sister's Sister's Hat. It seems improbable that all of these came from Sloane's own collection. The 'museum' was sold by auction in 1799 and its contents dispersed.

In none of these could one find high standards of scholarship, nor was there anywhere where the public, learned or not, could study and make use of the accumulated treasures of the past.

This state of affairs had long been deplored by thoughtful men. A few of the treasures of the monastic libraries dispersed at the Reformation had been saved by such men as Leland and Archbishop Parker and a generation or so later the first attempts were made to make books and manuscripts more freely available to scholars. In the middle of the sixteenth century the astrologer and reputed magician, John Dee, had vainly petitioned Mary Tudor to found a library, whilst later a group of scholars, amongst them Camden and the young Robert Cotton, had addressed a similar request to her sister Elizabeth. Despite their pleas and an elaborate scheme for the governance of this 'Library of Queen Elizabeth', which they had drawn up, nothing came of the proposal, nor is it certain that the petition was even delivered to the Queen.[1]

It may be that this failure to establish a national repository for the many precious manuscripts and books of which carelessness and blind fanaticism were already taking their toll induced Cotton to set about the formation of his own incomparable collection.

From the middle of the seventeenth century onwards, with the rise of a spirit of sceptical toleration, at least in intellectual circles, the possibility of the foundation of a national library in England became once more a subject of earnest discussion. In 1697 a proposal was made to refound the Royal Library, then under the care of Richard Bentley, and to have it properly endowed by Act of Parliament. Ten years later, in 1707, it was urged that the Library of the Royal Society, now enriched by the Arundel collection of manuscripts, should be joined to the Royal Library, together with the Cottonian manuscripts, then sharing with the Royal Library most inadequate and unsuitable quarters in old Cotton House, to form the nucleus of a national collection.

In 1743 Thomas Carte, a non-juring historian, stated: 'There is not a great City in Europe so ill provided with Public Libraries as London'. He went on to suggest that 'a gallery, or range of rooms for a Library' should be built on the top floor of the Mansion House, the official residence of the Lord Mayor of London. In these rooms should be placed, first of all, the manuscripts which had been collected by the two Harley Earls of Oxford and which, following the death of the second Earl, were at that moment in imminent danger of dispersal, a fate which had already overtaken the equally valuable collection of printed books. Carte points out that 'the late Earl designed it for public use', and would have been delighted to think that his collection should form part of a national library. To finance the project, Carte, knowing the parsimony of a Parliament which had left the Royal and Cottonian collections to be neglected in grossly unsuitable premises for many years, suggested that each of the twelve great City companies should contribute £2,000. The Harleian manuscripts might be bought for £20,000, and the rest of the money used to purchase books in all languages relating to trade, the arts and sciences, 'as well as the History and Antiquities of

1. Dee's petition to Queen Mary to found a royal library to counteract 'the spoil and destruction of so many and so notable libraries' is B. M. Cotton MS. Vitellius C.vii.b. 310, whilst the petition of Cotton and his friends to her sister is Cotton MS. Faustina E.v. ff. 67, 68. The petition suggested that the library be erected in some convenient place, such as the Hospital of the Savoy or St John's, Clerkenwell.

this Nation' and of her neighbours.[1] Nothing, unfortunately, came of this proposal.

Before telling of the events that led up to the foundation of the British Museum, we must go back and say something of those individual collections which were eventually to come together to form the basis of that great institution. The first of these was the Cottonian library. Sir Robert Cotton, or Sir Robert Bruce Cotton as he himself preferred to be called, to mark his descent from the mediaeval kings of Scotland, was born on 22 January 1571 at Denton in Huntingdonshire. He was educated at Westminster, where he came under the influence of the antiquary William Camden,[2] the second master, who became Cotton's lifelong friend. After taking his BA at Jesus College, Cambridge, in 1585, he became a member of the circle of learned men, deeply interested in the study of the mediaeval past, who were associated with the newly formed Society of Antiquaries.

Now settled in Westminster, close to Old Palace Yard, Cotton set himself the task of assembling the finest possible collection of manuscripts, miscellaneous coins and other antiquities in the fields of English history, literature and related subjects. It is therefore in these departments that the Cottonian library is richest. To a great series of mediaeval chronicles and monastic chartuleries must be added an unparalleled collection of State Papers, both mediaeval and Tudor, as well as such priceless relics as the manuscript of *Beowulf* (the earliest epic poem in the English or indeed in any other Germanic language), the Lindisfarne Gospels, the unique manuscripts of the Middle English

1. The first proposal, in an anonymous pamphlet, was almost certainly made by Richard Bentley (1662–1742). It was entitled 'A Proposal for building a Royal Library and establishing it by Act of Parliament,' London, 1697. In it the author laments the decay of the Library since its great days under James I. 'But in the succeeding Reigns, it has gradually gone to decay, to the great dishonour of the Crown and the whole Nation'; the valuable collection of coins embezzled; 'the Rooms miserably out of repair and so little that it will not contain the Books that belong to it'. He therefore proposes that a large and up to date library should be built on the south side of St James's Park and that Parliament grant to it the necessary annual revenue. It could, he points out, be used also for the conferences of learned societies and would attract readers from all over Europe. The money spent in England by such visitors would more than pay for the expense of building and maintaining such a library.

The plans of Thomas Carte (1686–1764), are given in Nichols *Literary Anecdotes*, vol. 2, pp. 509–10.

2. William Camden, 1551–1623, schoolmaster, antiquary and Clarenceux King at Arms. He left many of his books and papers to Cotton. (Hearne's *Curious Discourses*, vol. 2, pp. 390–2.)

poems, *Pearl* and *Gawaine and the Green Knight* and, two copies of Magna Carta, as well as the bull of Pope Innocent III, accepting the kingdom of England from the hands of King John. All these treasures and many others might well have perished but for Cotton's continued efforts.

Already, by the end of the century, Cotton's reputation as a collector and authority on the records of the kingdom was firmly established. A dispute over precedence between the English and Spanish ambassadors at Calais was referred to him by the Queen's government for elucidation and settlement.[1] In 1599 Cotton accompanied William Camden on a tour to the north of England. Together they explored the antiquities of that region, in particular the Roman Wall, and brought from thence several Latin inscriptions.

On the accession of James, who obligingly addressed him as 'cousin' on the strength of their supposed mutual relationship, Cotton's fortunes at first prospered. He had attached himself to the party of James's powerful favourite, Robert Carr, Earl of Somerset. This, however, was soon to be Cotton's undoing. For a time all went well. On 11 May 1603 he was knighted; on 25 June 1611 he was created a baronet, the thirty-fifth to be admitted to that order, the establishment of which Cotton himself was said to have done much to bring about. In 1601 he had been elected to Parliament[2] and did useful service there in investigating the manifold shortcomings of the Navy. Cotton was now frequently consulted by both James and the Court, and his opinion widely sought on antiquarian matters. All this time his collection was steadily growing. He was always generous in making his manuscripts available to other scholars, either by lending them or by allowing them to be consulted at his house in Westminster. There is no doubt that he regarded his collections already in some measure as a public trust and was genuinely anxious to establish a library, which should, as far as possible, be of service to the nation.

Dark days were now to come for both Cotton and his library and he was to pay dearly for his association with Somerset. The latter,

1. The tract by Cotton dealing with this dispute, *A Briefe Abstract of the Question of Precedence between England and Spaine*, is in *Cotton Posthuma*, London, 1651, pp. 73–79.
2. Cotton seems to have been returned first for Newtown, Isle of Wight in October 1601 and thus sat in Elizabeth's last Parliament. In February 1603–4 he was returned for the County of Huntingdon, along with Sir Oliver Cromwell, uncle of the future Lord Protector. He was next a member in 1625, when he sat for Thetford in Norfolk, and in the following Parliament of 1627–8 he represented the neighbouring borough of Castle Rising. Both these seats were Howard property; Cotton was closely associated with the head of that family.

implicated through his wife in the murder of Sir Thomas Overbury in the Tower, appealed to Cotton for help. Cotton, most unwisely, now inserted dates on a number of incriminating letters. There is no suggestion of deliberate forgery. It was done quite openly, in order to clarify the sequence of these letters and thereby help to establish Somerset's innocence. In the poisonous atmosphere of those days, however, such conduct was, to say the least, foolhardy.

In the meantime Cotton had been accused of revealing state secrets to the wily Spanish ambassador, Gondomar, a charge which Cotton denied, claiming he had acted entirely on the instructions of the King himself. On 26 October 1615, Cotton was summoned before a Royal Commission and within two months committed to the custody of one of the City aldermen. His library and papers were searched. His dating of Somerset's letters was also now revealed, leading to the presumption that in some way Cotton was involved in the Overbury plot. For a time things looked very black, but in the middle of 1616, he was at last released from custody on payment of a fine of £500, whereupon he at once received the royal pardon. The rest of James's reign passed quietly, with Cotton in correspondence with statesmen, scholars and men of letters, advising the new favourite, the all-powerful Buckingham, or being consulted by Ben Jonson on intricate points of Roman geography.

But these peaceful days were not to last. Already Cotton's growing association with the Parliamentary opposition, with men such as Sir John Elliott, Selden and Sir Symonds D'Ewes, had brought him into marked disfavour with the new king, Charles I. Suddenly the blow fell. An allegedly seditious pamphlet, found circulating in court circles, was traced to Cotton's library. The work in question was *The Proposicion for Your Majesties Service . . . to secure your Estate and to bridle the Impertinence of Parliaments*, written by Sir Robert Dudley in Florence some fifteen years before. Sir Robert was the probably illegitimate son of Robert Dudley, Earl of Leicester, Elizabeth's favourite. Denied what he considered to be his just claims to the Dukedom of Northumberland and to the Earldom of Warwick, in 1605, he went into self-imposed exile. Having become a Catholic, in 1612 he sent to his friend Sir David Foulis the pamphlet afterwards discovered in Cotton's library, with the hope, it is assumed, of ingratiating himself with James I and being restored to his honours and estates.

Although Cotton himself denied all knowledge of *The Proposicion*, he was summoned before the Court of Star Chamber and his library ordered to be sealed up. He was soon at liberty, but his library remained closed to him. In vain he petitioned the king, complaining that his manuscripts were perishing by this enforced neglect and that the sealing up of some of his best rooms made his domestic life impossible. The anxiety and frustration of these months took their toll and the old antiquary, deprived of his precious library, pined away. 'They had broken his heart who had locked up his library from him', he cried. Told on his death bed that Charles was at last reconciled to him, Cotton exclaimed 'You come too late. My heart is broken'.[1] On 6 May 1631 Sir Robert died, his beloved library still unrestored to him.

His son and heir, Sir Thomas Cotton, now petitioned for the return of the manuscripts on the grounds that all the books and papers in the collection were the undoubted property of the Cotton family. The bulk of the library then seems to have been given back to Sir Thomas. New perils, however, faced the collection. During the Civil War and Commonwealth, it seems to have been in danger of being sequestered, since Sir Thomas was lukewarm in his support of the new government. The library was probably saved only by the intervention of Sir Robert's old friend, John Selden, who was now a power to be reckoned with.[2]

When quieter times came, Sir Thomas began in his turn to add to his father's collections and he likewise made his library available to scholars. In due course, he was succeeded by his own son, Sir John, the third baronet, who continued the family tradition of adding to the

1. An incident related by John Rowland in The Epistle Dedicatory to his *A Choice Narrative of Count Gondomar's Transactions during his Embassy in England* (London, 1659). Cotton's first remark is mentioned by Joseph Planta in his Catalogue of the Cottonian Manuscripts. (J. Planta, *Catalogue of the Manuscripts in the Cottonian Library deposited in the British Museum*. London, 1802. *Preface*, p. xi.)

2. The antiquarian, William Stukeley states that the library was in the country during the Civil War: 'His great grandfather [Bromsal], high-sheriff of this county, preserv'd the invaluable Cottonian library from plunder in the time of the Commonwealth, whilst it was at Stratton in this county [Berks] about anno.1650'. (*Itinerarium Curiosum*. London, 1724. vol. I, p. 74.) By a coincidence, it was at Cotton House that Charles I was lodged for his trial at Westminster Hall and where he spent his last night before his execution. Details of Charles's cruel behaviour to Cotton, at the instance of the favourite, Buckingham, are given in Sir Symonds D'Ewes Autobiography (ii. pp. 173–4). Strype, in his edition of Stow's Survey (London, 1720, book 6, p.55) thus describes Cotton House: 'In the Passage out of Westminster Hall into the old Palace Yard, a little beyond the Stairs going up to St Stephen's Chapel (now the Parliament House) is the House belonging to the ancient and noble Family of the Cottons: Wherein is kept a most inestimable Library of Manuscript Volumes, famed both at Home and Abroad'. Later in the eighteenth century Cotton House was restored and converted into a residence for the Chief Clerk of the House of Commons. (Planta, *Preface*, p. xii.)

collection and permitting eminent writers access to it. It was this Sir John who earned the gratitude of posterity and fulfilled his grandfather's dearest wish, settling the Cotton Library on an unappreciative nation.

By an Act passed in 1700,[1] two years before the death of Sir John, it was laid down that: 'the Cottonian Library . . . should be kept and preserved . . . for publick Use and Advantage' and that at Sir John's death the 'Ancient Mansion House at Westminster' – old Cotton House, where the library still was – would be vested in trustees, whose duty it would be to care for both house and collections; the family, nevertheless, was to have full use of the property, other than the room in which was the library itself.

Soon, however, all was found to be far from well. As the House of Lords pointed out in a petition to the Queen of May 1706, the apartment in which the books were kept was quite unsuitable for the purpose. It was both narrow and damp, with one window only at each end, the arch over one of them being so dilapidated that it threatened at any moment to fall down, as did the arch on which the room itself was built. Sir Christopher Wren was consulted. He was firmly of the opinion that Cotton House was now so old and ruinous that nothing could be done to save it, except by demolishing and rebuilding at least a substantial portion of it. It was far better, he declared, to remove the library altogether and house it 'over the ushers near the House of Lords'. Wren was scathing about both the Cotton and the Royal Library, now also in Cotton House. 'I confesse', he wrote, 'both these libraries may be purged of much uselesse trash, but this must be the drudgery of librarians'.[2]

Luckily the great man's advice was not taken, but in 1707 a further Act was passed to remedy some of the defects of the original legislation.[3]

1. *An Act for the better Settling and Preserving the Library kept in the House at Westminster, called Cotton-house, in the Name and Family of the Cottons, for the Benefit of the Publick.* Elkanah Settle celebrated the occasion in some uninspired verses entitled *The Muses' Essay to the Honour of that generous Foundation the Cotton Library at Westminster, as it is now Given to the Publick* (London, 1701).

2. Public Record Office. *Calendar of Treasury Papers, 1702–7*, pp. 204, 434, 476. See also CJ, vol. XV, March 13, 1705–6 and the photographs of Wren's report and plans at B.M. MSS. Facs. Suppl. IId.

3. 5 Anne c.30. '*An Act for the better Securing Her Majesties Purchase of Cotton House in Westminster*'. It received the Royal Assent on 8 April 1707. (LJ, vol. 18, p. 302A). Cotton had petitioned Parliament to grant him a sum of £5,000 for the house and grounds, threatening otherwise to demolish it and sell the land for building 'a Square which might contain Four and Twenty Houses', highly convenient for members wishing to reside close to Parliament. (LJ, vol. 18, pp. 156, 157.)

It was obviously inconvenient that a national collection should be lodged in part of a private house. Nothing had as yet been done to construct the separate entrance 'a convenient Way, passage and resort' envisaged in the Act of 1700,[1] and visitors to the library had first to pass through the Cotton family's drawing room. Despite the eminence of the trustees appointed by the previous Act, namely the Speaker of the House of Commons, the Lord Chancellor, and the Lord Chief Justice (or perhaps because of this) almost nothing had been achieved. This new Act plainly said as much: 'Very little hath been done . . . to make the said Library useful to the Publick, except what has been done lately at Her Majesties charge', and it warned that 'so great a Treasure of books and manuscripts so generously given for the Publick Service . . . [is] in danger of Perishing for want of due Care'.[2] It was now decided to purchase both Cotton House and the surrounding grounds from the present Sir John Cotton, grandson of the third baronet, for £4,500, and ultimately to erect there a new and spacious building to be known as the Cotton Library. Arrangements were likewise envisaged for the preservation and custody of the collections. Nevertheless, nothing was done for these priceless relics. The old house became ever more ruinous, the Commissioners of Works making the excuse, still familiar, that it was not worth undertaking any repairs, as soon a magnificent library would be erected to house both the Cotton and Royal collections, as well as many of the other public records.[3] Needless to say, this bright vision never materialised. In 1722, with Cotton House near collapse, the two libraries were moved to a rented building, Essex House, near the Strand. From there, in 1730, the collections were brought back to a third house, close to the first, Ashburnham House, in Little Dean's Yard.

1. PGA, 12 and 13, Will. 3, p. 296.
2. PGA, 5 Anne, p.297.
3. The state of Cotton House was notorious. Before the passing of the 1707 Act, Sir John Cotton in his petition to Parliament had drawn attention to 'the Straitness of the Place and ruinous Condition of the Building wherein the Library is now kept' (LJ, vol. 18, p. 156) and in the years which followed its deteriorating condition became ever more marked. In 1716 the librarian, John Elphinstone, complained to the Treasury that 'the Library is contained in rooms near adjoining the river and will perish by dampness if provision is not made for firing'. (*Calendar of Treasury Papers, 1714–19*, p. 213.) David Casley, Deputy Keeper of His Majesty's and the Cotton Libraries, reported three years later on 'the ruinous condition of the house wherein the libraries are kept', but that Mr Benson of the Commissioners of Works 'raised a doubt whether the repair belonged to them'. The Treasury merely noted that the repairs 'ought to be a publique charge' and did nothing. (*Calendar of Treasury Papers, 1714–19*, p. 469.)

The reason for their second removal, besides the Board of Works's unwillingness to pay the increased rent demanded by the landlord of Essex House, was that the latter was surrounded by other buildings 'and therefore in Danger of Fire and in other respects very improper'[1] for such valuable collections. It was tragically ironical that, shortly after its installation in Ashburnham House, the Cottonian Library very nearly did perish completely in such a conflagration as had been foreseen. On Saturday, 23 October 1731, at about two o'clock in the morning, Dr Bentley, the former Keeper of the Royal Library, who was staying at Ashburnham House with his son, the then Keeper, awoke to find a smell of smoke proceeding from the room below that in which the Cotton Library was kept. A wooden mantle tree lying across a stove chimney in this lower room had caught fire and soon the flames spread to the panelling and were threatening the room above. Bentley and his servants first attempted to put it out where it had started and so the evacuation of the upper room was delayed until it was almost too late. Seeing, however, what was happening, David Casley, Deputy Librarian of both the Royal and Cottonian collections, carried off to safety the most precious volumes. The learned Dr Bentley, in nightgown and great wig, stalked out of the burning building with the priceless Codex Alexandrinus from the Royal Library tucked under his arm. But more vigorous action was now necessary. Despite every effort, the fire continued to spread. The engines were unaccountably delayed, already the backs of the presses in the library were ablaze and the books themselves beginning to burn. On learning the alarming news, the Speaker of the House of Commons, Arthur Onslow, by far the most conscientious of the Cotton trustees, came across from his residence nearby and directed the rescue of the remaining volumes and ensured the safety of those already got out. It was quickly realised that the only way to save the rest of the library was to smash open the cases and to throw the books, some of them already charred or burning out of the window to the court below. Certain of the surviving books and manuscripts were carried into the room of the Captain of Westminster School, others into the Little Cloisters and, after the fire was extinguished, into the great school boarding house opposite the gutted and smouldering building. On the following Monday they were transferred to another building belonging to the school which had recently been erected as a dormitory.

So Cotton's library was now forced to seek shelter within the confines

1. *Calendar of Treasury Papers, 1729–30*, pp. 109, 170, 333. *Report from the Committee appointed to view the Cottonian Library*, &c. *Commons Reports, First Series*, vol. 1, p. 445.

of his old school. On the same day Speaker Onslow, together with his fellow Trustees, went to look at the books as they lay scattered on the dormitory floor. Thanks almost entirely to Onslow's own efforts, the damage was less than had first been feared. The Royal Library had escaped almost unharmed, though many of the Cottonian manuscripts had suffered badly, not only from the flames, but from the water. The Speaker at once appointed an expert committee to examine the manuscripts and to make recommendations for their immediate care and rehabilitation. By November, the work of repair was in full swing. There can be no doubt that but for Onslow's speedy action in rescuing and carrying off to safety the bulk of the two libraries and at once placing them in expert hands for renovation, the number lost would have been far greater. Of the 958 volumes of which the library consisted, 114 were considered to be totally destroyed, 'lost, burnt, or entirely spoiled . . . burnt to a Crust' in the Committee's vivid phrase,[1] and a further 98 damaged. Bentley himself is said to have lost some valuable manuscripts which he had been collecting for ten years for his Greek Testament. During the course of the nineteenth century, however, many of these badly damaged manuscripts, even some hitherto regarded as utterly beyond repair, were wholly or partially restored and rendered once more useful to scholars.[2]

1. *Report*, pp. 450, 452. The Report implies that Casley was mainly responsible for saving the Codex Alexandrinus and the other more precious manuscripts. The story of Bentley carrying it out in his nightgown is given in a letter by Dr R. Friend, an eyewitness, to Lady Sundon (Nichols, *Literary Anecdotes*, vol. ix, p. 592). Arthur Onslow (1691–1768), Whig politician. He was Speaker of the House of Commons from January 1728 to March 1761.

2. A certain number of the Cotton manuscripts were repaired at the end of the eighteenth century under the direction of Joseph Planta, then Keeper of Manuscripts at the British Museum, a fact he proudly recalls in the preface to his catalogue of the Cottonian manuscripts published in 1802.

When the Cottonian Library came to the Museum in July 1756, of the 861 surviving volumes, 105 were no more than damaged bundles preserved in cases, with 'evident marks that leaves had been purloined and some had been bound up with much irregularity and disorder . . . persons by whom they had been occasionally handled, having thrown them into great and, in many cases, irretrievable, confusion'. Planta, assisted by 'great care and dexterity on the part of the bookbinder', succeeded in restoring 51 out of the 105 damaged manuscripts and had the remaining 61 volumes boxed. Of these, some, though sadly defective, were still usable. The rest, 61 bundles, Planta considered to be 'irretrievable' and, in any case, were no more than 'obscure tracts and fragments of little or no importance'. These were then placed in 62 cases. (Preface to *Catalogue of Cottonian Manuscripts*, p. xiv.)

Later in the nineteenth century, two of Planta's successors as Keeper of

The Committee of the House appointed to investigate the fire and the subsequent condition of the Cottonian Library was also empowered to investigate the state of the public records as a whole. They found that for the most part they were 'in great Confusion and Disorder'[1] and much in need of care and attention. The Committee recommended that steps should at once be taken to rectify this sorry state of affairs and in particular that the Cotton Library should be properly looked after. In their opinion, a new building should be erected on the land vested in the Crown by the Act of 1707, which would be designed to contain, not only the Cotton and Royal Libraries, but also such of the public records as might readily be accommodated there.[2] Plans were drawn up, but, as usual, nothing further was done. It needed the public spirited-ness of another collector to force Parliament into a realisation of its responsibility towards the treasures of the nation's past and the needs of present and future scholars.

This man was Sir Hans Sloane, the virtual founder of the British Museum. Born in Killyleagh, Ireland in 1660, Sloane was for many years a successful physician, who, in his time, had treated such diverse patients as Samuel Pepys and Queen Anne, and who had been largely responsible for the development in this country of the practice of inoculation against smallpox and the popularisation of milk chocolate.

After a medical education in both England and France, he settled in London and at once moved freely in scientific circles, becoming especially friendly with the great naturalist John Ray and the eminent scientist Robert Boyle, 'the father of chemistry'. In 1687 he was invited to accompany the Duke of Albemarle, the newly appointed Governor of Jamaica,[3] as his personal physician. Sloane had already shown an

1. *Commons Reports, First Series*, vol. 1, p. 446.
2. CJ, vol. 21, p. 918.
3. Christopher Monck, 1653–1688, second and last Duke of Albemarle, only surviving son of George Monck, restorer of the monarchy in 1660. Sloane attended him

Manuscripts, Josiah Forshall and Sir Frederic Madden, succeeded in restoring further damaged manuscripts. In July 1838, Sir Frederic examined the bundles afresh. (*Madden Journal*, 17 July 1838.) He worked on this delicate and arduous task off and on for many years. On 3 April 1845 he noted that he was still engaged on it and, a little later, on 8 January 1848, remarked that he had got no thanks for all the work he had done, in contrast to the praise showered on his rival, Antonio Panizzi, Keeper of Printed Books, 'this Italian . . . who does nothing but walk about with his hands in his pockets has a fulsome panegyric passed on him'. (*Madden Journal*, 8 January 1848.)

interest in both natural history and the collection of 'natural curiosities', and having consulted his friends, decided to accept the appointment. He set sail for Jamaica in September 1687 and was away for some eighteen months, returning in May 1689. Though the Duke had died shortly after reaching Jamaica, Sloane had enjoyed his stay in the West Indies. He had taken the opportunity to extend both his medical and botanical studies and to bring back such varied live specimens as a large yellow snake, a 'guana or Great Lizard', and a crocodile. None of these pets seem however to have survived the long voyage home.

On his return, Sloane established himself as a fashionable physician. For a while he settled at 'The Lord Montague's House', a building which sixty years later was to become the British Museum and to receive within its walls Sloane's own collections. He soon moved to a smaller house which still stands, on the north side of Great Russell Street, in what is now Bloomsbury Place, and occupied it until 1742. Despite the demands of a rapidly growing practice and of a wide circle of friends, Sloane had begun to lay the foundations of his immense collections. His professional position was now assured. He had been one of the doctors summoned to attend the Queen during her last illness and in April 1716 was created a baronet by her successor, George I, one of the earliest cases of a hereditary honour being bestowed upon a medical man. Shortly afterwards Sloane was elected President of the Royal College of Physicians and, in 1727, President of the Royal Society.

Sloane's first collections consisted for the most part of the specimens which he had brought back from Jamaica and were used by him in preparing his accounts of that journey. In 1691 Evelyn visited 'Dr Sloane's curiosities', which then consisted of 'plants, fruits, corails, minerals, stones, Earth, shells, animals, Insects &c collected by him with greate Judgement'.[1]

Gradually Sloane added further collections, of plants, fossils and minerals and of zoological, anatomical and pathological specimens. He likewise began to lay the foundations of an extensive and valuable

1. Evelyn, *Diary*, 16 April 1691, vol. 5, p. 48.

in his last illness and gives a detailed account of it in Sloane MS. 3984. It seems to have been aggravated, if not caused by his intemperate habits. His widow later married Ralph Montagu, the builder of Montagu House, Bloomsbury, in which, some sixty years later, Sloane's collections were to find a permanent resting place. Sloane's account of his experiences in the West Indies were published in his *A Voyage to . . . Jamaica*, 1707.

collection of antiquities and 'artificial curiosities'. Amongst them were Roman lamps, urns, gems and inscriptions, Etruscan, Egyptian and Assyrian antiquities and a few of later date, together with oriental and ethnographical specimens. To these were added drawings by Dürer, Holbein and others. In 1702 the famous collection of William Charleton or Courten – 'the most noble collection of natural and artificial curiosities, of ancient and modern coins and medals that any private person in the world enjoys[1]' – bequeathed to Sloane in Courten's will, was joined to his collections. In time other valuable collections, such as those of Petiver and Merrett, were added. Sloane had likewise gathered together a considerable number of books and manuscripts, mostly in the fields of medicine and natural history.

The value and importance of Sloane's collections were now widely recognised and many scholars, both English and foreign, turned to him for advice or offered him further specimens which they hoped would interest him. He had in 1708 taken the house next door to No. 4 Bloomsbury Place, to give himself sufficient room to accommodate his ever growing museum.[2] However, to keep such rare and magnificent objects in an ordinary dwelling was somewhat unwise, as an attempt to set fire to Sloane's house in order to rob it in April 1700 had clearly shown.[3] While he pursued the busy life of a fashionable doctor and man of science, there was little Sloane could do. In 1714 he had purchased the old Manor House at Chelsea, built by Henry VIII, and henceforth divided his time between this pleasant country retreat and his busy London life. More and more visitors now called, amongst them Voltaire, Benjamin Franklin, and Linnaeus, together with such distinguished, more or less native celebrities as Handel, who outraged Sir Hans by placing a hot buttered muffin on a valuable book. The composer is said to have believed that Sloane's obvious annoyance was

1. Ralph Thoresby, *Diary*, 24 May 1695. William Courten, 1642–1702, naturalist. For many years he lived under the assumed name of Charleton.
James Petiver (1663–1718), botanist and entomologist.
Christopher Merret or Merrett (1614–1698), physician and miscellaneous writer.
2. In 1695 Sloane had taken one of the row of houses, then newly built, to the east of Southampton House, the immediate neighbour of Montagu House, on the north side of the continuation of Great Russell Street, as it goes towards what is now Southampton Row. In 1708 he likewise rented the adjacent house in Bloomsbury Place and a large area of ground beyond the gardens of both houses, for the purpose, it is assumed, of growing medicinal herbs and other plants.
3. *An Account of the Apprehending, and Taking of John Davis, and Phillip Wake for setting Dr Sloan's House on Fire, to Robb the same, etc.* (London, 1700.)

institutions he regarded as distinctly unsatisfactory for his purpose. He particularly wished them to remain undivided, as they might not have done had they been left to the Royal Society, interested primarily in the scientific collections. He also wanted them to stay 'chiefly in and about the City of London . . . where they may, by the great confluence of people, be of most use'.[1]

He therefore devised a scheme whereby an institution which would look after his collections in a proper fashion might be created. In his will, dated 9 October 1739, and in subsequent codicils, he directed that the trustees he had appointed were first to offer the collections to the King for the nation, in return for the sum of £20,000, ('it not being, as I apprehend or believe, a fourth of their real and intrinsic value'[2]), payable to his executors on behalf of his daughters, Lady Cadogan and Mrs Stanley. Should the money not be forthcoming within six months of his death, his museum was to be offered at the same price successively to the Royal Society, to other English and Scottish institutions, and then to various comparable foreign societies. If none would accept his bequest, the collections were to be sold by auction.

On 11 January 1753 Sir Hans Sloane died, in his ninety-third year, peacefully, as he himself said he would, 'one day or other when you do not expect it,'[3] and was buried, alongside his wife, in Chelsea parish churchyard.

Sloane was a good physician, farsighted, practical, and a worthy successor to Newton as President of the Royal Society. But it is as the man who brought together the finest general collection of his time and then ensured that it should be bestowed upon his country, that Sir Hans Sloane earns the gratitude of succeeding generations.

1. *Sloane's Will*, p. 3.
2. *op. cit.*, p. 22.
3. Add. MS. 4, 241. f. 10.

CHAPTER TWO

The Foundation

IN little more than a fortnight after Sloane's death, the Trustees appointed under the terms of his will met. On Saturday 27 January 1753, summoned by his executors (Sloane's son-in-law, Lord Cadogan, his nephews, William Sloane and the Reverend Sloane Elsmere, Rector of Chelsea, and James Empson,[1] for many years the curator of the collections) the new Trustees gathered at the Manor House, Chelsea.[2] There were thirty-seven of them and all but two turned up that eventful Saturday morning. The most prominent amongst them was the Earl of Macclesfield, President of the Royal Society, who was elected to the chair. Others included Horace Walpole, William Stukeley, the antiquary, and Thomas Birch,[3] soon one of the most generous bene-factors to the infant Museum. The will having been produced and read by Lord Cadogan, the Trustees requested Empson to continue 'to take care of the museum – the same as he had done in Sir Hans Sloanes life

1. William Sloane, d.1767, was the son of Hans's elder brother, also called William, 1658–1728, who had likewise settled at Chelsea.

Sloane Elsmere, d.1766, was the son of Hans's only sister Alice, who had married John Elsmere of Belfast. Sloane Elsmere became Rector of Chelsea and officiated at his uncle's funeral.

Charles Cadogan, 1691–1776, second Baron Cadogan, soldier and member of Parliament. He succeeded his brother, Marlborough's chief of staff, in July 1726.

James Empson, d. 1766. One of the three original Under-Librarians or Keepers of the British Museum.

2. Accounts of this meeting and of other meetings of Sloane's Trustees and of the Parliamentary debates concerned with the offer of the collection to the nation are in the manuscript notes appended to a copy of Sloane's will, published in London in 1753, which was picked up by Sir Henry Ellis, then Principal Librarian of the Museum, in an antique shop at Sevenoaks in August 1836. (BM.C.61.b.13)

3. George Parker, second Earl of Macclesfield, c.1697–1764, FRS, FSA, MP for Wallingford (1722–27). President of the Royal Society (1752–1764). He did much to introduce the 'New Style' calendar. Was made a Trustee by the fourth codicil of 18 September 1750. (Will. p. 40.)

Horace Walpole, fourth Earl of Orford, 1717–1797. Author, wit, letter-writer and collector.

William Stukeley, 1687–1765.

time',[1] and elected him their secretary. A committee was appointed to draw up a petition to the King, as laid down by the will, which Lord Macclesfield was to present to His Majesty.[2]

Ten days later Macclesfield reported that the memorial had been handed to the King, who, having read it, replied curtly that 'he doubted if there was money sufficient in the Exchequer'.[3] Faced with this lack of royal enthusiasm, the trustees decided to make a direct appeal to Parliament. On Tuesday 6 March, a second petition was presented in the Commons by Edward Southwell, the Member for Bristol.[4] Henry Pelham,[5] Chancellor of the Exchequer and the most powerful man in the Government, was not wholly unsympathetic, but, like his royal master, considered that there was little money available to spend on such 'knick knackeries' even if offered to the nation on such apparently generous terms. He was likewise disturbed by the fact that considerable sums of public money were to be placed in the hands of Trustees, who would not be accountable to Parliament. Pelham, therefore, moved that the petition should lie on the Table, that is discussion of it should be indefinitely postponed. The general feeling of the House, however, probably under the benign influence of Speaker Onslow, always a warm advocate of a national collection, was distinctly against this dismissal of Sloane's handsome offer. To most members it seemed 'like thro-ing cold water on the generous gift of Sir Hans Sloane'.[6] In consequence the petition was referred to a Committee of the whole House.

Faced by a second rebuff, the Sloane Trustees meet once more at the King's Arms Tavern on Monday 12 March to decide how they might meet some of the objections to the scheme. The next day the matter was again warmly debated in the House. Pelham, now joined by Henry Fox, the Secretary at War, once more opposed the resolution that the House should go into a Committee to discuss the petition. At this, members

1. C.61.b.13.
2. The committee met at 7 p.m. on Tuesday 30 January 1753 in Lord Cadogan's house in Bruton Street, as did a second committee on 12 February, composed of Trustees who were also members of Parliament. They then drew up a petition to be presented to the House of Commons, which they laid before the main body of Trustees at the King's Arms on 28 February.
3. *op. cit.* Also letter of Walpole to Sir Horace Mann, 14 February 1753. Walpole, *Letters.* Yale edition, vol. 20, p. 358.
4. CJ, vol. 26, p. 647. Edward Southwell, 1705–1755.
5. Henry Pelham, 1695?–1754, Whig statesman. Brother of the Duke of Newcastle.
6. C.61.b.13.

asked what was expected of the present Trustees. Should they resign and new trustees, more acceptable to the Crown, be appointed? At length it was agreed that the whole matter should be considered by a Committee on the following Friday. (In the event, not till the Monday.)

The Trustees met yet once more to reconsider their position. After lengthy argument, they drew up a statement which they agreed if necessary to lay before the House. These resolutions they entitled *'Fundamental Principles from which the Trustees do not think they can in Honor or Conscience depart'*. Basically these were three: that the collections be preserved intact; that they be kept 'for the use and benefit of the publick, who may have free Access to view and peruse the same'; and most important, in contradiction to Sloane's wish that the collections should remain at Chelsea, 'that in case it should hereafter be judged the most beneficial and advantageous for the publick use, to remove the Collection from the Manor house at Chelsea, where the same is now deposited, that it be placed properly in the Cities of London or Westminster or the Suburbs thereof'.[1]

On Monday 19 March the House at length considered in committee the terms of Sir Hans' bequest. With Philip Yorke, son of Lord Chancellor Hardwicke, himself one of the Sloane Trustees, in the chair, the Committee heard Mr Gray,[2] another Trustee, speak enthusiastically of the collection and of how useful it would be to the learned world. James Empson was then summoned to give evidence that the collection was of much greater value than £20,000 and to estimate how much it would cost to maintain. Empson roundly declared that the collection was worth at least £80,000, 'that he heard Sir Hans Sloane say that they cost him a £100,000' and that the expense of looking after the collection would not be much more than '4 or £500 a Year'.[3] Faced by the evidence, the Committee resolved that the collection was worth far more than the £20,000 asked for and 'that it will be for the Honor and advantage of this country to accept of Sir Hans Sloane's Legacy'.[4]

Pelham was still not satisfied. In the subsequent debate, he drew

1. The *'Fundamental Principles'* are given in C.61.b.13.
2. Philip Yorke, 1720–1790, second Earl of Hardwicke. He succeeded his father on 16 March 1764.
George Gray, *c.* 1710–1773, MP for Winchelsea.
3. C. 61.b.13.
4. *op. cit.*

attention to the deplorable state of the Cottonian library, already in the possession of the nation for over fifty years, and urged that both that and the possibility of now purchasing the great Harleian collections should also be considered. Moreover, until it was known whether the Sloane Trustees would resign their trust, 'he could not give an opinion on the affair'.[1] After it had been made clear that the Trustees were prepared to resign, Arthur Onslow joined the debate. He emphasised that, in regard to the Cotton collection, 'the publick faith was pledged to erect a building proper to take care of them'[2] and that, as Pelham had also already urged, both the Sloane and Harleian collections should now be joined to the Cottonian library and all three properly housed. He was, however, against taking money from the Sinking Fund to finance all this – perhaps he realised that this would be asking too much from a parsimonious House – and had come to the reluctant conclusion that a lottery would be the best way to raise the necessary funds. Onslow's firm advocacy carried the day, and after a debate of over three hours, agreement was at last reached on what should be done.

On 6 April 1753 the Committee made their report. They agreed that Sloane's collections were worth far more than £20,000 and that this sum should be paid to the executors 'for the said Musaeum, to be kept intire, and maintained for the Use and Benefit of the Publick', that a 'proper Repository' be at last provided for the Cotton Library and for any additions to be made to it; that the sum of £7,000 bequeathed by a Major Edwards for this purpose be used for providing such a building or for adding to the library, and, finally, that the Harleian collection of manuscripts be purchased for £10,000. The necessary funds should be raised by that well tried, if unreliable, eighteenth century device, a public lottery.[3]

The Harleian manuscripts, which Pelham and Onslow both urged should now become national property, along with the Cottonian and Sloane collections, were the surviving portion of the magnificent library built up by Robert and Edward Harley, Earls of Oxford of the second creation. As Speaker of the House of Commons, Robert Harley had been closely associated with the acquisition of the Cottonian Library in 1700. With the able assistance of his librarian, Humfrey

1. *op. cit.*
2. *op. cit.*
3. The Report of the Committee is given in CJ, vol. 26, p. 747. For the whole course of the proceedings, see CJ, vol. 26, pp. 647, 701, 703, 747, 806, 827, 838.

Wanley,[1] he had built up, especially during the years of his political eclipse after the death of Anne, a truly noble collection. By the time of Robert Harley's death in 1724, it included more than 6,000 volumes of manuscripts, together with 14,500 charters and rolls. Edward, the second Earl, who for the most part shunned public life, devoted the greater part of his energies to the augmentation of the family collections. As his father had done, he made his great library freely available to any scholar who wanted to use it. Unfortunately for posterity, Edward Harley's magnificent style of living, his great generosity and ready sympathy for sometimes worthless dependants, led in later life, despite his great inherited wealth, to comparative impoverishment. So, at his death in 1741, the Harleian library of printed books, which at that time was estimated at more than 50,000 volumes, 400,000 pamphlets, and 41,000 prints, was sold off and dispersed by his widow and by his daughter and sole heiress, Margaret, Duchess of Portland. It was of this noble collection that Johnson wrote: 'It excels any Library that was ever yet offered to public Sale, in the Value as well Number of the Volumes which it contains'.[2]

Though often threatened, the manuscripts, fortunately, as yet remained undispersed. On learning of the Commons proposal, the Duchess wrote to Speaker Onslow to say, 'As I know it was my Father's and is my Mother's intention that they should be kept together, I will not bargain with the Publick', and on the further condition that 'this great valuable Collection shall be kept together in a proper repository, as an addition to the Cotton Library, and be called by the name of Harleian Collection of Manuscripts', agreed to part with them for £10,000.[3]

A bill was then speedily introduced into the House of Commons, embodying the various proposals, which on 7 June 1753 received the Royal Assent, less than six months after the death of Sloane. Rarely, especially in the eighteenth century, has Parliament acted so quickly. It was by this Act,[4] that the British Museum was to be governed, without any essential change, for the next two hundred years.

1. Humfrey Wanley, 1672–1726, antiquary. For details of his librarianship of Harley collections, see C. W. Wright, *Humfrey Wanley: Saxonist and Library-Keeper*, Proceedings of the British Academy, vol. XLVI, 1960, and C. E. Wright and R. C. Wright, *The Diary of Humfrey Wanley*. Bibliographical Society, London, 1966.
2. An Account of the Harleian Library p, .2. (*Catalogus Bibliothecae Harleianae*. Londini, 1743.)
3. Add. MS. 17,521, f. 38. Duchess of Portland to Arthur Onslow, 3 April 1753.
4. 26 Geo.II. c.22.

One fundamental problem remained. This was to raise sufficient money to purchase both the Sloane and the Harleian collections, to obtain 'one general Repository'[1] for all the collections near central London and to engage the staff necessary to launch the newly created Museum.

Notwithstanding the doubts of Onslow and the strongly expressed distaste of Pelham – an avowed enemy to lotteries – for any such expedients[2], the Act of 1753 stipulated that the money should be raised by these means. Since lotteries had long had an unsavoury reputation, elaborate safeguards were included in the Act to prevent chicanery and heavy penalties prescribed for any violation. Despite these precautions, however, the Sloane lottery succeeded in being more corrupt than had been feared and shocked even eighteenth century consciences. This lamentable state of affairs was for the most part due to the activities of a certain Peter Leheup, an 'odious character', who was already notorious for his questionable practices in both England and Hanover.

Despite his unsavoury past, Leheup was now made one of the receivers of contributions to the lottery and quickly rigged it in his favour. He at once circulated his friends on the most effectual means of evading the provisions of the Act, sold to one person more than three hundred tickets, under palpably false names, and so arranged it that the public sale of lottery tickets should be closed a few hours after it had been declared open, a mere six hours for the ostensible issue of one hundred thousand tickets, and despite the precise directions in the Act that it was to be kept open until 20 October, so as to allow time for foreign subscriptions to come in. In consequence, as the Parliamentary Committee of Inquiry afterwards remarked, 'the rise of the tickets above the true value was as much as ever'.[3] By now, tickets were changing hands for at least sixteen shillings. Leheup and his 'combination of stockjobbers', having bought their tickets at the lowest possible price, were now selling them 'to the deluded people at what profit they pleased to exact.' The Museum lottery had become 'a mere job for the benefit of the receivers and their favourites, who . . . extorted . . . at least £40,000 from the people'.[4]

This was too much for a now outraged House of Commons. Although Leheup's conduct was defended by Henry Fox, who probably had a

1. PGA 1753, p. 341.
2. *Parliamentary History*, vol. XV, col. 192n.
3. *op. cit.*
4. Speech of George Cook, *c.* 1704–1768, MP for Middlesex. *Op. cit.*, col. 192.

certain sympathy for a fellow profiteer, the Commons petitioned the King to instruct his Attorney-General to prosecute the too ingenious Receiver. Leheup was convicted of violations of the Lottery Act and fined £1,000, which sum 'he immediately paid', as no doubt he could well afford to do. But thanks to him and his accomplices, many poor but gullible people were 'utterly undone' and the custom of holding parliamentary lotteries to raise money for even the best of causes received a blow from which it never recovered.[1]

Nevertheless, when all was settled up, the Trustees of the new British Museum had at their disposal the considerable sum of £95,194 8s 2d with which to begin their activities. The Board, which had been appointed under the British Museum Act, was a distinguished one, inspired, no doubt by the precedent of the Cottonian Library. Headed by the three Principal Trustees, the Archbishop of Canterbury, the Lord Chancellor and the Speaker of the House of Commons, it consisted of most of the great officers of state and representatives of the Sloane, Cotton and Harley families. Added to over the years, but not fundamentally changed until the passing of the 1963 Act, the Board of Trustees was to render valuable service both to the Museum and to the nation at large during the next two centuries.

The Board's immediate care was now to see what it had taken into its charge. Its first meeting was held on 11 December 1753 at the Cockpit in Whitehall,[2] where it elected the unofficial members of the Board. There were fifteen in all, of whom the most prominent were the Duke of Argyll, the Earl of Northumberland, Philip Yorke and the Rev. Thomas Birch.[3] A second meeting was held in the rooms of the Harleian Library in Dover Street on 19 January 1754 and straight away they started to inspect this most valuable portion of their collections, the Harleian manuscripts. On the whole they found them in good condition, but were alarmed at finding that the ground floor, on which a number of manuscripts were kept, was damp.[4]

1. CJ, vol. 26, pp. 987–1001. *Parliamentary History*, vol. XV, col. 192–249.
2. *General Meetings, Minutes*, vol. I, p. 1.
3. Archibald Campbell, 3rd Duke of Argyll, 1682–1761, brother of John, the second Duke, soldier and statesman.
Hugh Percy, originally Smithson, Earl, later Duke of Northumberland, 1715–1786. He succeeded to the Percy estates in 1750, in virtue of his wife's descent from the Percies, Earls of Northumberland.
4. The room in which the manuscripts were had 'but one small fireplace [and they] seem too much expos'd to injury from the Damp attending Such a Situation'. (*Committee Minutes*, vol. I, pp. 2, 3.)

Three days later it was the turn of the Sloane collections. On 22 January 1754 the Standing Committee met at the Manor House, Chelsea to inspect them. They seemed in perfect condition, but the Trustees were by no means satisfied. In order to ensure that all was in order, they instructed James Empson to draw up a detailed inventory of every room, to note exactly what each contained, and to check it carefully against Sloane's own catalogues. Their Committee, on inspecting the Library, had 'found the Books disposed in a Very Irregular Manner, with but little regard to the Subjects or even Size of them'.[1] It was not only the books which were in confusion. The coins were in a worse state. Of the 32,000 coins said to be in the collection (actually only 22,000), many were missing, yet the heirs, as Dr Kaye, Dean of Ely and a Trustee, pointed out in 1776, took all the duplicates, including medals valued at half a guinea each. When the manuscripts were checked it was found that six or seven were missing, which had been lent to 'a person of rank'.[2]

On 5 February, accompanied by Speaker Onslow, the Trustees visited the old Dormitory of Westminster School to inspect the third of the founding collections, the remains of Cotton's library, still lying neglected and unused, with the dust of twenty years upon it. To their relief, the books were dry and in good condition underneath the dust.[3] The Trustees went on to remark that 'the present keeper of them is Mr David Casley, who is disabled by Age and Infirmity from Executing the Duty of his post in his own person, so that the whole care of the preservation of the said Library depends upon his wife, and that of shewing it lies in her with the Occasional Assistance of the Revd. Mr. Widmore, Keeper of the Library of the Collegiate Church of Westminster'.[4] When it is remembered that Casley was likewise responsible for the Royal Library, the neglect and virtual uselessness of both libraries to scholars is not to be wondered at. The Trustees were determined to remedy this state of affairs when it lay in their power to do so. For the moment the Cotton Library must stay where it was and they noted that, if necessary, the Harleian manuscripts could also be accommodated in the same spacious room.

1. *General Meeting, Minutes*, vol. I, p. 69.
2. Add. MS. 3,871. ff. 29–32.
3. 'Yet as it is Dry and Secure from the Weather, the MSS as well as Books appear to have Sustained no Injury from Damp . . . but they are in general so dusty, that a Speedy Care of them is Necessary in that respect'. (*Committee Minutes*, vol. I, p. 9.)
4. *Op. cit.*, p. 9.

The great need was to find suitable accommodation, quickly, under one roof, for all the collections and to allow for the expansion which was bound to occur once the new museum was properly established. At their meeting on 2 February, the Trustees resolved that the 'Providing of a General Repository . . . be taken into the Consideration'.[1] This was, however, easier said than done, for a building of the size which was clearly needed was not readily to be had for the money they could afford.

The first to be considered was Buckingham House, now Buckingham Palace. This was offered by Sir Charles Sheffield[2] for £30,000, 'with the gardens and field'. After thinking the matter over, the Trustees declined the offer on the grounds of 'the Greatness of the Sum demanded for it, the Inconvenience of the Situation, and other Circumstances'.[3] The 'other circumstances' were the possibility that an entirely new building might be erected for the museum in Old Palace Yard, Westminster, as part of a general plan for the redevelopment of this area, including a new Houses of Parliament. But the cost, at least £50,000 to £60,000, was far too great and this scheme was quickly shelved. Another possibility, fleetingly considered, was the use of the Banqueting House in Whitehall, but this was rejected as too small and offering little room for expansion.

The need for a decision was urgent. The collections had for far too long been largely unavailable to the public, and the Trustees were worried about the security of the Sloane collections, still housed in rural Chelsea.

They were now offered another building, which seemed eminently suitable for their purpose. This was Montagu House in Bloomsbury, on the every edge of London, a fine mansion, though somewhat fallen into decay.

A first house built in 1675 for the first Duke of Montagu to the designs of Hooke, the mathematician, with decorations by Verrio and other prominent artists, and one of the finest private houses in London, 'Mr Montague's new palace neere Bloomesbery', as John Evelyn described

1. *General Meetings, Minutes*, vol. I, p. 23.
2. Sir Charles Sheffield, ? –1762, originally known as Charles Herbert. He was the illegitimate son of John Sheffield, Duke of Buckingham. On the death of his legitimate half-brother, he was left the greater part of the family estates, taking the name of Sheffield. He was created a baronet in 1755. Buckingham House, built in 1703, was sold by him to George III in 1761.
3. *General Meetings, Minutes*, vol. I, p. 30, 3 April 1754.

it,[1] had been totally destroyed by fire on 19 January 1686. Montagu resolved to erect an even finer dwelling on the same spot. This time his architect was a Frenchman, Puget, who designed the great house very much on the lines of a contemporary Parisian hôtel. The magnificent staterooms and noble staircase with ceilings lavishly decorated by La Fosse, the walls covered with landscapes and architectural fantasies by Jacques Rousseau, whilst a third French artist, Jean Baptiste Monnoyer, 'scattered about him at every step a profusion of charming and gaily-hued flowers',[2] were the admiration of every visitor. As Horace Walpole wrote, 'What it wants in grace and beauty, is compensated by the spaciousness and lofty magnificence of the apartments'.[3]

This fine building, together with some seven and a half acres of garden, was now offered to the Trustees by the Earl of Cardigan and Sir Edward Montagu for £10,000.[4] At their meeting on 16 February 1754, the Standing Committee of the Trustees considered the offer and on the 22nd proceeded to inspect the property. They found it 'a Substantial, well built Brick Building . . . the Roof . . . Sound and in good Condition' and after certain repairs and suitable alterations, it seemed to them that it would be 'proper and convenient for the intended

1. Evelyn, *Diary*, 11 May 1676. By a coincidence, Evelyn had that very day dined with William Courten, whose collections were to come, with those of Sloane, many years later to Montagu House. (Evelyn, *Diary*, ed. E. S. De Beer, vol. IV, p. 90.)
Robert Hooke, 1635–1797, experimental philosopher.
Antonio Verrio, 1639–1707, decorative painter.

2. Knight's *London*, vol. 6, p. 163.
Charles de la Fosse, 1636–1716. Charles II was so taken with Fosse's designs for Lord Montagu that he was asked to carry out the decorations for Hampton Court, but was unable to accept the commission. (Bénézet. *Dictionnaire des peintres*, vol. 5, p. 334.) For his work at Montagu House La Fosse received £2,000 and an extra £500 for his diet.
Jean Baptiste Monnoyer, 1634–1699. He spent the last twenty years of his life in England, whence he had followed Montagu when the latter ceased to be Ambassador at Paris in 1678. He subsequently worked for Queen Mary II and Princess Anne. A portrait of him hangs in the Duty Officer's drawing room at the Museum.

3. Walpole, *Anecdotes of Painting*, vol. 2, p. 175.

4. George Brudenell, Earl of Cardigan, 1712–1790. Married the daughter of John Montagu, Duke of Montagu. On the death of his father-in-law in July 1749 he assumed the name of Montagu. He was himself created Duke of Montagu in November 1766.
Sir Edward Hussey-Montagu, later Earl of Beaulieu. He had married the Dowager Duchess of Manchester, heiress of John second Duke of Montagu, and had then adopted the name of Montagu. He died in 1802, aged 81.

purposes.'[1] After a few weeks' hesitation whilst they considered the possibility of incorporating a museum into the late Mr Kent's designs for new Houses of Parliament,[2] on 3 April 1754 the Trustees decided, subject to government approval, to accept the offer and purchase Montagu House and its grounds. In consequence, a private Act[3] was rapidly passed, enabling the Trustees to acquire it on payment of the sum of £10,000.[4]

Though Strype in 1720 had declared that 'for Stateliness of Building and curious Gardens, Montague-House hath the Pre-eminence, as indeed of all Houses within the Cities of London and Westminster, and the adjacent Parishes',[5] the great house had been empty and neglected for a number of years and the once lovely formal gardens were sadly overgrown, with the lawns a mass of anthills. The Trustees were now surprised and horrified to receive from their surveyor an estimate of over £7,000 for repairing and fitting out their new property. They indignantly ordered that new estimates should be prepared and the proposed expenditure was then reduced to a little less than £4,000. The original estimate, however, was far nearer the mark. In 1756 £3,000 was spent on repairs to the house; in 1757 £3,196, and in the following year £4,554. In all, before the Museum opened, money spent on maintenance and repair exceeded the sum originally spent on its purchase![6]

Nevertheless, it was obvious that Montagu House was the most suitable building for the Museum and the Trustees pressed on with arrangements for transferring their newly acquired collections to a permanent home.

Since the Duchess of Portland was anxious to get rid of them, it had already been decided to move the Harleian manuscripts direct to Montagu House, rather than to put them temporarily in the Dormitory of Westminster School alongside the Cottonian and Royal Libraries. In May and June 1755 they were safely transferred to the west wing of the old house, the first of the great founding collections to arrive.[7] The move was possibly premature, for it was found that some of the manu-

1. *Committee Minutes*, vol. I, p. 11, 22 February 1754.
2. *Op. cit.*, vol. I, p. 14, 26 February 1754.
3. 27 and 28 Geo. II. c.3.
4. *General Meetings, Minutes*, vol. I, p. 35. Private Acts, 27–28 Geo. II, p. 9.
5. Strype, *Continuation of Stow's Survey*, Book IV, p. 84. The gardens are clearly depicted in a '*Mapp of the Parish of St. Giles in the Fields*', contained in Strype.
6. Thompson, p. 652.
7. *General Meetings, Minutes*, vol. I, p. 65, 16 June 1755.

scripts were being damaged by rain leaking through the roof, as yet unrepaired. By the end of 1755, however, most of the repairs and alterations were completed and plans for assembling the remaining collections could go forward.

The Trustees were particularly desirous of making both the Sloane and Cottonian collections available to the public as soon as possible. Although visitors were still allowed to inspect Sir Hans's treasures in their old home at Chelsea, it was obviously not convenient and the Cottonian Library had been virtually inaccessible for over fifty years. The Trustees were likewise disturbed to hear a rumour that the Old Dormitory might be pulled down. It was obvious that speed was essential. Detailed plans and surveys were now made for the reception of the collections. Presses were built and shelves measured and fitted. It was calculated that the books in the Sloane collection would need 4,600 feet of shelving; the Harleian manuscripts, for the moment accommodated in the West Wing, 1,700 feet; the Cotton Library 384 feet, and the books bequeathed by Major Edwards 576 feet.[1] On 13 December 1755, tentative arrangements for their reception were complete. The bulk of the Sloane collections would go into seven rooms on the first state story; the Harleian manuscripts were to be transferred to four rooms on the second floor; Edwards's books and the Cotton manuscripts were each to be given a room there, while five rooms on the same story would take the rest of the Sloane collections. A few large items were to be accommodated in the Halls and landings.[2]

Soon the collections started to arrive and by the end of the year they were all assembled together in Montagu House.

The old building was not only cleaned and redecorated, the fine paintings by La Fosse and others were restored to their former glory, and the great gardens transformed into one of the sights of London. The formal pattern of the early eighteenth-century garden, with its terraces and plots laid out in a symmetrical arrangement of squares, rectangles and triangles, was redesigned to bring it into line with changing taste. The neglected lawns were cut and the numerous ant-hills removed. Paths were swept and gravelled and the borders planted with flowers. The Trustees took a keen interest in their garden. In May 1756 the Duke of Argyll presented 'a great Variety of Exotic Trees'[3]

1. Add. MS. 36,269, f. 274; *General Meetings, Minutes,* vol. I, p. 69, 13 December 1755.
2. *General Meetings, Minutes,* vol. I, p. 70.
3. *Committee Minutes,* vol. I, p. 83, 7 May 1756.

and other trustees, especially the eminent physician, Dr William Watson,[1] spent much time and money beautifying the grounds. By the beginning of 1757, the garden was ready to be opened to a few selected persons. Strict rules were laid down for their admission. 'No person . . . be admitted into the garden, except by particular leave of the Committee, unless they are accompanied during their continuance therein by a Trustee, by the lady of a Trustee, or by one of the officers of the Museum: and that they be desired not to tread upon the flower beds nor otherwise to injure the plants . . . That no plants or flowers be gathered but by leave of the Committee, for medical purposes, or as specimens for such studious and curious persons, as may be desirous of increasing their botanical knowledge.'[2]

All this work, on both house and garden, and the upset it entailed, annoyed the local authorities. In June 1756 the Trustees agreed that the street pavement outside Montagu House, which had become much damaged during the building operations, must be repaired or relaid without delay, 'as the Parish making great complaints about it' (sic). And this was done.[3]

Now the Trustees were to be offered a magnificent gift, the Royal Library of the Kings of England, which, since the early eighteenth century, had been stored alongside the Cotton Library. First at Old Cotton House, it had joined the latter on its travels to Essex House, to the ill-fated Ashburnham House, and finally had spent the last twenty-three years neglected in the dusty confines of Westminster Old Dormitory. Half a century after Sloane had written to Charlett on the possibility of merging the Cotton and Royal Libraries, the idea was at last coming to fruition.

The Old Royal Library had been founded by Edward IV in about 1471. It is probably more to the influence of his friend and ally, Charles the Bold of Burgundy, than to any bookish inclinations on Edward's own part that we owe the foundation of the collection. Added to by his successors, the library grew slowly. Under Henry VIII, John Leland, the famous antiquary, succeeded in acquiring many valuable manuscripts salvaged from the sack of the monasteries. A number, however, were destroyed a few years later in a drastic purge of 'all superstitious

1. Sir William Watson, 1715–1787, physician, naturalist and scientist. He devoted much of his time to experiments in electricity. He was knighted 1768.
2. *Committee Minutes*, vol. I, p. 204, March 4, 1757.
3. Add. MS. 36,269. f. 150. n.d.

bookes, as masse bookes, legondes and such like',[1] carried out during the reign of Henry's son, Edward VI. The remaining Tudor monarchs did comparatively little for the library, although the magnificent Queen Mary's Psalter, seized at the ports by a conscientious customs officer and presented to the Queen, was joined to the collection in her reign.[2] It was the first Stuart sovereign, James I, and his eldest son, Henry, Prince of Wales, who virtually refounded the Royal Library by the acquisition of such great collections as those of Lord Lumley, Isaac Casaubon,[3] and others. The greatest single event of this period, however, as far as the library was concerned, was the arrival in 1628 of the famous Codex Alexandrinus, a fifth-century manuscript of the Bible in Greek and still one of the greatest treasures of the Museum. This priceless manuscript was sent as a gift from Cyril Lucar, Patriarch of Constantinople, to Charles I, through Sir Thomas Roe, the English Ambassador.

During the Commonwealth, the Royal Library very nearly shared the fate of the royal collection of pictures. Shortly after the King's death, orders were given by the House of Commons for the books to be handed over with the intention 'to dispose of them . . . as they shall think fit'.[4] That the library escaped this fate, was probably due to the famous jurist, John Selden,[5] who had considerable influence over the new Council of State. A subsequent move by the authorities would have had, as it turned out, even more disastrous consequences. It was ordered that the library should be removed from 'James's House' to the Banqueting House in Whitehall[6] and from there to join the second, smaller royal library, which had existed within the Palace of Whitehall since the reign of Henry VIII. Had this been done, the books would undoubtedly have perished in the fire which destroyed the Palace, with

1. *Acts of Privy Council*, 1550–1552, p. 224.
2. This famous manuscript, now Royal MS. 2.B.VII. f.151, was in the possession of Henry Manners, Earl of Rutland, at the time of his arrest. Its exportation was stopped by Baldwin Smith, a customs officer, and it was later presented to the Queen.
3. John, Lord Lumley, c.1534–1609. He had inherited Cranmer's and other libraries and left at his own death some 3,000 volumes, including 400 manuscripts. It is possible that he presented his library to Prince Henry or that he allowed it to revert to the crown along with his palace of Nonesuch.
Isaac Casaubon, 1559–1614, classical scholar; born in Geneva, he became a naturalised Englishman in 1610.
4. *Cal. of S.P.Dom.*, 1649–50, pp. 10, 13. See also Bulstrode Whitelocke, *Memorials*, 1732, pp. 415, 416.
5. John Selden, 1584–1654, jurist, who was a personal friend of Sir Robert Cotton.
6. *Cal. of S.P.Dom.*, 1651–2, p. 151.

the exception of the Banqueting House, in January 1698. As it was, the conditions under which they continued could hardly have been worse. At St James's Palace, in which troops were quartered, it was reported that the books 'lie upon the floor in confused heaps, so that not only the rain and the dust, but the rats, mice, and other vermin can easily get at them'.[1] And things got no better. When Richard Bentley became Librarian, he declared that the room in which the books were was 'not fit to be seen'[2] and kept the Codex Alexandrinus in his own lodging, 'that Persons might see it, without seeing the Library'.[3] He proposed that the books should be transferred to the chapel in Whitehall, a proposal that was fortunately not acted upon, as again, the library would presumably have perished in the fire of 1698.

Early in the eighteenth century, despite the ruinous condition of Cotton House, the books were moved there and shared the fate of the Cotton Library. Now the Cotton Manuscripts had gone to the newly created British Museum, so it would seem right that the Royal Library should follow them. At all events, on 17 June 1757 the Trustees were informed that 'His Majesty had been graciously pleased to give orders for a Bill, to be prepared for his Royal Signature . . . for a Donation to the Trustees of the British Museum of . . . his Royal Library or libraries with the appurtenances whatsoever, now deposited in the old Dormitory at Westminster'[4] and 'whereas the said Library hath for many years past been placed in the Old Dormitory at Westminster, without due Convenience for the Custody thereof or the resort of Inquisitive and Learned Men; we . . . are Desirous that our said Library should not only be made useful to the present times, but be preserved and transmitted for the good of posterity under the care of Publick Trustees and Subject to proper Orders and Regulations, &c.'[5]

On 23 September 1757 the removal of the Royal Library began and by November 12 it was safely installed in its new home.[6] It was indeed

1. *op. cit.*, p. 468.
2. *Dissertation on Phalaris*, Ed. W. Wagner, Berlin, 1874. *Preface*, p. 41.
3. *op. cit.*, p. 40.
4. *General Meetings, Minutes*, vol. I, pp. 180, 181.
5. *Committee Minutes*, vol. I, p. 360.
6. *Committee Minutes*, vol. I, p. 376, 30 September 1756. The whole collection was in three rooms, the manuscripts in E22 on the second state story; the Printed Books in H61 and A60 on the first. It would seem most probable that it was on its arrival at Montagu House that the Royal Library was shelved according to the books' supposed original owner, that is, either the reigning monarch or else Arundel-Lumley, Cranmer,

a princely gift comprising some 12,000 volumes, of which 9,000 were printed books. Of the manuscripts, a few had been in the royal collection since the Middle Ages, but of the printed books, none can be identified with certainty from before the reign of Henry VII. Amongst those of the following reign which still survived were Henry VIII's copy of the *Summa de potestate ecclesiastica*, in which, against the passage that polygamy was not contrary to nature among the Patriarchs, he had written: '*ergo nec in nobis*' (therefore not in our case either), and also his *Assertio* against Luther, for which he received from the Pope the title of *Defender of the Faith*. But probably the most valuable gift that possession of the Royal Library brought to the Museum was the right of Copyright deposit. The various Licensing Acts from 1662 onwards and the Copyright Act of 1709[1] had laid it down that the Royal Library should receive a copy of every printed work registered at Stationers' Hall. Even though successive Royal Librarians had done little to substantiate that right, it was a valuable privilege and was to be of inestimable benefit, when subsequent acts and a more determined policy on the part of the Museum authorities enabled the regulations to be properly enforced.

Also included with the royal gift, was the reversion of the librarian's salary of £300 a year. Seventeen years later, in 1774, the Trustees at last came into possession of it and enjoyed its use till 1816 when, on the rearrangement of the Civil List, the payment was discontinued.[2] In all, the Museum received nearly £10,600 from this source, valuable income in days when money was scarce and parliamentary grants both modest and difficult to come by.

Other gifts were now arriving. The House of Lords deposited a collection of documents belonging to Thomas Rymer which had not been printed in his *Foedera*, together with sixty-four Rolls of Parliament;

1. 8 Anne C.19. *An Act for the Encouragement of Learning, by Vesting the Copies of Printed Books in the Authors or Purchasers of such Copies.* The Act laid down that nine copies of every work published were to be delivered to Stationers' Hall for the use of the Royal Library, the libraries of Oxford and Cambridge, the four Scottish Universities, Sion College, and the Advocates' Library, Edinburgh.
2. *General Meetings, Minutes*, p. 181, 17 June, 1757.

Isaac Casaubon, and so on. At the end of the eighteenth century when the printed books were re-arranged according to a broad subject classification, the Old Royal Library books were split up and the Library as such, ceased to exist. A number of books were subsequently disposed of as duplicates, including Henry VIII's presentation copy of his *Assertio Contra Lutheram*, now at Lambeth.

in February 1756, the collection of Egyptian antiquities, bequeathed to the Museum by Colonel William Lethieullier and augmented by other members of his family, were received, together with a few additional natural history specimens, including 'a Pelican of the Wilderness', presumably stuffed.[1]

It was obviously high time that a qualified staff should be engaged to administer and arrange the rapidly expanding museum. But at the beginning of 1756, the museum's annual income was £1,320, this being the interest on a capital sum of £44,000, all that remained out of the proceeds of the lottery, when all debts had been paid. Even by eighteenth-century standards, such a tiny sum would hardly support a large staff. Therefore, to make 'the State of the Officers and Servants and their respective Allowances consistent with the said Annual Income, the committee have endeavoured to reduce the Number of them as low as possible, and . . . settle their said Allowances in the most frugal manner'.[2]

Frugal it certainly was. The Principal Librarian, the only officer specifically mentioned in the Act of 1753, was to have an annual salary of £200. In addition, there were to be three Under-Librarians each in charge of a department, who were to receive £100 apiece. There were to be also three assistants, at £50 a head per year. After the wages of the various servants and of the estimated annual maintenance cost had been deducted, there was a surplus of £78 18s 5d 'for the keeping of the Garden, and other Expenses not yet thought of'.[3]

But two very necessary officers had been forgotten, a 'receiver and expeditor' or accountant, and a secretary. There was obviously no money left with which to pay them. A most ingenious solution was, however, devised to meet the situation. The salary of the Principal Librarian was cut to £160, but he was paid a further £40 as 'receiver and expeditor', whilst the three Under-Librarians had their salaries reduced to a mere £80 a year, each, in turn, acting as Secretary on an annual basis, and receiving £20 for so doing. They were, it is true, to be given the privilege of free coal and candles, but must provide their own furniture for the apartments in Montagu House now being prepared for them. It was expressly stated, moreover, that no fees might be accepted for

1. The pelican was a gift of Pitt Lethieullier on 23 February 1756. (Add. MS. 6,179. f. 40.)
2. General Meetings, Minutes, vol. I, p. 78, 17 January 1756. A note says that this report was actually made to the meeting of 16 June 1755.
3. op.cit., p. 79, 17 January 1756.

escorting visitors round the building, this being the principal occupation of the senior staff during the early days of the Museum.

Yet there seemed no lack of applicants for such badly rewarded positions. On 22 September 1754, Dr Gowin Knight, a distinguished physician and inventor, wrote to Lord Hardwicke, the Lord Chancellor, offering himself as a candidate for the post of Principal Librarian. The 'greatest part of my life [has been spent]', he claimed, 'in the pursuit of natural knowledge', and continued: 'A regular physician may . . . be allowed to deserve the Preference to such as were not of that Profession',[1] an indication that the Museum collections were regarded, at least by Dr Knight, as still primarily scientific, if no longer exclusively medical. Indeed it was not only Dr Knight who at this date thought of the collections, at least those of Sloane, as primarily scientific. An anonymous writer apostrophises the Sloane collections in the following terms: 'The Treasure which he bequeathed to his Country . . . may be attended with numberless Advantages to the Public. Here, the young Physician, Chemist & Apothecary may become well acquainted with every Substance, Animal, Vegetable or Mineral that is ever employ'd in Medicine. The Curious in Ores & Metals by viewing specimens of every sort will be instructed in what Beds of Stone . . . they are usually from and by that means will be inabled to judge what Metals or Metallic Bodies the Rocks or Mountains . . . may probably contain . . . and may lead to the finding of better Materials for the Potter, the Painter, the Glassmaker [and] . . . many other Artists to improve their Manufacture. In short the Naturalist will find in this Museum almost everything which he can wish & will be greatly assisted in his Inquiries and Observations'.[2]

Gowin Knight obtained the post, although only after keen competition with the self-styled 'Sir' John Hill, botanist, quack doctor and client of Lord Bute, the royal favourite, and with another physician, Dr John Mitchell,[3] whose name, along with that of Knight, was submitted to the sovereign on 17 May 1756.

To assist the new Principal Librarian, the Trustees appointed Dr

1. Add. MS. 36,269. ff. 29, 31. Gowin Knight, 1713–1772.
Philip Yorke, 1690–1764, 1st Earl of Hardwicke, Lord Chancellor, 1737–1756.

2. Add. MS. 4,241. ff. 27, 28.

3. S.P.Dom. Geo.II, vol. 134.f.71 (PRO.S.P./36). *General Meetings, Minutes*, vol. I, pp. 94, 95, 3 June 1756. For Mitchell's application to Lord Hardwicke for the post, see Add. MS. 36,269. f. 93.
John Hill, 1716?–1775, botanist and journalist. Johnson considered him 'an ingenious

Matthew Maty and Dr Charles Morton, two more physicians who, together with James Empson, for long the conscientious keeper of Sloane's Museum at Chelsea and his valued friend, constituted the three original Under-Librarians.[1] Even before the appointment of the three Under-Librarians, on 3 June 1756, the collections had been tentatively divided into three separate departments. The first consisted, for the most part, of the printed books and manuscripts of Sloane's library; the second, of the 'natural and artificial curiosities' from the same collection, whilst the third would contain the Cottonian and Harleian manuscripts, together with Major Edwards' library. Each would be in charge of an Under-Librarian with an Assistant. On the appointment of the three Under-Librarians, Maty was put in charge of all Sloane's library; Dr Morton of the Harleian and other remaining manuscripts; and Empson continued, as he had done for many years, to look after Sloane's natural history specimens and the various miscellaneous antiquities. With the arrival of further collections, a more logical arrangement was found necessary. Maty's department was henceforth to be exclusively of printed books, those of the Royal Library, for instance, coming to him, whilst all the manuscripts went to Morton. Similarly, the printed books from Edwards' library were now transferred to Maty, whilst the Sloane manuscripts came to Morton. The three departments, were, on 18 March 1758, given names corresponding to their new functions: the Department of Manuscripts; the Department of Printed Books, and the Department of Natural and Artificial Productions.

The Under-Librarians reported in turn on the state of the collections now entrusted to them. On the whole, they found a gloomy picture. Maty and his assistant, Henry Rimius,[2] for instance, discovered that the Cotton manuscripts would need to be carefully dried before they could come to Bloomsbury. Yet they said that despite the extensive damage, resulting both from the fire and the subsequent years of neglect, certain manuscripts, hitherto reported as wholly destroyed,

1. *General Meetings, Minutes*, vol. I, pp. 107–109.
Matthew Maty, 1718–1776, MD.
Charles Morton, 1716–1799, MD, FRS. He was a practising physician and was said to be a person of great uprightness and integrity, much admired as a scholar.
2. Henry Rimius, d. 1756.

man but [one who] had no veracity'. (Boswell, *Life*, vol. 2, p. 58.) He claimed to be 'Sir John' on the strength of being made a knight of the Swedish Order of Vasa by Gustavus III.

'may still be of some use in carefull hands'.[1] The medals in this collection, however, were in a most confused state, and needed careful sorting
before being transferred to Montagu House.

Similar reports were made on the other collections, and the Principal
Librarian was then ordered to consult with the officers of the three
departments as to the feasibility of compiling new catalogues of all the
collections or of making indexes to those catalogues which were already
in existence. Empson, meanwhile, was arranging the natural history
specimens, supplemented in May 1757 by the Brander collection of
'Minerals and other Fossils', into three sub-divisions of fossils, vegetables and animals, in that order, so that 'by this Arrangement the
Spectator will be gradually conducted from the simplest to the most
compound and most perfect of Nature's productions',[2] probably the
first example of display technique to be found at the Museum.

By the autumn of 1757, the arrangement of the collections was so far
advanced that the Trustees decided that small parties of important
visitors might now be allowed to take 'a transient view of the Museum'
or even, in exceptional circumstances, to consult specific books or
manuscripts.[3] Too many persons took advantage of this concession and
got in the way, both of the staff and of the workmen still engaged on the
building, so that on 14 July 1758, the Trustees passed a resolution
forbidding all further access to the Museum until it was formally open,
except on Saturday up to three in the afternoon.[4]

The first draft of the 'Statutes and Rules' for the conduct of the
Museum had been compiled by the Trustees in 1757. Heavily revised,
for the most part by Lord Macclesfield, they were at last issued in 1759.
From the first, it was decided that, in whatever limited and circum-
scribed a fashion, the contents of the Museum must be made available
to the general public, since, 'tho' chiefly designed for the use of learned
and studious men, both natives and foreigners, in their researches into
the several parts of knowledge, yet being a national establishment . . . it
may be judged reasonable, that the advantages accruing from it should
be rendered as general as possible'.[5] Some of the Trustees, however,

1. *Committee Minutes*, vol. I, p .104, 23 July 1756.
2. *General Meetings, Minutes*, vol. I, p. 165, 7 May 1756.
op. cit., pp. 175, 176, 14 January 1757.
3. *Committee Minutes*, vol. I., p. 381, 21 October 1757.
4. *op. cit.*, vol. I, pp. 451, 452.
5. *Statutes and Rules Relating to the Inspection and Use of the British Museum*, etc. London,
1759, pp. 5, 6.

had distinctly odd ideas as to what was 'consistent with the care and safety of the collections'. One at least, Dr John Ward, the elderly professor of rhetoric at Gresham College, London, was strongly of the opinion that 'ordinary people of all Ranks & Denominations' should not be admitted to the Museum, without the most stringent precautions, since 'many irregularities will be committed that cannot be prevented by a few Librarians, who will soon be insulted by such people if they offer to control or contradict them. . . . If any such people are in liquor & misbehave, they are rarely without their accomplices . . . who out of an Idle vanity in exerting what they will call their liberty will side with them & promote mischiefs that are to be more easily suppressed than . . . prevented . . . No persons of superior degree will care to come on such days . . . a great concourse of ordinary people will never be kept in order.' Dr Ward went on: 'If public days should be allowed, then it will be necessary for the Trustees to have the presence of a Committee of themselves attending, with at least two Justices of the Peace and the constables of the division of Bloomsbury . . . supported by a guard such as one as usually attends at the Play-House, & even after all this, Accidents must & will happen'.[1]

If the majority of the Trustees did not see the necessity for quite such stringent precautions, it was none the less firmly believed that the regulations governing admission to the Museum must be as strict as possible and be an effective deterrent to those members of society whose presence might harm the exhibits or give possible offence to their betters. Such fears may seem exaggerated or even risible, but it must never be forgotten that the eighteenth-century London mob could at times be a terrible threat both to property and persons. The Museum – situated on the outskirts of London – was always in danger of falling a victim. As late as 1815, Henry Ellis, then Keeper of the Department of Manuscripts, noted in his diary that a mob had attacked the house of the highly unpopular Lord Eldon, the Lord Chancellor, in nearby Bloomsbury Street and forced him to take refuge in the Museum gardens. The sergeant's guard, stationed there since the Gordon riots of 1780, had to clear the demonstrators out of Lord Eldon's house at the point of the bayonet.[2]

The Museum was to be 'kept open . . . every day, except Saturday and Sunday in each week; and likewise except Christmas-day and one

1. Add. MS. 6,179. f. 61. John Ward, 1679–1758, biographer, clerk in the Navy Office, schoolmaster and professor of rhetoric at Gresham College, London.
2. Ellis, *Diary*, p. 31. (Add. MS. 36,653.)

week after Easter-day and Whitsunday; Good Friday, and all days . . . specifically appointed for Thanksgivings or Feasts'.[1] For most of the year the hours during which the public might be admitted were from nine in the morning until three in the afternoon. During the summer, on certain days, the Museum was open from four in the afternoon until eight at night, a concession to those engaged in business and unable to come at any other time. But it was no easy matter to gain admission. Indeed, things seemed to be deliberately made as difficult as possible. Entry was strictly by ticket only. Such 'studious and curious persons' as desired to secure admission had to apply to the Porter well in advance, stating their 'names, condition and places of abode'.[2] Only after an application had been considered and approved by the Principal Librarian was a ticket issued. A second call was then necessary to receive it since the ticket was rarely for the day in question, and a third visit was probably necessary before the intending visitor was allowed, at last, to view the collections. No wonder that in those days of long working hours and scanty leisure, very few, other than those of independent means or foreign visitors, could spare sufficient time for the various preliminaries. No more than ten tickets were ever to be delivered for each hour of admittance, and parties, limited to five in number, were conducted round each department in turn by one or another of the Under-Librarians or his assistant.

Thus, its statutes drawn up, its collections tastefully arranged within the splendid rooms of Montagu House, both mansion and gardens looking as good as new, on 15 January 1759, the British Museum opened its doors to visitors for the first time.

1. *Statutes*, p. 7.
2. *op. cit.* p. 9.

CHAPTER THREE

The Early Years

1759–1799

DESPITE the difficulty of securing an entry and the limited time during which members of the public were permitted to look at the collections, the British Museum became at once one of the more popular sights in the metropolis. In 1761, there appeared the first of the many guide books: *'The General Contents of the British Museum: with remarks serving as a directory in viewing that noble cabinet'*.[1] Visitors were not at all numerous, the maximum being for some years about sixty a day, yet the task of showing them round took up the greater part of the officers' time.

The latter were, to be sure, not overworked. As the Trustees pointedly remarked: 'Requiring the attendance of the Officers during the whole six hours that the Museum is kept open is not a wanton or useless piece of severity, as the two vacant hours (if not thought too great a burden upon the Officers) might very usefully be employed by them in better ranging the several Collections'. The officers of the Department of Manuscripts, nevertheless, raised objections. They would prefer to have a day off instead to work on the collections, as they felt 'the impossibility of applying the two spare hours in any serious study, on account of the fatigue of the other four hours attendance',[2] that is, in escorting parties round the building, for the Trustees insisted that the officers must all take their full share 'in attendance upon the company'.[3]

The elegance and beauty of the house itself greatly impressed the majority of the early visitors. A 'stately edifice', one admiringly wrote, and particularly praised the 'many large and magnificent apartments'.[4] 'Of all the houses in London the largest, the completest, and the most magnificent' was the considered judgment of another foreign visitor.[5]

1. Printed for R. and J. Dodsley. London, 1761.
2. *General Meetings, Minutes*, vol. 2, pp. 267, 268, 21 June 1759.
3. *op. cit..* p. 268, 21 June 1759.
4. A. Thomson, *Letters on the British Museum*. London, 1767, p.3.
5. Grosley, *A Tour to London*. London, 1772, vol. 2, p. 23.

Sir Hans Sloane (1660–1753), physician and virtual founder of the British Museum.

Hall and staircase of old Montagu House.

La Fosse's elegant ceilings and the gaily decorated walls of the main staircase were particularly admired.

Having arrived on the landing and noticed the bust of Sir Hans Sloane at the top of the stairs, the party was conducted into a handsome saloon, furnished with a curious selection of miscellaneous objects, for the most part the Egyptian antiquities presented by the Lethieullier family, including the first of the Museum's famous collection of mummies, various specimens of coral, a vulture's head in spirits, and the stuffed flamingo. Here the visitor would await his turn to be conducted round the building, no doubt looking at the paintings on the walls and ceiling, examining the exhibits, or gazing through the tall, graceful windows onto the elegantly laid out gardens or across the fields, criss-crossed by hedges and by the pipes of the New River water company, to the wooded hills of Hampstead and Highgate. His turn at length come, the visitor would pass into a suite of rooms belonging to the Department of Manuscripts, Coins and Medals, the first of which contained part of the Royal Library, together with the Cottonian manuscripts, amongst which Cotton's copy of Magna Carta was admired by fervent patriots, and its partial destruction by the fire at Ashburnham House deplored. Next followed three rooms filled with the Harleian collection, including the Harleian medals, whilst in a fifth room were the medals belonging to Sloane's collection, to the number, it was claimed, of over twenty thousand, whilst in the sixth and last room of the department were to be found Sloane's manuscripts, mostly scientific or medical. The next room contained the greater part of the antiquities and then, crossing the vestibule once again, the visitor entered the west wing, in which were housed Sloane's natural history collections. Descending to the ground floor, by means of a secondary staircase, and passing the 'philosophical apparatus', designed by the Principal Librarian, the perambulation was continued through two rooms devoted to the bulk of the Royal Library, and then through the spacious and handsome suite, overlooking the terrace and the gardens to the north, which contained the printed library of Sir Hans Sloane. Finally, after going through the Trustees' room, the party would be conducted back towards the entrance by way of Major Edwards' library and the remaining portion of the old Royal Library, the rest of which had already been seen at the western extremity of the building.[1]

1. Another early guide to the contents of the Museum, together with plans, appears in *London and its Environs Described*, vol. 2. Dodsley. London, 1761.

c

Yet the Museum was still, to a large extent, in the true eighteenth-century sense, a cabinet of rarities. To the solid fare provided by the bulk of the great founding collections were added such attractions as a 'cyclops pig' and one of the horns which had grown out of the head of an unfortunate woman, Miss Mary Davies, whilst her portrait, complete with both horns, hung on the wall above.[1]

But the needs of the more serious student, for whose benefit the Museum had also been founded, were not forgotten. Even the earliest draft regulations, those of 1757, laid down 'that a particular room be allotted for the persons so admitted [to undertake research], in which they may sit, and read or write, without interruption, during the time the Museum is kept open'.[2] The room first allotted for this purpose was 'the corner room No. 90 in the base storey',[3] a narrow, dark room at the south-west angle of the building with only two windows, the light from which was quite inadequate at the farther end of the table. Nevertheless, it cannot have been wholly cheerless, at least in summer, as it looked out on to the trim lawns and gay flower beds of the well-kept garden. 'A proper wainscot table, covered with green bays in the same manner as those in the libraries',[4] and twenty chairs were more than sufficient for the comparatively few readers who took advantage of these new facilities. On the opening day, 15 January 1759, there were a mere eight readers, for the most part clergymen, and the number grew slowly, though amongst them were to be found such distinguished figures as the great jurist, Blackstone, David Hume and Thomas Gray, whose letters give a vivid picture of the Reading Room in its earliest days. In a letter of 8 August 1759 to his friend, James Brown, Gray wrote: 'Come and see me in my peaceful new settlement, [he had just gone to live in Southampton Row] from whence I have the command of Highgate, Hampstead, Bedford-Gardens & the Musæum. this last (as you will imagine) is my favourite Domain, where I often pass four hours in the day in the stillness & solitude of the reading room, wch is uninterrupted by any thing but Dr Stukeley the Antiquary, who comes there to talk nonsense; & Coffee-house news; the rest of the Learned are (I suppose) in the country, at least none of them come there,

1. *General Contents*, p. 97. 'A Picture of the same Woman and another Horn are shown at Oxford.'
2. *Statutes and Rules relating to the Inspection and Use of the British Museum.* 1757. p. 9.
3. *General Meetings, Minutes*, vol. 1, p. 234. 16 December 1758. The 'base storey' was actually, of course, at ground level.
4. *Committee Minutes*, vol. 2, p. 487. 8 December 1758.

except two Prussians & a man who writes for Ld. Royston. When I call it peaceful, you are to understand it only of us Visiters, for the Society itself, Trustees & all, are up in arms, like the Fellows of a College. the Keepers have broke off all intercourse with one another, & only lower a silent defiance as they pass by. Dr Knight has wall'd up the passage to the little-House, because some of the rest were obliged to pass by one of his windows in the way to it'.[1]

Gray's account of the mutual ill-feeling existing amongst the officers of the Museum is borne out by a passage in the *Statutes and Rules* of 1768 in which the Trustees urge 'that all of them [the senior officers] in general should consider themselves, and the other officers, as gentlemen living under the same roof, and equally engaged in carrying on the same noble design, and among whom, for that, as well as for other reasons, no personal pique or animosity should ever find the least place; but the most perfect harmony and a true spirit of benevolence ought always to be cultivated and prevail;'[2] At this time, it seems, one of the principal causes of the discord amongst the staff was Dr Peter Templeman,[3] first Keeper of the Reading Room, whose point of view differed radically from those of his colleagues. A physician, he was said to be so fond of literary leisure and of the society of learned men that, having independent means, he never troubled to acquire an extensive practice. Like two other medical men closely connected with the Museum, Matthew Maty and Dr William Watson, he was a member of the Medical Club which met every fortnight at the Queen's Arms in St Paul's Churchyard.

Templeman was of valetudinarian temper and resented the dreariness of the room in which his official life was passed. An entry in his note book shows how weary he was of it all. 'On Wednesday all the company going away a little after one of the clock, the Room being cold and the weather likely to rain, I thought it proper to move off too. Nothing material has happened that I know of'.[4] It was Templeman, too, when taking a breath of air in the gardens outside the Reading Room one sunny day was met by an irate Trustee who, horrified by this

1. Gray to Brown, 8 August 1759. *Correspondence*, vol. 2, p. 632. James Brown was President of Pembroke Hall, Cambridge. Gray himself was first admitted as a reader on 20 July 1759. 'Mr Gray of Southampton Row for two months'. *Committee Minutes*, vol. 2, p. 554. See also Gray's letter of 23 July 1759, to Mason. (*Correspondence*, vol.2, p. 629.)
2. *Statutes and Rules*, p. 74.
3. Peter Templeman, 1711–1769.
4. Quoted in Barwick, p. 24.

breach of the statutes, greeted the astonished Keeper with a severe 'Go back, Sir!'[1]

Certain manuscripts were never allowed to go into the Reading Room, the Codex Alexandrinus, two *codices aurei*, all the illuminated manuscripts, and three volumes of original royal letters. These were to be seen in the department of manuscripts by special arrangement, whilst not more than two books of prints were to be made available in the reading room in any one day. Even with so few readers, the lack of additional facilities for special classes of material was obviously felt, but these were not to be provided for well over a hundred years. A tentative step, however, in this direction was the order of the Trustees on 10 February 1759 that a special table, six feet by eight feet, was to be erected in the middle room of the first state story for the perusal of the maps and surveys from the Sloane collection, the humble forerunner of the present Map Room. On the day this order was made, it was learnt that Lord Egmont was to present a valuable collection of charts, 'said to be made by Mr Cambden', which arrived on 24 February.[2]

Templeman continued to be difficult. He complained that the long hours were gravely impairing his health. The Committee merely noted in answer, that they had 'no power to dispense with any part of the six hours of daily attendance required of him'[3]. He soon found other things to grumble at. He did not like the living quarters allotted to him in the Museum and complained bitterly. In the Trustees' view, he was also being too liberal in his attitude towards the readers. Unauthorised copyists, that useful breed of literary 'devils', had been allowed in, and he was actually assisting readers to get hold of books and manuscripts more quickly than was normal, to the indignation of his colleagues, who saw no reason why readers should want books from *their* departments to study. The Trustees first ordered, on 3 February 1759, 'that Dr Templeman do not suffer any person to be brought into the reading room by persons who have leave to study therein, in order to take copies or make drawings from them, without their having obtain'd leave of the Committee for that purpose'.[4] This disposed of the copyists. Then on 14 September, after vigorous representations by his colleagues, Templeman was firmly reminded that the officers of Printed Books and

1. *op. cit.*, p. 24.
2. *Committee Minutes*, vol. 2, pp. 509, 510, 515, 10, 24 February 1759. John Perceval, 2nd Earl of Egmont, 1711–1770, First Lord of the Admiralty, 1763–1766.
3. *op. cit.*, vol. 3, p. 643. 17 October 1760.
4. *op. cit.*, vol. 2, p. 508, 3 February 1759.

of Manuscripts 'are the proper Judges' as to whether or not a book or manuscript was to go into the Reading Room 'without special leave'.[1] Finally, on 27 June 1760, 'a Complaint having been made that the Duty of the several officers and servants has been rendered burthensome by disorderly applications from the Reading Room for Books of which no previous notice had been given the day before', Templeman was ordered strictly to enforce the rule that a day's notice must be given for any book or manuscript, except in the most extraordinary circumstances.[2]

So much for the first attempt to expedite the supply of books to readers, no more successful than the many which have succeeded it. All this was too much for poor Templeman. On the 18 December 1760 he resigned on grounds of ill-health, to be succeeded by the Rev. Richard Penneck. Penneck, described in a testimonial presented at the time to the Trustees as 'a young clergyman . . . whose sobriety and morality in general are without exception',[3] got on well with both the readers and his colleagues. During his long tenure, from 1761 to 1803, the services of the reading room developed steadily, though numbers still remained few.

It must not be thought that the Trustees, even at this early period, were indifferent to the needs of the readers. Only fears for the safety of the great collections entrusted to them made them, at times, unduly cautious. On 19 June 1760 they minuted: 'As admission into the Reading Room is by all regulations hitherto made, entirely left to the Committee, they think it necessary to observe that the liberty of studying in the Museum is the part of this Institution from which the Publick is like to reap the greatest benefit; and that therefore admission into the Reading Room should be made as convenient as possible: that as the number of persons applying for the liberty of the Reading Room or at least of those making use of it when granted has not hitherto caused any inconvenience the only case necessary at present is to prevent improper persons from being admitted.' And they went on to suggest that the Principal Librarian should be empowered to grant admission on those days on which the Committee was not sitting, a reversal of the original tendency to grant tickets of admission only to those individuals known personally to the Trustees or the officers, or recommended by persons of rank.[4]

1. op. cit., vol. 2, p. 565, 14 September 1759.
2. op. cit., vol. 3, p. 628, 27 June 1760.
3. Add. MS. 32,903. f. 380.
4. General Meetings, Minutes, vol. 2, p. 327, 19 January 1760.

Nevertheless, readers and prospective readers were scarcely pampered, and it was lucky that to most of them time was of no importance. The twenty-four hour rule was again strictly enforced and notice had to be given the day before to the officer in charge of the room by each reader 'what Book or Manuscript he will be desirous of perusing the following day'.[1] In due course, the book would be handed over to him personally by one of the officers. He might, if he so wished, make notes, but if for any reason he left the room, even for a moment, he must hand back the book and claim it on his return.

The temporary reader, the chance enquirer, was not forgotten. Those having 'occasion to consult or inspect any Book, Charter or Deed for Evidence or Information other than for Studying' might be admitted on application to the Trustees or, in an emergency, to the Principal Librarian. Such readers might, however, only consult a book or manuscript in the presence of the Principal Librarian himself or of one of the officers of the department to which it belonged. Not surprisingly for many years there were few temporary readers.[2] Efforts were made to improve the Reading Room and make it more comfortable. In 1765 the Trustees ordered the floor covered with rush matting and the window frames – doubtless rattling with the September gales – repaired and made tight.[3]

The Museum was now set on the course it was to maintain for so long, despite the perennial shortage of money, at times of enough for even the most pressing bills. Again and again the Trustees were forced to petition Parliament for additional grants. As early as April 1760 they had appealed to the Treasury for more money. 'Without some additional support,' they declared, 'it [the Museum] cannot possibly be carried on'.[4]

In 1762, Parliament granted the sum of £2,000, the same two years later, and further subventions of the same amount, increased eventually to £3,000. Paltry sums, even at that date, and already grossly inadequate for a national collection, as politicians as diverse in their outlooks as Edmund Burke and John Wilkes indignantly pointed out. Wilkes, in particular, was a strong advocate of increasing government grants to the Museum, and also of establishing a proper national gallery of art, possibly in 'the spacious garden of the British Museum'. Burke

1. *Statutes and Rules,* 1759, p. 21.
2. *op. cit.,* p. 24.
3. *Committee Minutes,* vol. 4, p. 1021, 27 September 1765.
4. *General Meetings, Minutes,* vol. 2, p. 316, 22 April 1760.

supported the motion, and demanded as well that the Museum's grant be increased from £3,000 to £5,000.[1]

The Museum was undoubtedly getting crowded. Maty, as Principal Librarian, had reported to a Committee of the House of Commons that all the tickets to visit the Museum were engaged for a week ahead and that over 300 persons were waiting to visit the galleries. The previous summer, at one time more than 2,000 applicants had awaited admission and there had been three months delay in granting tickets. There was no other museum in Europe, he stated, in such a position, with 10,000 visitors a year. Neither Maty nor the Committee seem to have considered that a reform of the cumbersome system of admission was the real answer. The Principal Librarian likewise pointed out that it was unpleasant for the officers, who had to be men of liberal education and have 'considerable Knowledge in the modern as well as in the antient languages', to have to take round the Museum 'the lower kind of people, who, in many instances, have behaved improperly to them'. The Committee were of the opinion that all this arose from letting people in without paying and that the Trustees should be empowered 'to demand and receive money for the admission of Persons to see the said Museum, some days and hours being still allotted for receiving Persons gratis'. The Trustees themselves were of a different opinion. On 31 January 1784 they resolved 'That it appears to them that no dependence can be placed on the regularity of any revenue that might accrue from admitting persons to the sight of the Museum for money and that even if the amount of such revenue could be in any ways ascertained . . . it would be but a small proportion to the deficiencies of the regular expenditure of the Museum.' To the relief of the Trustees, the bill authorising the entrance charges was defeated in the House of Commons, and so for many years the Museum managed as best it could on what, even by contemporary standards, was a mere pittance.[2]

With so small an income there was little money to spare for buying books, or indeed, anything else. In 1766, £2 8s 6d was spent on printed books, and no manuscripts at all were bought for many years. The total expenses for the museum amounted annually to about £1,850, whilst the average income from the endowment was rarely more than £900. The difference had to be made good from money grudgingly voted by Parliament and from the proceeds from sale of duplicates.[3]

1. *Parliamentary History*, vol. 19, col. 187–192.
2. CJ, vol. 34, pp. 73, 89. *General Meetings, Minutes*, pp. 858, 9 January 1784.
3. This was authorised by the Act 7 Geo. II. c.18. *An Act to enable the Trustees of the*

Only the interest on the money bequeathed to the Museum by Major Edwards which had at last reverted to the Trustees in January 1769, and the salary of the Royal Librarian, also eventually paid to the Trustees, permitted the formation of a tiny purchase fund. It was very small, £300 from the Edwards fund and £248 from the Royal Library, but without it, the prospect would have been bleak indeed.[1] Gray was hardly exaggerating when he wrote in 1759: 'the Trustees lay out 500£ more than their income; so you may expect, all the books & the crocodiles will soon be put up to auction'.[2] It must have seemed monstrous to the Trustees when, in April 1798, they were assessed on their meagre resources for the newly introduced income tax. They were presented with a demand for £675 16s 6d yet, as they indignantly pointed out, their whole regular income being £1,149 1s 0d this would leave them with almost nothing either to pay their staff or to maintain the buildings. Eventually the Commission agreed to levy only a moderate tax, but it left the Trustees' finances more straitened than ever.[3]

Yet despite this official parsimony, the collections grew through the generosity of many individual donors, often themselves Trustees. Horace Walpole, as so often, clearly realised what would happen. 'The Establishment of the British Museum', he wrote, 'seems a charter for incorporating the arts, a new era of *vertu.*' A collector who 'should destine his collection to the British Museum' would feel 'he was

1. The reversion of the salary of the Royal Librarian came to the Trustees in 1774, on the death of Claudius Amyand, who had purchased the office from the younger Bentley in 1745. Amyand was said to have paid £2,300 for it, but, subsequently, the price was said to have been less than half of that amount. Details of the money received from Major Edwards' fund is given in *Appendix 19* to the *Report of the Select Committee on the British Museum*, 1835. (PP, 1835, vol. 7, p. 423.) The original amount paid by his executors in 1769 was £7,500, which was invested and the interest, for many years, expended solely on the purchase of printed books. In September 1785 the Edwards and Royal Library funds were amalgamated. From 1785 until the closure of the fund in June 1815, £16,135 was spent on every type of acquisition – books, manuscripts, coins, prints, antiquities and so on. It was finally extinguished in order to help pay for the von Moll collection of books and fossils.
2. *Correspondence*, vol. 2, pp. 632, 633.
3. *Committee Minutes*, vol. 8, p. 2150, 12 May 1798.

British Museum to exchange, sell or dispose of any Duplicates, etc. A number of valuable works were lost to the Museum in these sales of duplicates, some of which were subsequently bought back by the Trustees. The last of such sales was held in 1832.

collecting for his country. . . . If pictures and statues flow into books and medals and curiosities of every kind, may we not flatter ourselves that a British Academy of Arts will arise'.[1]

One of the most munificent gifts was made in 1762, when the great collection of tracts formed by the London bookseller George Thomason of the Rose and Crown, St Pauls, during the Civil War, was bought and presented to the Museum by the young George III on the advice of the favourite Lord Bute for £300, far less than they had cost the original owner. This wonderful collection, containing almost every tract or pamphlet issued by London booksellers between 1640 and 1661, more than 33,000 publications, had been painstakingly gathered by Thomason who realised the interest to posterity of the host of pamphlets and other ephemera which poured from the press during these turbulent years. In addition he secured many manuscripts, which the conditions of those days made it difficult or impossible to print, and a considerable number of foreign pamphlets, thanks to his position as a prominent London bookseller and the friend of distinguished Presbyterians and other persons of influence. At the Restoration, his collection was refused by both the King and the University of Oxford, to whom Thomason had wished to sell it. It had remained in the hands of the descendants of Samuel Mearne, Charles II's bookseller, who had taken charge of the collection when its purchase was being considered by the King, until its acquisition in 1762 by George III.[2]

Another important gift of these early days was that of Solomon Da Costa, a Dutch Jew from Amsterdam who had settled in England early in the eighteenth century. Having made a fortune 'without scandal or meanness', he spent it in philanthropic works, not only amongst members of his own community, but also on the poor of every race and creed. Early in life Da Costa had come across a rich collection of Hebrew books, superbly bound with the Royal cypher on the covers, which had apparently been acquired by Charles II, sent to the royal stationer for binding and then left there, since there was no money to pay the bill. In 1759 Da Costa wrote to the Trustees offering his treasured collection to the Museum 'as a small token of my esteem, love, reverence, and gratitude to this most magnanimous nation; and as a thanksgiving offering, in part, for the generous protection and numberless blessings

1. Add. MS. 38,791. f. 1.
2. G. K. Fortescue, *Catalogue of the Pamphlets . . . collected by George Thomason, 1640–1661*. London, 1908. Preface.

which I have enjoyed under it'.[1] The Trustees accepted Da Costa's generous offer and so this small but fine collection of Hebrew Biblical manuscripts and of early printed books in that tongue took its place in the Museum library.

Even before the opening, a number of additions to the original collection of antiquities had been received. The majority of these were gifts of three members of the Lethieullier family. Between them, from 1756 to 1770, they bequeathed or donated several valuable antiquities. The Lethieullier collection of Egyptian curios, for example, consisted of about thirty miscellaneous pieces, including two mummies, which immediately proved a popular attraction.[2]

The natural history collections were the next to benefit, when they obtained the remarkable collection of fossils found in Hampshire by Gustavus Brander,[3] one of the Trustees. Although their true significance was not yet appreciated, such fossils were already receiving considerable attention from scientific men and arousing wide interest amongst the general public. The Brander collection was carefully examined and described by the eminent Swedish scientist, Daniel Solander,[4] who had been first a reader, and then an increasingly important member of the Museum staff, which he had joined in 1763. Solander's name is forever linked with that of a younger and more famous man, Joseph Banks, whose long and intimate connection with the British Museum lasted from the day in August 1765 when he was admitted to the Reading Room as a young man of twenty-one, till his death in 1819, a Trustee and one of the greatest of the Museum's benefactors.

It was largely owing to Banks and Solander that the Museum aquired so many valuable accessions to its collections from the voyages of the great explorers of the latter part of the eighteenth century. Cook and Menzies, for example, both bestowed valuable gifts upon the

1. *Memoirs of Thomas Hollis. Appendix*, p. 614. Another version of Da Costa's letter is in GM, February 1760.
2. The Lethieullier family were distinguished City merchants, originally from Brabant. Smart Lethieullier, 1701–1760, one of the original Sloane trustees, was perhaps the best known, both as an antiquary and as a man of letters. His cousin, Colonel William Lethieullier, FSA, had travelled extensively in Egypt and it was his collection, added to by Smart and by William's son, Pitt Lethieullier, which was presented to the Museum.
3. Gustavus Brander, 1720–1787, merchant and antiquary, of Swedish descent.
4. Daniel Charles Solander, 1736–1782, born at Norrland, Sweden. It was Linnaeus who, in 1759, urged his 'much loved pupil' to visit England and furnished him with the necessary letters of introduction.

Museum.[1] Here, the presence amongst Sloane's collections of a number of ethnographical specimens (though relatively few) was of paramount importance. The fact that the Museum from the very beginning had possessed examples of the arts and crafts of primitive peoples undoubtedly led to other and more valuable objects of the same kind being sent to join them. But for Sloane, perhaps Cook, Banks, George III, and other benefactors of the ethnographical collections would not have bequeathed their treasures so readily to a young and comparatively unknown institution.

From the great first voyage of HMS *Endeavour* came several outstanding specimens of Polynesian art, and the later voyages again contributed much. On 26 September 1775, Maty wrote to Hardwicke: 'The Museum is going to be enriched with a complete and most superb collection of all the natural as well as artificial curiosities which have been found in the expedition to the South Seas'. The Admiralty, Maty stressed, was insistent that these collections must be displayed at the Museum 'in a particular manner and in a distinguished place as a monument of these national exertions of British munificence and industry'. Even though it was difficult in the confined space available, 'a room has been fixed up in the house for their reception' papered by the Trustees in 1778 'with a neat Mosaic pattern', at a cost of about £3 12s 6d.[2] This 'Otaheiti or South Sea Room' was always popular. A description of 1807 gives a picture of it as it was at that date: 'In the left corner is the mourning dress of an Otaheitean lady; opposite are rich cloaks and helmets of feathers from the Sandwich Islands. Over the fire place are the Cava bowls and, above them, battoons [and] various other implements of war. The idols of the various islands, present, in their hideous rudeness, a singular contrast with many of the works of art'.[3] The 'mourning dress' has always been considered one collected during Cook's voyages. There is little doubt that the tradition is correct and most probably the dress was presented by Cook himself. George

1. James Cook, 1728–1779, the circumnavigator. Archibald Menzies, 1754–1842, naval surgeon and explorer. 'An ample collection of natural and artificial curiosities brought home by Menzies from North West America and the South Sea Islands' was deposited by His Majesty in 1796. (*General Meetings, Minutes*, vol. 4, p. 922, February 13, 1796.) On 13 January 1792 Banks presented 'numerous animals, most of them in spirits', collected by himself on Cook's first voyage or by Cook on the two subsequent voyages. (*Committee Minutes*, vol. 8, p.2049.)
2. Add. MS. 35,612. f. 323. *Committee Minutes*, vol. 6, p. 1063, 6 March 1778.
3. David Hughson [i.e., David Pugh.] *London, being an Accurate History of the British Metropolis*. London, 1805–9, vol. 4, p. 390.

Forster the younger, one of the naturalists who accompanied Cook on his second voyage, wrote of these dresses, 'Captain Cook has given one to the British Museum'.[1] When, in 1966, the dress was dismantled for more effective conservation, it was found to be mounted on a European made easel and, most surprisingly, a small wooden figure, whose existence was previously unsuspected, was found inside the head covering. Both the little figure, an image representing a minor spirit, and the easel, were probably incorporated when the dress was made up, presumably on board Cook's ship HMS *Resolution*. The figure was almost certainly placed there by the Tahitians who assembled the dress for Cook, as a charm to ward off the evil effects of taking such a sacred object as the mourning dress away from Tahiti, and so its existence remained unsuspected, to Cook and his crew and to all subsequent observers until its recent discovery.[2]

The natural history collections likewise benefited from the gifts of the great navigators and discoverers. Cook, for instance, gave to the Museum, it is said, the first kangaroo ever to be seen in Europe.[3]

Of the hundred odd pieces in the present ethnographical collections acquired during this period only the mourning dress, however, is known to have been given by Cook himself. Many articles originally collected by Cook came to the Museum when the Vancouver collection was purchased. Another early donation resulting from Cook's second voyage was 'a collection from New Zealand & Amsterdam in the South Seas [Tongatapu, visited by Furneaux on the second voyage and revisited by Cook on the third voyage] brought by capt[n] Furneaux, consisting of 18 articles, domestic and military', presented by the Admiralty on 3 February 1775.[4]

During all this time, further small collections were being acquired. In April 1766, the King presented a collection of Egyptian antiquities and natural products formed by Edward Wortley Montagu,[5] husband of the celebrated blue-stocking, Mrs Montagu. Dr Maty, Under-Librarian of the Department of Printed Books, made extensive purchases at the same sale of the famous sculptor Roubillac's studio in May 1762 and, on the

1. G. Forster, *A Voyage round the World*. London, 1777, vol. 2, p. 72.
2. B. Cranstone, *The Tahitian Mourner's Dress*. BMQ, vol. 32, pp. 138–144.
3. Edwards, *Lives of the Founders of the British Museum*. p. 334.
4. *Committee Minutes*, vol. 6, p. 1454. It was the arrival of this collection which so greatly excited Matthew Maty.
Tobias Furneaux, 1735–1781, commanded the *Adventure* on Cook's second voyage.
5. Edward Wortley Montagu, 1678–1761, diplomatist.

28th of that month, presented seventeen busts to the Museum, together with several pictures, all portraits, and other busts and pictures on subsequent occasions between 1760 and 1776. He also invited his friend Casanova to look round the Museum. It is improbable that the famous amorist found at that date much to interest him within its sober walls.[1] Casanova did succeed in selling to Maty a bogus antique gem, 'un onyx d'une grande beauté', said to be by the classical sculptor Sostratis, whose signature it allegedly bore. In his *Mémoires* Casanova wonders whether 'elle est peut-être encore au Musée britannique'[2] but it no longer seems to be, if indeed it ever was.

A few books were bought out of the Edwards fund, then almost the sole source of ready money for any purchases, whilst in 1767 an interesting collection of specimens of volcanic origin and of other geological items, including, in 1769, a 'mushroom stone', were presented by William Hamilton, the newly appointed envoy to the court of Naples who, in Gibbon's words, was 'wisely diverting his correspondence from the Secretary of State to the Royal Society and British Museum'.[3]

But it was not Hamilton's specimens of volcanic rock, for the most part personally gathered on the slopes of Vesuvius, that were to make the Museum so much his debtor, but a more magnificent collection which over the years he had been building up.

William Hamilton, though well born, and despite many close connections with aristocratic and even royal personages, was as poor as befitted the younger son of a younger son. His upbringing in the household of Frederick, Prince of Wales, had led to an intimate friendship with that unfortunate Prince's son, the future George III, a friendship he was only to lose in old age through his disastrous second marriage. After a relatively undistinguished military and parliamentary career, Hamilton was appointed Envoy Extraordinary to the Court of Naples in 1764, a post he was destined to hold for over thirty years. He had early been bitten by the mania for collecting and brought to it taste and discrimination rare at that period. Always in comparatively modest circumstances, he formed his successive collections mainly as a form of investment, hoping to recoup his considerable outlay by selling his accumulated treasures at a profit. Long before he took up his appointment at

1. Casanova, *Mémoires*. Pléiade edition, vol. 3, p. 323.
2. *op. cit.*, vol. 2, p. 807.
3. *The Autobiography of Edward Gibbon*, ed. by John Murray. London, 1896, p. 268. Sir William Hamilton, 1730–1803, diplomatist and antiquary.

Naples, he had moved at ease amongst the cognoscenti and lovers of fine things to be found in the circle of Horace Walpole, who had prophesied that Hamilton would soon 'ruin himself in virtuland',[1] as, indeed, he more than once nearly did. As a young officer, he had formed a small but choice collection of pictures, which he had soon to sell to pay his mounting debts. 'I was obliged to sell my collection of pictures . . . on which I doted, rather than bear to be dunned',[2] and this, to his sorrow, was to a large extent to be the fate of his subsequent acquisitions.

In the Kingdom of Naples Hamilton found a setting worthy of his scientific and archaeological talents. His excursions on the slopes of Vesuvius and Etna, often at great personal risk, resulted in the fine volcanological collection, given to the Museum in 1767. It also led to his election to the Royal Society in 1766, and to the title bestowed on him by French savants of *Le Pline moderne de Vésuve*. But in the field of archaeology he was to achieve greater renown and to benefit both the British Museum and other institutions. Almost from his earliest days in Naples, Hamilton had set about forming as fine a collection of Greek vases as his means would allow. He was the first to collect seriously these relics and the first 'who recognised the value of these unpretentious vessels for forming and ennobling modern art-taste'.[3] By 1772, he had gathered together about seven hundred and thirty pottery vases; a hundred and seventy five terracottas; about three hundred specimens of ancient glass, including some extremely fine funerary urns; six hundred bronzes, including arms and armour, and a great many miscellaneous antiquities, amongst them a first-class collection of more than six thousand coins. Hamilton published a description of his collection, with numerous plates, the text being by a French savant, D'Hancarville,[4] and it soon became widely known among connoisseurs. Many of the vases and other antiquities which are now considered to be of Greek origin, were regarded by Hamilton and his contemporaries as the visible remains of the Etruscan people, whose mysterious origins and shadowy existence appealed to the romantic taste of the late eighteenth century.

1. Walpole to Mann, 8 June 1764. *Correspondence*, vol. 22, p. 243.
2. Hamilton to Charles Greville, 12 September 1780. A. Morrison, *The Hamilton and Nelson Papers*, no. 95.
3. A. Michaelis, *Ancient Marbles in Great Britain*, p. 110.
4. *A Collection of Etruscan, Greek and Roman Antiquities from the Cabinet of the Hon. W. Hamilton*. 4 vol. Naples, 1766-7.

Hamilton arranged for some of his plates to be circulated in proof and these were brought to the notice of the great potter, Josiah Wedgewood. Such examples of the potter's art greatly excited him and were the inspiration of much of his finest work. The name of his factory, 'Etruria', was an acknowledgment of the debt he owed to the supposed creators of these masterly specimens of his craft, and he celebrated the opening of these new works in 1769 by producing six handsome black vases, decorated with three figures taken from Hamilton's book.

In 1772 Hamilton travelled to England in order to sell his collection and approached the Trustees of the British Museum to see if they were interested. Alexander Thomson, author of *Letters on the British Museum*, had already remarked in 1767, 'I am sorry to acquaint you that the collection of these antiquaries [of Greece and Rome] is far short of what I hoped to find',[1] none of the founding collections being, in this aspect, at all distinguished. The Trustees were fortunately not slow to grasp this unparalleled opportunity. They applied to Parliament for a special grant to obtain Hamilton's vases – the first time that this had been done – and on 20 March 1772, having given a committee of the House an opportunity to satisfy themselves of its real value, Parliament voted a sum of £8,410 to purchase the collection 'for the Use of the Publick', together with a further £840 to enable the Trustees 'to provide a Proper Repository'.[2] However, for the moment no extension to the existing building was considered necessary, and the vases were exhibited in the twelfth room of Montagu House, an elegant and spacious room upstairs. It needed the arrival of an even more famous collection of classical antiquities before any addition was made to the rapidly filling rooms of the old mansion. In the rest of his time at Naples, Sir William Hamilton formed a second and even finer collection of antiquities. This was not destined to reach the Museum. Much of it was lost at sea and the rest was gradually dispersed.

But the Trustees did not always behave with the foresight they displayed in the case of the Hamilton vases, even though they were supported by the testimony of Josiah Wedgewood, who told a committee of the House of Commons that, within two years, he had himself by his imitation of Hamilton's vases, brought into the country about three times the sum which the collection had cost.[3] The antiquary and

1. *Letters on the British Museum*, p. 28.
2. CJ, vol.33, p. 602, 20 March 1772.
3. Edwards, *Founders*, p. 353.

pioneer of geographical studies, Richard Gough,[1] had a high opinion of the Museum as a suitable repository for the nation's treasures. 'Many capital collections of MSS have been dispersed irrecoverably ... a public library is the safest port, and of all public libraries the British Museum is on the most liberal plan, deficient only in the want of a sufficeint fund to furnish itself with what it may not suit the wishes or the finances of many good collectors to bestow on it.'[2]

Nevertheless, when some time later Gough approached Samuel Harper, Keeper of Printed Books, for permission to deposit at the Museum the plates illustrating his book *Sepulchral Monuments*, he met with a decided rebuff, one Trustee allegedly saying that he 'would not be his warehouseman'.[3] Enraged at this cavalier treatment, Gough made arrangements for his collections of maps and charts to go at his death to the Bodleian Library.

The other two departments were growing, though for the moment, their acquisitions were perhaps less outstanding than those of the department of Natural and Artificial Productions. The most valuable donation to come to the Library during the last decades of the eighteenth century was the collection of plays bequeathed in 1779 by David Garrick.[4] The earlier collections had been lacking in works of popular literature. Thus the Lumley Library which formed the basis of much of the Old Royal Library, though formed during the greatest years of the Elizabethan and Jacobean drama, contained not one specimen of a play, even by the most eminent authors, still less of popular tales and ballads. Serious students had no time for such 'baggage books', as Sir Thomas Bodley called them. The Garrick plays, therefore, consisting of the dramatic works of most of the great Elizabethan and Jacobean writers, as well as of a host of minor and anonymous authors, supplied a major deficiency in the Museum collections and enabled Charles Lamb and other writers, shaping the taste of the new generation, to introduce such forgotten figures as Webster, Middleton and Tourneur to a more appreciative public.

The Department of Manuscripts had already acquired the large

1. Richard Gough, 1735–1809, antiquarian.
2. *British Topography*. London, 1780. Preface, p. xlvii.
3. There is no direct evidence that this abusive remark was ever made, but Gough certainly believed that it had been. (Nichols, *Literary History*, p. 577.)
4. David Garrick, 1717–1779, the actor. On 27 May 1770 the Trustees noted that the plays had been received, 'except a few volumes which have not hitherto been found'. (*General Meetings, Minutes*, vol. 4, p. 814.)

manuscript collections of Dr Thomas Birch, one of the original Trustees.[1] Birch, an energetic and zealous Trustee, and a close friend of Sloane, had done much to help the Museum during these early years, at times acting as secretary if one of the Under-Librarians was unable to fulfill that task. On his death in 1766, he bequeathed many valuable manuscripts, for the most part dealing with English history and biography, together with a considerable number of printed books on the same subjects. Amongst his other duties, Matthew Maty, then Under-Librarian in charge of Printed Books, busied himself in sorting out the Birch collections, as he tells Lord Hardwicke in a letter of July 1766. Maty goes on to say that he hopes to produce a short account of Birch's life and writings, but apparently he never did so. Hardwicke comments somewhat acidly, 'This Account has never been given not much to Dr Matys credit [?] who had obligations to poor Dr B.'[2]

It is now time to look more closely at those who guided the early steps of the Museum.

The first Principal Librarian, that learned physician and experimental scientist, Dr Gowin Knight, seems to have been a somewhat irascible man. Not only did he quarrel with most of his senior colleagues, as gleefully noted by Gray, but also found himself at variance on more than one occasion with the Trustees, being first rebuked by them in April 1760 for an implied criticism of their conduct. Knight had questioned the draft of the proposed regulations in a manner 'which appeared . . . to contain a very unjust & disrespectful Reflexions (sic) on the proceedings of the Standing Committee'.[3]

Two years later there was again trouble. The Principal Librarian, in the opinion of some of the Trustees, was maintaining improper relations with the contractors and, without due authority, employing tradesmen and workmen of his own choosing. Dr Knight, in reply, accused the Committee of prejudice and spoke bitterly of his endless disputes with both the Museum Surveyor and various tradesmen, not, one presumes, with those whom he himself favoured.[4] The Trustees came to believe however, that 'there does not appear any ground to suspect any collusive or unfair practice between them'.[5] The dispute seems to have been

1. Thomas Birch, 1705–1766, historian and biographer, one of the original Sloane Trustees and later among the first elected Trustees of the Museum.
2. M. Maty to Lord Hardwicke, 26 July 1766. Add. MS. 35,607. f. 284.
3. *General Meetings, Minutes*, vol. 2, p. 304, 5 April 1760.
4. *op. cit.*, vol. 2, p. 398, 6 February 1762.
5. *op. cit.*, vol. 2, p. 422, 26 June 1762.

caused entirely by Knight's irascible temper. Through all these re-criminations he went on with his inventions – inventions such as his improved compass widely used in the Navy – for which he was best known to his contemporaries. On 18 April 1760, for instance, he was granted a patent for 'a new Machine Window-Blind far superior to any that have hitherto been used'.[1]

Knight died in 1772, to be succeeded by Dr Matthew Maty, a Dutchman born in Utrecht in 1718 of French Protestant parents. Like Knight he was a doctor of medicine, having received his degree at Leyden in 1740. On coming to England in the following year, he practised as a physician, but soon deserted medicine for more congenial literary fields. During his medical career he had been an early and active advocate for the practice of inoculation against smallpox, experimenting on himself unknown to his family.

Maty was appointed on 19 June 1756 as one of the three original Under-Librarians, being described by the writer of a testimonial on that occasion as a 'sensible, prudent & civil writer'[2] despite, the handicap of a slight foreign accent which he never succeeded in overcoming. His courtesy and urbanity whilst showing visitors the Museum collections were warmly praised by Grosley.[3]

Starting as the Under-Librarian in charge of Printed Books, in 1765 Maty was transferred to the Department of Natural and Artificial Productions, exchanging departments with Samuel Harper, newly created an Under-Librarian, who had expressed a strong preference to stay in Printed Books.[4]

The lack of specialisation and the fluid state of the establishment is well marked throughout this period and, indeed, for many years later. Like Secretaries of State, Under-Librarians, in theory at least, had no regular department and might, at the wishes of the Trustees, move anywhere within the Museum and take charge of any part of the collections.

Not everyone, however, thought highly of Maty. Doctor Johnson had a marked dislike for the little Dutchman, who had made disparaging

1. Add. MS. 36,123. f. 197.
2. Add. MS. 36,269. f. 105. Maty's application for the post of Under-Librarian is Add. MS. 36,269. f. 102.
3. Grosley, vol. 2, p. 25.
4. Harper had succeeded Empson. On 1 June 1765, Maty wrote to Lord Hardwicke, 'Poor Mr Empson is now very near his end, being hardly able to get out of his bed'. (Add. MS. 35,607. f. 175.)

remarks about his *Dictionary* and, in addition, had alluded to Johnson in unfriendly terms in the *Journal Britannique*, a periodical which Maty had for long conducted. When a friend suggested that Johnson should be Maty's assistant in running the *Journal*, the former was furious. 'He', exclaimed the Doctor, 'the little black dog. I'd throw him into the Thames!'[1]

Johnson was more friendly with Maty's successor as Principal Librarian, the Keeper of Manuscripts, Dr Morton whose long reign lasted the rest of the century. Johnson had been granted a ticket, on Morton's recommendation, in May 1761 but there is no evidence that he actually used the Reading Room itself. If he came to the Museum, he probably worked in Dr Morton's private room and so avoided any contact with the Keeper of Printed Books whom he so much disliked. As with so many of the early officers, Maty regarded his Museum duties as merely a part-time occupation. Thus, when in 1760 he was considering taking the post of Secretary of the Society for the Encouragement of Arts, Manufactures and Commerce, he wrote to Lord Hardwicke pointing out that his Museum hours would not interfere in any way with this additional post and that the books and plants available there would greatly assist him in his work as secretary to the Society. The salary he received from the British Museum was not, in his opinion, compatible with the amount of work he was expected to do and, in any case, it was insufficient to support a large and growing family. As a foreigner, he continued, he was excluded from all places of 'trust and profit', and though an Under-Librarian's post at the British Museum was, presumably, a place of trust, it certainly was not one of profit. Though he was unsuccessful in obtaining this post, a few years later he was appointed the foreign secretary of the Royal Society, an office he held for the rest of his life. In this capacity he seems also to have fallen out with Joseph Banks, the young president of that Society, but for the most part he was agreeable and well disposed, with a wide circle of friends. When he became Principal Librarian in 1772, his health was already failing and, 'siezed with a languishing disorder'[2] he died, to be succeeded at the head of the Museum by Dr Charles Morton, Keeper of the Department of Manuscripts and another of the original Under-Librarians.

A physician, like his two predecessors, Morton was a man of sedentary habits, extremely idle, disposed to let things run on from day to day and rarely to show the slightest initiative. During the twenty-three years

1. Boswell, p. 284.
2. Nichols, *Illustrations*, vol. 3, p. 217.

of his Principal Librarianship, he did little to enhance the reputation of the institution. True, he had insufficient funds, but all was wrapped in a sleepy torpor and it needed the energy and skill of younger men to bring the Museum more into line with the radical spirit of the coming century. Morton and his fellows were, on the whole, content to wait for generous bequests to be made to them rather than pursue an active policy. The Trustees were to complain more than once of his failure to carry out his duties in a satisfactory manner. On the 26 May 1781, they angrily commented that they had the 'undoubted right' to the constant attendance of the officers, whenever the Museum was opened, that this applied just as much to the Principal Librarian as to anyone else. He was under their orders, as if directly appointed by them, and the general care and superintendence of the institution were particularly his concern.

Dr Morton certainly took his duties lightly. Even when, as in 1780, the very existence of the Museum was threatened by savage mobs during the Gordon riots and both house and grounds were full of troops, he could not be bothered to return from leave. The Trustees considered his conduct in this respect, 'highly improper and irregular'.[1] He must not live away from the Museum, they insisted, without leave from the Board. The following September they were still complaining of his absences. His attendance, they considered 'is not adequate to the duty required from a principal Librarian'.[2] All Morton could plead in extenuation was that his health was bad, but this failed to satisfy the Trustees, and the good doctor survived for another eighteen years.

Amongst those who had tried unsuccessfully to obtain the post of Principal Librarian at Maty's death was the Rev. Samuel Ayscough.[3] Ayscough had a passion for indexing. It was not without reason that he

1. *General Meetings, Minutes,* vol. 4, p. 832, 26 May 1781.
Committee Minutes, vol. 7, p. 1761, 18 May 1781.
2. *General Meetings, Minutes,* vol. 4, p. 835, 29 September 1781.
3. Samuel Ayscough, 1745–1804. On first entering the Museum in about 1785 – he had already waited fifteen years and applied in vain for five earlier vacancies – he was attached to the Department of Natural History. On the death of K. G. Woide in 1790, he was, in the following February, transferred to Printed Books, and his place in Natural History taken by Dr George Shaw.
Karl Gottfried Woide, 1725–1790, was Assistant Librarian in the Department of Manuscripts from 1782 onwards. Born in Poland, he was the Museum's first distinguished orientalist, an outstanding Coptic scholar. At the time of his appointment to the Museum, with the assistance of Harper, Woide was working on his critical edition of the Codex Alexandrinus New Testament, which appeared in 1786. From June 1770 until his death he was preacher at the Dutch Chapel Royal at St James Palace.

was known as 'The Prince of Index-Makers'. Even before joining the permanent staff of the museum he had compiled a catalogue of the Sloane, Birch and Additional manuscripts, arranged according to a classification system of his own, a further catalogue of Rolls and Charters, and had started work on a catalogue of the printed books, for which last he was paid the handsome sum of 12s a week.

Assisted by Samuel Harper and P. H. Maty, the son of the former Principal Librarian, Ayscough eventually produced this in 1787, under the title *Librorum impressorum qui in Museo Britannico adservantur catalogus*. Although it has many faults, it was a remarkable achievement for its day – the first catalogue of the collection of printed books – and formed the basis of subsequent compilations. An interleaved copy with manuscript additions long served as the Reading Room catalogue, until it was replaced by a new version during the second decade of the nineteenth century.

During his last years at the Museum, Ayscough turned his logical and methodical mind to the task of rearranging the library by classes and to cataloguing the Thomason collection, a task that was not to be completed till a hundred years after his death.

But perhaps the officer of the British Museum best known to the general public during this early period was Daniel Solander, a Swede, and a favourite pupil of the great botanist, Linnaeus. He had come to England in 1760 to seek his fortune and had soon found himself a member of the circle of scholars and dilettanti which was gathering round that young and enthusiastic patron of both arts and sciences, Joseph Banks.[1] 'The learned and ingenious Dr Solander' was now engaged on various projects, including the cataloguing of the famous collection of the Duchess of Portland, Edward Harley's daughter. In 1763 he had become an assistant in the Department of Natural and Artificial Productions and was soon at work compiling a systematic catalogue of the 'natural productions'. In 1768 he was selected by Banks to be his principal scientific companion on Cook's first voyage in the *Endeavour*, and special leave was granted to him by the Trustees for that purpose.

Of the details of that fruitful collaboration, it is not necessary to speak here, but it led to a close relationship between the Museum and the great voyages of discovery which were taking place during the closing years of the century. Thus, when in 1775, James Cook arrived from his second voyage, he sent all his 'curiosities' to Solander's apartments at

1. Sir Joseph Banks 1743–1820. President of the Royal Society, 1780–1820.

the Museum. Solander writes excitedly to Banks, 'This moment Cook is arrived. I have not yet had an opportunity of conversing with him, as he is in the Board room . . . all the shells go to Lord Bristol. Four cases have your name on them, and I understand they contain Birds and Fishes'.[1] The treasures, or at least the greater part of them, were to be divided up between the Museum, the Royal Society and various interested scholars.

Not only the great discoverers brought rare gifts from afar to Solander. 'I have sent Solander', writes Sir William Hamilton to Joseph Banks in February 1779, 'a collection of corals for our Museum',[2] and other donors were equally generous. When in 1773, Maty succeeded Knight as Principal Librarian, Solander took his place as Under-Librarian or Keeper in charge of the Department of Natural and Artificial Productions, the first scientifically trained member of the staff to hold this office. His sudden death, in 1782, at the comparatively early age of 46, was a great loss both to science and to the Museum. He had already acted as Principal Librarian in Morton's absence and would most probably have been his successor rather than Joseph Planta.

Another stalwart of these early days was Dr Samuel Harper,[3] like others of his colleagues a clergyman, the second Keeper of Printed Books, who was made Under-Librarian on 15 February 1765, the same day that Solander had become an Assistant. Harper was a man of strict views, at least as far as the Museum was concerned. In 1765 the Trustees noted with approval his action in turning out of the Museum garden a Miss Keate who, had been improperly admitted by the porter. The Trustees were always somewhat jealous of their garden and of those permitted to enter it. On 21 July 1769 they minuted that the garden might be opened from seven in the morning till half an hour after sunset, when a hand bell would be rung to announce its closing.[4] Those not leaving at once would henceforth be excluded.

The gardens were also the scene of great activity during the Gordon riots of 1780 when they were used by the troops engaged belatedly in

---

1. Solander to Banks, 1, 22 August 1775. *Banks*, p. 772. E. Smith, *Life of Banks*, p. 42.
2. Hamilton to Banks, 9 February 1779. Smith, *Life*, p. 62. *Banks*, p. 382.
3. Samuel Harper, d.1803. Curate of Gamston, Notts., and from 1775, Vicar of Rothwell, Leeds. The son of Robert Harper of Lincolns Inn. The Museum acquired the latter's magnificent working library of petitions to Parliament, private acts and similar material, built up by him during his long career as a parliamentary agent, at the sale of Samuel Harper's library in 1802. It is now in the State Paper Room.
4. *Committee Minutes*, vol. 5, p. 1218. 21 July 1769.

putting down that display of arson and mob violence. The men of the York Regiment were accommodated in tents erected on the lawns, whilst the old reading room and other parts of the basement were appropriated for the officers on duty. Harper, Solander, Planta and others gave up part of their own residences to provide further accommodation, whilst the garden shed was turned into the officers' mess kitchen. It was a scene which added colour and excitement to the humdrum lives of the Museum staff. On 7 July the young Prince of Wales and his brother, Prince Frederick, joined the admiring crowds of their father's subjects and paid a short visit to the encampment. It was, however, decided that whilst the troops were there it would not be possible to permit as many visitors as usual to the Museum, and the numbers were in consequence restricted. When, on 10 August, the regiment at last left, they expressed their thanks to the Trustees for the hospitality they had received during their doubtless not unpleasant stay in Bloomsbury.[1]

Five years later the gates of the Museum, still guarded by a detachment of troops as they were to be for another hundred years, were illuminated with 'G. R. and a Crown composed of Lamps' in thanksgiving for George III's recovery.[2] Few institutions in the kingdom had better cause to wish that monarch well than had the British Museum, of which he had long been a generous benefactor.

The original reading room over which Dr Templeman had grumblingly presided was now quite inadequate. In addition, its basement situation rendered it exceedingly damp and, in the opinion of Templeman's successor Dr Penneck, most unhealthy. On 18 February 1774 he complained to the Trustees that the reading room's excessive dampness was adversely affecting his health. Certain of the readers, too, were complaining of the general unpleasantness of the old room. Penneck strongly urged that new and more adequate accommodation should now be provided. The Trustees, on the recommendation of the Principal Librarian, decided to appropriate the 'two corner rooms of the Library' on the west side of the house for the reception of such persons as wished to read printed books or to examine manuscripts. In May 1774 estimates were received for converting the 'South West-angle room upon the first State Story' and the 'small corner room' into a suitable reading room. In October the new room was opened, far more light and airy than the old one, whose general air of gloom had been enhanced by the

1. *General Meetings, Minutes*, vol. 4, p. 824, 30 September 1780.
2. *Committee Minutes*, vol. 8, p. 2004, 24 April 1789.

cases of stuffed birds which lined every wall.[1] This new reading room was to serve several generations of readers, until in its turn it was superseded by still better accommodation in 1803.

It was of this reading room that Isaac D'Israeli gives a picture in his *The Illustrator Illustrated:* 'I passed two years in agreeable researches at the British Museum, which then was so rare a circumstance, that it had been difficult to have made up a jury of all the spirits of study which haunted the reading room. . . . There we were, little attended to, musing in silence and oblivion; for sometimes we had to wait a day or two, till the volumes, so eagerly demanded, slowly appeared'. According to Lord Beaconsfield, his father's companions in the reading room 'never numbered half a dozen',[2] though this number certainly increased after the turn of the century.

As the eighteenth century drew to a close, the Museum, still under the calm and peaceful rule of Dr Charles Morton, was steadily growing, both in reputation and size. Grosley, in his *Tour of London* of 1772, speaks warmly of the institution, both 'of the treasures which it contains and of the eagerness of the English to raise it to the utmost perfection'. But he complains of what seemed to him, as to many others, the inadequate arrangements for viewing the collections, despite, it would seem, 'the obliging readiness' of the staff. Yet, only a slight increase in the funds, grudgingly provided by Parliament, would enable 'this magnificent establishment' to be really worthy of the British nation. Amongst Grosley's suggestions was one for a chief trustee, paid by the state, whose principal duty would be 'to keep open house for foreigners of distinction and do the honours of the Museum'. Printed Books, however, he considered to be 'the most inconsiderable part of this immense collection'. If the library were to be made truly 'worthy of so great and magnificent a metropolis', it could never be contained in the quite inadequate space now available for it at Bloomsbury. The printed book collection should therefore, he considered, be transferred *en bloc* to the 'Banquetting-house, in Whitehall, where there would be ample space, not only for the existing stock but for all necessary expansion'[3]. Thus, early in the Museum's history, we get the theme that is to dominate all thinking on it for the next two hundred

1. *op. cit.*, vol. 5, p. 1403, 18 February 1774.
op. cit., vol. 6, p. 1444, 4 November 1774.
2. Isaac D'Israeli. *The Illustrator Illustrated.* London, 1838, p. 5. Preface by B. Disraeli to I. D'Israeli, *Curiosities of Literature.* [London], 1881, vol. 1, p. XXIX.
3. Grosley, vol. 2, pp. 20–5.

years. There was no room at Bloomsbury for all the collections. Something must go elsewhere. What shall it be? Different generations have given different answers, but the question remains the same and is still, as always, unresolved. At this time, however, there was scarcely any real urgency. New acquisitions were on a comparatively modest scale and the money available for any purchases was as yet ridiculously inadequate. It was only in the next century, with the conversion of the small collection of printed books into a great national library, unexampled for richness and size in the Western world, that the problem was to become genuinely pressing.

But in the late eighteenth century, even valuable gifts were looked upon with a certain suspicion. This sort of thing was always liable to happen with the Museum ruled by a supine administration, with no real desire either to collect new treasures or to display adequately those already in their possession. However, as the century ended, two collections were received which did much to raise the library departments to a new level. The first was the fine collection of manuscripts, which, together with a large number of printed books, mostly biography, were bequeathed to the Museum in 1799 by Sir William Musgrave,[1] an able and zealous Trustee, who had devoted many years and considerable sums to the formation of his collection. But the Musgrave bequest, and indeed all earlier ones, were completely eclipsed by the Cracherode collection, which came to the Museum in the last year of the eighteenth century.

Clayton Mordaunt Cracherode[2] was a typical product of the later eighteenth century. A man of great inherited wealth, he had few interests outside the building up of his collections of books, prints, coins, drawings, minerals and gems. Despite the possession of wide estates in various parts of the country, Cracherode never travelled farther afield than Oxford. His whole life was passed in London, leaving his house in Queen Square, Westminster only to walk round the bookshops in the Strand or to make his way slowly towards the Museum. He had been ordained early in life, but always refused to accept any ecclesiastical preferment. His many acts of kindness and charity to those less fortunate than himself were done without any suspicion of patronage. He had long been a Trustee, taking his duties quietly and seriously, and showing a keen interest in every aspect of Museum affairs. On his death, in the latter part of 1799, except for two volumes left to close personal friends,

1. Sir William Musgrave, d. 1799. Elected a Trustee 23 Jan. 1783.
2. Clayton Mordaunt Cracherode, 1730–1799.

'mild Cracherode' bequeathed the whole of his vast and extremely valuable collection to the Museum. It consisted of about 4,500 rare and for the most part, very fine volumes; a collection of prints and drawings which were his special favourites; a collection of coins and gems, and a smaller cabinet of minerals.

The British Museum thus entered the new century as a famous institution, its treasures many, but on the whole still not really comparable with the great continental collections, which had mostly been formed by the enlightened despots of the *ancien régime*. Foreign travellers, in particular, tended to compare it unfavourably with similar institutions abroad or even with other museums in Great Britain. Thus two visitors, Barthélemi Faujas de Saint-Fond and Louis Simond, who visited London at the end of the eighteenth and the beginning of the nineteenth century were far from complimentary. Saint-Fond wrote, 'The British Museum contains many valuable collections in natural history, but nothing is in order, everything is out of its place; and this assemblage appears rather an immense magazine, in which things have been thrown at random, rather than a scientific collection, destined to instruct and honour a great nation'.[1]

Simond likewise complains of the way his party were escorted round at a gallop by 'a German ciceroni' [sic] 'treating the company with double *entendres* and witticisms on various subjects of natural history, in a style of vulgarity and impudence which I should not have expected to have met in this place and this country'.[2] He, however, acknowledges in a footnote that more recently things had greatly improved. It should be noted that both visitors still regarded the Museum primarily as a scientific institution.

The nineteenth century was to bring fresh problems and challenges to the Museum. Thanks however, to the great men who were to be its servants in the years that lay ahead, it survived, strengthened by the ordeals which it had undergone, and emerged by the end of the century a British, indeed a universal institution, almost without parallel in the civilised world.

1. B. F. de Saint-Fond. *Travels in England, Scotland and the Hebrides.* London, 1779, vol. 1, p. 89.
2. Simond, vol. 1, p. 84.

CHAPTER FOUR

A Time of Growth and Change

THE year 1799 marked the death of Dr Charles Morton, last of the three original Under-Librarians, and the second to become Principal Librarian. In 1796 the Earl of Hardwicke had died, last of the original elected Trustees. Even in 1799 almost all the senior staff were still either physicians or clergymen. Most were elderly and since there were no pensions, they retained their positions if they possibly could until death released them. Under Morton there would be no real alteration. Despite his long connection with the Museum, he had done little to improve or to enlarge the collections. It was time for a change and the Trustees realised it. They chose the one man on the staff who was neither an elderly clergyman nor a non-practising physician, the one man with the energy and vision to bring the Museum, however haltingly, into the new century.

The new Principal Librarian was Joseph Planta, son of Andrew Planta,[1] a Protestant pastor from Castasegna in Switzerland. The elder Planta had settled in London in 1752, bringing with him his young son, then scarcely eight years old. Andrew Planta became an Assistant Librarian at the newly founded Museum, pastor of a German church and, not least, 'reader' to Queen Charlotte, wife of George III.[2] His father's connections, both at Court and at the Museum, were to stand his son, Joseph, in good stead. Initially, they procured him an appointment as secretary to the British Legation at Brussels, which he only relinquished in 1773 to take up the position which his father had held before him of an Assistant Librarian in the Museum. On Morton's becoming Principal Librarian, Joseph Planta, despite his comparative youth and lack of seniority, was appointed an Under Librarian on 20 December, 1776, and took charge of the Department of Manuscripts. In the same year he also succeeded Morton's predecessor Maty, as secretary to the Royal Society, a tribute to the high regard in which he

1. Joseph Planta, 1744–1827, FRS. As well as being an officer of the Museum, he held the post, from 1788 to 1811, of Paymaster of Exchequer Bills.
2. Andrew Planta, d. 1773. Assistant Keeper of Natural History, 1758–1765; Assistant Keeper of Printed Books, 1765–1773.

was already held. For the next twenty-three years he patiently and successfully ran his department, being especially responsible for the repair and restoration of the Cottonian manuscripts damaged in the fire of 1731. Now this urbane, scholarly, good-tempered man of fifty-five became Principal Librarian, an office he was to hold with great distinction for twenty-eight years.

A man of liberal and enlightened views, he did not share that fear of the common people so noticeable in his predecessors and in at least one of his successors. Despite renewed threats of popular tumults, the Principal Librarian was determined to try to abandon the restrictions which hampered the popular enjoyment of the Museum collections. Conditions of entry were bit by bit made easier, though only gradually did these enlightened policies prevail. Regulations still demanded that a prospective reader must 'if not known to any Trustee or Officer, . . . produce a recommendation from some person of known and approved character as it might be dangerous, in so populous a Metropolis as London, to admit perfect strangers'.[1]

This fear of the mob was to bedevil all attempts to make entry to the Museum more widespread throughout much of the first half of the nineteenth century, which was one cause of the hostility with which it was regarded by so many radicals. But, under Planta's rule, reading room admissions grew from under two hundred in 1799 to over five hundred a year by 1820. The small reading room, more than adequate for 1774, was now quite insufficient to cope with the flood of new readers, many of them refugees from the French Revolution. In 1803, therefore, it was abandoned and another room, no. XIV, was adapted for use as a reading room, 'larger and more commodious', as the *Gentleman's Magazine* reported. It was a particularly handsome corner room, with three large windows on the north side, as well as one on the south, and several portraits on the wall. Two long tables, covered with green cloth, extended across the room from north to south, one on each side, with the Superintendent's table facing a large marble fireplace in the south wall. The *Gentleman's Magazine* also warmly praised the improved service

1. *Directions respecting the Reading Room of the British Museum*, 3 July 1804, p. 2. (P.P., H. of C., 1803–4, vol. 48, pp. 67–9.). *A Plan for the more easy Admission to the British Museum. Approved . . . 8 of June 1804.* A few years later, at the height of the invasion scare and with the growing political unrest, a less liberal policy was adopted which lasted until the end of the war in 1814. In October of that year, a writer in *The Times* complained of the Trustees' suspicious attitude towards readers and demanded, 'Is the Library to be for the use of those who keep the keys or for those who pay for the books?' (*The Times*, 14 October 1814).

to readers: 'An officer is in attendance to assist the readers . . . in general, I have found much more alacrity in fetching the books and manuscripts that are called for.'[1]

This new alacrity may have been due to changes in the administration of the Reading Room. Dr Penneck had died in 1803 and no Keeper of the Reading Room was appointed to succeed him. His duties devolved first on the Assistant Librarians, an extension of the previous arrangement of May 1778, whereby the Keeper of the Reading Room had to be present there for two-thirds of the time, the other Assistant Librarians dividing the remaining hours between them. In 1806 it was found necessary to add the Under-Librarians to the rota. All officers had, however, been relieved in June 1801 of the 'unimportant office of daily exhibiting the curiosities'. Three attendants were now engaged who were in future to perform these duties with the help of a guidebook.[2]

This unsatisfactory method of supervising the Reading Room lasted until 1814, when further changes were made. There was now to be only one Assistant Librarian, available for two days in each week, the readers at other times having to make do with what help the attendants were able to give them.[3] A little later, Thomas Maurice, Assistant Keeper of the Department of Manuscripts, was given the title of Chief Superintendent, but with little real power.[4] This scheme continued until 1824, when all responsibility for the running of the Reading Room was taken away from the senior staff. The Reading Room was henceforth to be supervised merely by a senior attendant, to be known as the Clerk of the Reading Room, with limited powers and responsible to the Principal Librarian alone. The first Superintendent under the new arrangements was James Cates, who was to be in charge of successive reading rooms

1. GM, vol. 73, pp. 99–100, February 1803.

2. *General Meetinge, Minutes*, vol. 4, p. 949, 3 June 1801.

3. As early as 1778 Penneck had complained of the excessively long hours that continual superintendence of the Reading Room involved. Arrangements were therefore made for his duties to be divided between himself and the other three Assistant Librarians, the latter receiving an allowance of £40 for this additional responsibility. (*Committee Minutes*, vol. 6, p. 614, 15 May 1778). In 1801, on a renewed complaint by Penneck, the order was reiterated. (*Committee Minutes*, vol. 8, p. 2212, 12 June 1801). At his death two years later, the arrangements already mentioned were brought into force. (*General Meetings, Minutes*, vol. 4, p. 961, 12 February 1803. *Statutes and Rules*, 1805, p. 110).

4. Rev. Thomas Maurice, 1754–1824. Assistant Keeper, Department of Manuscripts, 1799–1824. An accomplished oriental scholar, he was the Museum's first expert in Indian languages.

until his death in 1855. He had been engaged as an ordinary attendant on 24 April 1810, having previously been a servant in the household of the fourth Duke of Grafton. 'Mr Cates was remarkable for the extreme neatness of his attire, and looked very much like an old English clergy-man',[1] and was said to have been, in his youth, one of the best amateur boxers of his day.

This divided rule, with the Keeper of Printed Books responsible for supplying books to readers, but not for the administration of the room in which they were read, led to constant friction during the next thirty or so years.

The 'new room' of 1803 was soon found to be insufficient. In 1809 it was therefore decided to use two other rooms. However, these too soon proved to be inadequate for the ever increasing number of readers and on 12 April 1817, Planta reported that room no. 5 on the Upper Floor, hitherto assigned for the accommodation of the Harleian manu-scripts, should also be used. In 1823, the Trustees ordered that 'the room which adjoins the present Reading Room towards the Saloon be forthwith prepared for . . . readers',[2] and on 10 December 1825 that a third from the Department of Manuscripts be added to those already in use.

This increasing number of readers meant an increasing demand for books, no longer simply for the standard theological and antiquarian works, which had been the staple fare of an older generation of readers. The demand henceforth was for new books and, to the dismay of the readers, all too often the Museum had never received them. The right to a copy of every book delivered to Stationers' Hall had been loosely enforced and a mere handful of books had been received. With the rising demand for recent books and the passing of a new Copyright Act in 1814,[3] the Trustees hesitantly decided to assert their privilege. Already, in 1806, they had sought the opinion of the Law Officers as to whether their right to receive books under the Act was valid, and had

1. Cowtan, pp. 200–1.
2. *General Meetings, Minutes*, vol. 5, p. 1205, 15 March 1823.
3. 54 Geo. III. c. 156. *An Act to amend the several Acts for the Encouragement of Learning, by securing the Copies and Copyright of printed Books, to the Authors of such Books or their Assigns.* It was replaced by the more comprehensive, but still imperfect Act of 1842. The Law Officers in 1806 had considered that 'printed and published as aforesaid', in 8 Anne c.19, meant printed and published after entry at Stationers' Hall, 'the result of which opinion is that no books can be demanded unless the Publishers chuse to enter them at Stationers' Hall', which the majority did not. (*General Meetings, Minutes*, vol. 4, p. 988, 19 April 1806.)

received an unsatisfactory answer. In 1815 the Rev. Henry Baber,[1] now Keeper of Printed Books, was instructed to do what he could to secure all new books from Stationers' Hall. A collector was appointed to receive them for the Museum, but the system was still defective.

On 20 July 1816, James Bean, Baber's Assistant Keeper, wrote urgently to Stationers' Hall to complain that certain books had not been delivered, and pointed out that he was 'authorised . . . to demand the same on the best paper, of the respective Publishers, for the use of the Public Library'.[2] The situation remained highly unsatisfactory as Baber pointed out in the strongest possible terms to a Parliamentary committee in 1836: 'Every dirty trick', he declared, was resorted to on the part of the publishers 'to impose on us, and to evade the Act'.[3] It was not until the passing of the Act of 1842[4] and its drastic enforcement by Panizzi between 1850 and 1856 that modern books came into the Museum in any considerable numbers. But for the moment the library carried on as best it could. As Grosley had said in 1772, 'Printed books are the most inconsiderable part of this immense collection'[5] and for many years yet this was only too true. Planta did indeed make great efforts to improve his library departments. In 1812 the Trustees at his earnest instigation petitioned Parliament for special grants to remedy the worst of the deficiencies, the Library being, as they said 'very defective . . . in that part of the collection which respects the British Islands and the several Possessions of the British Empire'.[6] Faced with this frank appeal to the patriotism of members, Parliament, after some hesitation, gave on 25 June 1812 the sum of £1,000 'to enable the Trustees . . . to proceed in making the necessary purchases for improving the Collection of printed Books'.[7] The grant was continued annually until 1815 when, in the

1. Rev. Henry Hervey Baber, 1775–1869. Assistant Keeper of Printed Books, 1807–1812; Keeper, 1812–1837. Rector of Streatham, Cambs., 1827–1869.

2. Add. MS. 33,498. f. 118. Rev. James Bean, d. 1826. Assistant Keeper of Printed Books, 1812–1826.

3. Baber was emphatic. On being asked what proportion of published books were received under the Act, he answered 'We lose, I conjecture, about one-fifth'. (*Select Committee, 1836. Minutes*, para. 4630.)

4. 5 & 6 Vict. c. 45. *An Act to amend the Law of Copyright*. This in turn was replaced by the far Better Act of 1911. The important change in the 1842 Act was that all books were now ordered 'to be delivered for the Use of the British Museum' to the Museum itself within one month of publication, rather than to be got as hitherto through a Collector from Stationers' Hall.

5. Grosley, vol. 2, p. 20.

6. CJ, vol. 67, pp. 267–268.

7. *op. cit.*, p. 475.

post-war economic climate it was discontinued. Parliament had never-theless purchased for the Museum the Lansdowne manuscripts in 1805 at a cost of £4,925, and were shortly to grant further sums for the acquisition of Francis Hargrave's legal library in 1813 and Charles Burney's great classical library five years later. But for many years yet a regular acquisitions policy was impossible. Funds just did not permit. Not until the achievement of regular annual purchase grants by Panizzi forty years later did the library at last really start to rival and soon to outshine all other great national libraries.

Nevertheless in the conditions of the early nineteenth century, with the country waging a life and death struggle against Napoleon and accumulating what, to contemporary eyes, was an impossibly large national debt, Parliament's comparative parsimony was, if not justified, understandable. The Museum had, despite a Parliamentary grant of nearly £8,000 in 1811, shown a deficiency of £1,272 2s 11d. This was not due to any extravagant overspending. Much of the money, £4,101 18s 5d in fact, was laid out in endeavouring to keep the old building in a proper state of repair.[1] However, as the years passed and the Museum slowly grew, Montagu House was becoming an ever less suitable place to contain both antiquities and natural history collections and the national Library.

For the Museum was now indeed expanding at an increasing rate, from 13,406 visitors in 1807–8, to no less than 27,479 four years later. And now there was so much more to see. In 1802 the many antiquities captured from the French as a result of the campaigns which destroyed Napoleon's armies in Egypt were given to the British Museum by George III. Napoleon had taken to Egypt with him a whole team of archaeologists and from 1798 to 1801 they busily explored and excavated the remains of ancient Egypt, the first systematic exploration ever carried out. According to the sixteenth article of the Capitulation of Alexandria of 31 August 1801, all collections of marbles, manuscripts and other antiquities, together with specimens of natural history and drawings then in the possession of the French, became the property of the victors. Subsequently, after much argument, it was agreed that the antiquities should be retained by the British, but that the natural history specimens and a few other objects might be taken away by the French, as the personal property of the scientists who had discovered them.

So the archaeological specimens, which included the famous Rosetta

1. *op. cit.*, p. 646. Appendix 3. The repairs to the 'West Side of the Buildings, in the Great Court', alone cost £1,160 5s. 1d.

Encampment of the York Regiment at the British Museum during the Gordon Riots (1780).

Soldiers at the gatehouse of old Montagu House.

Joseph Planta, Principal Librarian (1799–1827).

Stone – its triple inscription soon to be the key to the decipherment of the hieroglyphic writing of the ancient Egyptians – the great sarcophagus, then thought by some to be that of Alexander the Great, and many other precious objects became the property of the British government. The Rosetta stone itself was nearly lost to the Museum. Realising its great potential value to science and justly proud of having discovered it, the French savants succeeded in hiding it aboard one of the transports bound for France. The young W. R. Hamilton – to be intimately connected with the Museum for many years – got news of the stone's whereabouts and, rowing over to the vessel on which it was hidden, successfully obtained its release.

Brought back from the Mediterranean by the Navy, the Egyptian objects reached the Museum early in 1802. There was nowhere to put them in old Montagu House, and they had to be accommodated in wooden sheds in the garden. This was obviously no fit place for such treasures, 'acquired by His Majesty's victorious Arms'.[1] Even had there been room, however, these heavy masses of stone would have undoubtedly caused the collapse of the already sagging floors of the old building, never designed for such a purpose and already supported in many places by iron props to prevent their breaking up altogether.

The Trustees again petitioned Parliament for money to meet the expense of a new building. Somewhat reluctantly £8,000 was granted, to be followed in 1805 by a further £8,000 and by subsequent sums in 1806 and 1808 to complete the new gallery. But now the Trustees had another problem to consider.

The finest collection of classical sculptures then existing in England was that formed by Charles Towneley,[2] the head of an ancient Catholic family, who, during the previous forty years, had built up an incomparable collection of antique sculpture, in marble, bronze and terra cotta, largely derived from the excavations being carried out at Rome and its neighbourhood in the closing decades of the eighteenth century. Towneley was a modest man, devoted to his hobby. His 'learning and sagacity', wrote a contemporary critic 'in explaining the

1. *Petition of the Trustees to the House of Commons.* CJ vol. 59, p. 378, 2 July 1804. One of the earliest mentions of the Rosetta Stone at the Museum is in Simond: 'We remarked a treble inscription on a large block of dark porphyry, brought from Rosetta . . . All three saying the same thing serve as a glossary to each other.' (Simond, vol. 1, p. 83.)

2. Charles Towneley, 1737–1805. The name is variously spelled 'Townley' and 'Towneley', but the latter form is more common.

works of antient art were equal to his taste and judgement in selecting them'.[1] On his return to England, Towneley had exhibited his marbles at a fine house in Park Street, Westminster, where, as the property of a notorious Papist, they had narrowly escaped destruction at the hands of the mob during the Gordon riots.

He continued to add to them the choicest specimens of classical art. In 1791 he had become a Trustee of the Museum and had subsequently expressed his intention of bequeathing his great collection to that institution. However, by a codicil to his will made on 22 December 1804, only twelve days before his death, Towneley left the collection first to his brother and then to his uncle, on condition that the recipient should be responsible for the erection of a suitable repository at the cost of at least £4,500. Should either decline, it was to go to the Museum. The Towneley estate was now heavily encumbered. Neither Towneley's brother nor his uncle were able to meet the expenses involved in retaining the marbles in the family. The Trustees of the British Museum, therefore, petitioned Parliament for a substantial grant for the purchase of this magnificent collection.[2]

A Committee was set up to consider the matter. Planta proposed that the Museum should purchase the whole collection for £20,000, and the nomination of two Trustees to be vested in the Towneley family. The original will had stipulated that in the event of the collection being accepted, the Trustees should 'set apart a room or rooms which now is ... or which may hereafter be erected ... sufficiently spacious and elegant to exhibit these Antiquities most advantageously to the Public'[3] and it was revealed that such a building could also contain the newly acquired Egyptian antiquities. The committee examined the most eminent sculptors of the day, such as Nollekens and Flaxman, who testified that the marbles were worth at least £20,000. Nollekens remarked, 'I should think it worth £30,000 honestly',[4] and Payne Knight pointed out that £20,000 would be a cheap price for an individual to pay, 'buying it on speculation'.[5]

1. Society of Dilettanti. *Specimens of Ancient Sculpture*, vol. 1. f. 61.
2. C J,vol. 60, pp. 342, 343, 5 June 1805.
3. *Copy of Mr Townley's Will. Report on British Museum Petition respecting Mr Townley's Collection of Sculptured Marbles*, p. 3. (P.P., H. of C., 1805, vol. 3, p. 347.)
4. *Report*, p. 6. Joseph Nollekens, RA, 1737–1823, sculptor; John Flaxman, RA, 1755–1826, sculptor and draughtsman and first professor of sculpture at the Royal Academy.
5. *op. cit.*, p. 6. Richard Payne Knight, 1750–1824, himself a trustee and a great benefactor of the Museum. MP for Leominster, 1780–1784; for Ludlow, 1784–1806.

The Museum architect, George Saunders, presented to the committee the plans for a new building,[1] which it was hoped would be completed by Michaelmas 1806. Towneley himself had seen the plans before his death and had warmly approved them. He considered that the exterior should not be a copy of old Montagu House, which was not in his opinion 'a pattern to be followed in this improved age',[2] and greatly preferred the neat classical design proposed by Saunders. Negotiations were still going on with the Towneley family, who were reluctant to part with the bronzes, prints, pictures and books, which they considered entailed with the estate and therefore theirs to keep. The committee, too, were of the opinion that the new building might well prove inadequate, especially as it was to contain other collections besides Towneley's. Nevertheless, it was resolved to recommend to the House the purchase of the collection 'for public Inspection and Use; particularly if measures were taken to afford Artists free access to the said Collection', for £20,000.[3]

So the Towneley collection came to the Museum and was put in the new gallery erected at the north-west corner of Montagu House and joined to it by a short corridor, the first building to be specifically erected at Bloomsbury as an exhibition gallery.

The Museum now possessed a superb collection of antiquities, equal to if not surpassing its other collections. It was henceforth unsuitable that antiquities should continue to form a subordinate part of the department of Natural and Artificial Products. In 1803 Taylor Combe had been appointed an Assistant Librarian, in charge of antiquities, then mostly coins.

Though Charles Towneley himself had written to Sir Joseph Banks on 4 February 1803, pointing out that someone was specifically needed to look after the collection of coins, medals and miscellaneous antiquities, 'which has now become extensive' and recommending 'young Mr

1. *op. cit.*, p. 6. George Saunders, FSA, FRS, 1762–1832. Architect; Surveyor for Middlesex. In May 1833 Saunders' plans for the Towneley gallery were found by Ellis in one of the garrets of Montagu House. Apparently they had been carried up there in 1809, when the Prince of Wales, accompanied by his mother and sisters, visited the Museum to view the new gallery. George had 'ridiculed what he called our "Colfichets", and the framed Cuttings in paper, small pictures, and all that was deemed rubbishing and unnecessary mounted to the Garrets'. Add. MS. 42,506. f. 112, 113.
2. Add. MS. 36,524. ff. 33–36.
3. *Report*, p. 6.

Combe' for the post,[1] Combe was still nominally under the direction of the Keeper of the Natural History Department.[2] In 1806 when the Keeper of the Natural History Department E. W. Gray, died, Planta decided that the time had now come for a change. In 1807 therefore, the old department was split into the Department of Natural History and Modern Curiosities and the Department of Antiquities and Coins, the first of many such proliferations.[3] Taylor Combe was put in charge of the new Department of Antiquities, whilst Shaw[4] became Keeper of Natural History and Modern Curiosities, which included, not only the Natural History collections proper, but also those ethnographical specimens collected by Cook, Banks, Menzies and others, together with other objects that could not easily be fitted in elsewhere.

The Towneley galleries, as finally organised by Taylor Combe, consisted of thirteen rooms in which all the antiquities were displayed, not only the Towneley marbles and the Egyptian antiquities, but also the Cracherode collection of gems, coins and medals; the Sloane and Cottonian coins and medals; the Sloane antiquities, the Hamilton vases and all

1. Add. MS. 36,524. f. 34. Andrew Gifford, 1700–1784, a Baptist minister, was the Museum's first numismatist, and also the first Assistant Keeper of the Department of Manuscripts. He was followed, as the Museum's coin specialist and as second in command of the Department of Manuscripts, by the Rev. Richard Southgate, 1749–1795, an expert on Anglo-Saxon coins and curate of St Giles-in-the-Fields, in which sordid parish his colleague, Samuel Ayscough, was assistant curate.

2. Taylor Combe, FRS, 1774–1826, numismatist, son of Charles Combe, also a well-known numismatist. In 1803 the national collection of coins and medals was transferred from the Department of Manuscripts, where it had been since the Museum's foundation, and combined with the Hamilton vases and other miscellaneous antiquities in the Department of Natural and Artificial Productions. Combe was specially enjoined 'to take the immediate Custody of the Collection of coins &c.' and to make a catalogue of them as speedily as possible. (*Committee Minutes*, vol. 8, p. 2336. 5 Aug. 1803.)

3. *General Meetings, Minutes*, vol.5, p. 1008. Combe, who already had the title of Keeper of Coins and Medals, with the rank of Assistant Librarian in the Department of Natural and Artificial Productions (*Committee Minutes*, vol. 8, p. 2236, 5 August 1803), was now promoted Under-Librarian. The post of Extra-Assistant Librarian was transferred from Printed Books to the new department, with its holder H. W. Bedford, who was then made an Assistant Librarian. On Bedford's death three years later, the post was given to William Alexander, the first Keeper of Prints.

4. George Shaw, MD, 1751–1813, naturalist and physician. He had been ordained, but had abandoned the Church for medicine. Joint founder and Vice-President of the Linnaean Society.

the other miscellaneous antiquities which had accumulated since the founding of the Museum.[1]

Also to be seen among them from June 1810 onwards was the Portland vase, which has been for over 160 years one of the most famous of all the Museum's treasures. The Portland Vase's presence in the collections, indeed, its presence in England, was once again due to that indefatigable collector, Sir William Hamilton. 'Except the Apollo Belvedere, the Niobes, and two or three others of the first class marbles', wrote Sir William enthusiastically, 'I do not believe that there are any monuments of antiquity existing that were executed by so great an artist'.[2] And although modern taste may not entirely share this un- critical admiration for such works of the Roman period, the Portland vase is indeed an object of great beauty. It is first recorded as being in the possession of the noble Roman family of Barberini by 1642, whence its earlier name of 'Barberini Vase'. It is not known when or from where it came in to their possession. The old tales that it was once the cinerary urn of the Emperor Alexander Severus, and that it was discovered within a marble sarcophagus excavated in 1582, are mostly discounted by modern scholars. By the latter half of the eighteenth century, the once immensely wealthy Barberini family had grown impoverished, and in 1780 the vase was sold by the last of the line to James Byres, a Scottish antique dealer resident in Rome. In 1783 Byres sold it to Hamilton for £1,000, a price which that impecunious ambassador could not easily afford.

On a visit to England in December 1784, Hamilton brought the vase with him, with the express intention of selling it to the highest bidder. Through the good offices of his niece Mary Hamilton, he finally managed to dispose of it early in 1785 to the Dowager Duchess of Portland, who was eager to add it to her already extensive collection, the same that Daniel Solander had been employed in cataloguing on his first arrival in England. The negotiations were undertaken in complete secrecy, so that when the whereabouts of the vase was finally revealed it excited considerable comment. 'I have heard', wrote Walpole, 'that Sir

1. On the opening of the new gallery the Egyptian antiquities were transferred there from the sheds in the gardens where they had been housed since 1802, to join the other antiquities. The Towneley building contained a principal room, 50' × 33' × 25', suitable for the display of larger antiquities, such as the Egyptian ones, whilst above was another spacious room, 12' high for 'Etruscan vases and other matters of elegant antiquity'. (*General Meetings, Minutes*, vol. 4, p. 964, 14 May 1803.)
2. Walpole, *Letters*, ed. P. Cunningham, vol. 8, p. 408.

William Hamilton's renowned vase, which had disappeared with so
much mystery, is again recovered – not in the tomb, but in the treasury
of the Duchess of Portland, in which, I fancy, it had made ample room
for itself'.[1] The Duchess had in fact paid Hamilton 1800 guineas for the
vase, together with four less important antiquities. The Duchess was not
fated to enjoy her new and highly treasured possession for long. In July
1785 she died and at the sale of her great collection it was bought by her
son, the third Duke of Portland, for 980 guineas. Twenty-four years
later in 1810, he deposited it on permanent loan in the British Museum,
where it has remained ever since. In 1945 it was purchased from the
Portland family by the Museum.

The Portland Vase is the finest surviving example of 'cameo-glass',
and depicts in white relief on a blue background the marriage of Peleus
and Thetis. Probably made as a wedding gift, it is thought to date from
about 25 AD. Soon, however, the young Department of Antiquities was
to receive an even more magnificent treasure. In 1816, the Earl of Elgin
offered to the nation his collection of Greek statuary, taken for the most
part from the Parthenon at Athens.

Thomas Bruce, seventh Earl of Elgin, had succeeded to the title at
the age of five and had received the conventional upbringing of an
eighteenth-century nobleman. Commissioned into the army in 1785,
he had reached the rank of major-general by 1835 without having seen
active service in any form. After undertaking various diplomatic
missions to Vienna, Brussels and Berlin, in 1799 he was appointed
Ambassador to the Sublime Porte at Constantinople. From the outset
of his appointment, Elgin seems to have considered what services he
might be able to render to art and archaeology.

Not much was then known concerning the remains of classical Greek
sculpture and buildings still buried in the lands held for centuries past
by the Turks. Greece itself was little explored and wartime conditions
made travel in the Near East even more difficult than usual. Elgin
conceived the idea of taking with him a staff of artists, architects, and
formatori, or makers of casts, so as to record accurately for the first time
the treasures of Greece and of the Near East. Receiving no official
encouragement, he persevered none the less and approached, amongst
others, the young J. M. W. Turner with a view to engaging him as the
principal artist to the expedition. Turner, even though only twenty-four,
demanded a high salary and the right to retain at least some of the
drawings made during his travels. Elgin therefore took the advice of Sir

1. Walpole to Lady Ossory, 10 August 1785. *Letters*, vol. 3, p. 485.

William Hamilton, whom he met at Palermo, and engaged Italian artists and craftsmen, who could be got far cheaper and with less trouble than their English equivalents. With some difficulty he eventually obtained Turkish permission to send a staff of six artists to Athens to make drawings and casts and to copy inscriptions from the ancient buildings.

On his own arrival at Athens – then no more than a small and not particularly wholesome village – Elgin realised that something far more drastic than merely making drawings and taking casts would be necessary if the sculptures of the Parthenon and other monuments of classical Greece were to be saved for posterity. Not only were many of the finest surviving statues being constantly ground down for mortar (as a friendly Turk told Elgin, 'A great part of the Citadel has been built with mortar made in the same way [from ground up statues]. That marble makes capital lime'),[1] but even more aimless destruction of buildings and other remains was continually going on. With great difficulty, but aided considerably by Britain's new-found prestige from her recent victories over the French in Egypt, Elgin at last obtained a firman or official licence from Constantinople to take away 'any pieces of stone with old inscriptions or figures thereon'.[2] Slowly, with frustrating delays and constant obstruction by the local authorities, the great sculptured friezes were removed from the Parthenon and then carefully packed and embarked on a British man-of-war for transport to England. Elgin was now convinced that the operation, drastic as it undoubtedly was, was the only certain means of saving the precious sculptures. 'I am sure', his principal artist, Lusieri, told him, 'that in half a century there will not remain one stone on another'.[3]

More and more sculptures were sawn off and embarked for England. But soon Elgin had more than Turkish obstruction and French intrigues to contend with. The brig *Mentor*, carrying sculptures and other antiquities, was wrecked on its voyage from Athens to Malta. Although some things, including several valuable papyri, were lost, the bulk of the cargo was eventually salvaged and dispatched without further mishap to England. Elgin's difficulties did not end here. Caught travelling across France by the renewed outbreak of the war against Napoleon, he was

1. Edwards, *Founders*, p. 383.
2. *Report from the Select Committee on the Earl of Elgin's Collection of Marbles*. p. 69. (PP, H. of C., 1816, vol. 3, p. 49.)
3. Smith, p. 198. Giovanni Battista Lusieri, d. 1 March 1821, draughtsman and topographical artist, known as Don Tita.

arrested and interned, for a time under stringent conditions, from 1803 to 1806.

Nevertheless, despite ever increasing difficulties with both Turks and French, and the imprisonment of its instigator, the work at Athens went on. By March 1810, all the remaining marbles, save for certain large fragments, were embarked, together with Lord Byron, on a transport for Malta and, by 1812, the three last boxes had arrived safely in England, where these wonderful sculptures, so very much to the taste of the age, were already enjoying wide publicity.

The first marbles had arrived in England on 12 August 1802, the bulk of them following eighteen months later. Charles Towneley wrote, 'I have lost no opportunity of informing persons of taste and judgment in the Fine Arts of the interesting operations which Lord Elgin is now so eagerly carrying on. His Lordship's zeal is most highly approved and admired, and every hope and wish is entertained for his final success. But our Government is universally blamed for not contributing their political influence, as well as pecuniary aid towards these operations, for the advancement of the Fine Arts in this country'.[1] Educated opinion, in general was equally enthusiastic and Elgin and his marbles became the rage.

On his return in 1806 from imprisonment in France, Elgin decided to put the marbles on permanent exhibition, calling in sculptors and dilletanti, such as Flaxman and W. R. Hamilton,[2] to assist him. On Flaxman's advice, a scheme to restore the statues to what was considered to be their pristine state, was fortunately abandoned. Flaxman estimated that it would cost at least £20,000 and would 'lower rather than raise the intrinsic value of the collection'.[3] He agreed, however to replace any missing arms and other limbs, where this might be considered necessary. The marbles now began to attract numerous visitors. The Swiss artist Fuseli exclaimed rapturously, 'De Greeks were Godes! De Greeks were Godes',[4] and others were equally impressed, despite the 'damp, dirty

1. Towneley to W. R. Hamilton, 8 February 1803. (Elgin. Appendix, p. 68.)
2. William Richard Hamilton, 1777–1859, antiquarian, civil servant and diplomat. He became a Trustee of the Museum in 1838.
3. Hamilton to Elgin, 23 June 1807. Quoted in Smith, p. 297.
4. B. R. Haydon, Life, vol. 1, pp.82–86. Quoted in Smith, p. 301.
   Henry Fuseli, 1741–1825, painter and author.
   Thomas Bruce, Seventh Earl of Elgin, 1766–1841, was very conscious of the value of his great collection. In a letter to Lord Mulgrave, First Lord of the Admiralty, of 16 February 1808, in which he requests a 'demonstration in force' by the Navy in Greek waters close to Athens so as to frighten the Turks and make them release the

penthouse'[1] in which they were exhibited. The feeling grew that so valuable a collection should no longer remain in private hands, however eminent, but that Parliament should purchase it for the nation 'and build a well-lighted museum to contain it'.[2]

After schemes to finance his exhibition by charging admission had been rejected, Elgin opened negotiations with the British Museum through his agent W. R. Hamilton. He was more and more convinced that only by placing his treasures in a public collection would their safety and integrity be assured. In May 1811, Elgin formally approached the government. In his letter he stressed the fact that the whole cost of the recovery and removal of the marbles was more than £62,440, an immense sum for any private individual to lay down on a highly speculative venture. Elgin had clearly considered that it was in some way part of his ambassadorial duties to save these treasures of Western civilisation from destruction and yet he had not received a penny from official sources to assist him on this rescue operation. The government, still burdened by the expenses of the war, would offer no more than £30,000, a sum Elgin indignantly refused.

A few years later in 1816 the question of their purchase for the nation was raised again. During all this time, the marbles, to which had been added in May 1812 eighty-six large cases of further specimens, were still on public exhibition. Burlington House, with the garden shed in which they were now stored, had just been sold and it was urgent that permanent arrangement be made for their custody. Hamilton urged Planta to deposit them, if only temporarily, at the Museum, and the Trustees resolved to communicate at once with Hamilton and the Government as to the possible purchase of the whole collection.

Not all the authorities agreed on their value or even authenticity. Payne Knight, a Trustee, and soon himself a great benefactor of the

1. Haydon, *Life*, vol. 1, p. 84.
2. G. Cumberland in *Monthly Magazine* for July 1808. Quoted in Smith, p. 302.

remaining marbles still held by them, he says 'My exertions and expences for seven years have amply shown the importance I attach to the collection, which even now is I believe in London superior far to anything of the kind elsewhere'. Add. MS. 40,096, f. 54.

Henry Phipps, first Earl of Mulgrave and Viscount Normanby. 1755–1831, Secretary of State for Foreign Affairs, 1805–6. First Lord of the Admiralty, 1807–1810.

England had declared war on Turkey in February 1807, and the cases were not released until long after the end of the war in January 1809.

Museum, considered 'some of them were added in the time of Hadrian'[1] but most experts agreed both on their real antiquity and on their artistic importance. In February 1816 a committee of the House of Commons was set up to go into the whole matter. Elgin testified to the urgency there had been of saving the sculptures from destruction and emphasised how badly they had been defaced, even during the last fifty years, by neglect and by Turkish barbarism. He told the committee of the great expense, now reckoned as over £74,000, to which he had been put to bring them safely back to England. As Lord Aberdeen said, it seemed impossible 'that a private individual could have accomplished the removal of the remains',[2] and emphasised that, but for Elgin's prompt action, the French would have carried them off to Paris. The experts too were enthusiastic, speaking of the works 'simplicity and grandeur', 'the finest I have ever seen', and so on.[3] Even the still suspicious Payne Knight remarked, 'I think, my Lord Elgin, in bringing them away, is entitled to the gratitude of the Country; because, otherwise, they would have been all broken by the Turks' and he suggested that the possession of such a collection 'will contribute to the improvement of the Arts'.[4] This practical aspect of the matter – the use of such sculptures in the training of young artists – was, of course quite natural at the period when neo-classical enthusiasm was at its height, when Canova, for instance, viewed the marbles 'with breathless enthusiasm', and felt he could not see them often enough,[5] and classical sculpture of the Periclean period was regarded the noblest form of art. Swayed by such considerations as these, the Select Committee recommended that the sculptures should be purchased for £35,000, to cover the estimated value of the collection, the expenses of obtaining them being ignored. The committee's recommendation was accepted and the necessary Act passed.[6] Lord Elgin was therefore considerably out of pocket over the whole business, but he had had the satisfaction of saving the sculptures for posterity, and the sum granted was not ungenerous, given the prevailing mood of post-war frugality.

Now came the question of moving them to the Museum. The fears

1. Elgin, p. 39.
2. Op. cit., p. 49.
3. Op. cit., pp. 36, 37. Evidence of Chauntry and Rossi.
4. op. cit., p. 43.
5. Antonio Canova, 1757–1822, sculptor. Smith, p. 344.
6. 56 Geo. III. c. 99. *An Act to vest the Elgin Collection of ancient Marbles and Sculpture in the Trustees of the British Museum for the Use of the Public.* (1 July 1816.)

which had already been expressed that the Museum would have no room for these treasures within its existing buildings, already crowded, were well justified. Henry Ellis,[1] the Trustees' Secretary, wrote to the government, giving details of the temporary building which would be needed until proper accommodation could be provided. Such a building, he estimated, would cost about £1,700 whilst the removal would cost at least £800. In fact, it cost a trifle less. On 8 August 1816 the sculptures were brought to the Museum at a cost of £798, and housed in a temporary shed, somewhat misleadingly described by an enthusiastic contributor to the *Gentleman's Magazine* as 'two spacious rooms on the ground floor . . . adjoining the Towneley and Egyptian Galleries',[2] which was to contain the Elgin marbles, the Phigalian marbles, and other classical statuary, in particular a frieze depicting combats between Centaurs and Lapiths, and between Greeks and Amazons, which had been acquired for £19,000 in 1814. There, in this inadequate accommodation, the Elgin marbles had to stay until 1831, when a proper building was provided. Already they were amongst the most popular of the exhibits, admired by public and expert alike.

Under the guidance of Planta, the Museum was slowly recovering from its long years of lethargy. His liberalisation of the admission regulations had resulted in a dramatic rise in the number of visitors.[3] He had likewise eased the regulations for admitting students to the Department of Antiquities to draw the sculptures, for any idea of the scientific study of the antiquities was as yet scarcely dreamed of. Permission for the study of prints, coins and medals, although with certain restrictions, was likewise now more readily granted. For the first time the Museum began issuing scholarly publications dealing with some of the contents, a duty which has since come to be regarded as one of its principal functions. Amongst the earliest was a facsimile of the

1. Sir Henry Ellis, KH, LL.D., 1777–1869. Born in Bishopsgate, he became in 1796 together with his future colleague, Henry Baber, one of the Under Librarians at the Bodleian. The following year he obtained a law fellowship at St John's College, Oxford. In August 1801 he was made an extra assistant in the Department of Printed Books, 'to be employed at the rate of £4 a month so long as his services shall be required in the Library'. (*Committee Minutes*, vol. 8, p. 2197, 7 Nov. 1800.) In March 1805 he succeeded Ayscough as Assistant Librarian and on Beloe's dismissal in 1806 became Keeper of Printed Books. Keeper of Manuscripts, 1812–1828; Secretary, 1814–1828; Principal Librarian, 1828–1856.
2. GM, Jan. 1817, p. 80.
3. The rise was indeed dramatic, from 11,989 visitors in 1805–6 to 15,390 in 1808–9; then 29,152 only two years later, 33,074 in 1814–15 and 40,500 by 1817.

Old Testament from the Codex Alexandrinus, edited with scholarly
care by the Rev. Henry Baber, who had become Keeper of Printed
Books in 1812.[1] Another was the new catalogue of printed books,
compiled by Baber and Ellis, a vast improvement on the earlier catalogue by Ayscough, though itself not without faults, as time showed.[2]
There were other similar publications, Planta himself, for instance,
writing much of the catalogue of the Cottonian manuscripts published
in 1802. On all sides valuable acquisitions were fast arriving, especially
for the rapidly expanding Department of Antiquities, which now
received the caryatid figure from the Erechtheum at Athens, as well as
other classical remains, including, in 1819, the famous 'Apotheosis of
Homer'. The coins and gems from the Towneley collection, which had
been retained by the family when the marbles came to the Museum,
were now acquired, as were various pieces of Egyptian sculture, the first
beginnings of the Assyrian collections – within a few years to be
enriched to an extent beyond the imagination of the early nineteenth
century – and, in 1825, the superb collection of Richard Payne Knight.
Knight, a wealthy dilettante, had been collecting classical antiquities
regardless of expense for many years, buying up not only rare pieces
which came upon the market from other collections – and the closing
years of the eighteenth and early nineteenth century saw the break-up of
many such – but also those antiquities newly unearthed in Italy and the
Near East. Bronzes, many of the greatest rarity, coins, gems, drawings
and almost every sort of classical antiquity except marbles, for which
he had little taste, were added, piece by piece, to his collection. For
many years a Trustee, when he died in 1824 at the age of seventy-
five, he bequeathed his magnificent collection, on the sole condition
that his family should be added to the number of family Trustees.
This was done by a special Bill, Knight being the last benefactor so
honoured.

The long neglected departments of Printed Books and Manuscripts
were likewise beginning their slow climb to the heights they reached
later in the century, though they were still below the level achieved by
the principal continental libraries. Henry Baber was the new Keeper of

1. In 1814 and 1815 Parliament granted £4,000 towards printing the Codex, which
appeared between 1816 and 1828. Carl Woide, Assistant Keeper of Printed Books had
produced an edition of the New Testament some thirty years before in 1786. Another
publication issued during this period was the *Synopsis of the Contents of the British Museum*,
of which the first edition appeared in 1808.
2. *Librorum impressorum qui in Museo Britannico adservantur catalogus*, London, 1813–19.

Printed Books, a more energetic and a finer scholar than any of his predecessors. Baber was at last trying to force publishers to implement the Copyright Act of 1814, though, because of its manifest inadequacies, with comparatively little success. On 10 February 1816, Baber and his Assistant Keeper, James Bean, were ordered by the Trustees to produce examples of the more important works not being received under the Copyright Act and to submit them to the Law Officers for their opinion on whether the offending publishers should be prosecuted.[1] No prosecutions, however, seem to have been undertaken. As Baber later pointed out to the Select Committee of the House of Commons of 1836, the Trustees on the whole refrained from prosecuting and the books, if considered necessary, were bought. The number of books received by copyright continued to be very few – no more, for instance, than 2,679 between May 1834 and April 1836.

But books were at last coming in, though still in the case of contemporary works with many gaps. It was becoming difficult for his tiny staff to catalogue the increasing intake. On 19 July 1817, Baber reported his difficulties to the Trustees and requested that one of the assistants who was willing to do so might be permitted to work all day on Saturdays to clear off the arrears.[2]

In 1817 the Museum was offered the book and manuscript collection, (principally of classical authors) of the Rev. Charles Burney,[3] brother of Fanny Burney and son of Dr Burney, the musicologist and friend of Johnson. On 23 February 1818, the Trustees petitioned Parliament for the funds to acquire this library of about 14,000 books and 525 manuscript volumes. The Trustees' petition was granted with certain conditions. £13,500 was allowed for the purchase, but duplicates were to be sold off, a sum of between £3,000 and £4,000 was taken off the annual grant and the Book Fund of £1,000 a year was likewise withdrawn.[4] With these harsh conditions, the Trustees had to be content. After all, they did have a bargain: a superb collection of editions of Greek authors, both printed and in manuscript, many with marginal notes by such scholars as Bentley and Casaubon. Of the major dramatists,

1. *General Meetings, Minutes*, vol.5, p.1135, 11 February, 1816.
2. *Committee Minutes*, vol. 10, p. 2670. 19 July 1817.
3. Rev. Charles Burney, DD, 1757–1817.
4. 'In consideration of so ample and costly an accession being made to the existing stock of Books, it may be proper to suspend or reduce, for a time, the annual grant of £1,000 to the Book Fund, with the exception of such parts of that annual sum as are applied in subscriptions to Works now in progress of publication.' *Report*, p. 4, PP, H. of C. 1818, vol. 3, p. 353.

Burney had 47 editions of Aeschylus, 102 of Sophocles and 166 of Euripides, and of other Greek authors, the array was equally impressive. Although Latin writers were less numerous, there were rarities amongst them, in particular a fourteenth-century Plautus, containing twenty of his plays. In addition there was the collection of English newspapers, dating from the seventeenth and eighteenth centuries, including many unique examples, for long known simply as the Burney newspapers, and nearly 400 volumes containing material for a projected history of the British stage which Burney had never carried out.[1]

Other smaller collections were now also received; those of Francis Hargrave, of legal manuscripts and printed books in 1813; that of Guingené, of Italian and French literature, obtained in 1818 for only £1,000; and that of Baron Von Moll, scientific works, with a cabinet of coins and a valuable herbarium, had been obtained in Munich three years earlier. Thus, the Department of Printed Books was at last receiving acquisitions at a rate worthy of the national library of a great country. These four libraries, received between 1813 and 1818, added 35,000 volumes. In addition, though the annual grant of £1,000 was received only from 1812 to 1815, it had transformed the situation entirely. For the first time the Trustees could buy rare and important books or libraries as they came on the open market, instead of having to rely on gifts, and on the few purchases they were able to make from money obtained from the Edwards fund or from the sale of duplicates.

The Department of Manuscripts was also helped by these annual grants, its share being a little under half of that allotted to Printed Books, and it had likewise received many valuable manuscripts from the Burney and Hargrave libraries. But at this time it also made two fine acquisitions, from one of which the Department still benefits.

The first was the collection of political and historical manuscripts amassed by Lord Shelburne, the Whig statesman who had died in 1805.[2] This wonderful collection was the occasion of the first petition of the Trustees for a special grant for one of the library departments. No such public grants had as yet been made for either of the two library departments, since the Harleian and other founding collections

1. Another important acquisition from the Burney collections was the earliest manuscript then known of Ptolemy's *Geographia*, which had formerly belonged to Talleyrand and was bought by Burney in 1816.
2. William Petty, 1st Marquess of Lansdowne and 2nd Earl of Shelburne, 1737–1805.

had been acquired fifty years before. The Lansdowne manuscripts were now secured for the comparatively small sum of £4,925, an amount far short of its real value.[1]

But it was the second great gift to the Department of Manuscripts which really secured for that Department the outstanding place it has ever since enjoyed amongst such collections. This was the collection of the Rev. Francis Egerton, for a short while in his old age eighth and last Earl of Bridgewater.[2] A country clergyman, he pursued his varied classical and genealogical studies with great tenacity. His last years were spent in Paris, where the frequent sight of his smart carriage, occupied solely by his many dogs, attended with elaborate ceremony, scandalised and amused the inhabitants. He died in 1829, at the age of seventy-two, and by the terms of his will bequeathed to the British Museum his whole collection of manuscripts, rolls, charters and other papers, including a considerable number of original letters by French historical figures. But far more important were estates in Shropshire, also left to the Museum 'for the continued augmentation of the aforesaid Collection of Manuscripts'.[3] By a codicil, permission was given for the Trustees to sell these estates if it were thought beneficial to the Museum to do so. An additional sum of £5,000 was also left to the Trustees for acquiring manuscripts and augmenting the salary of the Keeper of the Department. The Trustees decided that the interest from this sum should indeed be paid to the Keeper, but that his normal salary must be reduced by an equal amount.[4] From 1832 onwards, the Trustees made frequent use of this fund for buying manuscripts, all of which are still known as Egerton manuscripts, and are kept distinct from the Additional Manuscripts, which form the main collections.

It now remains to tell something of the slower, though marked expansion of the Natural History Department. In the closing years of the eighteenth century, the department, still containing 'artificial' as

1. *Report from the Committee on the Lansdowne Manuscripts*, p. 6. (PP, H. of C., 1807, vol. 2, p. 19.) Planta promised that to make room for the Lansdowne manuscripts he would get rid of 'anatomical preparations . . . and a Number of other Articles of a trifling nature'. (*Op. cit.*, p. 5.)
2. Francis Henry Egerton, 8th Earl of Bridgewater, 1756–1829.
3. Edwards, *Founders*, p. 454.
4. It was, however, not always paid to the Keeper. To Madden's disgust, in May 1852 E. A. Bond was appointed Egerton Librarian though still merely an Assistant. His Keeper commented acidly; 'A pitiful and unworthy trick to take away the money from me to augment Bond's salary . . . This is my reward for my labours in the service of the Trustees since 1827!' (*Madden Journal*, 8 May 1852.)

well as 'natural curiosities', had been in charge of Dr E. W. Gray, who had succeeded the Rev. P. H. Maty, son of the second Principal Librarian, in 1787.[1] From 24 December 1801 to 14 December 1805, when he resigned on the grounds of ill-health, Gray acted also as Secretary. He was a quiet man, who seems somewhat overshadowed by his assistant, the naturalist Dr George Shaw. Shaw, who had joined the Museum service as an Assistant Librarian on 11 February 1791, quickly fell foul of authority. A request by him in 1795 to give lectures in the basement of the Museum was turned down by the Trustees, on the grounds that it 'was not justified to give permission to read lectures within the walls of this house'.[2]

Four years later he was again in trouble. Unknown either to his Keeper, Gray, or to the Trustees, Shaw had apparently authorised a doctor friend to dissect several curious and rare animals in the collection and had further transgressed by irregularly admitting a draughtsman into the galleries to make sketches of objects in the collections, whether for his own use or not is not clear. He was summoned before the Board, censured for this 'highly irregular conduct', and suspended from the execution of his office for the space of a calendar month, his salary being given to three other officers appointed to do his work for that period.[3] A harsh sentence, but Shaw was lucky not to be dismissed on the spot, as others had been before.

When Gray died in 1806, Shaw succeeded him as Keeper of the Department, which now covered the botanical, zoological, geological and mineral collections, as well as Ethnography. On Shaw's death in

1. Rev. Paul Henry Maty, 1745–1787. Assistant Keeper of Printed Books, 1776–1782; Keeper of the Department of Natural and Artificial Productions, 1782–1787. Foreign Secretary, Royal Society, 1776; Principal Secretary, 1778.

Edward Whitaker Gray, MD, 1748–1806, botanist and physician, Keeper of the Department of Natural and Artificial Products, 1787–1806. Secretary to the Royal Society and Librarian to the College of Physicians. His great-nephew, John Edward Gray, was the Museum's Keeper of Zoology for much of the nineteenth century.

The elder Maty had a high opinion of the natural history collections as they then were. In a letter to Lord Hardwicke of 5 May 1775, he gives considerable praise to the ornithological specimens. Even though some were imperfect or damaged by insects, 'upon the whole I think that part of our Collection the most brilliant as well as the most complete in Europe, excepting perhaps, the Cabinet du Roi at Paris'. No opportunity, he considered, should be lost to add to it. 'It would tend to make that part, as I trust the whole will be, immortal.' (Add. MS. 35,612. f. 215.)

2. *Committee Minutes*, vol. 8, p. 2107, 11 July 1795.

3. *op. cit.*, vol. 8, pp. 2175–7, Dec. 14, 1799; 10 Jan. 1800.

1813, he was succeeded by Charles König,[1] who remained Keeper until 1851, years which were to see great changes in the departments under his control.

Sloane's original collections included many botanical specimens acquired on his Jamaican voyage, a few fossils, a record pair of Indian buffalo horns, 14 feet from tip to tip, said to have been given to him in lieu of a fee by a barber in East London, and miscellaneous bits and pieces. In 1781 the collection of 'natural and artificial curiosities' which had been formed since the middle of the seventeenth century by the Royal Society, and contained many valuable specimens, was transferred to the Museum. Other collections, small and large, were being acquired throughout the rest of the century. Amongst them were the fossils and other natural history specimens, including minerals, in the Cracherode collections and the series of valuable gifts made over a span of some sixty years by Sir Joseph Banks. The foundations of the Museum's great collection of minerals were laid by the Hatchett collection, received in 1799, and that of Charles Greville,[2] nephew of Sir William Hamilton, which was offered to the Museum by his heirs in March 1810.[3] The collection was found to consist of about 20,000 specimens, most of them very rare and in excellent condition. It was valued by experts consulted by the Parliamentary committee at at least £13,727, being in their opinion, far finer than that in the Jardin des Plantes at Paris. The money was forthcoming, and in May 1810 the collection started to arrive. At one stroke the British Museum had outdone in this particular field every possible rival. As Robert Greville wrote: 'Possession [of the collection] . . . would without doubt, *at once*, render the Cabinet of Minerals in the British Museum the *first in the world*'.[4] König, the first mineralogist as such to be on the staff, was from

1. Charles Dietrich Eberhard König, 1774–1851, mineralogist, Keeper of the Mineralogical and Geological Branch of that Department, 1837–1851, with a general supervision over the whole.
2. Hon. Charles Francis Greville, 1749–1810. It was he who passed on to his uncle his mistress, the celebrated Emma Hart, afterwards the second Lady Hamilton.
3. Add. MS. 40,716.ff.70, 73. Charles Greville's brother, Robert, in a memorandum on Planta's visit on 13 March 1810, wrote, 'I mentioned my preference, if possible, to treat with the British Museum for the *Greville Collection of Minerals* . . . a collection so complete and valuable & which had been collected by my Brother [to be] placed in the British Museum & this seemed to the advantage of the British Nation & perpetuating the Memory of the Person by whom this collection had been so industriously & scientifically made'.
4. *op. cit.*, f. 77.

his appointment in 1807 employed in cataloguing and arranging the mineralogical collections, which had been somewhat neglected till then. On becoming Keeper in 1813 he continued to devote the greater part of his time to management of this portion of the department. In 1815 Baber and he were sent by the Trustees to Munich to inspect the collections of books and mineralogical specimens offered by the Baron von Moll, with authority to buy it on the spot if they considered it advisable, and they did.[1]

The Trustees had designated the Saloon of old Montagu House as a 'proper place' for the display of their greatly enlarged collections of minerals, soon to be one of the Museum's principal atrrerations.[2] Its floor was strengthened with cast-iron pillars in order to bear the additional weight, and the necessary table cases speedily provided. König was then ordered to incorporate the earlier collections with those now acquired from Charles Greville.[3]

At the same time a thorough reorganisation of the department took place. It lost its reputation as a place where obscure natural curiosities might be deposited and became the truly scientific department it was to remain. In February 1806 it was laid down that all the cases should bear proper inscriptions, indicating clearly their respective contents,[4] and in the following year the officers of the department were directed to prepare a classed catalogue of all the books on natural history to be found in the general library, and also to arrange the botanical collections in proper sequence.[5] In May 1808 Shaw was ordered to reorganise the basement rooms, in which much of the natural history collections were then stored. Those objects likely to interest or instruct the visitor were to be brought up and placed in the main rooms, whilst duplicates were to go down to the basement.

The following year an even more drastic reorganisation took place. Certain objects, mostly of a medical or anatomical nature, were declared 'unfit to be preserved in the Museum', and ordered to be disposed of to the Hunterian Museum, which, as a professional medical collection, was

1. £4,578 was paid for Von Moll's collections, which consisted of a library of 20,000 volumes, a small but choice collection of minerals, and a herbarium. To raise the money Edwards' fund was sold out and the Museum thus lost this source of income. Baber and König were paid £187 for their fares and incidental expenses during their trip, and a further £300 as remuneration for their trouble.
2. *Committee Minutes*, vol. 9, p. 2441, 10 March 1801.
3. *op. cit.*, vol. 9, p. 2487, 9 March 1811.
4. *General Meetings, Minutes*, vol. 4, p. 985, 8 February 1806.
5. *op. cit.*, vol. 5, p. 1013, 28 February 1807.

considered a more suitable home for them. They were a mixed bag: the oteological collections; 'monsters in spirits'; anatomical preparations, injections and paintings; a few tattered stuffed quadrupeds, hitherto kept out of sight in the basement, and all the remaining duplicates. A fine collection of animal horns was, however, considered too valuable to be so disposed of, and was rescued from the basement room in which it had long remained hidden and brought upstairs. For most of the nineteenth century, these horns were to be displayed over the cases of stuffed birds in the ornithological gallery above the King's Library, leaving only when all the natural history collections were transferred to South Kensington late in the century.[1] The ubiquitous Sir Joseph Banks was deputed by the Trustees to supervise the purge. This he did, with characteristic enthusiasm and thoroughness, even though advancing age and gout prevented him from going into every one of the many narrow basement rooms where the collections were stored.[2] At times Dr Shaw was somewhat drastic in his efforts to clear away the unwanted specimens which had accumulated. König remembered his ordering the burying or burning of 'zoological rubbish' and that 'some persons in the neighbourhood complained and threatened with an action, because they thought the moths were introduced into their houses by the cremations in the Museum gardens'.[3]

Nevertheless, in the basement cleared of its former dross, Charles König laid out a new arrangement of the collection of seeds and plants, to be inspected and approved of in its turn by Sir Joseph. Upstairs in the room formerly occupied by the minerals was arranged a comprehensive display of fossils, objects which more and more were coming to appeal to the popular imagination.

Thus with the last traces of the 'old curiosity shop' appearance of the past carefully removed, 'all the refuse which ought to be either sold or destroyed'[4] cleared away, the Natural History departments faced the future, eager despite the doubts of some of their colleagues to take full advantage of the growing scientific spirit of the new century.

1. *op. cit.*, vol. 5, pp. 1051, 1052, 1055, 1056, 15, 20 April 1809.
2. *Select Committee*, 1835. *Minutes*, para. 1613.
3. *op. cit.*, para. 2755.
4. *Committee Minutes*, vol. 9, p. 2393, 29 June 1808.

CHAPTER FIVE

A New Era Begins

OLD Montagu House was beginning to feel its age. More and more of the Trustees' scanty funds were being devoted to its upkeep, and its inadequacy was becoming increasingly apparent. In 1780 the stone vases above the colonnade had had to be removed, because dangerously decayed. One had already fallen, damaging the carriage of a gentleman visiting the Museum. In May 1792 the Museum surveyor George Saunders reported the whole house, and especially the cornice, badly in need of repairs.[1] On 1 January 1779, a great storm had caused considerable destruction. Windows were broken, tiles and chimneys flew away and the Principal Librarian's wall fell down. More seriously, in May 1800, it was found that dry rot had caused extensive damage in the basement rooms, which were damp and quite unsuitable for housing the collections. With space so limited, however, it was imperative to use every available corner. The paintings on the walls and ceilings of the great staircase had been once more cleaned and repaired at considerable cost, and all the time the petty expenses of keeping an old building in order for a purpose it was never intended to fill mounted. Some relief was obtained in June 1815 when the care of the building was taken out of the hands of the Trustees and given to the Office of Works, a government department, which with its successors, has looked after the Museum ever since.

No wonder, when plans for the Towneley gallery were being discussed, great emphasis was put on making the new gallery as unlike Montagu House as possible. An alternative scheme, imitating the old building, was drawn up, but the sub-committee of Trustees expressed its preference for something more simple, specifically designed to be a Museum gallery and not a converted 'family Mansion'. After all, Montagu House was built during what they considered to be the very worst period of French architecture, whilst the new building would probably still be in use a century after the old had fallen down.[2] They

1. *Committee Minutes*, vol. 8, p. 2056. 5 May 1792.
2. *General Meetings, Minutes*, vol. 4, p. 965, 14 May 1803.
Committee Minutes, vol. 8, p. 2232, 30 April 1803.

did not know that within a few years both would disappear simultaneously beneath Smirke's gigantic Greek revival museum.

The area too was changing. Gone or going were the green fields,
stretching from the garden walls of the Museum up towards the distant
hills of Hampstead and Highgate, the pipes of the New River water
company, the only sign of urban development, standing high above the
grass on wooden supports. In Great Russell Street the fine houses were
being demolished and, to Dr Morton's disgust, smaller ones took their
places, necessitating a high wall between them and the Principal
Librarian's garden. In August 1799, news was received that the Duke of
Bedford was granting building leases on all the lands to the north of the
Museum. The Trustees were offered a part of this area for the future
expansion of the Museum. Reluctantly, they had to refuse the Duke's
proposal. Their financial position prevented them, and they supposed
they lacked authority to do so, without specific Parliamentary sanction.[1]
Thus a great chance to obtain badly needed space was lost through
financial stringency, as was frequently to happen in the future. The
Trustees did, however, insist that their former right of way out of the
Museum northwards must be maintained. It was agreed that a footpath,
twenty feet wide, would therefore lead out of the north gate of the
Museum, through the midst of the new houses, as it had done formerly
through the open fields.

And so the encirclement of the Museum began. Within its walls,
space, especially in the library, was becoming ever more precious. The
antiquities now had ample room in their fine new building. The Natural
History Department continued its somewhat confined existence in
the many basement rooms of the old house, but its period of growth
had scarcely begun. The Library, on the other hand, thanks to
Planta's energy, was beginning to expand rapidly. In June 1815,
the post of Extra-Assistant Librarian, lost in February 1807, was
granted once more to the Department of Printed Books, 'owing to the
great increase of the Library', and the additional help was much
appreciated.[2]

A further basement room was allotted to Printed Books, but this

1. *op. cit.*, vol. 8, p. 2170, 2171, 9 August; 6 September 1799.
2. *op. cit.*, vol. 9, p. 2608, 8 July 1815. The Extra Assistants were H. W. Bedford,
1805, transferred to the Department of Antiquities; N. Schlichtegroll, 1816–19;
G. H. Noehden, 1819–22; Philip Bliss, 1822; F. A. Walter, 1822–31; and Antonio
Panizzi, 1831–7. The post was then abolished. J. T. Smith, Keeper of Prints and
Drawings, also ranked for a time as an Extra Assistant Librarian.

soon became unusable. Water was discovered seeping from a pipe and forming pools on the floor, and the basement rooms, with bull's-eye windows looking out on to the courtyard, were not really suitable for the storage of books or anything else. In May 1807 Planta had had all reviews and literary journals moved from the basement into a gallery built round a small ante-room of the reading room, convenient for readers, as well as better for the books themselves.

In the meantime, the whole library was being reorganised. The old system of housing the books according to the original collections was at last abandoned and all were now rearranged by subjects. William Beloe,[1] the Keeper of Printed Books, reported somewhat disconsolately to the Trustees on the new system. The former arrangement was in his opinion the most convenient, but he agreed reluctantly that it was far from satisfactory. The various moves as envisaged by the Trustees would, he feared, 'take long and continual labour by many persons!' All the pressmarks in both books and catalogues would have to be changed. It was really all too much.[2] Nevertheless, the Trustees ordered him to continue arranging the books by classes and report back. Poor Beloe! He soon had other things to worry about. An unscrupulous artist and dealer, Robert Dighton, had succeeded in extracting a number of prints from the Cracherode collection and selling them to various dealers and private individuals. Beloe, as the officer responsible for the custody of the prints, was accused by the Trustees of 'negligence in the discharge of his duties and . . . dismissed accordingly.[3]'

Beloe, an easygoing man, appears to have been taken in by the unscrupulous Dighton, and there was nothing criminal in his conduct, except his carelessness in the handling of such valuable prints. The thefts were discovered when Samuel Woodburn, an art dealer, called at the Museum to see the Cracherode copy of Rembrandt's 'Coach Landscape'. Beloe being away, it was looked for by Ellis, who was unable to find it. Woodburn then revealed that he had been sold a copy

1. Rev. William Beloe, 1756–1817, miscellaneous writer. Rector of Allhallows, London Wall and Prebendary both of Lincoln and St Paul's Cathedrals. Appointed Under-Librarian and Keeper of Printed Books in August 1803, in succession to Harper, an outside appointment due, presumably, to Ayscough's advanced age. He was dismissed from the Museum in July 1806.

2. *General Meetings, Minutes*, vol. 4, p. 984, 8 February 1806. Ellis remembered that when he first came to the Museum in 1801 'the floors of several of the rooms were then covered with books sorted out into classes'. (*Select Committee*, 1835. Minutes, para. 1029.)

3. *General Meetings, Minutes*, vol. 4, p. 993, 10 July 1806.

of this print and several other valuable Rembrandts and Dürers with 'on the back . . . some appearance of Mr Cracherode's mark'. A search warrant was issued, and a considerable number of the missing prints recovered from Dighton's house and various dealers. It was clear that the depredation was extensive and had been going on for some time. Beloe, when summoned before the Trustees, denied that Dighton had ever been left alone with the collection. 'I made a point of it religiously never to leave him alone unless I was accidentally called out', and then either Ellis or one of the messengers undertook the necessary supervision. Dighton, who had been introduced to Beloe by a mutual friend, had gained considerable influence over him and had made him several presents: 'Having been always treated with great courtesy by Mr Beloe, I two or three times sent him presents of fish when I knew he had company and once of green peas when they were a guinea a quart.'

The Trustees asked for legal advice about the likelihood of securing a conviction against Dighton, and were told that it was doubtful without absolute proof, as opposed to strong presumptive evidence, that the prints were, in fact, in the Cracherode collection when it came to the Museum, and also that Beloe had admitted that 'he did not examine the Portfolio . . . after he had the inspection'. On a promise that he would not be prosecuted, Dighton confessed everything. He had been systematically robbing the Museum since May 1795, but after meeting Beloe had been able to do it far more extensively. 'My acquaintance with Mr Beloe increased & my admissions were facilitated.' Since the prints were only loosely pasted in, it was easy to extract them. 'I twice carried with me a Portfolio to shew Mr Beloe some drawings and availed myself of that means of conveying prints away. I never found occasion to be particularly guarded in the manner of taking them away: Sometimes in my pocket; sometimes in the bosom of my Coat; Often in a Roll in my hand.'[1]

So Beloe went, complaining pitifully of the injustice of his fate, while the real criminal was allowed to go scot-free. 'Comparison will infallibly be drawn,' he wrote, 'between the case of the real offender who cannot perhaps be brought to punishment and that of the person on whom his dishonesty imposed and who is doomed to positive ruin.'[2] He did have the faint consolation that the Trustees publicly declared that he had been guilty only 'of negligence, in one particular Branch

1. *Original Letters and Papers*, vol. 2, 1785–1809, pp. 802–823.
2. *op. cit.*, p. 825.

of his Duty'.[1] Beloe was however deeply embittered by the treatment
he had received and never fully recovered from it.

Taylor Combe had kept Henry Ellis, Beloe's Assistant Keeper, who
was on leave, informed as to the fast changing situation. In a letter of
11 July 1806, Combe wrote, 'A very large meeting of the Trustees was
convened yesterday, at which, after a long consultation, it was determined, that Mr Beloe should be dismissed from the Museum, and the
painful task of communicating to him this heavy sentence was imposed
on Mr Planta. I need not tell you how this has agitated us all. Poor Beloe
(for I must now call him so) is, with his family, thrown into the deepest
affliction.' Combe goes on to tell Ellis that it had now been 'whispered
to me that you either already were, or are very speedily to be promoted'.[2]
The rumour was true and on 11 September Ellis was promoted Under-
Librarian and made Keeper of Printed Books.

Thanks to prompt action on the part of the authorities concerned,
most of the prints were recovered, but it was obvious that they must in
future be properly looked after. First, in February 1807 engravings were
transferred from Printed Books to the Department of Manuscripts; a
detailed catalogue of all the prints was ordered to be made by a visiting
specialist, who was at the same time to mark them, and finally, in 1808,
drawings and engravings were transferred to the newly created Department of Antiquities. A special room was allotted to them in the new
building, as well as a smaller room for coins and medals, and an extra
assistant, with the title of Keeper of Prints, appointed to look after
them. The specialist was a Mr Philipe, who had done much to unmask
the criminal activities of Robert Dighton. The prints were first placed
under the care of the artist William Alexander, 1767–1816, who, in
1808, was appointed Keeper of Prints, with the rank of Assistant
Librarian and who also acted as draughtsman for other departments. On
Alexander's death in 1816, he was succeeded by John Thomas Smith,
1766–1833 (born, as he was fond of telling, in a hackney coach),
Keeper of Prints and Drawings for the next seventeen years. Smith was
the author of *Nollekens and his Times*, whose pupil he had been, and *A Book
for a Rainy Day*, published posthumously.

The Library was also going through a difficult time. To crown every-
thing, the readers complained, not unreasonably, of the activities of the
St Giles Association of Volunteers. In these days of fear of invasion by
Bonaparte, the Military Association of the Inhabitants of the United

1. *General Meetings, Minutes*, vol. 4, p. 997, 12 July 1806.
2. Combe to Ellis, 11 July 1806. Add. MS. 41,312. f. 12.

Parishes of St Giles and St George had been given permission by the Trustees to 'drill and discipline the said corps' in the courtyard and garden of the Museum,[1] provided they did not damage the Egyptian antiquities stacked in the garden, awaiting transfer to the Towneley galleries, or harm the flower-beds. The readers were indignant. They were 'much disturbed and interrupted', 'by the Military Music of the Association who are permitted to exercise in the Garden'. The Trustees were sympathetic. There was to be no more military music or man-oeuvres such 'as will give serious disturbances to the silence necesary for Study'.[2]

The St Giles Volunteers were indeed becoming a nuisance. First, they placed several barrels of gunpowder in the Engine Room of the Museum, until the alarmed Trustees heard about it and ordered its instant removal. Then they asked for and obtained a small room in the base-ment in which to store their arms, and next got reluctant permission for the erection of an ammunition shed in the north-west corner of the garden – one presumes as far from the Museum buildings as possible – and turned the tool shed into a guard room. The secretary of the Association brought two dogs into the grounds contrary to the statutes, and complained that the guardroom was damp and unhealthy. The soldiers' habits of going round with naked lights and of making fires on the Museum premises also had to be stopped. At last, in 1809 the Trustees could stand no more. All real danger of an invasion was now long past and the St Giles Volunteers could surely go and exercise elsewhere. The room in the basement was needed, or so it was alleged. But the gallant volunteers refused to budge. They declared that they had nowhere else to go. If they left the Museum, they must be disbanded. Lord Amhurst, the Commander-in-Chief, pleaded with the Trustees. Reluctantly they gave the Volunteers first till 1 May and then to 2 July to make other arrangements. At last they went, the basement room they had used as a guard room was vacated and the armourer's shed in which they had stored their ammunition was demolished.

This was not the end of a military presence at the Museum. In view of the new streets springing up all round and the upset caused by the erection of the new building on their own premises, the Trustees in 1807 asked for and obtained a permanent sergeant's guard, increased to a subaltern's guard at times of crisis or when the mob threatened. The

1. *Committee Minutes*, vol. 8, p. 2237, 5 August 1803.
2. *op. cit.*, vol. 8, p. 224, 20 April 1804.

troops in their 'centry boxes' in fact stayed on at the Museum for more than fifty years.[1]

With the volunteers gone, the Trustees surveyed the ruins of their once lovely gardens. It was becoming ever more difficult and expensive to maintain them. The walks were again newly gravelled, but in 1809 when several trees had to be cut down, it was decided not to replace them. The days of the peaceful Museum garden with its shady grove of elegant lime trees and gay flower-beds were clearly numbered.

It was clear too that patching up was not really the solution for the house. An established architect, Robert Smirke, had been commissioned in 1815 to design the temporary shed for the Elgin marbles. He had likewise drawn up plans to make some extra space in Printed Books, for a gallery round three sides of each room of the library and for new floors in some of the rooms, with, if necessary, additional supports below. But this was again mere patching. Something more radical was necessary. On 10 February 1816 Planta reported to the Trustees concerning the deficiencies of the existing building and proposed the erection of a new suite of rooms. But the only really practical solution to the Museum's growing problems was a vast rebuilding programme, involving the replacement of old Montagu House and the utilisation of the entire site.

Plans were, however, set in train for the extra galleries, and the opinion of the Attorney-General sought as to the legal position should the Trustees construct these buildings in their garden. The Duke of Bedford was being difficult. In his view, such buildings would lessen the value of his estates now being laid out in the seemly squares and broad streets of Bloomsbury and he filed a suit in Chancery against the Trustees.

The Museum was being attacked on all sides. Gone was the easy eighteenth-century acceptance of both sinecure and sloth, and though the Museum under Planta was certainly not slothful, nor were many of its official positions mere sinecures, the first rumblings were heard of a storm of criticism, that 'small black cloud of radical reform mania'[2], which, by the middle of the century was to shake the Museum to its foundations and come near destroying it.

As early as 1814, the Trustees had declared, in the face of mounting

1. *General Meetings, Minutes*, vol. 5, p. 1018, April 23 1807. The guard was finally withdrawn on 29 December 1863. The old guard house still exists, having been used for many years as an office for the works staff.
2. *The British Museum, Quarterly Review*, CLXXV, p. 145.

criticism, that 'for long time past [they had] endeavoured to increase the facilities allowed to the public for inspecting every part of the Museum'.[1] They pointed out that between 28,000 and 30,000 persons had visited the Natural History and Antiquities collections during the past year and that additional facilities had recently been granted for examining drawings, engravings, coins and gems. On security grounds it was simply not possible to admit all comers freely. It was true that the Reading Room was inadequate, but funds were lacking for convert-ing more rooms and engaging more staff. The officers were always most liberal in granting admission and it was scarcely ever refused. If Parliament provided the necessary funds, the Trustees would provide more accommodation for readers and the general public.

But the voice of criticism was by no means stilled. More and more scholars and others wanted to use the Reading Room, and more and more of the public wanted to view the collections. Then was heard what was described as 'the blue & buff signal of war to the knife', as both the *Edinburgh Review* and the *Westminster Review*, amongst others, attacked the Museum, in a display of that 'antagonism between the aristocracy of talent and the aristocracy of birth'[2] characteristic of the Age of Reform. A letter to *The Times* in October 1823 complained that 'The reading rooms of this great establishment are hermetically sealed against the majority of those who would wish to frequent them for scientific purposes.' The writer went on to blame Henry Bankes, MP, for the Trustees' reactionary attitude. 'With his usual love for every-thing antiquated,' he had 'declared himself hostile to all innovations' and seemed to think that 'the regulations of the Museum were the best of all possible regulations'. This disappointed reader admitted that he had failed to get in because he had refused to make formal application to the Trustees. Books and manuscripts were properly, he declared, 'collected and preserved, not for the inspection of a select few, but for the use and benefit of the whole literary republic'.[3]

In response one correspondent condemned the 'pompous and inquisi-torial ordeal'[4] of asking for a temporary ticket of admission, whilst

1. *General Meetings, Minutes*, vol. 5, p. 1131, 1132; December 10, 1814.
2. *Quarterly Review*, CLXXV, p. 144.
3. *The Times*, 10 October 1823. Henry Bankes, 1757–1834, politician and author, MP for Corfe Castle and for Dorset. He acted as the Museum's Parliamentary spokesman. A strong Tory, he was opposed to any change. Panizzi thought little of him and considered that he had harmed the Museum by his illiberal attitudes.
4. *op. cit.*, 20 October 1823.

another praised the help he had received and for the 'civilities' of the officers of this 'noble institution'.[1] Another correspondent, however, some time later, was less kind and attacked both Planta and Baber for allowing the books 'to become food for moths'. The Museum was (this was to be a mounting criticism) 'a kind of rookery for certain favourites and dependents, where each has a snug nest and a comfortable maintenance, and each will do as little as he possibly can for his bread and butter'. All is summed up in the sweeping criticism: 'Bad editions, bad catalogues, a bad reading room and tedious and frequent delays.'[2]

The volume of criticism grew. Few knew or cared about the difficulties and frustrations with which the officers had to cope: little money, inadequate accommodation, and wavering and uncertain support from both government and Parliament. It was so easy to lay all blame for these deficiencies on the poor quality of the staff and the misgovernment or worse of the Trustees.

It was lucky that not all thought of the Museum in this way, for it was now on the point of receiving the most magnificent bequest ever made to it, and even in high places prejudice against the Museum was very strong.

On 15 January 1823, George IV wrote to his Prime Minister Lord Liverpool: 'The King, My late revered and excellent Father, having formed during a long series of years, a most valuable and extensive Library . . . I have resolved to present this collection to the British Nation'.[3] The following day, the government communicated a letter, together with a minute of their own, to the Trustees of the British Museum and requested their opinion as to the best way in which 'His Majesty's most gracious intentions can be carried into effect'.[4] The Trustees recommended that the royal library come to the Museum, be kept there distinct from the rest of the library in a separate repository, the catalogue of it be finished, and drew the government's attention to the fact that 'a new building will be indispensably requisite for that purpose' which could be completed in two years.[5] What lay behind this sudden and generous offer?

George III, on coming to the throne in 1760, found that the library of his ancestors had been bestowed on the Museum by his grandfather

1. *op. cit.*, 24 October 1823.
2. *op. cit.*, 18 November 1825. A blistering attack, particularly on the Reading Room.
3. *The King's Library. Copies of Papers presented by Command*, p. 1. (PP, H. of C., 1823, vol. 4, p. 56.)
4. *op. cit.*, p. 2.
5. *op. cit.*, p. 3.

three years before. To George, a fine library was part of the royal prerogative and, though no reader himself, he conscientiously built up over the next sixty years one of the finest libraries ever created by one man. The king was, in the words of one who knew him well, 'the most judicious of Collectors',[1] and was aided by his librarian, Sir Frederick Barnard,[2] and advised by Dr Johnson and Consul Smith at Venice among others. Special attention was paid to maps, charts and topo-graphical drawings, at that date still obtainable cheaply, and thus the Museum's present important map collection was begun. Even in the last years of his reign, when the King was no longer responsible for his own actions, books were bought on a lavish scale. George was always most generous in allowing scholars the freedom of his library and he explicitly forbade Barnard to bid against 'a literary man who wants books for study, or against a known Collector of small means'.[3]

There was, in fact, more than one royal collection. Thomas Amyot, in a letter to Ellis written probably sometime in 1825, mentions three. The first, the 'Little Library' had been removed to Brighton. 'It was what the old King used to call his "Gentleman's" Library, that at Windsor being his "Nobleman's", & this [the King's Library] his "Royal" Library. They were all admirably selected with a view to their respective objects.'[4]

By the time of the King's death the collection amounted to 65,250 volumes, besides 19,000 unbound tracts, which in February 1823 was offered by George IV 'to the British Nation'. Not it would appear without some difficulty. George IV was anxious to get rid of it, because it cost a minimum of £2,500 a year to maintain and in his opinion, took up far too much room. The grandiose reconstruction of Bucking-ham House – henceforth known as Buckingham Palace – which the King began early in his reign involved the subdivision of the apartments hitherto used for the library and their conversion to other purposes. He needed therefore to move the old King's library as speedily as possible.

It was said that the King had first proposed selling the books to

1. Thomas Amyot, FRS, 1775–1850, antiquary and civil servant. Treasurer of the Society of Antiquaries. (Add. MS. 41,312. f. 45.)
2. Sir Frederick Augusta Barnard. It was alleged that he was an illegitimate son of Frederick, Prince of Wales, but this is by no means proved. His second name, that of the Prince's own wife, seems to make the tale unlikely. The Prince is known for certain to have had only one natural son, who died young.
3. Edwards, *Founders*, p. 473.
4. Amyot to Ellis, n.d., *c*. 1825. Add. MS. 41,312. f. 45.

Alexander I of Russia and was only dissuaded with difficulty by the Prime Minister, Lord Liverpool, and the Home Secretary, Lord Sidmouth, and then demanded to be paid from government funds the amount which he would have received from the Tsar. The story, as told in the *Quarterly Review* of 1850, was that Richard Heber, the book collector, heard of the King's intentions and went to the Home Secretary, Sidmouth, who arranged to pay the King an equivalent amount from public funds. It was also alleged that the Prime Minister, Liverpool, was approached, either through Princess Lieven, the wife of the Russian Ambassador, or through other prominent persons.[1] The story, which seems to have been fairly widely circulated, was quickly denied by J. W. Croker, who would undoubtedly have known the truth, and by Princess Lieven herself. It is possible that the story originated with Frederick, Duke of York, who was extremely annoyed with his brother over the disposal of their father's property and who told Greville that George 'even had a design of selling the Library collected by the late King, but this he was obliged to abandon'.[2] William IV is likewise said to have been so furious at his predecessor's action that, according to Macaulay, he would never even visit the King's library. 'Now what did it matter to Wm IV whether his palace contained a Library or not'.[3]

Even then it was uncertain that the library would come to the Museum. Many, such as W. R. Hamilton, Elgin's former agent and now Under-Secretary of State at the Foreign Office, considered that it was unsuitable to go to Bloomsbury, where it would be 'melted and lost as it were amid the more numerous objects of a more general and National Library'. It must be kept entire, as the old King had wished, and yet to send it to the British Museum would duplicate existing stocks in the library. Would it not be better, he wrote to Peel as late as March 1827, to put it somewhere else at the other end of London, say in the Banqueting House in Whitehall or in some other building near Westminster? After all, an additional library in the south-west of London would relieve pressure on the Museum and the money spent on providing new accommodation at Bloomsbury might be better spent in erecting entirely new premises elsewhere.[4] Peel replied that the King stipulated that his father's library should go to the Museum, and,

1. *Quarterly Review*, no. CLXXV, December 1850 p. 143.
2. Greville, 8 January 1823. vol. 1, p. 108.
3. Macaulay, *Journal*, 29 November 1849.
4. W. R. Hamilton to Sir Robert Peel, 25 March 1827. Add. MS. 40,393. f. 52.

indeed, it was generally believed that the old King himself would certainly have so wished. In his own opinion, Peel told Hamilton, either the library should have remained the personal property of the Crown, as he himself would have preferred, or else it should have gone to the 'Chapel at Whitehall'.[1] Many of the Trustees, who, after all, were some of the most powerful men in the country, had however been making strenuous efforts to ensure that the royal library did come to the Museum.

A committee was set up by the House of Commons to consider the whole matter, its deliberations being watched with anxiety by the Museum staff. Despite continued attempts in some quarters to prevent the library's coming to Bloomsbury, the committee finally came down on the side of the Museum, their main reasons being that the old Royal Library was already there; that George III's interest in that institution had been well-known, and that the King's Library was 'very rich in many of those classes in which the latter [the Museum] is very deficient'.[2] The duplication was, in fact, far less than many had supposed. Of the Department of Printed Books' approximately 125,000 volumes, not more than 21,000, and probably less, were duplicates of those in the King's Library. The committee declared on 23 April that 'the Public will derive the greatest benefit from placing this noble donation under the care of the Trustees of the Museum'.[3] The Library, however, must be 'kept distinct and entire' and 'a separate room should be appropriated for its reception'.[4] The Museum could breathe again. All was well, Baber wrote delightedly to his friend Philip Bliss at Oxford on 10 May that 'Very many attempts have been made to get this Library placed elsewhere at the west end of the metropolis and to be made a separate literary establishment, but these efforts have all proved futile'.[5]

Parliament fortunately agreed with the recommendations of the committee and made arrangements for the necessary financial provisions.[6] Ellis also wrote to Bliss a few weeks earlier, before the final result was known in an equally triumphant strain. 'The gift of the King's

1. Sir R. Peel to W. R. Hamilton, 27 March 1827, op. cit., f. 58.
2. *Report from the Committee on Papers relating to the Royal Library*, p. 6. (PP, H. of C., 1823, vol. 4, p. 41.)
3. op. cit., p. 7.
4. op. cit., p. 8.
5. Add. MS. 34,568. f. 569.
6. CJ, vol. 78, p. 227, 379, 443, 444. £40,000 was granted 'towards defraying the expense of Buildings at the *British Museum* for the reception of the Royal Library . . . for the year 1823.' (op. cit., p. 444).

Library to the Nation and, of course, to the National Repository is truly magnificent . . . Between ourselves the Coins and Medals will accompany the books to us, as will the Geographical and Topographical Collection, except the Military Maps. Avaunt Bodley, thou now second rate Library! [Planta] is delighted with the Gift, but he blundered sadly in the outset . . . It is intended for the Royal Library to remain for ever entire, a very proper respect to the memory of the King, who was more than fifty years forming it.'[1]

As well as laying it down that the the Library must be accommodated separately, the committee had recognised that a gallery specially designed to house it must now be constructed. The 'present edifice', they reported, 'in which treasures of very high value are desposited is in a decaying state', was by no means fire proof and was not 'well calculated for the purposes to which it is applied'.

New buildings were an absolute necessity, not only for the King's Library, but as part of a general rebuilding scheme for the whole museum. 'The part of it which shall be first begun should be appropriated for this Library, and for a safe depository of the many valuable manuscripts now at the Museum, and . . . care should be taken in its construction, to render it fire proof'.[2]

A few weeks later the Commons granted £40,000 towards the expenses, the first of many such payments over the next twenty-five years. By 1827, £157,000 had been voted for the rebuilding of the Museum and work on the major reconstruction of the galleries had, as yet, scarcely begun. In June 1823 the Trustees asked Smirke to draw up plans for 'a proper Building for the reception of the Royal Library, and a Picture Gallery over it' and also for 'providing a fit place for the safe deposit of the manuscripts'.[3] Such buildings were to form part of a plan for the erection of a completely new museum and the demolition of old Montagu House.

Smirke pressed on with his plans for the new galleries, which were to be, in Baber's words, 'chaste and grand and truly classical', and which would 'exhibit to the best advantage the various collections of literature, sciences and art which we now have and still expect and hope to obtain'.[4] The inhabitants of the south side of Montagu Place complained of the 'large solid building,' being erected immediately

1. Add. MS. 34,568. f. 528.
2. *Report*, p. 8.
3. *General Meetings, Minutes*, vol. 5, p. 1211, 26 June 1823.
4. Add. MS. 34,568. f. 569.

The old British Museum Reading Room, in use from 1834 till 1857.

The King's Library (1823–1827), the oldest existing part of the British Museum.

A pictorial criticism of the British Museum's failure to open its doors to the public on general holidays.

A. Archer's painting of trustees and officers of the British Museum assembled in the temporary Elgin gallery, 1819.

behind their houses, but to no avail.[1] By December 1824 the southern part of the new wing, destined for the manuscript collections, was ready to the height of the roof. Only the unusually wet weather was delaying things. By May 1826, the Department of Manuscripts was asked to prepare plans for the imminent move; on 14 April 1827 the manuscript collections were ordered to be moved into the new East Wing, which they were the following June. They were not, however, to have all of these new apartments. Baber was promised some as a Reading Room, whilst others were allotted to the overcrowded Natural History departments. Pressure on the existing Reading Rooms was already so great that in 1828 one of the new rooms of the Department of Manuscripts was made available to be used as an extra Reading Room should the need for it arise.

Meanwhile, all was almost ready for the reception of the King's Library, by this time moved to temporary premises at Kensington Palace. On 9 June 1827 Planta was instructed to take the King's Library formally into his possession. But still there were delays. In June 1828 the Treasury approved 'the immediate removal of the King's Library to the British Museum'[2] and finally in August it arrived. But not before an alarming development had occurred. In July the Trustees learnt that 'certain Books belonging to the Royal Library' were being withheld. J. H. Glover, one of the assistant librarians of the Royal Library, was asked for an explanation. He told the Trustees that he had instructions from Sir Frederick Barnard to withhold thirty-three books, of which he gave a list, and that two further volumes were being withheld on the King's express command. But worse was to follow. Glover also revealed that on the authority of a second letter from Barnard he was ordered to retain 'the whole of The Military Plans, The Charts, Topography and Geography, the catalogue whereof are contained in Six Volumes folio, exclusive of the Military Plans'.[2]

The Trustees learnt that Nicholas Carlisle, the King's under-librarian, had authorised Glover 'to deliver The Charts and the Whole of the Geography and Topography to Capt. Parry, whenever Capt. Parry should demand them'. The Trustees wrote in haste to Peel, the Home Secretary, requesting him to ask His Majesty for all the books on Barnard's list 'and more especially The Charts and the Collections of Geography and Topography, particularly adverted to in the Reports of the Committee of the House of Commons'. Peel was likewise requested

---

1. *Committee Minutes*, vol. 10, p. 3110, 14 June 1826.
2. *General Meetings, Minutes*, vol. 5, pp. 1292–1294, 12 July 1828.

E

to point out that 'the Trustees feel the great advantage of making the British Museum the general depository of all these valuable Collections'. They promised to make them freely available to any department of state which wished to see them and to supply such department 'with Catalogues of every Branch of these Collections and with such Copies of any particular portion as may from time to time be required for the Public Service'.[1]

Peel now took the matter up with the King. The Trustees wished, he said, to know His Majesty's pleasure as to what books he himself wanted to retain and, above all, what was to happen to the charts and to the geographical and topographical collections. The Home Secretary suggested that the charts might go to the Admiralty, and the rest to the Museum.[2] George replied, somewhat testily, that he had not expected to be 'catechised' on the subject of his gifts and sarcastically observed that he '*unfortunately* did not think it *necessary to ask Permission*' to retain the few books he had decided to keep. There was, he went on, 'a *Domestick* Feeling attached to those Books that are Reserved and which the King retains for Windsor Castle'. He agreed, however, in general with Peel's proposals.[3] In his reply of the following day Peel tactfully pointed out that it was consistent with the King's original intention to order 'that the Nautical Charts should be deposited in the Archives of the Public Department which is most interested in their careful preservation'.[4]

A draft letter to the Trustees was prepared for the royal signature, confirming 'that the Nautical charts only shall be transmitted to the Admiralty' and that the other collections might come with the rest to the Museum, since on enquiry it had been found that there was 'not room for their proper Custody in those offices to which the Topographical and Geographical collections might have been most useful'. Any other interested department must be given the 'utmost facility of access for the purpose of consulting them'.[5] So by a narrow chance, these

1. *op. cit.*, vol. 5, pp. 1300, 1301, 16 July 1828.
2. Peel to George IV, 24 July 1828. Add. MS. 40,300. f. 246.
3. George IV to Peel, 25 July 1828. *op. cit.*, f. 248.
A list of these books appears in a memorandum in the handwriting of Nicholas Carlisle, dated 19 June 1828. (BM Department of Printed Books. 11912. b.55.)
4. Peel to George IV, 26 July 1828. *op. cit.*, f. 250. Peel tells the King that he will convey His Majesty's pleasure to the Directors of the British Museum, but will 'avoid all controversy of an unpleasant nature'.
5. *op. cit.*, f. 252. In his evidence eight years later before the Select Committee, Panizzi stated that there had been protracted negotiations between the Trustees and

superb collections came to the Museum. Some fifteen years later, the Admiralty, finding no further use for them, permitted the nautical charts also to be transferred.

The following November the public were allowed in to view this gift in the room specially designed for it. The gallery above, intended for the pictures of the national collection, was never so used, since the opening of the National Gallery rendered it unnecessary. It contained, for much of the nineteenth century, the bird collection of the Natural History department, and on their departure was given over to the display of ethnographical specimens.

In the meantime, important changes had taken place at the Museum. On 3 December 1827, Planta died, still in office after fifty-three years, 'at the advanced age of 84',[1] and had been succeeded as Principal Librarian on 20 December by the Keeper of the Department of Manuscripts, Henry Ellis. It had been a near thing. The distinguished antiquary, Henry Fynes Clinton had, even before Planta's death, obtained the ear of the Archbishop of Canterbury, who remarked: 'There is that about him which would make his nomination . . . acceptable to the public.'[2] On learning of Planta's death, Fynes Clinton hurried to London to find that the Archbishop, as good as his word, had taken steps to secure his appointment as Principal Librarian. All three Principal Trustees, the Archbishop, the Lord Chancellor, and the Speaker, were said to favour his nomination, rather than that of Ellis, 'who had for many years filled a subordinate position at the Museum'.[3] Ellis now began to pull every possible string to secure the nomination for himself. All his most influential friends were begged to do what they could. One Trustee, Lord Farnborough, told Ellis that 'the King thought of another Person as the successor to Mr Planta' and whilst he considered that this candidate 'was not half as fit as Mr Ellis', refused to interfere, since the Archbishop considered all appointments 'as

1. John Caley to Ellis, 4 Decemb 1827. Add. MS. 41,312. f. 71. It was Charles König who had told him the news.
2. H. Fynes Clinton *Literary Remains*, London, 1854. p. 256. Henry Fynes Clinton, 1781–1852, author of *Fasti Hellenici* and other works.
3. *op. cit.*, p. 266.

the King 'in order to procure the direction of such a donation to the British Museum'. He concluded, 'Yes, I think both Trustees and officers worked very hard to get the library then and exerted all their influence both public and private.' (*Select Committee*, 1836. *Minutes*, para. 4900, 4901.)

belonging virtually to him'.[1] However, Ellis's patron, Lord Aberdeen, persuaded Lord Lansdowne to intervene on his behalf. On 19 December Lansdowne informed the anxious Ellis, 'You are probably aware that the official Trustees have selected the names 1st of Mr Fynes Clinton, 2ndly of your own as fit candidates to succeed the late Mr Planta at the British Museum as head librarian. It gives me great pleasure to inform you that having thought it my duty in repeating their names to His Majesty without any derogation to the merits of Mr Clinton to call his particular attention to the claim arising from your long and able services to the establishment.'[2] The King took the hint and Lansdowne was 'authorised to direct your appointment to be made out accordingly'.[3] So on 20 December, to his mortification, Fynes Clinton learnt that, after all, His Majesty 'in consequence of the long services in the Museum of Mr Ellis has been pleased to appoint him successor to Mr Planta'.[4] Thanks to Lord Lansdowne, who twenty-eight years later, was instrumental in promoting Ellis's great successor, Antonio Panizzi, Ellis was now Principal Librarian, an office he occupied with dignity and increasing bewilderment, the still centre of the tempests that raged round him for another thirty years.

Henry Ellis had been successively Assistant Keeper and Keeper of Printed Books and since 1812, on the sudden resignation of Francis Douce,[5] Keeper of Manuscripts. With his scholarly tastes and capacity

1. Lord Farnborough to Ellis, 4 December 1827. Add. MS. 41,312. f. 80. Charles Long, 1st Baron Farnborough, 1761–1831, politician and art expert. He assisted George III and George IV in the decoration of the royal palaces.

2. op. cit., ff. 84, 89. George Hamilton Gordon, 4th Earl of Aberdeen, 1784–1860, Prime Minister, 1852–55.
Henry Petty FitzMaurice, 3rd Marquess of Lansdowne, 1780–1862, Whig statesman.

3. op. cit., f. 89. This is the only definitely known case in which the sovereign chose the second of the two names customarily presented to him by the Trustees. Museum tradition has it, however, that the same was done with Frederic Kenyon, ninety-odd years later. Ellis was alleged to have pursued on foot the all-powerful favourite Sir William Knighton, the King's physician, who was driving off in his carriage, in order to secure the reversal of the names. The intervention of the King's even more powerful female favourite, Lady Conyngham, was also dreaded. Bliss wrote despondently to Madden on 6 December 1827, 'If my Lady C. puts her finger on the Librarianship goodbye to Ellis, & Baber & yourself, for there will then be no vacancy.' (Egerton MS. 2837. f. 253.) Madden was trying for the Assistant Keepership of the Department of Manuscripts, which was expected to fall vacant on the promotion of Ellis.

4. Literary Remains, p. 267. How Fynes Clinton could have coped with the problems he would have faced, in particular Antonio Panizzi, makes interesting speculation.

5. Francis Douce, 1757–1834, antiquary. He bequeathed his manuscripts, coins, prints and drawings to the Bodleian and his unpublished essays to the British Museum.

for hard work, Ellis proved to be an excellent Keeper, though not in the opinion of his distinguished successor, Sir Frederic Madden. He continued in conjunction with Baber to work on the catalogue of Printed Books, despite his transfer to a new Department. From 1814 onwards, he was also Secretary to the Trustees, a post he likewise filled with distinction. A little, fat, Pickwickian man of High Tory opinions, Ellis was not, however, really the type of Principal Librarian to lead the Museum into a new era. Jolly, liked by almost all, telling his juniors improper stories whenever he had the chance, he buzzed anxiously through those long years, overshadowed by his mighty subordinates, Panizzi, Madden and Forshall.[1] Madden detested him. 'The little great man', he scornfully called him, who always acted 'in a most childish manner', and who was quite incapable, in Sir Frederic's opinion, of worthily maintaining the high office which he held.

But this was still in the future. In 1828 all looked promising. He had a good team. In Printed Books was the wise and learned Henry Baber, modest and unassuming, a good scholar and a devoted librarian. Baber's assistant was the great Dante scholar and friend of Charles Lamb, Henry Cary.[2] In the Department of Manuscripts, Ellis' successor was the Rev. Josiah Forshall, who had already established a reputation as an administrator and was, like Ellis before him, Secretary to the Trustees. With him was the redoubtable Frederic Madden,[3] one of the outstanding personalities of the nineteenth-century Museum. Madden came from a military family; his father was a captain of Marines, and his uncle, Sir

1. Rev. Josiah Forshall, 1795–1863, chaplain of the Foundling Hospital, 1829–1863.
2. Rev. Henry Francis Cary, 1772–1844, translator of Dante's *Inferno*, 1805, and *Purgatorio* and *Paradiso*, 1812. Assistant Keeper, Department of Printed Books, 1826–1837. The other senior member of Baber's staff was Francis Augustus Walter, Extra Assistant Librarian, Department of Printed Books, 1822–1831, formerly a member of the staff of the King's Library.
3. Sir Frederic Madden, KH, 1801–1873.

Ellis claimed for the Museum Douce's *Table Talk*, not to be opened before 1900. Madden commented, 'This will be a *valuable acquisition to those who are* alive in the year 1900, when his *treasures* are to be open to the public. I could not have believed Douce would have acted so absurdly.' (*Madden Journal*, April 28, 1840.)
Ellis told the Committee of 1835 that Douce, being a man of independent means, was disinclined 'to give up his time, so much as the collection of manuscripts required . . . He preferred ease'. (*Select Committee, 1835. Minutes*, para. 1479.) Ellis could or would not give any other definite reason for Douce's departure except, vaguely, that he had quarrelled with some trustee. Douce was odd, 'whimsical and apt to murmer'. (*op. cit.*, para. 1482, 83.)

George Madden, a major-general. Hard-working and conscientious, a brilliant antiquarian, Madden was an exceptionally difficult man, whose obsessive hatred of Ellis and Panizzi amounted almost to mania. The Journals which he kept for the greater part of his life are a mine of information on the nineteenth-century Museum.

He had first tried for the Keepership of the Department of Antiquities on the death of Taylor Combe, as had Cary, but the post had gone to Edward Hawkins,[1] who held it for nearly forty years. In July 1826 Madden had been engaged to help in the projected classed catalogue, but now wanted a more permanent appointment. When Forshall became Keeper of Manuscripts in 1828, Madden had secured the post of Assistant Keeper and since much of Forshall's time was occupied with his duties as Secretary, he more or less ran the department on his own, a task he performed with devotion and skill. The Natural History collections were under the direction of Charles König, assisted by J. G. Children,[2] whilst Antiquities were under the care of the distinguished numismatist, Edward Hawkins.

In 1831 the man came who was to transform the whole Museum, to create a truly National Library and to be the centre of endless controversies, both within and without the Museum. This was Antonio Panizzi,[3] a refugee from the tiny Duchy of Modena in northern Italy, and perhaps the greatest administrative librarian who has ever lived. He had arrived in England in May 1823, penniless and scarcely speaking a word of the language, having given up a promising legal career in the cause of Italian freedom and been executed in effigy by the Modenese authorities. By his industry and charm, within a few years, he had become a successful teacher of Italian in Liverpool, then Professor of Italian at the newly founded London University, and had gained the friendship and affection

1. Edward Hawkins, 1780–1867, numismatist, Keeper of Antiquities, 1826–60. His fine collections of medals and political cartoons were bought by the Museum.

2. John George Children, 1777–1852, Assistant Keeper, Department of Natural History, 1816–1837; Keeper of Zoology, 1837–1840.

3. Antonio Genesio Maria Panizzi (Sir Anthony Panizzi, KCB.), 1797–1879, born at Brescello, in the Duchy of Modena, the son of a village chemist. This remarkable man, becoming more English than the English, served not only the British Museum, which he virtually recreated, for nearly forty years, but through his close friendship with some of the most distinguished men of the day, Palmerston, Russell and Gladstone amongst them, did much to bring about the unification of Italy. Having twice previously refused high honours, he at last accepted a KCB from Gladstone in 1869. In April 1879 he died in his house in Bloomsbury Square near the Museum he had been reluctant to leave.

of such men as Lord Brougham, Lord Chancellor in the victorious Whig government of 1831, Thomas Campbell, the poet, William Roscoe of Liverpool,[1] and many others. Already he was laying the foundations of an outstanding career, which was to win him the devotion of many of the most prominent men of his generation and to transform the Museum from an institution of comparatively little repute – what Sir Humphrey Davy had called, 'this ancient, misapplied and, one might almost say, useless Museum'[2] into a great library and national collection of antiquities, the envy and admiration of the world.

Ellis' was an able, hard-working team, and if for the most part they were arrogant, quarrelsome men, they were nevertheless of real scholarship and ability, each, in his own way devoted to the betterment of the Museum as he saw it. Most of them were still comparatively young and all very different from the handful of elderly clergymen and physicians with whom Planta in his early days had to make do as best he could. It was a team that benign, placid Sir Henry, for all his great powers of scholarship, was never to succeed in mastering.

Ellis was faced from the outset with a multitude of problems. The buildings were still going up, but more slowly than the Trustees wished. Pressure on the small and malodorous reading rooms was growing (1,556 readers in 1827, 1,954 readers three years later), but what really worried the Trustees was the dangerous state of the old House. Most of the floors were supported by props concealed by the bookcases, and the danger of fire was ever present. When in 1816 Smirke had put galleries round the main library rooms, he found on taking down the hangings that there were open holes in the walls leading directly into the flues. Though every posssible precaution was now taken, the risk was very serious. The situation seemed so dangerous that at one time the Trustees considered the immediate evacuation of the whole collection.[3]

They now pressed on a reluctant Treasury the scheme of erecting the north wing to take the library department, even before the west wing

1. Henry Peter Brougham, Baron Brougham and Vaux, 1778–1868. He had known Panizzi in Liverpool and had helped him to obtain the post of Professor of Italian at London University.
William Roscoe, 1753–1831, historian.
Thomas Campbell, 1777–1844, the poet, befriended Panizzi on the latter's arrival in London, and introduced him to Roscoe.
2. John Davy, *Life of Humphrey Davy*, vol. II, p. 342.
3. Smirke's evidence before the Select Committee of 1836. *Select Committee, 1836, Minutes*, para. 5425.

for the antiquities was complete. New rooms had already been constructed to house the Elgin marbles, at last released from their shed in the gardens, and for the recently acquired Egyptian sculptures. To extend that gallery further southwards would involve the destruction of the Towneley building which the Trustees thought was premature, when so much remained to be done elsewhere. So on Ellis fell the cares of the protracted negotiations, though assisted by Josiah Forshall, his successor as Keeper of Manuscripts and Secretary to the Trustees, whose influence over the Board, and in particular over the Archbishop,[1] was to be a sinister feature of the next two decades.

The Museum was becoming more unpopular. As a writer in the *Quarterly Review* wrote later, it 'had become too prominent a mark for nuisance-abaters and notoriety-hunters to be passed over'.[2] Men of science attacked it for its obscurantism and its failure to recruit practical scientists to its Board; radicals for its inefficiency, exclusiveness, and lack of facilities for the common man, and all for the high-handed fashion in which the Trustees allegedly spurned numerous offers of desirable acquisitions. Many scholars, too, were justifiably aggrieved at the lack of facilities in the reading rooms, whilst the whole service provided by the Museum was felt, by a more critical and educated public, to be grossly inadequate.

The attacks on the Museum became ever more virulent. William Cobbett denounced the Museum in the House of Commons 'as a place intended only for the amusement of the curious and the rich'.[3] In that age of transition, when change was so much the fashion and all things were, it seemed, to be made new, the British Museum, with its air of a more leisurely and perhaps less efficient past, could find few friends to defend it.

The need for an up-to-date catalogue of printed books was increasingly felt. Readers had merely the catalogue of the main collections prepared by Ellis and Baber some twenty years before, with additions to it on interleaved sheets, and the catalogue of the King's Library, drawn up by the royal librarian, Sir Frederick Barnard. There were also the catalogues of the different manuscript collections, now being revised and reorganised by the industrious Madden. In April 1834

1. William Howley, 1766–1848. Archbishop of Canterbury, 1828–1848, Bishop of London, 1813–1828. Despite his strong Tory sympathies Madden detested him.
2. *Quarterly Review*, CLXXV, p. 145.
3. William Cobbett, 1762–1835, essayist and politician. He lost no opportunity of attacking the Museum.

Baber presented a detailed scheme for a new and comprehensive catalogue with his brilliant young Italian colleague as sole editor, supervising the work of three 'well educated young men' who would be engaged to assist him. 'Mr Panizzi's age,' Baber wrote, 'activity of mind and various literary acquirements eminently qualify him as the supervising officer.'[1] The Trustees were not so sure. They rather hankered after a classed catalogue, a type of subject catalogue which seemed to scientific men perhaps more useful than an alphabetical one arranged by authors. Such a catalogue had actually been in preparation since 1825, but was still very far from complete.

More ominously, Baber's eminently practical plan was regarded with deep suspicion by Ellis, who could conceive of no better way to compile a catalogue than that which he himself had attempted many years before. Swayed by Ellis, the Trustees rejected their Keeper's advice and produced a plan of their own which Baber was ordered to put into operation. This was to divide the task up among the existing staff working independently, whilst Baber and Cary between them would exercise a mild supervision over the whole in the interval of their other duties. Despite the protests of Baber and Panizzi at the emasculation of their original plan, the Trustees persisted in their own scheme. In this clumsy fashion, the first steps were taken in an ever more disastrous project lasting fifteen years.

By December, all the titles had been arranged in their respective classes and 13,000 titles already revised. Of this number the energetic Panizzi had revised almost as many titles as all the other cataloguers put together, a feat which aroused the surprise and admiration of the Trustees. Work was also started on the transcription of the old catalogue, for which a new grade, Transcribers, intermediate between assistants and attendants, was engaged. Although wretchedly paid, it provided an opening into the Museum service for young men without much formal education.[2] By 1835 this freshly transcribed copy of the Reading Room catalogue had got as far as the letter A and B was well on its way.

Soon all work on the catalogues was suspended as the staff prepared to meet a new attack on the venerable institution. Many radicals, and

1. Report by Baber to the Special Committee of Trustees, 26, April 1834. *Royal Commission on British Museum. Appendix*, p. 104.
2. Edward Roy, for instance, who from a Transcriber rose to be Assistant Keeper. It was he who first devised the compilation of the Reading Room catalogue on movable slips.

not radicals alone, would have echoed Cobbett's words: 'Whatever in
the wide world was this British Museum and to whom, to what class of
persons, was it useful . . . The management . . . as bad as bad could be.
The officers . . . were . . . clergymen, who employed poor curates to
perform their duty . . . whilst they were living in indolence and affluence
here in London.'[1]

The immediate cause of the enquiry was a certain Mr John Millard,
who had formerly held a post as a supernumerary in the Department of
Manuscripts. He had been engaged to compile an index to the manuscripts in November 1824 and had been subsequently dismissed for
inefficiency. He had interested in his case not only the *Edinburgh
Review*, but also Benjamin Hawes,[2] the radical MP for Lambeth. Here
was an opportunity for a long overdue investigation of the affairs of the
Museum. Consequently the House of Commons appointed a Select
Committee to enquire into the condition, management and affairs of
the Museum under the chairmanship of Southeron Estcourt, the
Conservative member for Devizes, with Hawes and two active Trustees
– Lord Stanley, later Prime Minister and Sir Robert Inglis[3] – among its
members. The real purpose of this committee was to reveal the
nepotism, corruption, inefficiency and maladministration said to be rife
within the Museum. Also under attack was its alleged neglect of the
physical sciences and the virtual absence of men of science and other
specialists from the Board.

From the very first day, 18 May 1835, the committee harried the
calm and imperturbable Sir Henry Ellis in an effort to establish
the truth of their allegations. The main attack was directed against the
Board of Trustees, its excessive powers, its inefficiency, and the rank
and status of its members.

Sir Henry, acknowledging that his own powers of patronage were
limited – 'The housemaids' places are in my gift and I also appoint the
watchmen' – was quite unmoved by their attacks. To him, the system
was as perfect as any that could be devised. 'I believe it [the Museum]
to be as faithfully administered and as perfectly administered as such an

1. *Hansard*, 3. S., vol. 20. c. 617.
2. Sir Benjamin Hawes, 1797–1862, MP for Lambeth. He advocated many pro-
gressive ideas, including the penny post and the electric telegraph.
Thomas Southeron Estcourt, 1801–1876, Home Secretary, 1859.
Edward Stanley, fourteenth Earl of Derby, 1799–1869, three times Prime Minister.
Sir Robert Harry Inglis, 1786–1855, a strong Tory who opposed all the principal
reforms of his day.
3. *Select Committee, 1835. Minutes*, para. 6.

institution can allow'.[1] In his opinion literary and scientific men were quite unsuitable to become trustees. 'I look to the benefit of the Museum, not to the general benefit of science',[2] he exclaimed. As to literary men, 'it never entered into the contemplation of the trustees to select poets and historians'.[3] No, to Ellis the present board of great officers of state, assisted by noblemen and others of distinguished birth, with a keen, if amateur, love of the humanities or, more rarely, of science, was far more effective.

Baffled, though by no means satisfied, by Ellis's calm self-satisfaction, the committee moved on to the question of longer hours of opening, in particular hours during which the working classes might avail themselves of the Museum. Sir Henry here was equally adamant. To open in Easter week, for instance, would be disastrous, further 'the most mischievous portion of the population is abroad and about at such a time . . . the more vulgar class would crowd into the Museum . . . the mere gazing at our curiosities is not one of the . . . objects of the Museum'.

Sir Henry was appalled at the thought. 'The more important class of the population . . . would be discontented', if it had to associate with sailors from the dockyards and their girls. When asked, somewhat acidly, if he had ever known a sailor from the dockyards to bring a girl into the Museum, Ellis replied that in all events the class of people who would come at such a time 'would be of a very low description'.[4]

It was the same when the committee ventured to suggest that the Reading Room might be open longer, so that more readers might take advantage of it. 'My own opinion,' said Sir Henry very decidedly, 'is that the Museum library is rather too much used than too little used, taking a comprehensive and prospective view of what might conduce to the public good.'[5] The readers preferred the hours of 10 to 4. They 'clamoured' so much when the hours were changed to 11 to 5 that after only two days Sir Henry had himself to go to the Archbishop to have them altered back again. As for evening opening, a very different type of being from the 'men of research' who now used the room might get admitted, 'a class of persons for whom it would be hardly necessary

1. *op. cit.*, para. 245.
2. *op. cit.*, para. 146.
3. *op. cit.*, para. 162.
4. *op. cit.*, para. 1320–1322, 1328–1330.
5. *op. cit.*, para. 1303.

to provide such a library as that of the British Museum; they would be lawyers' clerks, and persons who would read voyages and travels, novels, and light literatures; a class, I conceive, the Museum library was not intended for'.[1] When it was pointed out that even lawyers' clerks might have literary aspirations and that even quite respectable individuals, such as barristers or businessmen, might find it more convenient to come in the evening, Sir Henry loftily remarked that he could not conceive it possible that such as they would not be able to come during the present hours.

The committee then expressed some anxiety as to what other duties members of the staff might have, which might hamper them in their Museum work. Ellis pointed out that the duties of neither Forshall, as chaplain to the Foundling Hospital, nor Panizzi, as titular Professor of Italian at London University, interfered with their Museum duties in any way. Panizzi certainly had 'nothing that ever calls him away. There is no man more punctual in his attendance'.[2]

Ellis was successful in rebutting the charge made by Sir Harris Nicolas that he had mismanaged an opportunity to acquire a collection of French manuscripts offered to the Museum and other charges that important collections, such as Gough's topographical collection and the Douce manuscripts (both left to the Bodleian), the Fitzwilliam collection and others, had failed to come to the Museum through the Trustees' negligence or because the prospective donor had considered that his bequest would not be properly looked after. An otherwise friendly writer in the *Quarterly Review* ascribed their reluctance, at least in part, to the former hasty habit of the Museum in disposing of alleged duplicates. It was for this reason that Douce and Gough had left their collections to the Bodleian, Fitzwilliam his to Cambridge and 'Soane steered clear of the careless triton of Great Russell Street in order to found his minnow Museum in Lincoln's Inn Fields'.[3]

So far, the worst suspicions of the committee seemed to be unfounded, but they pressed on to the question of a classed catalogue. Would not such a catalogue be preferable to an alphabetical one? Ellis was vague, and referred them to Baber, who had not yet given evidence. He did, however, give his opinion, an opinion that was to be echoed by Baber and Panizzi. 'I do not know that a classed catalogue is indispensable, an alphabetical one is; An alphabetical one is referred to

1. *op. cit.*, para. 1313.
2. *op.cit.*, para. 334.
3. *Quarterly Review*, CLXXV, p. 142.

500 times where a classed one is referred to once.'[1] But the committee, having learnt the words 'classed catalogue', were determined to return to this theme. With a few words more on the Reading Rooms, which he earlier had admitted were too small and moreover 'a little offensive', owing to poor ventilation, Ellis's evidence for the moment closed.

Before finishing, he had stated that he was himself perfectly satisfied with the conduct of Mr John Millard, the ostensible object of the whole enquiry. If he was, Forshall, Keeper of Manuscripts and Secretary to the Trustees, who next gave evidence, certainly wasn't. Millard had 'become very inefficient'. He had made paltry excuses for his constant absence from duty and his work was distinguished by its 'reckless negligence'.[1] This opinion, now supported, in a vague way, by Sir Henry, was more than echoed by the fiery Madden, who denounced the unfortunate Millard as being 'totally incompetent for the task to which he had been appointed'.[3] Poor Millard! He was now called in to give his own version of his dismissal, and it was henceforth abundantly clear even to the committee, that the Museum had been right to dispense with his services.

It was now the turn of the scientific departments. Their officers had far more complaints to make than had their colleagues. Perhaps they felt themselves likely to obtain a more sympathetic hearing. Charles König, Keeper of the Natural History departments, complained of the lack of trained assistance, so that much of his time was frittered away on manual jobs. He considered the Museum had 'a very miserable collection', compared with that of Paris or Berlin, the insect collection of the latter being ten times larger.[4]

König had other complaints. The new rooms allotted to the department were not really suitable, nor had he at any time been consulted by Smirke – a charge which the architect later convincingly rebutted. Little or no cooperation was received from the government in obtaining specimens from abroad, nor did they feel the importance of getting specimens from returning explorers or other travellers for the Museum, rather than for such private bodies as the Zoological Society of London. In his opinion, too little attention was paid to making the exhibits attractive and interesting to visitors (a very modern point of view for 1835). His sentiments were echoed by his colleagues, in

1. *Select Committee, 1835. Minutes*, para. 1690.
2. *op. cit.*, para. 1827, 1845, etc.
3. *op. cit.*, para. 2080.
4. *op. cit.*, para. 2628, 2705.

particular John Children and J. R. Gray, then beginning a distinguished career in the Natural History department.

Brown, the Banksian librarian, described by König as 'the greatest botanist in the world',[1] was also in favour of scientific men on the Board, but with reservations. 'Scientific qualifications', he exclaimed, 'should not be overlooked' in the selection of Trustees,[2] but on the whole scientists were 'not particularly fitted for the management of such an establishment.[3] The committee's report was inconclusive, and suggested that a new committee should be appointed to go further into the matter the following session.

So far, therefore, the Museum had survived. There was no evidence of corruption or nepotism, and little of gross mismanagement. It was lack of money rather than of goodwill which had prevented the Museum from giving the service and acquiring the collections which many considered it should have done. As Ellis said: 'The Museum Library is not decidedly poor in any class . . . It is as rich as the money granted to the Museum would allow it to be made.'[4]

It was certain, however, that when the committee reassembled the following year, the principal object of its investigations would be the Department of Printed Books, that Department with which the majority of the educated public had the most contact and with which there was already deep and widespread dissatisfaction. Its resources and methods would undoubtedly be closely compared with that of similar libraries elsewhere. As early as 1833, it had seemed probable that sooner or later an enquiry into the workings of the Library would be held. Baber, in consultation with Panizzi, decided to collect information on the management of the principal foreign libraries in advance. Panizzi therefore drew up a questionnaire and circulated it, largely through the medium of his own foreign acquaintances, to as many libraries as possible.

Replies were received from thirty-six institutions, but it was obvious that these would have to be supplemented by personal visits. In the winter of 1835 Panizzi visited the main libraries of western Europe, except for Austria and much of Italy, in which it would still have been unsafe for him to travel with a death sentence hanging over his head. Baber wrote to his colleague at Paris: 'I look with impatience to your

1. op. cit., para. 2854.
2. op. cit., para. 3721.
3. op. cit., para. 3718.
4. op. cit., para. 2459, 2467.

return, as I am confident you will bring back with you much interesting information respecting the management of the libraries you may have visited'.[1]

The new committee which assembled the following February was a smaller and more able body than that of the previous session. Some of the more belligerent members had gone and it was probable that the new committee would spend less time smelling out imaginary scandals and seek instead to discover impartially what was really wrong with the Museum and to suggest remedies.[2]

Millard still hoped to influence the findings of the committee. On 16 February 1836, he wrote to the editor of the Edinburgh Review, a virulently anti-Museum publication, asking him to examine the evidence of the committee and to issue an article which would confer 'a real benefit upon the public'. 'The present Executive [Board of Trustees],' he considered, 'need only some stimulus to induce them to meet the views of those who have brought forward the present inquiry.'[3] Millard stressed the contrast between the Museum and foreign libraries, especially the Bibliothèque Royale at Paris, a contrast of which the officers of the library were only too painfully aware. Ellis had nevertheless pointed out the previous year that the Museum was more liberal in its attitude towards its readers than was its French counterpart.[4]

One member of the Museum staff, at any rate, was not looking forward to the committee. The irascible Madden confided to the pages of his journal that he would certainly not give evidence unless forced to. A pamphlet published by 'that blockhead Millard' roused him to new heights of anger. 'When I see such humbug brought prominently forward and such ignorance and negligence find supporters, it disgusts me beyond endurance.' The 'son of a bitch', he snarled, was now 'puffed up in the eyes of the public as a wonderfully talented and injured man'.[5] Sir Frederic would have more than enough opportunity shortly to indulge his spleen.

On 2 June 1836, after some preliminary hearings on the scientific

1. Add. MS. 36,714. f. 420.
2. The 1836 committee consisted of 15 members, of whom not more than four appear to have been radicals.
3. Add. MS. 34,617. f. 326.
4. 'Our own system was infinitely superior . . . as to the management of the Library, its hours, and its numerous accommodation.' (Select Committee, 1835. Minutes, para. 246.)
5. Madden Journal, 9 July 1836.

collections, it was at last the turn of Printed Books. Its Keeper, Baber, presented his evidence in a firm, clear and resolute way. He was a good librarian, he knew his job, and he had undoubtedly been well primed by Panizzi. Much of the evidence was still taken up with the merits of a classed catalogue. In his opinion, such a catalogue was of far less importance than a really good up-to-date alphabetical one. All their efforts and whatever money was available should be directed solely to that end. Baber refuted some of the allegations which had been made as to supposed deficiencies in the collections.

On 7 June, Panizzi himself was called, this tough, brawny man, with the face and something of the manners of a bandit, about whom so many tales were told.

He was quite frank. In his opinion the Museum library was quite unworthy of so great and prosperous a nation, decidedly less good than libraries of far smaller countries. 'As a national establishment for this nation it is very poor . . . far inferior to the king's library at Paris . . . the finest in the world'.[1] Government support for the national library had been, and continued to be, meagre. From 1820 to 1824 only about £200 a year had been voted as a purchase grant for the Library. Of recent years there had been a slight increase, the total allowance for both books and manuscripts having in 1834 risen to the dizzy height of £1,974 per annum. It was a pitiful sum to be allotted to such a purpose by the richest nation in the world. The tiny Duchy of Parma, for instance, had spent more than £4,000 on one collection alone and other countries had been equally lavish in their expenditure.

The only solution, the only possible way to build up a worthy national library, was regular and generous Parliamentary grants. Unless the staff knew what money would be available, there could be no proper planning. At least £10,000 a year was needed, together with additional grants for the purchase of modern books, above all in fields which had not yet been properly covered. He would, moreover, get rid of the Natural History collections. Their presence was an anachronism and they took up valuable room. Space would soon become a pressing question again and one must look well ahead. Panizzi certainly did not want specialists on the Board, above all scientists, of whom he had an extremely low opinion. Far better, he thought, to have men of rank and of liberal sympathies for Trustees, men who had so greatly benefited the Museum in the past and would, he was sure, do so in future.

Panizzi concluded by stating with his usual clarity what he considered

1. *Select Committee, 1836. Minutes*, para. 4773, 4774.

the goal at which all should aim. 'As to its most important and most noble purpose, as an establishment for the furtherance of education, for study and research, the public seem to be, almost, indifferent'.[1] It was to be Panizzi's life work, in so far as it lay in his power, to change all this, to make the library, the antiquities and indeed every department, a centre for the latest research and to recruit a staff able to carry out this function. Some gleamings of such a feeling may indeed lie behind Sir Henry's High Tory prejudices against admitting the 'vulgar': a realisation that the Museum should never at any time be a mere peep-show. To Panizzi it was far more than this. All, even the humblest should they wish, must be able to share freely in the riches provided by the Museum. His famous and oft-quoted dictum reveals his fundamental position, from which he never wavered. 'I want a poor student to have the same means of indulging his learned curiosity, of following his rational pursuits, of consulting the same authorities, of fathoming the most intricate inquiry as the richest man in the kingdom, as far as books go, and I contend that the Government is bound to give him the most liberal and unlimited assistance in this respect.'[2] A proud challenge to throw at the feet of men who represented the castebound and *laissez faire* England of the day, especially by a man, a foreigner who, a few years before, had himself been a penniless and hunted fugitive.

The committee were suitably impressed by this vigorous outburst and the sustained evidence with which he backed his demands. It was clear that here was a man who, given the chance, would spare no one, least of all himself, to bring his ideas to fruition. With Panizzi's evidence completed, the work of the committee was almost over. The Archbishop explained briefly how this remarkable man had joined the Museum, not, as so many whispered, through the favouritism of a corrupt Whig administration, a 'job', engineered by the unscrupulous Brougham for services rendered, but clearly and decisively on Panizzi's own merits, 'a man of great acquirements and talents, peculiarly well suited for the British Museum; that was represented to me by several persons who were not connected with the Museum, and it was strongly pressed by several Trustees . . . and considering the qualifications of that gentleman, his knowledge of foreign languages, his eminent ability, and extensive attainments, I could not doubt the propriety of acceding to their wishes'.[3] Though not all of Panizzi's colleagues, then or later, would

1. *op. cit.*, para. 4936.
2. *op. cit.*, para. 4795.
3. *op. cit.*, para. 5511.

have echoed Archbishop Howley's sentiments, there can be little doubt that the Museum and the world of scholarship in general benefited immeasurably from the decision. Reformed the Museum would have been, willy-nilly. It was its great good fortune that the reformation was not imposed on it from outside but carried out by a member of its own staff, with a boldness, imagination and administrative zeal which amounted to genius.

After a number of readers had testified, in the face of frequently hostile questioning by members of the committee, that the services offered by the British Museum were superior to those of any comparable foreign library and that its only defect was a shortage of books, due 'entirely from the niggardly disposition of the Government',[1] the committee's last days were taken up by a detailed examination of Sir Robert Smirke. He revealed how for more than twenty years the Trustees had been making plans for the proper housing of their collections and had been hampered by the parsimony of the Treasury and by a vexatious law suit as to their right to carry out such alterations. Smirke did admit that growth of interest in the Museum had considerably falsified his first calculations. Both general visitors and readers had increased more than had been anticipated, from 35,581 persons in 1815–16 to 99,112 in 1830–31. 'This increase has increased in a degree far beyond the expectations of the Trustees and officers in every department.' When the reading rooms were first planned the daily average was probably not more than about thirty readers; now it was frequently over two hundred, 'and yet more accommodation was wanted'.[2]

On 14 July 1836, the committee issued its report. It was brief and explicit, consisting, essentially, of eighteen resolutions. There was, to the relief of the non-scientific members of the staff, no fundamental change recommended in the general composition of the Board. Four important recommendations were made: further departments should be created; there should be more frequent consultations between the Trustees and their Keepers; Parliament must be more generous in its grants, and most influential for the future: the officers should receive salaries more in keeping with their responsibilities, but be strictly forbidden 'to hold any other situation conferring emolument or entailing duties'.[3]

1. *op. cit.*, para. 5013.
2. *op. cit.*, para. 5313.
3. *Select Committee, 1836. Report*, p. iv.

It was quite obvious that, for the majority of the senior members of the staff, a choice must now be made whether to resign such outside appointments or leave the Trustees' service.

Sir Frederic, for one, was furious. He considered that the 'exceedingly unjust' recommendation concerning outside appointments would 'put an end to any hopes I may have formed of becoming richer'. With dismay he adds, 'I do not at all like the present aspect of things . . . and only wish to God I could escape from it.'[1] He was soon to like things much less.

On 11 March 1837, the Trustees resolved that any outside appointment was incompatible with the retention of an officer in their service. The blow had fallen. Now each must make up his mind what to do.

For Panizzi and most of the younger men the choice was easy. Even Sir Frederic, grumbling furiously, had no real option.[2] But what about Baber? The attractions of his quiet country parish must have seemed very tempting to this kindly, cautious man, who, though seeing quite clearly what needed to be done to revitalise the Museum, in order to bring it into the main stream of contemporary thought, yet knew that another was far more capable than he of achieving this aim. In Baber's opinion this could only be Antonio Panizzi, whose great abilities and potential for leadership he had come to recognise. The Keeper did not think much of his nominal second-in-command, Henry Cary, despite his scholarship and pleasant manner.[3] The years ahead would, he knew, need a harder, tougher man than poor, sick, gentle Henry Cary, and none could be harder or tougher, both on himself and on others, than the ex-Carbonaro from Modena. The whole Museum was now in a state of tension and rumours were rife. Would Baber go? Would Forshall resign the Keepership of Manuscripts to concentrate on the Secretary-ship, where every day he was acquiring more and more real power? And if so, who would succeed them? In the Trustees' new instructions to their staff no outside employment would be permitted without express

1. *Madden Journal*, 21 July 1836.
2. Edward Edwards, later on the staff of Printed Books, had written *A Letter to Benjamin Hawes*, in which he strongly criticised Madden for working at the Public Record Office on private work in official time. Sir Frederic was furious and in his copy of Edwards' pamphlet denies this accusation in no uncertain terms. (Edwards, *Letter*, pp. 40–1 in *Madden Collection*.)
3. In a letter of 20 January 1836 to Panizzi, who was in Paris, collecting evidence to answer the charges of the Select Committee, Baber tartly observes that 'Cary was no bigot to any plan of my own'. (Add. MS. 36,714. f. 20.)

sanction and the list of absolute prohibitions was wide. In future, too, apartments at the Museum would be allotted only to Keepers; non-residential Keepers and all Assistant Keepers must live not more than one mile from the Museum. Although there would be a slight rise in salaries, leave was drastically reduced and the long-established extra-duty payment abolished. Madden once more complained bitterly of the injustice of it all.[1]

Almost at once Baber gave formal notice of his intention of resigning, whilst Forshall told Madden he would resign the Keepership of Manu-scripts as soon as the Trustees permitted him to. In Printed Books, most people still favoured Cary. He was highly regarded, both as a scholar and as a man, and would in normal times undoubtedly have quietly succeeded his old Keeper. But Cary was in poor health. On the death of his wife in 1832, he had had a nervous breakdown from which he had never fully recovered. The Trustees began to have doubts as to whether, after all, Cary was the right man to take charge of an expanding department at a critical time.

On 24 June the post of Keeper of Printed Books was officially declared vacant. The same day Cary personally applied for the position, only to be told that in view of his indifferent health considerable objections had been raised by certain Trustees to his nomination. Poor Cary! He was indeed 'the sport of fortune', as Madden called him.[2] He returned crest-fallen to the department, where he told Baber and Panizzi what had happened. The latter at once realised that this was his chance, and straight away, in the presence of both Baber and Cary himself, applied to the Archbishop for the position of Keeper of Printed Books. Already the names of other candidates, from other departments and from outside the Museum, were being mentioned. The claims of Ernest Hawkins of the Bodleian[3] and of the writer, Richard Garnett[4] were freely canvassed. Cary now had second thoughts and resolved to appeal once more to the Archbishop, who always favoured fellow churchmen. This time the Archbishop told him that he would himself support his candidature, but that, if his health should again fail, he must at once resign the Keepership. So the matter stood for a week, but

1. *Madden Journal*, 9 March 1837.
2. *op. cit.*, 10 July 1837.
3. Ernest Hawkins, 1802–1865. He was then under librarian at the Bodleian and subsequently became Secretary of the Society for the Propagation of the Gospel.
4. Richard Garnett, 1789–1850, afterwards Assistant Keeper, Department of Printed Books, 1838–1850. He was ancestor of a long line of distinguished literary figures.

the Speaker Abercromby,[1] among others, now felt that in the circumstances Panizzi was the only possible choice, and took active steps on his behalf, despite Forshall's attempts to delay until Madden had been safely installed as Keeper of Manuscripts.

On 17 July the House of Commons was due to be dissolved, and after that there would be for a time no Speaker. On the 15th Abercromby ordered Forshall to prepare immediately a certificate of appointment, so that it might be signed at once. Forshall took the blank certificate round to the Speaker's secretary, who filled in Panizzi's name. Abercromby then signed it, as did Cottenham, the Lord Chancellor.[2] Forshall then took the certificate down to the Archbishop, who had gone to the country for the weekend (much to Madden's annoyance, as his Grace had left town without signing *his* certificate) got him to sign it, and returned it to the Museum. The following Wednesday, 19 July 1837, Panizzi was officially informed that he had been appointed Keeper of Printed Books and at once wrote to the Archbishop as the senior of the three Principal Trustees to thank him and to assure his Grace 'that it will be the height of my ambition to show myself not unworthy of the honourable trust reposed on me by a zealous discharge of the arduous duties of my office to the utmost of my humble powers'.[3]

Cary, and indeed most of his contemporaries, wondered how the Trustees could prefer an intriguing Italian Papist, this mere hanger-on of the Whigs, to honest, scholarly, hard working *Protestant* Mr Cary? I could only be another example of the 'Melbourne-Rads' usual habit of finding comfortable sinecures for their friends. Bitter articles appeared in the papers comparing the successful candidate, 'a mere scissors-and-paste compiler of editions of Italian authors, without one particle of original genius', 'unknown to this country and unhonoured in his own',[4] with Henry Cary, 'a scholar and a poet of European reputation'. Equal indignation was felt by many within the Museum. To Madden it was utterly wrong to promote an inferior over a superior, and that inferior a foreigner. Ellis was so furious that when asked to give a formal testimonial as to Panizzi's suitability he politely but firmly refused.

Cary himself had made the mistake of sending to *The Times* a copy of an indignant letter he had written to the Lord Chancellor, an

1. James Abercromby, first Baron Dunfermline, 1776–1858, Speaker, 1835–1839.
2. Sir Charles Pepys, first Earl of Cottenham, 1781–1851, Lord Chancellor, 1836–2841.
3. Fagan, vol. 1, p. 140.
4. *The Times*, 26 July 1837.

unforgivable sin in a serving officer, and though as Madden said of 'Poor Cary's letter', 'We all think him ill-used',[1] neither the sending of the letter nor its contents were likely to make the Trustees regret their choice. Cary wrote: 'My age, between 64 and 65 years, it was plain might rather ask for me that alleviation of labour which in this, as in many of the public offices, is gained by promotion'.[2] No longer was this to be so in the Museum; the days of slothful ease were over.

Sir Frederic, in the meantime, was nursing his resentment, both against 'the foreigner' and the Trustees. He was particularly angry with the Archbishop, who had not signed *his* certificate, though it had been prepared some days before, until he had signed Panizzi's and then, despite the pleas of Forshall and Madden himself to insert an earlier date, had dated it 18 July, 'the day on which he actually received it – thus leaving Mr Panizzi the seniority over me by two days! I am a good deal mortified at the result . . . However, it is now of no use to complain and I must content myself with having obtained the house which is the more important of the two'.[3] This refers to the wily Sir Frederic's successful plan to obtain the suite of rooms at the Museum previously occupied by Baber. The new Keeper of Printed Books, despite his indignant protests, was forced to be content with inferior apartments, those formerly allotted to a junior officer. Panizzi was resolved never to be so tricked again and determined to uphold his rights at all costs next time. The incident, trivial in itself, was another skirmish in the long drawn out feud between the two men, into which, sooner or later, almost all the staff of the Museum were drawn. For the next twenty years their bitter disputes set all Bloomsbury by the ears, a raging storm in which poor Sir Henry was tossed and turned, a surprised and indignant victim of the powerful currents sweeping away for ever the placid old Museum he had known so long. It needed the authority of a Royal Commission to still these quarrels at last and to leave a weary Panizzi vindicated and triumphant.

1. Madden to Bliss, 19 July 1837. Add. MS. 34,572. f. 235.
2. Cary, vol. 2, p. 286.
3. *Madden Journal*, 26 July 1837.

CHAPTER SIX

The Making of a National Library
1837–1847

FOR the moment, the two rivals were both too busy reorganising
their departments to take very much notice of each other. Madden,
who writes in his journal that nothing had been done 'worth notice' in
the department whilst its Keeper was away on his honeymoon with his
second wife, was soon hard at work.[1] The department had been badly
neglected for years. Forshall, like Ellis before him, had been largely
occupied by his duties as Secretary to the Trustees, and Ellis's predecessor Francis Douce had been a wealthy dilletante with no inclination for
humdrum routine. So Madden, painstaking, hard-working, and like his
great rival, determined to make *his* department the best in the Museum,
first made a thorough search through the collections to see what was
there. There were many skeletons in the cupboards. Three large boxes were
discovered filled with the charred remains of the Cottonian collection.
Further boxes came to light, some containing the 'refuse' of the
Hargrave collection, others with charters from the Lansdowne collection,
never looked at since they first came to the Museum in 1806. As
Madden sarcastically noted, 'The then Keeper of Manuscripts [Nares],
presuming that it would give him *some trouble* to catalogue these
charters *wisely* determined to NAIL them up . . . So much for the zeal of
Messrs. Douce, Ellis and Forshall! For my part, I am determined not to
suffer a scrap to be put away which I have not thoroughly examined and
I am resolved to rescue from oblivion every paper of the least value'.[2]

Madden was likewise revising all the departmental catalogues and
making new ones wherever needed, of the charters, the seals, and all the
papyri in the department. Like Panizzi, he had his differences with the
Trustees, although, thanks to Forshall's unswerving support, to nothing
like the same extent. But there were constant pinpricks. Certain
Trustees interfered with the day to day running of the department, and
so on 13 October 1838, Madden complained that, when he presented

1. *Madden Journal*, 24 October 1837.
2. *op. cit.*, 24 November 1837.

an important catalogue to the Trustees, the historian Hallam[1] (whom Madden disliked intensely) merely glanced at the catalogue and then announced that nothing it it was of any importance. 'The rest of the sapient Trustees, not one of whom ever read a manuscript in his life or could judge of its value, offered to allow the sum of £150 to be expended',[2] which Madden had, perforce, to accept. The services of a skilled restorer, deemed essential by Madden, were brusquely refused. When, in the previous January, Madden had obtained permission to spend £200 in buying manuscripts, the Trustees wanted to know first which he intended to buy. 'Surely if they can trust my judgement at an auction, they can in a Bookseller's shop', the angry Keeper wrote.[3]

But on the whole Madden was far too busy and far too pleased, with his new department and his new wife, to give full vent to his usual spleen. He could even appreciate the attacks made by Panizzi on the Royal Society, with whom at that time the Keeper of Printed Books was engaged in a characteristically violent dispute. When the Society's reply was shown to him, Madden remarked nonetheless that it was 'done very neatly and as far as it goes completely, because it proves negligence and inaccuracy on the part of Panizzi, yet by no means proves that bibliographical notes are at all useful in forming a catalogue of a library'.[4]

Yet on the whole, he could say at the end of 1838, 'I have not a wish, except to be somewhat richer . . . Perhaps if I live, I may yet be able to rise with a *white face*',[5] a hint, one presumes, at his rival's swarthy countenance.

Madden, too, was fortunate in his second-in-command. This was the Reverend William Cureton, who served the Museum for many years as Assistant Keeper of the Department of Manuscripts and after his resignation, as the Royal Trustee. Cureton had arrived on 8 August 1837 and Madden, for once, was distinctly impressed. His new colleague had, 'a pleasing way of speaking . . . I hope to proceed very satisfactorily with him'.[6] A few years later, however, when relations

1. Henry Hallam, 1777–1859, historian. He had strongly supported Panizzi for Keeper of Printed Books.
2. *Madden Journal*, 13 October 1838.
3. *op. cit.*, 30 January 1838.
4. *op. cit.*, 14 January 1838.
5. *op. cit.*, 31 December 1838.
6. *op. cit.*, 8 August 1837. William Cureton, 1808–1864, Syriac scholar, Canon of Westminster, 1849–1864, Assistant Keeper, Department of Manuscripts, 1837–1850. Royal Trustee, 1859–1864.

between Madden and his deputy were cooler, Madden noted snobbishly that Cureton was merely the son of a yeoman farmer, had been a servitor at Christ Church and had only got a double third. He did, however, subsequently add that Cureton had originally been entered as an undergraduate, but his mother's income being greatly reduced at the death of his father, 'generously resolved to take the footing of a servitor, in order to contribute to the increase of his mother's resources'.[1]

Cureton, a brilliant orientalist, was to be valuable in quite a different way in the difficult days to come. When, in their bitter anger, Panizzi and Madden would not speak to each other, Cureton, who always got on well with Panizzi, acted as an intermediary and tried unsuccessfully to smooth things over between these two inveterate enemies. Madden never forgave Cureton for maintaining good relations with his hated rival, and on the occasion of Cureton's resignation confided to his journal that his Assistant Keeper was lazy, spending far too long doing very little. In an earlier entry he berates Cureton 'for throwing himself at Panizzi's feet', and says that to advance his own views, he had harmed his Keeper. 'In regard to the general management of the Department and services to the Public, he has done nothing.'[2] The usual opinion of Cureton's character and capabilities was more favourable than that of the irascible Madden.

Of the other members of the staff there were John Holmes,[3] a pleasant, hard-working individual, who succeeded Cureton as Assistant Keeper and who would have gone further, but for his comparatively early death, and E. A. Bond,[4] who joined the department in 1838 and was to prove a tower of strength, a quiet man, whom all respected. In due course, Bond was to succeed Madden as Keeper of Manuscripts and then, twelve years later, to become a highly successful Principal Librarian.

Panizzi too was engaged in building up his staff, that small band of devoted young men who in a few years were to transform the Department of Printed Books beyond recognition. The first of these, John

1. *Madden Journal*, 9 February 1834.
2. *op. cit.*, 9 April 1850; 3 November 1849.
3. John Holmes, 1800–1854. His son, Sir Richard Holmes also served for a time in the Department of Manuscripts. In 1869 he became the Royal Librarian at Windsor Castle.
4. Sir Edward Augustus Bond, 1815–1898, Assistant Keeper of Manuscripts, 1854–1866; Keeper, 1866–1878; Principal Librarian 1878–1888. He had entered the Record Office in 1833 and transferred to the Museum five years later.

Winter Jones,[1] had arrived a few months before Panizzi had become
Keeper. Jones was the perfect lieutenant; Richard Garnett the younger,
long afterwards commented that he was far more suited to be one who
carried out loyally and conscientiously the policies of others than to
initiate policies of his own.[2] From the start Panizzi thought highly of
him and when, at the end of 1837 Cary left,[3] Jones, backed by Panizzi,
put in for the vacant Assistant Keepership. But 'Mr Panizzi was
obnoxious to persons influential with the Archbishop',[4] (*i.e.* the
Secretary, Forshall). Jones was rejected on the grounds of not having
been sufficiently long in the Trustees' service. In his place the Rev.
Richard Garnett was appointed, who had been considered the previous
year as a possible successor to Baber. Garnett, who arrived on 16 April
1838, without Panizzi's having been informed of his coming, was to be
a good second-in-command during the next few difficult years. Although
Panizzi never felt for him the affection which he felt for Winter Jones,
he came to respect the quiet clergyman, a man so different from himself,
and his early death was a heavy blow.

Madden was surprised that Garnett had troubled to come to the
Museum. Even though 'he certainly is an able man', Madden thought
he would have preferred to continue doing his own work, 'to the fag and
toil of cataloguing'.[5]

It was decided that the additional staff who had come with the
King's Library were not to be replaced when they left and that the
senior officers would consist merely of the Keeper, the Assistant Keeper
and an Extra-Assistant Keeper, still to be appointed. In a letter of 12
October 1837, Panizzi asked the Trustees to provide him with further
staff. He was to get his staff, but always too few for the many duties
that a fast expanding library thrust upon them. The first to arrive was

1. John Winter Jones, 1805–1881. Of a literary family originally from Carmarthen-
shire, he had read for the bar, but was prevented from completing his studies by the
temporary loss of his voice. The open air life of two years as travelling secretary to the
Charity Commissioners restored him to health. In 1850 he became Assistant Keeper
and, six years later, Keeper of Printed Books. On Panizzi's retirement in 1866 he was
made Principal Librarian. He resigned in August 1878.
2. R. Garnett, *The Late John Winter Jones*, p. 11.
3. Cary had submitted his resignation to the Trustees on 14 October 1837, complaining that 'under the present circumstances of his situation . . . he felt he could not
continue'. (*Committee Minutes*, vol. 16, p. 4579.)
4. *The Late John Winter Jones*, p. 6.
5. *Madden Journal*, 1 March 1838.

Thomas Watts,[1] who, with Jones, was destined to be Panizzi's principal assistant. With administrative ability, gift for languages, and remarkable memory, Thomas Watts, despite his 'outward guise of a blunt-spoken farmer',[2] was the most outstanding of the young men who now gathered round the new Keeper of Printed Books.

Panizzi's first task was the Reading Room. Here he had to behave with unaccustomed tact. The Reading Room was under the direct control of the Principal Librarian and Sir Henry was most jealous of his rights. The task of the Library was merely to supply the books to the readers and to maintain the catalogues. Many of the attacks made on Panizzi thus concerned matters over which he had no personal control. However, with the grudging assent of Sir Henry, he now started to make reforms in the service of the Reading Room. In September 1837 he introduced the use of printed application forms for books, basically the sort still employed, instead of the odd scraps of paper hitherto used by readers. He likewise insisted that readers should themselves return their books when finished with them, and then receive back their application tickets, and that until they had done so they would be responsible for the books they had had out. These, and other similar reforms, were bitterly resented by certain readers and much ill-feeling was expressed in various quarters against these schemes of the 'Italian Harlequin'.

In January 1838 began the move of the Library from the old and crumbling rooms of Montagu House to the apartments prepared for them by Smirke. Panizzi must have been glad to see them go. Already it contained more than 230,000 volumes and it was growing fast. Smirke, misled by Forshall, had underestimated the rate of growth, and within a few years the space question was to become, once again, a nightmare. In his evidence before the Parliamentary Committee of 1836, Panizzi had described the Library as then contained in 'the ground floor of Montague-house, three rooms in the basement, four rooms on the first floor, and part of the reading rooms. I do not include the King's library. It becomes daily more and more difficult to put up books'. He also stated that it would be now impossible to accommodate

1. Thomas Watts, 1811–1869, Superintendent of the Reading Room, 1857–1866; Keeper of Printed Books, 1866–1869. He was first engaged on a temporary basis on 17 January 1838 and was not formally appointed till 27 November.
2. Edwards, *Founders*, p. 561. Many years later, W. B. Rye wrote jokingly to Winter Jones of Watts' 'usual ursine amiability of temper'. Rye to Jones, 20 October 1867. (*Miscellaneous Departmental Papers.*)

any further large bequests. The new building would contain only some 20,000 volumes more than the old library and in consequence would once again be filled in four or five years time, even at the present rate of growth.[1] However, for the moment, under the direction of Watts, supervised by Panizzi, all went well.[2] The plan was to classify every book before it was moved, to transfer a whole class at a time and so place them on the new shelves. A press-mark was allotted to each book and such press-marks recorded in the catalogue against the relevant entry. It was slow work and though Panizzi reported to the Trustees in April 1838 that 'no inconvenience of any consequence has hitherto arisen to the readers',[3] he wished devoutly that things might somehow be speeded up.

On 9 January 1838 the new reading rooms, also in the north wing, were opened. Even though a marked improvement, they were soon too small. Subsequently, by a re-arrangement of the furniture, more space was made for reference books and the number of readers' places increased to a maximum of 208. No wonder that readers strongly disliked the torrid atmosphere, which made 'your head very hot and heavy and your feet cold',[4] and which gave rise to the notorious 'Museum headache', of which Carlyle, among others, bitterly complained. It also provided a breeding ground for that animal widely spoken of, yet unknown to science, the 'Museum flea' which, for many years was said to plague the more susceptible readers.[5] The lighting of the new rooms was inadequate, the windows being high and, in one room, only on one side. So the complaints of readers who constantly grumbled and wrote to the papers were by no means unjustified.

For ten years the controversy over the new catalogue embittered relations between Panizzi and his staff and the Trustees, their Principal Librarian and their Secretary. It was a dispute about whether a printed alphabetical catalogue should be published, and about whether to wait until the whole alphabetical sequence was ready in manuscript before printing. Panizzi had always supported Baber's plan of a single editor responsible for the entire project, but, probably

1. *Select Committee, 1836. Minutes*, para. 4804, 4806.
2. Among the archives of the Department of Printed Books is a *'Register of Persons employed each day in the removal of the Library'*. From this it would seem that Panizzi had a greater share in supervising the move and Watts somewhat less than is usually thought.
3. *Panizzi Papers*, 1837. f. 31.
4. Private letter, quoted in Fagan, I, p. 347.
5. *op. cit.*

under Ellis's influence, the Trustees would have none of it. They wanted a printed catalogue 'and that at the earliest practicable period'.[1] Panizzi attempted to carry out their instructions, but was appalled to hear that his masters now wanted the first volume printed as soon as possible. It could be done, he agreed, but not well done. He would be willing to undertake the task if the Trustees wished, but he must have more staff. With the aid of Jones and other members of Printed Books, he prepared the rules for the new catalogue, which, though criticised then and now, became the basis of all Museum cataloguing for 130 years.

Panizzi was determined to carry out the Trustees' instructions to the best of his ability, even though he was convinced they were misled and bitterly resented their constant interference. 'All our efforts', he ordered his staff, 'must be directed to this end',[2] that of completing the catalogue in the shortest possible time. 'No effort is spared in order that the catalogue may be printed before the end of 1844 . . . even at a sacrifice of much of its correctness and utility,' he reported.[3] By the end of 1840, the first volume, A, came out, full of errors, as Panizzi had foreseen. Already the Keeper of Printed Books was being widely criticised, both for the imperfections of the first volume and for the non-appearance of subsequent ones, every mistake being attributed to his ignorance, laziness and folly. Panizzi resented these accusations. He was not responsible for the delay. 'I . . . never took any step that could improve the catalogue if that tended to prolong its completion,'[4] he remarked. Neither Trustees nor the general public had any idea of the magnitude of the job involved.

By January 1846 patience on both sides was exhausted. The Trustees were determined to have their printed catalogue and wanted to know why no further volumes had appeared. Panizzi replied that it was not desirable to issue such a work until the whole was ready for the press and asked the Trustees to consider carefully whether such a work, in at least forty volumes costing as many thousand pounds which would be long out of date when published, was really worth all the trouble involved. 'It appears to me,' wrote Panizzi in despair, '. . . that there cannot be any doubt as to whether it is better to have a GOOD

1. Sub-Committee Minute of 18 November 1837. (*Royal Commission, Appendix*, p. 160.)
2. Circular letter to staff of Printed Books, 8 August 1839. (*Royal Commission, Appendix*, p. 228. *Panizzi Papers*, 1839. f. 144.)
3. Report to Trustees, 25 January 1840. (*Royal Commission, Appendix*, p. 234).
4. Panizzi to Jones, 20 January 1841. (*op. cit*, p. 265.)

catalogue in manuscript or a bad one in print. A bad catalogue, like other bad books, ought not to be printed at all . . . it does more harm the more it is propagated.'[1]

Sir Henry Ellis, as the only serving officer who had actually produced a catalogue, though nearly thirty years before, was now called in by the Trustees to advise. His proposals were inadequate and easily demolished by Panizzi, who gleefully pointed out the many errors in Ellis's own catalogue. He demanded that the Trustees make up their minds: whether or not it was worth publishing 'a catalogue which, when published, will be subject to the ridicule and indignation of all persons who understand what a catalogue of a splendid national library ought to be'.[2] Panizzi was now winning, despite a further 'triumphant refutation' of his criticism by the indignant Sir Henry.[3] The more reasonable Trustees were willing to accept the considered judgment of their Keeper of Printed Books. On 27 November 1847, Panizzi's moment of triumph came. The Trustees admitted by implication the errors of their former policy and asked Panizzi 'to proceed with the utmost dispatch in the compilation of a full and complete catalogue in manuscript, of the books in his custody'.[4] By a combination of expertise and resolution Panizzi had confounded his critics and got his way. But further troubles menaced him.

Madden was again being difficult. He had not forgiven Panizzi for his two days' seniority and, like Ellis, was a Tory of the old school, who disliked and distrusted all foreigners, especially those with revolutionary pasts and more particularly one who was the boon companion of leading Whigs like Russell and Palmerston. Relations had been deteriorating again for some time. Unless absolutely compelled to, Madden refused to speak to his colleague. Notes were left on Panizzi's desk in his absence, as if, he contemptuously remarked, they were communications from some foreign and hostile power. There was constant bickering over things like the duties of their respective attendants. Madden objected that his were being used in the Reading Room; Panizzi retorted that Madden couldn't handle his staff anyhow. Madden then complained

1. Panizzi to Ellis, 2 October 1846. (*op. cit*, pp. 290, 291.)
2. *op. cit.*, p. 308.
3. *Report of Sir H. Ellis*, 14 January 1847. (*op. cit.*, p. 334.) Madden's opinion of Sir Henry for failing to stand up to Panizzi is expressed in characteristically blunt terms: 'He is a pitiful fellow and though he has been so often & so grossly insulted by that Italian blackguard, he is still ready to fall down at his feet'. (*Madden Journal*, 12 February 1847.)
4. *Royal Commission, Appendix*, p. 446.

that it was said that *his* attendants were allowed to do as they pleased and set a bad example to others in the Museum. Madden was likewise furious at Panizzi's order forbidding anyone other than a library attendant to remove a book from the shelves of the library or to return one to it. 'As long as this Italian librarian has the ear of the Trustees . . . every measure however monstrous and unjust is sure to be passed'[1].

It was not, however, the duties, or lack of them, of the attendants which now caused an almost irreparable breach, but a more fundamental question, that of the manuscripts in the King's Library. Madden had always considered these as belonging more properly to his own department than to Printed Books and so in February 1840 he advised the Trustees that he intended to remove them and had Panizzi's permission to do so. Nothing was done; then, suddenly, about a year later, early one morning without telling anyone what he intended, he had them carried off to his own department. Panizzi, not unnaturally, was furious at this high-handed action. He denied that he had ever given his consent. He considered it a violation of the conditions under which the Library had been bestowed upon the Museum.[2] But there was little he could do. The Trustees, probably influenced by Forshall, supported Madden's action, a bad omen for the future and for any hope of co-operation between the embittered rivals.

Three years later Madden again had his eye on some manuscripts contained in the Printed Book collections. On 17 June 1845 he wrote a note to Panizzi, requesting him 'before he took his *three months* vacation (allowed by his friends the Trustees) to transfer to my department the manuscript maps and geographical MSS presented by the Lords of the Admiralty in 1844'. Panizzi declined to hand them over, since, he claimed, they formed part of the geographical collection of George III. 'Now this dog knows as well as I do that a number of these MSS were never in George III's library, but came direct from the Admiralty.' The Trustees must decide. Panizzi, in any case, was now off to Italy. 'God grant he may never return! Amen.'[3] Madden was once more feeling at odds with the Museum, which he increasingly came to regard with loathing and mistrust. He wrote to his friend Bliss on 9 April 1840 'All here as usual or *rather worse*',[4] and again on 18 February 1846 told Bliss

1. *op. cit.*, 31 December 1844.
2. The formally polite but catty exchange of letters is Egerton MSS. 2,842. f. 320, 322. Panizzi's account of the incident is in *Royal Commission, Minutes*, para. 2545.
3. *Madden Journal*. 17 June 1845.
4. Madden to Bliss, 9 April 1840. Add. MS. 34,573. f. 433.

that he and his wife were about to go on holiday. 'We propose to leave the Museum for a fortnight . . . I wish I could say never to return to it.'[1]

To his jaundiced eye every incident, however trivial, was a personal insult. When Panizzi introduced the not unreasonable rule that officers of other departments should no longer wander through the library at any hour, taking books off the shelves as they pleased without telling what they had taken, but must ask for them through the proper channels, Sir Frederic was once more furious. 'By the present arrange-ments, the Officers are almost *excluded* from the use of the books, & can only procure them at all through an attendant's hands. So much for the new System! Yet so highly do our Masters and the Treasury think of its management that they are going to vote an *extra* allowance of £10,000 per annum for ten years – which, with the sum now annually granted, will amount in that period to £200,000 for buying and binding books!! Are all the world mad about this gentleman?'[2]

This is a sarcastic reference to Panizzi's latest achievement. Although distracted by the worry of preparing the new catalogue, Panizzi was engaged at the same time in building up the library, in particular with those English works whose absence from the national collection had so long been a disgrace. 'This emphatically *British* library,' he had written in 1837, on first becoming Keeper, 'ought to be directed most particular-ly to British works and to works relating to the British Empire, its religious, political and literary as well as scientific history, its laws, institutions, commerce, art, etc. The rarer and more expensive a work of this description is the more . . . efforts ought to be made to secure it for the library.'[3] Although by a quirk of official policy, the acquisition of modern copyright books was not under his control but in the feeble hands of the Secretary's office, he had done his best to rectify these defects. The rate of accessions was becoming phenomenal, yet the books must be got and must be housed. Madden is most eloquent when discussing the goings on of his rival. 'For my own part I am lost in astonishment at his proceedings. How is he to spend the money . . . Within what period are the books to be catalogued. And this too at a time when he refused to let me see the maps sent by the Admiralty for fear when I printed a list of them *the public should ask for them and he would not be able to find them*', and concludes by wishing some

1. Madden to Bliss, 18 February 1846. Add. MS. 34,576. f. 24.
2. Madden to Bliss, 15 March 1846. Add. MS. 34,576. f. 53.
3. *Panizzi Papers*, 1837. f. 11.

Sir Henry Ellis, K. H., Principal Librarian (1827–1856).

South front of the old British Museum, early 19th century.

South front of the British Museum designed by Smirke: an artist's impression. The various pieces of statuary were never erected.

The new Coral Room (mid 19th century).

The Bird Gallery (mid 19th century).

Sir Anthony Panizzi, K.C.B., Keeper of Printed Books (1837–1856), Principal Librarian (1856–1866).

member of the House of Commons would put a stop to such reckless doings.[1]

Yet during these same years Panizzi laid the foundations not only of the general library but also of the great supplementary collections of maps, music, newspapers and of both English and foreign official publications. Almost alone amongst his contemporaries, he realised the importance of apparently worthless political pamphlets, manifestoes and the like as raw material for future historians. In all this work, but particularly in the realm of foreign purchasing, Panizzi was greatly helped by Thomas Watts, with his facility in so many languages. In 1861 he reported to Panizzi, by then Principal Librarian, on what had been their joint policy for the previous quarter century, to 'bring together from all quarters the useful, the elegant, and the curious literature of every language; to unite with the best English Library in England or the world, the best Russian Library out of Russia, the best German out of Germany . . . and so with every language from Italian to Icelandic, from Polish to Portuguese . . . I have the pleasure of reflecting that every future student of the less-known literatures of Europe will find riches where I found poverty'.[2]

And it was not only Europe in which they were interested. Panizzi, with the help of a young American, Henry Stevens of Vermont, was busy building up the American collections. In Panizzi's own words, he was getting Stevens 'to sweep America for us as you have done London for America',[3] so that by 1865, the year of Panizzi's retirement, 10,000 American works had been added to the collections. As Stevens noted in 1873, the American collection in the Museum had grown from 1,000 volumes in 1843 to between 70,000 and 75,000 volumes thirty years later, 'a total of American Books . . . far surpassing that of any other library in Europe or America'. Stevens half jokingly remarked, 'It is becoming a matter of pride with many Americans to be well represented in the Museum Catalogue . . . Indeed the British Museum Catalogue is becoming a sort of *Campo Santo*, where all good American authors desire to be buried. No miner [sic] catalogue, not even the best in America, seems to satisfy them in this respect.'[4]

1. *Madden Journal*, 29 January 1846.
2. Thomas Watts, Letter to Panizzi, 20 February 1861. *Papers relating to Salaries of Officers employed in the British Museum*, p. 17. (PP, H. of C., 1866, vol. XXXIX, p. 199.)
3. Library Association, *Transactions*, 1884, p. 117.
4. Henry Stevens to W. B. Rye, 27 October 1873. (*P.B. Departmental Archives*.) Henry Stevens, 1819–1886. He described himself as a 'bibliographer and lover of books'. Garnett called him 'genial, expansive, sanguine, both crafty and candid'.

Even by 1856, when Panizzi succeeded Ellis as Principal Librarian, the Library had grown from 150,000 volumes in 1827 to more than 520,000 and was to exceed a million in fifteen years. Such a rate of growth cost money – a great deal of money, even by Victorian standards. Here Panizzi, with his powerful friends and entrée into the inner councils of the Whig leaders, could be especially helpful. In 1843 he had made a detailed survey of the state of the Library and its deficiencies, class by class and language by language. Two years later he presented this report to the Trustees, declared that the only sure means of achieving his aim was regular and generous parliamentary grants, so that a consistent accessions policy might be maintained. The Trustees approved Panizzi's scheme and in the autumn of 1845 a request for £10,000 a year for the next ten years for the purchase of old books, £5,000 for new books, and £2,500 for binding was made. This was to be in addition to the normal grant.[1]

No wonder Madden was sick with jealousy! The Treasury had emphasised, in view of the large grants being given to Printed Books, the necessity of *postponing* during that period any additions (however desirable) to the other departments of the Museum!!! Can such folly really be believed?'[2] Such sums were indeed very large by the standards of the day, yet, surprisingly, the government granted them with only a slight modification, an annual grant of £10,000 for the purchase of *all* books and the condition that a certain saving should be made on purchases for other departments. Madden could nevertheless reasonably complain a few years later: 'If money had always been forthcoming, the number of the manuscripts acquired during the last 15 years might have been more than doubled . . . The liberality of the Treasury becomes very small when compared with the expenditure of individuals . . . Lord Ashburnham, during the last 10 years, has paid nearly as large a sum for MSS as has been expended on the national collections since the Museum was founded.'[3] Poor Sir Frederic. He truly loved his department and much of his jealousy and testiness was due, as the Royal Commission of 1850 pointed out, to misplaced zeal and affection.

1. P.P., H. of C., 1846, vol. XXV. p. 229. A copy of Panizzi's report with notes by Rye is among the papers in the Archives of the Department of Printed Books.
2. *Madden Journal*, 24 April 1846.
3. *Communications relating to the Enlargement of the British Museum*, p. 11. (PP, H. of C., 1852, vol. XXVIII, p. 201.) Bertram, Fourth Earl of Ashburnham, 1797–1878. He spent very large sums on acquiring a collection of manuscripts almost unrivalled in its day.

The rival department was, however, now to receive another magnificent gift, the greatest, after the King's Library, which it has ever received, further exacerbating the strained relations between Panizzi and Madden.

This was the wonderful library which had been collected over many years by the eminent bibliophile, Thomas Grenville,[1] younger son of the eighteenth-century premier, George Grenville, the friend and follower of the elder Pitt. He had himself briefly held office in the Whig administration early in the nineteenth century, but had long since given up any thought of a political career in order to devote himself to the formation of his library. Enjoying a comfortable sinecure, he used the money in the discriminating purchase of rare books and in private charities. He had for many years been on terms of affectionate friendship with Panizzi, valuing his 'unceasing kindness to the wreck of an old man'.[2] Panizzi was deeply concerned as to the fate of the great library 'formed and preserved', as he later wrote, 'with the exquisite taste of an accomplished bibliographer, with the learning of a profound and elegant scholar and the splendid liberality of a gentleman in affluent circumstances'.[3]

Grenville had a low opinion of the Museum Trustees, of whom he himself was one, and had seriously considered leaving the whole collection to his great nephew, the Duke of Buckingham. However, he eventually decided to bequeath his beloved books to the Museum, merely expressing the wish that they should all be kept together and a catalogue of them published. Panizzi was privately informed of his old friend's decision, and was 'strongly moved almost to tears',[4] by the generosity and warm affection towards himself shown by Grenville. It was agreed that the offer should remain a secret, known only to Panizzi and the donor, until the latter's death. Grenville died on 17 December 1846, and Panizzi at once revealed the details of the bequest to the Trustees. The magnificent gift was accepted, though with a little hesitation as there really seemed no place to house it. On Ellis's suggestion it was decided to put it in the new Western Manuscript

1. Thomas Grenville, 1755–1848, an adherent of Fox. In 1782 he had begun the negotiations which were to end the American war. He was First Lord of the Admiralty, 1806–1807.
2. Grenville to Panizzi, 2 December 1845. Add. MS. 36,715. f. 242.
3. *Account of the Income and Expenditure of the British Museum for the Year 1847*, p. 9. (PP, H. of C., 1847–48. vol. XXXIX, p. 273.)
4. Fagan I, p. 271.

Saloon for the time being. Panizzi had already reported that there was absolutely nowhere in Printed Books where it could go, although it might be possible to accommodate it later in the long narrow room to the east of the King's Library, which was then in process of construction.

Madden of course was furious at his rival's 'grasping projects'. But he dared not disobey a direct order of the Trustees, though he proceeded to hamper the move in every possible way. When first designated as the future home of the Grenville Library, the shelves were almost all empty. Now they suddenly began to fill with manuscripts, which Madden said had to go there. Panizzi denied that he had ever said that all he needed were the unoccupied shelves. The whole of the Saloon would undoubtedly be wanted to accommodate the Grenville books in a fitting manner and he refused even to consider moving the library from Grenville's house in Hamilton Place, Piccadilly, despite pressure from the executors, until he had a definite order from the Trustees to do so and was assured that there would be a safe place provided for its reception at the Museum. Madden was beside himself, and said he had been told by Ellis that Panizzi needed only six bays. That was bad enough, but now the 'vagabond Italian' must have 'the entire room delivered up to him'.[1]

On 28 January 1847, a bitterly cold day with driving snow, the removal of the priceless collection to the Museum took place. Panizzi had arranged for a number of special vans to be fitted with shelving so that the collection might be transported shelf by shelf. As each van was loaded under strict supervision, it set off for Bloomsbury through the snow, an attendant walking behind. On arrival the vans were unloaded by Panizzi and his staff[2] and the precious volumes carried into the Saloon where Madden had by now filled up almost every available press. Panizzi had requested the keys of the glazed cases, which still had manuscript department locks, the locksmith so far having neglected to change them. Madden refused, on the grounds that the keys fitted the locks of those cases where the select manuscripts were kept and it was unthinkable that anyone but a member of his own department should have access to these. A flustered Ellis thereupon gave Panizzi *his* pass-key to the locks, only to request it back the following morning, overwhelmed by the upbraidings of Madden. The locks were at last changed and honour satisfied. But as Panizzi had foreseen, there was insufficient room. To his mortification many of the treasures of his old friend were

1. *Madden Journal*, 13, January 1847.
2. *Panizzi Papers*, 1844. f. 57b.

laid out on trestle tables covered by dust sheets, those less precious being put on planks on the floor. The Trustees noted that about five hundred volumes 'for want of room on the shelves [were] lying on the floor of the Galleries'.[1]

Still more blows were to come. Madden was loudly demanding that all manuscripts in the Grenville collection should be transferred to his department, despite the wish of the donor that the collection should remain entire and the fact that the majority of such manuscripts were copies of printed books not otherwise found in the library. Sir Frederic was determined to get hold of the Grenville manuscripts, and had the support of Forshall, always ready to thwart Panizzi's schemes. Madden gleefully noted that the Secretary considered his demands to be 'only just and proper'. Despite the bitter dispute now raging between Ellis and Panizzi over the catalogue question, the Keeper of Manuscripts was less sure of the Principal Librarian than he ought to have been. Ellis, who had, in Sir Frederic's opinion, 'not the spirit of a mouse', was always an uncertain factor and, to avoid further trouble, 'will no doubt put the whole into Mr Panizzi's hands'.[2] But, with the aid of Forshall, Madden managed to secure an order from the Trustees for the manuscripts to be transferred to him,[3] an order that was blandly ignored by Panizzi on the grounds that he couldn't find them, hidden as they were on the floor.[4]

Madden's final blow was to get hold of the precious volume of plates by the artist Julio Clovio on the excuse that he had to show it to a royal visitor and refused to return it, incorporating it instead in his own collections. Madden surpassed himself with this particular piece of academic skulduggery. First, on 2 March, he reminded Ellis that the Trustees' resolution transferring the Grenville manuscripts to his department had not been complied with and demanded that it be enforced without delay, as he wished to show the Clovio to his visitor, the Duchess of Cambridge. Panizzi claimed in return that all news of this intending visit was deliberately kept from him, solely 'for the purpose of taking away the manuscript'.[5] At all events, Ellis sent a note

1. *Committee Minutes*, vol. 22, p. 7160. 13 February 1847.
2. *Madden Journal*, 18 January 1847.
3. *Committee Minutes*, vol. 22, p. 7159, 13 February 1847. Madden was ordered to keep the Grenville Manuscripts together and distinct from the rest of the collections.
4. *Committee Minutes*, vol. 22, p. 7183. 27 February 1847. Panizzi told the Trustees that he would pass the Manuscripts over to Madden 'as soon as they were found and a list made of them'.
5. *Royal Commission, Minutes*, para. 2553.

to Panizzi, asking him to bring the manuscript immediately. A message came back that the Keeper of Printed Books was out and the Clovio locked in his cupboard, 'either a lie or a pitiful mode of evasion', snarled Madden.

When the Duchess arrived Madden told her that unfortunately he was not able to show her the Julio Clovio, though the Trustees had repeatedly ordered it to be transferred to him. Lord Cadogan, the Trustee escorting the Duchess, pointed out that 'the person' in whose hands it was placed was absent. Panizzi then appeared, the Clovio was produced, briefly admired by Her Royal Highness, and then snatched away by Madden, to be locked up in one of *his* cases, to which he alone had the key. 'Having obtained this one,' he gloated, 'and that the most valuable of the MSS of the Collection, I shall certainly persist in endeavouring to get the remainder with as little delay as possible.'[1] Eventually the Royal Commission ordered the Clovio to be handed over to the Department of Prints and Drawings, as Panizzi himself had advocated, as a sensible alternative to it remaining with the rest of the Grenville collection.

Madden had been further infuriated to receive a letter from Lord Cawdor, one of his few supporters among the Trustees. Cawdor wrote that he knew Panizzi had no time for the scientific collections, but had hoped he would have respected the manuscripts. ' "*Hoped!*" ' exclaimed Sir Frederic, 'what right has a fellow like this to be *allowed* to act in the manner he does. It is thoroughly disgraceful and humiliating. Had this blackguard not come from Italy, had he been a plain Englishman, no person would have thought of countenancing his abominable proceedings.'[2]

Panizzi waited, confident that time would justify him. Yet, thanks almost entirely to himself, his department was the proud possessor of the Grenville library of 20,240 volumes 'which cost upwards of 54,00 l., and would sell for more now' and which, for books on vellum, outdid any foreign library except the King's Library at Paris'.[3]

1. *Madden Journal*, 1, 3 March 1847.
2. *op. cit.*, 17 January 1847. Madden, of course, was of Irish extraction. Earl Cawdor of Castlemartin, 1790–1860. Harleian Trustee of the British Museum, 1834–1860.
3. *Accounts &c of British Museum*, 1847. pp. 9, 11. (PP, H. of C., vol. XXXIV, p. 223.) Others felt differently. Lord Ellesmere, while praising Grenville's generosity, asks Peel 'to avoid any expressions which might encourage *similar* donations from others. The time is gone by when they would be of real advantage to the Nation'. (Add. MS. 40,601. f. 374.)

CHAPTER SEVEN

Danger from every Side

A NEW threat now disturbed the uneasy peace of the Museum, that of armed insurrection. The year was 1848, the year of revolutions, whose progress on the Continent was followed with considerable attention by the ex-Carbonaro, now Keeper of Printed Books, his German agent, Asher, sending him details of the latest events in Vienna and Berlin.[1] But at home, in England, things seemed different. However much Panizzi might welcome the discomfiture of his old enemy, Austria, he would tolerate no threat to his beloved Museum.

Encouraged by the success of the various revolutionary movements abroad, the Chartists, the most vocal and radical of contemporary movements in England, decided that their hour had come. Five million of them had signed a petition setting forth their grievances, which was now to be presented to Parliament, by force if necessary. With vivid memories of the Gordon riots of 1780 and of later disturbances, the authorities took alarm and fears were expressed for the safety of the Museum and of other public buildings. The Duke of Wellington, despite his almost eighty years, was said to be in 'a prodigious state of excitement'[2] and fully prepared to use troops if need be to prevent the Chartists crossing the Thames bridges, should they decide to march on London from Kennington Common, at which spot they were to assemble.

Sir Henry Ellis, to whom a Bank Holiday crowd conjured up visions of a riotous mob, was beside himself with anxiety. He had, according to Madden, behaved 'like a child from the first, taking no responsibility, giving no orders, except such as were positively injurious, and finally shutting himself up in his own home'.[3] His apprehensions were increased when it was learnt that another Chartist meeting was to

1. Panizzi scandalised the Tory Ellis by introducing into the Reading Room later that year the notorious French socialist, Louis Blanc, 'a short, plebeian-looking man . . . Nothing prepossessing in his appearance'. Note by Ellis, 20 October 1848. (Add. MS. 42.506. f. 123.) Louis Blanc, 1811–1882, French politician and historian.
2. Greville, vol. 2, p. 288.
3. *Madden Journal*, 10 April 1848.

be held in Russell Square, almost at the gates of the Museum. Threats were said to have been uttered to burn that institution to the ground and neither the Trustees nor the officers dared take any risks over the safety of the collections. Madden was a little sceptical about the whole business. 'All this seems very ridiculous, yet the reports current would make us suppose that every public office is to be attacked by an armed mob.'[1] The Museum was at the moment particularly vulnerable. Old Montagu House and the various residences were then being demolished to make way for Smirke's new building and most of the stout wall which had once protected the Museum along Great Russell Street had been taken down.

Madden, greatly alarmed for the safety of his wife, who was expecting another child, pointed out that if the Chartists assembled in Russell Square were 'bent on mischief', their first object of attack would be the Museum. 'The long range of wooden hoarding facing the street presented so *tempting* a means of entry that no one could contemplate a mob rushing in across such a frail barrier without dismay and once in the court, the isolated block of ancient building forming my house would inevitably fall a sacrifice either to plunder or complete destruction'.[2] Lady Madden and the children were evacuated to Forshall's new house, nearer the main building and easier to defend, its windows already barricaded and its front door hurriedly sealed up. As with other public offices, the staff were sworn in as special constables, led by Antony Panizzi, who, according to Robert Cowtan, then a young attendant and present on the great day, had now assumed virtual command of the Museum and of its defences. He was thoroughly enjoying himself putting the Museum into a state of defence. He had some 250 men recruited from the staff and from the men working on the new buildings, supported by two officers and fifty-seven other ranks of the regular army and twenty Chelsea pensioners. Fifty muskets and the necessary ammunition had been sent from the Board of Ordnance, as well as cutlasses and two to three hundred pikes, and these assorted arms were issued to the garrison.[3]

1. *op. cit.*, 8 April 1848.
2. *op. cit.*, 10 April 1848.
3. Of the three surviving accounts by eye witnesses, Panizzi's share in the defence of the Museum is mentioned only by Cowtan, whose narrative was followed largely by Fagan, who, as Panizzi's close friend and virtually adopted son, had every opportunity of verifying Cowtan's story by asking Panizzi himself. But nearly twenty-five years had elapsed since these events had occurred, and Panizzi was now a very old and sick man. Cowtan worshipped Panizzi, but the main burden of his story rings true. Both Edwards

An officer from the Royal Engineers had been sent to the Museum to advise on the construction of suitable barricades and other obstacles.[1] On the evening of 9 April, Panizzi toured the defences, looking for weak places through which the mob might force their way. He noted 'that the Museum can be well defended by a well-directed fire of musketry from the roof which commands not only every side of the building but every approach to it as well as some most important points of the interior'.[2] Stones were taken up to the roof to be thrown down on to the heads of the Chartists should they succeed in overwhelming the outer defences, stretchers and medical supplies prepared, and fire engines were to stand by to deal with any possible conflagration.

All was now ready. Provisions for a three-day siege had been laid in, and on the morning of the 10th the staff, assembled under the command of the Keeper of Printed Books, impatiently awaited the coming of the foe. Sir Robert Inglis, the only Trustee present, gave the order to the troops to open fire on the mob immediately on the first stone being thrown. Cowtan remarked in after years, 'Fergus O'Connor or any of his confederates would have found rather a warm reception if they had ventured to force their way into the Museum.'[3] Madden, with perhaps more truth, judged it somewhat differently. He considered that the soldiers would probably have been a match for the mob had they broken into the Museum but, in any case, 'the rest would have scattered like sheep'.[4]

Another member of the staff also viewed the situation, though in a different light. Edward Edwards of Printed Books – very much of a radical – had stoutly refused to be made a special constable, to the indignation of his Keeper, who witheringly exclaimed 'What! not

1. This officer, Major Barrow, arrived on the Sunday morning, 9 April, and at once had constructed 'very strong permanent and temporary barricades along the whole of the windows looking into the front court'. 'Measures,' Madden noted, 'had also been taken to protect the Coin Room by cutting through the timbers of the wooden staircase leading to it, so as to give way under the pressure of a number of persons. (*Madden Journal*, 10 April.) Arrangements were also made with owners of neighbouring houses 'to secure a retreat if thought necessary'. (*op. cit.*)
2. Fagan, 1, p. 282.
2. Cowtan, p.150, Feargus O'Connor, 1794–1855, the principal Chartist leader.
3. *Madden Journal*, 10 April 1848.

and Madden would naturally not mention the activities of a man they so detested. Madden contents himself with abusing Ellis and stressing the part played by his allies, Gray and Hawkins, and particularly by himself, in the day's events.

defend the place from which you get your living'.[1] Edwards, the self-educated son of a bricklayer, had first distinguished himself by the evidence he had given before the Select Committee on the Museum in 1837. He had subsequently joined the staff of the Department of Printed Books as a temporary assistant but unfortunately had quickly fallen foul of Panizzi. Two such hot-tempered individualists as Edwards and his Keeper were not likely to remain long in the same department without quarrelling. Already they were barely on speaking terms, and the events of April 1848 were to render their relationship even more difficult. 'Mr Panizzi asked me if I was willing to be sworn in as a special constable!' he remarked sardonically in his diary. 'It seems that Ellis, etc. are in great alarm at the announced Chartist demonstration.' And when all was over and the great 'rebellion' had ended in a pitiful anticlimax, 'not in blood, but in ridicule',[2] Edwards mockingly remarks: "The superior 'special constables'' [were] firmly convinced that their "magnificent display" yesterday alone prevented the Chartists from attempting a bloody insurrection.'[3]

All the morning, the determined garrison waited for the expected attack to develop. Nothing happened. Only a confused murmuring was heard from the great crowd of demonstrators assembled in Russell Square. Panizzi, like a prudent commander, sent out patrols to contact the enemy, but they returned with little or no information, except the news that some 2,000 Chartists had marched off at about eleven o'clock to join the main body on Kennington Common 'and were not *armed*'.[4] To hearten his men, Panizzi exhorted them in his strong Italian accent, which, even after a lifetime spent here, he never quite lost, 'England expects that every man this day will do his duty', a Nelsonian phrase which to many must have seemed in the circumstances a little comic.[5] At midday the garrison were regaled by a generous meal of beef, bread and beer, though even the imminent danger of attack would not permit the relaxation of the rule against smoking.[6] The dinner was brought across from the public-house opposite, now the Museum Tavern. It was served, to Madden's disgust, 'in my new rooms communicating with the Hall, in which also the Pensioners slept'.

1. Edwards, *Diary*, 4 April 1848.
2. Halèvy, *History of England*, 1841–1852, p. 211.
3. Edwards, *Diary*, 4, 10, 11 April. Edward Edwards, 1812–1886, Assistant at the Museum from 1839 to 1850.
4. *Madden Journal*, 10 April 1848.
5. Cowtan, p. 150.
6. *Madden Journal*, 10 April 1848.

By the evening it was clear that the demonstration had failed. 'All had evaporated in smoke.' The Chartists' leader, Feargus O'Connor, advised them to disperse, 'advice they instantly obeyed, and with great alacrity and good humour'. O'Connor himself told the Home Secretary that he would not return to the meeting, as his toes had been trodden on until he was lame, and his pocket had been picked.[1]

At eight o'clock, after entertaining 'the gentlemen of my department', Bond, Holmes and Oliphant,[2] to a scratch dinner, Madden walked across to the Front Hall to find a milling crowd of dissatisfied attendants, who had had nothing to eat since midday, and were anxious to get home. Ellis was nowhere to be found, but eventually some tea was brought over for the staff, 'but so miserably managed that but few got anything'. Hawkins told Madden that the police had ordered a guard maintained until at least ten o'clock. But Madden and Hawkins, 'the only two officers . . . who endeavoured to preserve something like discipline' (in Madden's version), decided that most of the staff could return home, if forty volunteers agreed to stay on. So at last the weary defenders went off to rejoin their families.

The troops were staying the night. The Chelsea Pensioners, like true old soldiers (but contrary to Museum regulations) were smoking, 'snugly arranged in the new MS rooms, (and as afterwards appeared by the extraordinary management of Sir Henry Ellis,) with their ammunition close beside them in open barrels, so that a spark might have blown them all up, together with the front of the apartment'.[3] So the Museum faced that day worse perils than the Chartists.

Madden went home and got what sleep he could curled up on the sofa in the drawing room. 'Thus ended the memorable day of the 300 special constables in defence of the National Museum'. Madden thought it was very lucky that things had not turned out worse. There was 'not the slightest attempt at organisation & combination; nobody knew what his neighbour did and the whole, from the highest to the lowest, presented the most lamentable proof of the want of a Head who had energy & judgement sufficient for such an emergency'.[4] Although ignoring his rival Panizzi's efforts to bring order out of the chaos, Madden was right in stressing how lamentably the Museum's nominal

1. Greville, vol. 2, p. 289.
2. Thomas Oliphant, 1799–1873, musical composer and writer. He had been the first person specifically engaged to look after the Museum's music collections.
3. *Madden Journal*, 10 April 1848.
4. *op. cit.*

heads, its Principal Librarian and the majority of its Trustees, had failed to meet the challenge to its existence.

Now things at the Museum, to the relief of Sir Henry, returned to normal, that is to a state of continual internecine warfare, in which the powerful Secretary Forshall treated the departmental heads with scant respect; where Panizzi and Madden were at times just short of coming to blows; where the relations between König and Gray in the Natural History department were scarcely less bitter, and where the distinguished Keeper of Antiquities Edward Hawkins was never consulted by the Trustees about new arrangements for one of his own galleries.

A new cloud was gathering over the Museum, a cloud of greater menace than the half-hearted demonstrations of the Chartists. The endless quarrels among the senior members of its staff were common knowledge, and many still regarded it, for all its recent improvements, as a monument of incompetence and folly. As the *Saturday Review* said, some years later, 'If discord, envy, hatred, wrath, malice, and all uncharitableness have a favourite house in England, it will be found between Bloomsbury Square and Tottenham Court Road.'[1]

Letters were constantly appearing in *The Times* and other newspapers criticising the Museum. Bad feeling was likewise aroused when, on 1 February 1842, the King of Prussia visited the Museum and Sir Henry Ellis on his own initiative refused admission to a reporter from *The Times*, and, according to the jealous Madden, thrust himself unduly forward, drawing up a statement for release to the press which omitted almost all mention of the Trustees and emphasised his own importance. Ellis, wrote Madden, 'is a great man for *little affairs*'.[2]

The difficulty of getting reading room tickets without the recommendation of some prominent person was widely resented, and further trouble arose over Smirke's plan for retaining a high brick wall along part of Great Russell Street, instead of ornamental iron railings.[3] The façade itself was also widely criticised. Nothing seemed right. 'Situations in the Museum, as they become vacant by death – no one ever retires – are given to German and Italian boys; so that in time our great national institution will be one *grande maison des étrangers*'.[4] Such were the comments of the contemporary press.

Mounting criticism was expressed in the literary world concerning

1. *Saturday Review*, 8 March 1856.
2. *Madden Journal*, 2 February 1842.
3. *The Times*, 2 October, 4 October 1850, *et seq.*
4. 'Correspondent of the *Edinburgh Review*', 1845, *Madden Collection*, fol. 85.

the non-appearance of further volumes of the printed catalogue, the overcrowding and the lack of facilities in the reading rooms. Perhaps most important, the scientific men, already a power in the land, felt that the Natural History departments were neglected and deplored the lack of eminent scientists on the Board of Trustees. Attacks were constantly made in Parliament, in particular by the radical Joseph Hume[1] and by Edwards's friend, William Ewart,[2] a tireless advocate of more public libraries.

The spokesmen for the Trustees in the House answered as best they might. Their facts were doubtless correct, but prejudice against the Museum and, in particular, against its Italian-born Keeper of Printed Books, ran deep.

Two things at last brought matters to a head. The first was an acrimonious public exchange of letters between Panizzi and the distinguished antiquary, Sir Nicholas Harris Nicolas.[3] Bitter feelings were aroused. Panizzi quoted with relish Nicolas's former tribute to the reforms which he had earlier introduced – a tribute which Nicolas had apparently forgotten, unless Madden is correct in saying that it was John Gray who wrote the attacks on his colleague, under Nicolas's name. At all events, it gravely weakened Nicolas's case – Panizzi was not a successful lawyer for nothing – and further aroused the wrath of his enemies. It was, said Madden, 'conduct every Englishman would blush to imitate',[4] but was none the less a telling riposte, and emphasised Panizzi's argument that no reliance could be placed on his adversary's opinions. Nicolas, in turn, accused Panizzi, 'an Italian notary . . . undistinguished even in the literature of his own country', of deceit, of improper influence over the Trustees and of sheer incompetence in failing to produce a proper printed catalogue, the present one being full of 'eternal cross-references' and suchlike 'frivolities'.[5]

Demands were made in Parliament for a thorough investigation into this apparently hopelessly old-fashioned and corrupt institution, demands that were echoed, both privately and publicly by Panizzi, who

1. Joseph Hume, 1777–1855, radical politician.
2. William Ewart, 1798–1868, radical MP who promoted Acts for the abolition of capital punishment and for the establishment of free public libraries. Panizzi had known Ewart and other members of his family well during his Liverpool days, but they were now estranged.
3. Sir Nicholas Harris Nicolas, 1799–1848, antiquary, originally a naval officer. According to Madden he eventually fled abroad to avoid imprisonment for debt.
4. *Madden Journal*, 11 July 1846.
5. Nicolas, *Animadversions on the Library*, pp. 27, 51.

longed to clear his name and that of the Museum before an impartial tribunal. The Prime Minister Lord John Russell listened to this growing volume of criticism, but for the moment would only make vague promises a commission might be set up. On 3 March Madden received a letter from Nicolas, enclosing one from Joseph Hume informing Nicolas that he is 'preparing for an enquiry into the state of the Museum in all its branches' and asking for advice as to what was the best course to take and what particular objects required special enquiry. 'I certainly shall not commit myself by furnishing information gratuitously to such a person as Mr. Joseph Hume,' snorted Sir Frederic, 'for whom I have the utmost contempt.'[1] In the end it was the scientists who precipitated the enquiry.

On 10 March 1847, a memorial was addressed to Russell by members of the British Association and other scientific bodies expressing dissatisfaction at what appeared to be undue weight given to non-scientific men in appointments to the Board of Trustees.[2] On 17 June, a Royal Commission was appointed to enquire 'in what manner that National Institution may be made most effective for the advancement of Literature, Science and the Arts'.[3] The Commission was a powerful one, the Chairman being Lord Ellesmere,[4] a distinguished scholar, as well as a great nobleman, and the Museum could be assured that the investigation would be thorough. The secretary to the Commission, John Payne Collier,[5] was perhaps not so happy a choice. He was opinionated and, as a lifelong habitué of the Reading Room, considered he had greater knowledge of what was needed at the Museum than any of its officers. Had not the Commission been so able, his influence and lack of impartiality might well have proved disastrous.

1. *Madden Journal*, 3 March 1847.
2. *Memorial to the First Lord of the Treasury presented 10 March 1847, by members of the British Association for the Advancement of Science and other Scientific Societies respecting the management of the British Museum.* (PP, H. of C., 1847. vol. XXXIV, p. 253.) There was, they claimed, 'no effective provision for the proper guidance of the Natural History Department'.
3. *Royal Commission. Report*, p. iii. (PP, H. of C., 1850, vol. XXIV, p.1.)
4. Francis Leverson-Gower, 1800–1857, the youngest son of the first Duke of Sutherland, changed his name to Egerton. After being created Lord Ellesmere, he signed his name Egerton Ellesmere. A 'liberal conservative' in politics, 'he gave me the impression of being a shy man. There was about him an air of pensive gravity which was peculiar'. (8th Duke of Argyll, *Autobiography*. Quoted in GEC, vol. 5, p. 55.)
5. John Payne Collier, 1789–1883, critic. He had worked in the Bridgewater Library under Ellesmere. Subsequently he was widely believed to be guilty of numerous literary forgeries.

Ellis was the Royal Commission's first witness, and to him, as always, all was well with the Museum. In his opinion, no changes were either desirable or necessary, apart from such minor inconveniences as having no room of his own and being forced therefore to work either in the Manuscripts Department or in his own house. It was a pity, too, that there was no way into the Department of Printed Books except through Manuscripts. The attendants going to and from their dinner kicked up a dust cloud as they passed, damaging the books and annoying their superiors. Of the bitter feuds going on around him, the Principal Librarian professed ignorance. There were 'no serious disputes'. 'They are all upon very fair terms. I do not know of any absolute disputes among them.'[1]

Forshall was next called, by now an ailing man.[2] His evidence clearly showed that here was one cause of the situation in which the Museum now found itself.[3] No proper accounts were kept. The Secretary had assumed many powers that more properly belonged to the Principal Librarian, and his department, grossly inflated as it was, was conspicuously inefficient. Forshall himself, with his influence over the Archbishop, was able to run the Board pretty much as he liked. Trustees were summoned or not at his pleasure and he might present them 'with such minutes as he pleased'.[4] He formed an almost insuperable barrier between the Trustees and the other officers, causing endless frustration and bad feeling. It was by no means only the library which had suffered in this respect. Orders from the Trustees for the arrangement of the new Lycian marbles gallery had gone through Forshall to the Museum sculptor, Sir Richard Westmacott. Hawkins, the Keeper of the

1. *Royal Commission, Minutes*, para. 2544.
2. A few weeks later Forshall was again seriously ill. Alarmed at the probable loss of his most powerful ally, Madden noted that the excitement brought on by appearing before the Commission had made Forshall 'utterly incapable of attending to any business'. He continues: 'Should his mind be seriously affected, as it was on a former occasion, the views and wishes of that Scoundrel Panizzi will be carried into effect. Through him it is that Cary's heart was broken, Ellis's hair turned grey by mental agony and, as to myself, God knows how much older a man he has made me by his infamous conduct and the conduct of those who supported him.' (*Madden Journal*, 23 July 1847.)
3. The cross-examination was conducted for the most part by Andrew Rutherfurd, the Lord Advocate, 'who is nothing more or less than an avowed partisan of Mr Panizzi and acts under his instructions. Of course, it is easy to see the object he has in view'. (*Madden Journal*, 13 July 1847.) Andrew Rutherfurd, Lord Rutherfurd, 1791–1854, Scottish judge and politician.
4. *Royal Commission, Minutes*, para. 1042.

Department of Antiquities, had been ignored. No wonder that a distinguished witness commented on the marked 'want of power'[1] in that department. Hawkins, indeed, was very bitter. He felt that he was competent to arrange these or any other marbles. Sir Richard, who was constantly employed in arranging and re-arranging the sculpture galleries, was in Hawkins' opinion continually guilty of sacrificing scientific accuracy for the merely picturesque.

Madden was now called. (To his disgust he had been out when the Commission assembled and so missed the first meeting altogether.) He was, as usual, full of complaints and highly conscious of his moral rectitude. 'The old servant,' a sardonic critic remarked, 'feels himself to be a treasure.'[2] He had no space; he had no staff; there was not enough room for students to consult manuscripts (a justifiable complaint); *he* never got generous grants, such as *other* departments had. The Manuscripts Department had equal or greater claims than theirs on the generosity of the Treasury. All the old grievances were revived. The residences, Panizzi's seniority, the injustice of his own belated appointment, the dispute over both the King's and the Grenville manuscripts (which latter, incidentally, the Keeper of Printed Books had not handed over to him, despite four orders by the Trustees to do so) – the tale of woe goes on. To make ends meet, the poor man had to write for three or four hours every night of his life and the whole work of the department devolved solely on him.[3]

Madden was, undoubtedly, a good and conscientious Keeper and certainly had the well-being of his own department at heart. He had made it more efficient and worked hard to repair the neglect into which it had fallen under his predecessors. Even his grumbles are often as much for the better running of his department as for his own troubles. But if ever a man had a chip on his shoulder, it was Frederic Madden, forced against his will to labour among colleagues whom he considered his social inferiors. Life was made unbearable 'by the constant annoyance I feel in not being in the station of society I am intitled to and being associated here with men who have little or no pretensions to the name of gentleman'.[4] It must have particularly infuriated the snobbish

1. Evidence of Sir Charles Fellows, *Minutes*, para. 1686.
2. *Quarterly Review*, CLXXV, p. 157.
3. *Minutes*, para. 2164, etc. The *Quarterly Review* remarked about all this that Madden was obviously 'a gentleman who doesn't know *what* he wants'. (*Quarterly Review*, CLXXV, p. 157.)
4. *Madden Journal*, 31 December 1841.

Madden that whilst he had to be content with a humdrum, middle-class circle of acquaintances his hated rival, 'this scoundrel Italian', though merely the son of a village chemist, was the welcome guest of some of the greatest in the land, spending Christmas with the Palmerstons at No. 10 Downing Street or a week or more with Lord Clarendon, the Foreign Secretary, or at the country houses of other Whig grandees. Panizzi was on terms of close friendship with Lord and Lady Holland – particularly with the latter during her long widowhood[1] – with both the exiled Orleanist princes and with Napoleon III and his Empress, not to mention Cavour and other distinguished statesmen. Panizzi wintered abroad at Naples or Baden-Baden. Madden thought himself lucky to be able to take the family to Brighton or the Isle of Wight. It was all most unfair.

It was now the turn of this strange and remarkable man, Antonio Panizzi, to appear before the Commissioners to answer the many charges that had been brought against his administration. Tall and dignified, his rugged face still handsome, he now stood at bay to face his accusers, before that higher tribunal to which he had for so long wished to appeal. Slowly and carefully he answered his critics. It was clearly proved that the delays and inconsistencies that had bedevilled the production of the new printed catalogue were the result of the Trustees' policy and the mismanagement, if no worse interpretation was to be put on his conduct, of the Secretary, Forshall. In addition, Panizzi told the full story of how the Grenville Library had come to the Museum, though minimising his own share in the acquisition. As to how the bequest had been slighted and misused, the Commissioners were left to draw their own conclusions.

Panizzi then spoke of the attendants in his department, of the poor conditions and of how they were forced to supplement their slender incomes by waiting and similar activities (a practice which lasted at the Museum until very recently), a side of Museum life of which the Commissioners were no doubt quite ignorant.[2]

After Panizzi had further clarified the position with regard to the

1. All Madden ever got was an occasional present of game from a minor peer.
Henry Edward Fox, second and eldest legitimate son of the third Lord and Lady Holland, 1802–1859. He married in 1833 Mary Augusta, daughter of the Earl of Coventry, 1812–1889.
2. Madden, for all his faults, could be very generous in helping his own attendants, such as Richard Sims, who through no fault of his own landed himself in a debtor's prison. Panizzi, too, spent large sums out of his own pocket in assisting those attendants who were in financial difficulties, as Robert Cowtan gratefully acknowledged.

projected printed catalogue, it was the turn of the heads of the other departments, in particular König, Hawkins and Gray. König, elderly, ailing and clearly jealous of Gray, Keeper of the Department of Zoology, with whom his relations were little better than those between Panizzi and Madden, resented his former department's being split and his being reduced to *primus inter pares* with Botany and Zoology. 'Strictly speaking, I have no department,' he complained, 'I formerly was head of the Department of Natural History, but since its partition in 1837, I am Keeper of only one of its branches, sometimes called "Mineralogy and Geology"; sometimes "Mineralogy, including the Fossils".'[1] The fossils were a constant cause of dispute between König and Gray. Each claimed exclusive authority over them, and their squabbles were endless. Like all the other scientists, König felt that the scientific departments were the Cinderellas of the Museum, especially when it was considered that the 'Department of Natural History was the most ancient, and [the one] for which the British Museum was mainly founded',[2] a pre-eminence he felt that had now been usurped by the Library and by the Antiquities Department.

And so the Commission worked on, ferreting out the causes of all complaints, whether justifiable or not. The more experienced praised the Reading Room and its services; another declared, 'I am unwilling to go to the Museum, there is so much time wasted in hunting over the present catalogue.'[3] Another, equally indignant, objected to Panizzi's rule that readers should themselves return their books: 'Sir Henry Ellis did not wish any gentleman to carry up his books, if he objected to it.'[4]

A clearer picture of the Museum was beginning to emerge. Much of the discontent was due to the power improperly acquired by Forshall over the Trustees and to the vacillating behaviour of Sir Henry. All the officers had sound ideas for their own departments and very often knew what the Museum as a whole was most in need of, whether expansion into new fields, such as British and medieval antiquities, the improvement of the long neglected ethnographical collections, or the urgent necessity of bettering the conditions under which the staff laboured. Gray, as well as Panizzi, was extremely bitter about this. In a long letter to Ellis which he laid before the Commission, he stated his conviction as a medical man that 'the miserable state of health and

1. *Royal Commission, Minutes*, para. 3092.
2. *op. cit.*, para. 3148.
3. *op. cit.*, para. 4835.
4. *op. cit.*, para. 6144.

mind of several officers, who have either died or left the Museum . . .
have been in a great degree referable to this want of some provision for
their retirement without being placed under the necessity of over-
working their powers by study at night and at other times . . . in the
hopes of making some provision for themselves'.[1] These sentiments
found many echoes. But it was Panizzi who obtained vastly improved
conditions of service and an adequate pensions scheme ten years later.

Now once more the Keeper of Printed Books took over, and
rebutted his various challengers. In May 1849 – such was the length of
the commission – he faced the Commissioners for the last time. He
again showed how he had built up the library almost from nothing,
despite the handicap of a defective Copyright Act. He carefully replied
to justified criticisms. For instance a better educated Superintendent,
able to deal at once and effectively with readers' queries, was much to be
desired. And as always, the crying need was for more money, more staff,
and more space.

As to the other critics, whether they were such prominent personages as Thomas Carlyle or John Payne Collier or the host of ignorant
scribblers, who constantly hounded him, such were beneath contempt.
'The more ignorant people are, the more troublesome they are,' he
sourly commented.[2] Proudly he concluded, though perhaps showing a
little of that over-sensitiveness to criticism on which the Commission
was to remark: 'As to the management of the library, I do not think I
have done less than my predecessors who were Englishmen or less than
my present colleagues who are Englishmen have done for their
departments.'[3]

Three of the most active Trustees also gave evidence, one, Sir Robert
Inglis, a bitter opponent of Panizzi, the others, Henry Hallam the
historian, and W. R. Hamilton, his warm supporters.[4] Inglis went as
far as to say that the Trustees should have refused the government grant
of £10,000 a year for books until new and adequate accommodation
was provided. Both Inglis and Hallam agreed that there was a deplorable
lack of communication between the Trustees and their senior staff and

1. *op. cit.*, para. 8689.
2. *op. cit.*, para. 10016.
3. *op. cit.*, para. 9985.
4. Madden hated Hamilton almost as much as he did Ellis or Panizzi. 'I still trust
my life may be spared to see the day when the Museum may be freed from three such
men as Ellis, Hamilton and Panizzi; the first a bully and a slave; the second a prejudiced, ill-tempered partisan and the third a knave and a blackguard.' (*Madden Journal*,
12 June 1849.)

that many of the staff were at loggerheads with each other, as they had 'painful reason to know'.[1] Hamilton, after telling the Commissioners that Panizzi was 'one of the best public servants I ever knew',[2] dwelt on the deficiencies of Smirke's new buildings, in which 'internal uses . . . have been sacrificed for the external form',[3] and expressed the view that more consideration and more time should have been given to their design and construction. At long last the hearings came to an end, with Madden popping up to have the last word.

On 28 March 1850, after a number of inspired leaks[4] and much speculation in the press, the Commissioners delivered their report. It was a gentle but firm rebuke to the Trustees and to their Secretary, and an unqualified vindication of the Keeper of Printed Books and the policies he had pursued or had vainly advocated during the previous thirteen years.

In the opinion of the Royal Commission, the Trustees, despite their individual integrity, had not really proved worthy of the trust reposed in them, especially when it was considered that £1,100,000 of public money had been spent on the maintenance of the Museum since 1755. The Trustees had ignored their own rules. There was no regularly established standing Committee – merely those Trustees able to attend whom the Secretary deigned to invite – and there had been no proper visitations of the individual departments since 1829.

It was made abundantly clear that the overpowerful Secretary, Forshall, was the cause of much of the mischief and that his usurpation had been due to the supine acquiescence of the majority of the Trustees and the bumbling inefficiency of the Principal Librarian. 'The administration' the Commissioners reported, 'from the neglect of those rules' had fallen 'into hands to which it was never intended to be entrusted'.[5]

1. *Royal Commission, Minutes*, para. 10217.
2. *op. cit.*, para. 10586.
3. *op. cit.*, para. 10581.
4. Gray told Madden as early as September 1849 that he had seen part of the draft report. 'They are "very complimentary" to me and my Department, but not quite so much as to Mr Panizzi and Mr Brown (!), but very much more so than to himself.' (*Madden Journal*, 9 September 1849.) The following April Gray showed Madden another draft of the final report which he had also got hold of through one of the attendants who had been Joseph Hume's secretary. It apparently differed little from the published report, except that certain details on the Natural History departments had been struck out, 'and wisely'. (*Madden Journal*, 4 April 1850.)
5. *Royal Commission, Report*, p. 6.

Step by step they showed how the power of the Secretary had been built up. He alone knew the proposed agenda beforehand and could arrange it, adding or deleting items as he pleased. Every report from the officers had to be in writing and he alone read what extracts he chose to the Board. He alone attended all meetings. Neither the Principal Librarian nor any other officers were permitted to be present. 'The systematic exclusion from the Board when the affairs of his department are under consideration of the Keeper joined to that of the Principal Librarian leaves them [the Keepers] under the painful but natural impression where their suggestions are disallowed that they have not been properly represented.'[1] The Secretary's department, despite its ever-increasing size, was inefficient and badly organised. The Commission therefore recommended the abolition of the posts of Principal Librarian and Secretary and in its place the establishment of a responsible Executive Council to run the Museum, though exactly how this should be composed they could not agree.[2]

Madden and Gray were rebuked for the 'manifestation of similar feelings . . . of ill judged criticism',[3] as had been shown by outside critics of the library. Panizzi's administration was vindicated, and Grenville and other manuscripts taken by Madden were ordered to be returned. The running of Madden's own department was commended and his 'many subjects of complaint, and of dissatisfaction'[4] were found to be frequently justified. He *did* not have enough staff; the Oriental manuscripts ought to be formed into a separate department and valuable manuscript collections had indeed been lost to the nation through lethargy and unfair allocation of resources. Yet all this did not justify 'the want of harmony and good understanding between the heads of departments',[5] though much of the conduct of the malcontents sprang from misplaced zeal and from the lack of a 'more prompt and

1. *op. cit.*, p. 7.
2. Madden was alarmed to hear that when a new governing body for the Museum was set up as recommended in the Report, either Ellesmere or Macaulay would be the Chairman, with Panizzi in charge of the library and antiquities and Professor Owen, the naturalist, as the other 'director' of the scientific collections. Both of them would have the pay of Keepers 'for doing nothing or for doing mischief'. (*Madden Journal*, 4 April 1850.) As it turned out, the only part of this section of the Report to be implemented was the appointment of Owen as Superintendent of the Natural History Departments.
3. *Royal Commission, Report*, p. 13.
4. *op. cit.*, p. 29.
5. *op. cit.*, p. 31.

vigorous system of management'[1] by the Trustees and Principal Librarian.

The Commissioners showed anxiety about the inadequate buildings. Extra money had been obtained for further excavations in Mesopotamia, but there was no room to receive the treasures that were being unearthed there. The present building, they concluded, was 'a warning rather than a model to the architect of any additional structure'.[2]

As to the antiquities, the Commission advocated the formation of a national collection of British antiquities, of which there were still too few, and condemned the practice of permitting an outsider to arrange the sculpture rather than having it done by the Museum's own experts. The difficulty which had arisen in the Natural History departments over the disposition of the fossil collections was regretted and the consequent jealousy between König and Gray deplored. To resolve the differences the reform of the departments of Zoology and Mineralogy was highly desirable.

The report was well received. *The Times* remarked that it offered 'ample proof of the diligence, care and impartiality with which they have investigated the large and intricate subject',[3] whilst the *Athenaeum* remarked that Panizzi, Jones and Watts had been shown to be 'a race of bibliographical giants and the first of these commanded our admiration by the manly spirit in which he faced all difficulties and grappled with all opponents'.[4] Madden, of course, had other views. 'A more partial enquiry never yet was made and it is disgraceful to the character of English gentlemen to lend themselves to the plans of an Italian vagabond, whose only merit lies in his powers of misrepresentation'.[5]

The Trustees, in a minute of 4 May 1850, affirmed their dislike of the proposal for an Executive Committee and appointed a sub-committee to examine the Commission's recommendations in detail. Their

---

1. *op. cit.*, p. 31.
2. *op. cit.*, p. 32. Madden, too, was contemptuous of Smirke's buildings and of Hamilton's warm advocacy of their fashionable Grecian appearance, to which all other considerations would appear to have been sacrificed. Hamilton had suggested to Madden, whom he had met on a bus, that as a clock would spoil the look of the new front, one should be put up on one of the houses facing the Museum, so that the gate-keepers would still be able to tell the time, and a sum of money paid to the owner of the house to take care of it. 'O, worthy Trustee! He is afraid that an arch will hide the least portion of his beautiful Greek front of the Museum.' (*Madden Journal*, 27 August 1850.)
3. *The Times*, 29 March 1850.
4. *Athenaeum*, 11 May 1850.
5. *Madden Journal*, 26 May 1849.

report stressed the favourable comments made by the Commission on their conduct and denied that any drastic changes in their constitution or administration were either desirable or necessary.[1] The government, for their part, as so very often happens, did little, despite much public criticism, to implement any of the Commission's proposals.

Some of the difficulties, however, now resolved themselves. Forshall, a very sick man, was forced to retire and Ellis took over his duties, finding them, as he had already told the Commissioners, surprisingly light.[2] Forshall took his dismissal badly. In a letter to one of the Trustees he complained bitterly of what seemed to him the iniquity of his enforced resignation. Like the other officers, he had always considered that his appointment was 'legally as well as morally for life', but since that appointment had been unjustly 'revoked', would it not be possible, he asked, for him to be given a rich living as a compensation?[3]

Panizzi was now the dominant figure in the library, and the rapidly ageing Ellis leant more and more on him. In September 1850 Panizzi's Assistant Keeper, Garnett, died[4] and was succeeded by his faithful follower, John Winter Jones, who had been his choice for the post fourteen years before. Jones was an ideal second-in-command, the perfect foil to the great man, whose devoted friend and assistant he ever was. And now he supported his chief in what were to be the two great questions for the library during the next few years, the enforcement of the Copyright Act, and the threat of inadequate space.

The passing of a better act in 1842 and the transfer of the duty of enforcing it from the feeble hands of the Secretary's department to the vigorous grip of the Keeper of Printed Books presented the Museum with an opportunity of obtaining these books to which it had always

1. The draft of this report, largely the work of Peel, was found in his pocket after his fatal accident on Constitution Hill on 29 June 1850. The report is in PP, H. of C. 1850, vol. XXXIII, p. 249. Madden, not surprisingly, disliked Peel intensely and considered him to be 'a real Philistine'.
2. *Royal Commission, Minutes*, para. 1002.
3. Add. MS. 41,396. f. 248.
4. Panizzi had secured the appointment of Garnett's sixteen-year-old son Richard, who was to be the outstanding figure of the next generation at the Museum. This typical act of kindness drew a warm letter of thanks from the boy's widowed mother. (*Panizzi Papers*, 1851. f. 79.) On hearing of Garnett's death, Madden remarked, 'He is a great loss and I regret his death much . . . we would better have spared the head of his department, or any other member of it.' (*Madden Journal*, 28 September 1850.)

been entitled but which publishers, 'by every dirty trick',[1] had avoided sending.

Panizzi would stand no such nonsense. Armed with adequate legal powers, he strictly enforced the Act, if necessary prosecuting defaulting publishers, and thereby incurring further abuse. Though hurt by the malevolent criticism which his actions aroused, since he was only doing his duty, he pressed on. The London publishers dealt with, he passed to the provinces, and then to Scotland, Wales and even Ireland, travelling everywhere to see how the Act was being enforced and what further books he might obtain. The results fully justified the hard work, the spiteful and unmerited abuse. 'When I entered upon the Keepership of Printed Books,' Panizzi wrote, 'the Library was very defective; – when I gave up that office, thanks to increased outlay and to the enforcement of the Copyright Act, the Library was rich.'[2]

But all this and an ever-increasing flow of books from other sources meant that the library was rapidly filling up. The plan then advocated was to buy and demolish certain neighbouring houses and to construct new buildings 'continuing the north side of the Museum into Russell-Square', which would contain 'a gallery for the library of Mr. Grenville, corresponding with the value and dignity of the bequest, space for . . . much enlarged reading-rooms with an easy and suitable access to them'.[3]

It was not only the library, though, which needed more room. The zoological collection was 'now at least ten times as numerous in kinds and specimens as it was in the year 1836'.[4] The provision of a new mineralogical gallery was a necessity, and the lack of space for the proper exhibition of antiquities was notorious: 'The present possessions of the Museum are in almost every room crowded together and piled over each other like goods in a warehouse.'[5] The Assyrian sculptures which were exciting nation-wide interest were in no better state. 'It can scarcely be said that any accommodation is provided,'[6] said Hawkins, in despair. In short, as Ellis informed Trevelyan of the Treasury in July 1851, 'a considerable addition to the building'[7] was urgently necessary

1. Baber's evidence to Select Committee, 1836. *Select Committee, 1836, Minutes*, para. 4630.
2. *Panizzi, Passages*, p. 22.
3. *Communications* p. 3.
4. Report to the Trustees by Gray, *op. cit.*, p. 12.
5. Report by Hawkins, *op. cit.*, p. 13.
6. *op. cit.*, p. 14.
7. *op. cit.*, p. 17.

or, as Panizzi said more dramatically, the lack of suitable accommodation was becoming 'daily, hourly, more pressing'.[1]

The scheme envisaged for the Museum involved the demolition of twelve houses in Montague Street and of six more adjoining in Russell Square, to the east and northeast of Smirke's main buildings. But to do this would obviously be expensive and would take a considerable time. And time was the very thing which the Museum, and, particularly, Printed Books, had not got. In any case, the Treasury thought the scheme, which would cost at least £300,000, too expensive. A partial solution to the problem was, however, at hand. Panizzi, who had long advocated the erection of new buildings to the northeast, realised that alternative accommodation, at least a new reading room and Library, should be provided immediately.

For nearly twenty years various proposals had been put forward for making use of the inner quadrangle formed by the four wings of Smirke's buildings, a gloomy grass-covered plot, called sarcastically by Thomas Grenville, 'the finest mason's yard in Europe';[2] where Madden's two small boys played alone. Watts had suggested in an article in the *Mechanics' Magazine* back in 1837[3] building a reading room within the quadrangle, whilst Professor Hosking, of London University, had evolved a plan, which was actually submitted to the Trustees, for turning the northern half of the King's Library into a reading room, whilst a domed rotunda would be erected within the quadrangle for the display of sculpture and other antiquities.[4]

On the evening of 18 April 1852, Panizzi drew a rough sketch of what seemed to him to be needed and on the back of the sheet scribbled down the dimensions: a square of 197 feet and a square within it of 170 feet; within this second square a circle 100 feet in diameter and in this second circle another 40 feet in diameter.

This sketch, warmly approved by the colleagues to whom he showed

1. Letter from Panizzi to Ellis, 3 March 1851. (*Communications*, p. 8.)
2. *Quarterly Review*, CLXXV. p. 153.
3. *Mechanics' Magazine*, vol. 26, pp. 454–9. *The New Buildings at The British Museum*, signed PPCR: 'Peerless Pool, City Road', as Watts told Garnett, the open air swimming pool in Islington owned by his family.
4. Ellesmere, writing to Peel in a letter of 17 Jan. 1850, discusses, somewhat disparagingly, Hosking's plan 'to show how space left unoccupied by the existing buildings might be applied to meet the demand which has grown up since they were designed'. He likewise thinks that such a plan, 'to build . . . a kind of modified copy of the Pantheon at Rome' will not receive Treasury sanction. (Add. MS. 40, 603. f. 26.) William Hosking, 1800–1861, architect and civil engineer.

it the next morning, was soon transformed into architectural drawings, and submitted to the Trustees. In his report of 5 May 1852, Panizzi emphasised that the 'claims of the readers require the immediate and special consideration of the Trustees', and by his new scheme, 'the inconveniences now felt can be completely remedied . . . in a short time, and at a comparatively small cost by the erection of a suitable building in the inner quadrangle which is at present, useless'.[1] 'Something,' he went on, 'must be done immediately.'[2] Any other scheme would take years to complete and then would have to be related to the requirements of the Museum as a whole, rather than directly to the reading room and its supporting book-stacks, whose needs were the most urgent. 'The whole of this building, which . . . would be unique, promises to be striking as well as elegant and cheerful, and capable of being as well lighted, ventilated and warmed, as can possibly be wished.'[3] These were certainly improvements which would delight every reader, as the present rooms were badly lighted, badly ventilated, and often bitterly cold. In a further report of 1 June, Panizzi emphasized more strongly how quickly the library was filling up. During the period between 1846 and 1850, 87,087 works had been purchased, a yearly average of 17,417, and a further 139,853 received by copyright and donation, an average of 27,970 each year. As a result, 'the collection of printed books, which has been more than doubled during the last 15 years, would be double of what it is now in 20 years from the present time'.[4] Panizzi's proposed new building would afford ample room even for such a phenomenal increase.

Despite these appeals, accompanied, like all Panizzi's reports, by a wealth of statistics, the Trustees hesitated. It was then learnt that the Treasury had rejected the previous proposals for northward extensions. Though it was now Panizzi's scheme or nothing, the Trustees hankered after some larger and more ambitious scheme which would provide for other departments. Articles praising and attacking the 'ingenious suggestions of Mr Panizzi'[5] appeared in the press. One of the most dangerous attacks came from the *Quarterly Review*, a publication friendly to the Museum. It condemned Panizzi's proposed 'bird-cage' and suggested roofing over the whole of the quadrangle with glass so as to

1. *Communications*, p. 27.
2. *op. cit.*, p. 28.
3. *op. cit.*, p. 28.
4. *op. cit.*, p. 31.
5. *Critic*, 11 August 1860.

form a court suitable for exhibiting the Museum's collection of statuary. Printed Books might be accommodated in the vacant galleries, and a new reading room or rooms constructed in the north wing. Despite Panizzi's scorn of this plan, 'suggested by an amateur',[1] it was seriously considered by the Trustees and backed by the authoritative opinion of Sir Charles Barry, the architect of the newly erected Houses of Parliament. Panizzi was angry and alarmed at this development and, supported by Ellis and Sidney Smirke, the Museum architect, did what he could, by detailed criticism and indefatigable lobbying, to defeat Barry's 'preposterous' proposals.[2]

For two anxious months he waited, while the Trustees and then the government made up their minds. At last, on 26 January 1854 Panizzi was informed by Ellis in a triumphant note, 'I have this moment received the Treasury letter approving the plans and proposed the expenditure of £86,000.'[3]

Once approved, the plans quickly went ahead under Panizzi's energetic supervision. In September 1854 the first brick was laid; in January 1855 the first iron standard erected. By March of that year, *The Builder* could give a detailed description of the proposed reading room, 'the largest and may be made the handsomest in the world'.[4] 'The public, instead of creeping in at an ignoble entrance by a dirty lane will pass at once through the grand hall into their new reading

1. *Quarterly Review*, vol. XVII, p. 157. *Panizzi Papers*, 1853. f. 270.
2. Sir Charles Barry, 1795–1860, architect also of the Reform Club and of Bridgewater House, which he designed for Lord Ellesmere. Smirke thought little of his plan. 'The more I consider it in detail, the more preposterous it seems.' (*Panizzi Papers*, 1853. f. 113.) Ellis likewise poured scorn on Barry's plans in a letter to Bliss of 29 November 1853. Barry intended to cover over the whole of the 'Inner Court' with a glass roof, supported on forty or fifty 'iron pillars of enormous height'. It would be, said Ellis, 'nearly two acres of ground covered by a sky-light! It will not be carried into effect. That matter is settled'. (Add. MS. 34,579. f. 473.) Another possible, though, of course, remote source for Panizzi's idea for a great unsupported domed roof, was the conservatory erected at Brighton in 1833, to the designs of A. H. Wilds, a local architect. Owing to the elimination of a central supporting pillar, the whole edifice suddenly collapsed, fortunately without any loss of life. In 1850 or thereabouts Joseph Paxton travelled to Brighton to inspect the heap of debris and twisted girders. Panizzi knew Paxton, and it is therefore possible that the former's Reading Room and the latter's Crystal Palace were derived from Wilds' ill-conceived scheme. (Anthony Dale, *Fashionable Brighton*, pp. 154, 155.) The author is indebted to his colleague, George Painter, for drawing his attention to this parallel.
3. *Panizzi Papers*, 1854. f. 81.
4. *Builder*, vol. XIII, no. 633, 24 March 1858.

saloons, the chief of which with a dome not much less in size than the Pantheon at Rome, will be filled with light and fresh air.'[1] It was even proposed to introduce a series of statues around the room at the base of the dome, but this scheme was abandoned before it got too far.

By May 1857 all was ready and, on the 2nd of that month, the new Reading Room was formally opened, to the delighted plaudits of most of the press and public. On 8 May, the general public were admitted to the Room for one week and thereafter it began its career as a reading room, with 'ample and comfortable accommodation for 300 readers'.[2] It was, of course, not only the Reading Room which was new, but also the four 'quadrants', the 'iron library' which surrounded it. Constructed with the utmost regard for safety from fire, and with the maximum use of natural light, essential in foggy Victorian London, these stacks were a marvel of technical achievement and an example of the ingenuity of Panizzi who, as in the case of the Reading Room itself, was responsible for the design in almost every detail. *The Times* wrote: 'His indefatigable industry and his untiring interest in the Museum have been devoted to the daily inspection of the works and he has originated constant and valuable suggestions in the course of their progress.'[3]

Not everyone joined in the chorus of praise. Madden, for one, was still bitter. The Room, though 'splendid', he considered, 'unsuited . . . to its purpose & an example of reckless extravagance (having cost £150,000), occasioned through the undue influence of a Foreigner. Had Mr P. been an Englishman, the Treasury would not have granted £20,000 for such a purpose'.[4]

On the day of the opening, 2 May, a great breakfast was given to celebrate the occasion. It was served in the Reading Room itself, and Panizzi was the hero of the hour. Madden walked out in disgust. 'It was wholly a *private* party of Mr P's . . . and I rejoice much I had nothing to do with it.'[5]

Once more his rival had defeated him – on 4 March 1856, Panizzi had become Principal Librarian. It had by no means been a certainty. Many, both inside and outside the Museum, still looked askance at the promotion to high office of a foreign-born former revolutionary, as 'a wrong to the Museum and an insult to the literature and science of the

1. *The Times*, 5 July 1854.
2. *op. cit.*, 21 April 1857.
3. *op. cit.*
4. *Madden Journal*, 21 April 1857.
5. *op. cit.*, 2 May 1857.

country'.[1] Nevertheless, it had happened, though until all was success-fully concluded, Panizzi had no peace.

It had long been clear that poor old Sir Henry, now in his seventy-ninth year, must go, both for his own good and that of the Museum. Early in 1856 it was discreetly suggested to him that if he resigned, he would continue to be paid his full salary and emoluments. Surprisingly, Sir Henry agreed. Ellis strongly favoured Panizzi, whom he had grown to admire to succeed him. Although by no means the senior Keeper, Panizzi ran the Museum during Ellis's not infrequent absences. Panizzi, conscious as he was of his own merits, was determined to use his considerable influence to obtain the position he so much desired. Although Ellis told him not to worry, there were setbacks. His old acquaintance, Lord Lansdowne, seemed to be turning against him and then suddenly one of the Trustees, Sir David Dundas,[2] suggested himself as a possible candidate. Panizzi was horrified. 'Why a man who has never succeeded in anything should be deemed good enough for us and rob those who have served faithfully the Trustees (of which he is one!) for many years of their legitimate rewards, it is not for me to say',[3] wrote Panizzi to his friend Lord Holland.

However, all was well. As Panizzi got a considerable number of influential people to point out, he would not be the first foreigner to preside over the destinies of the Museum. On 19 February the Arch-bishop assured Cureton that Panizzi would have his support and so 'all is right in that quarter'.[4] Ten days later, Panizzi's name and that of the distinguished historian, John Kemble, were submitted to the Cabinet for the final decision.[5]

1. *Saturday Review*, 8 March 1856.
2. Sir David Dundas, 1799–1877, Solicitor-General under Russell, Judge-Advocate-General, 1849–1853. Dundas seems to have been an odd character. Panizzi wrote to Lord Holland, 'Many think he is not quite, quite right and at times I think so too.' (Panizzi to Lord Holland, 14 February 1856. Add. MS. 52,009. f. 66.)
3. *op. cit.*
4. Cureton to Panizzi, 19 February 1856. *Passages*, p. 35.
5. John Kemble, 1807–1857, philologist and historian, the eldest son of Charles Kemble, the famous actor.

Madden, of course, was almost out of his mind with rage. Having failed to win the expected support from Gray and Hawkins, he had himself, on 25 February, written to the three Principal Trustees asking to be considered for the post of Principal Librarian. 'I am, after Mr. Hawkins, the senior Assistant Officer in the Museum.' Hawkins had already refused to allow his name to be put forward despite Madden's pleas to him to do so. On 4 March Madden was told by Ellis that only Kemble's and Panizzi's names had been submitted, 'as there were no other applicants'. Madden had not even been

On 4 March Panizzi was officially informed that he was the new Principal Librarian. 'The devil choke him with it say I,' growled Madden. 'It is hard to think that if this cursed fellow had never come to England with a rope round his neck . . . I should now have had the finest chance of a good house and £1,000 per annum. And what has *he* done for the Museum & the Public that I have not done, ay and ten times more. My bitter ban upon him'.[1] It is difficult not to feel sorry for Madden. Throughout the years he had stayed on at the Museum hoping against hope for something to turn up and now all was over. But for the majority of the staff, Panizzi was the right man for the job. 'What pleases me,' he wrote to a friend, 'is that in this house all – excepting of course Madden and Hawkins who looked to the promotion themselves, are strongly for me.'[2]

Most of the papers acquiesced in the appointment of one whom many still regarded as foreigner whose sole claim to fame was that 'he shines, we are told, in society'.[3] But the next few years were to show clearly that this appointment, even though 'an example of patronage at once corrupt and detrimental to the interests of this great national institution'[4] was not so disastrous as many feared.

1. *Madden Journal*, 1, 5 March 1856.
2. Fagan, II, p. 14.
3. *Saturday Review*, 8 March 1856.
4. *Literary Gazette*, 1 March 1856.

---

seriously considered. As to Kemble, in Sir Frederic's opinion, 'I feel satisfied that his name was taken *on purpose* as a block to keep any other Officer of the Museum in the background, except Mr. P. and then to secure the appointment of the latter . . . But should I even survive this *Italian* I have no certainty of promotion . . . It makes me feel quite sick at heart.' (*Madden Journal*, 19, 25 February; 4, 5 March 1856.)

CHAPTER EIGHT

The Department of Antiquities

1820–1860

FROM the second decade of the nineteenth century onwards, the widespread interest in classical antiquities began to fade. The German scholar Millingen, who visited England in 1826, noted with surprise 'the disregard entertained in this country for Archaeological pursuits'[1] and by this he meant the study of the antiquities of Greece and Rome. The age of Adam, of Wood's *Ruins of Palmyra* and similar volumes, of the Grand Tour and of the dilettanti, was passing away. In its place was an ever-growing appreciation of non-classical antiquities, reflected the Romantic movement's love of Gothick and the exotic generally, and the nineteenth-century devotion to Biblical studies.

To begin with the emphasis was on the discovery and acquisition of imposing single objects, for the most part still from the Near East. Gradually, with acceptance of the geologists' theories of the true age of the earth and of man's place in evolution, there was a quickening interest in every aspect of non-classical antiquities. In particular from about the 1840s onwards there was a growing appreciation of the pre-historic remains being discovered in increasing quantities, and one may date the foundation of archaeology as an exact science from the middle of the century.

These changes are reflected in the history of the Department of Antiquities. For long, the men of the older generation, such as Hamilton and Panizzi, brought up in the traditions of the eighteenth century, showed a marked distaste for all non-classical antiquities and would willingly have purged the Museum of such unworthy accretions. As late as 1857, Panizzi was strongly urging 'limiting the British Museum collections of antiquities to classical or pagan art, as was in a great measure the case a few years ago' and the valuable space now occupied by medieval antiquities, 'by what are called British or Irish Antiquities, and by the ethnological collection, might thus be turned to better

1. James V. Millingen, *Ancient Unedited Monuments*. Pt. II, *Preface* p. ii.

account. It does not seem right that such valuable space should be taken up by Esquimaux dresses, canoes and hideous feather idols, broken flints and so on'.[1]

A few years before, William Vaux, then an assistant in the Department of Antiquities, subsequently the first Keeper of the Department of Coins and Medals, had written to Henry Layard, the discoverer of Nineveh, pointing out that W. R. Hamilton, one of the most influential of the Trustees, thoroughly disliked the wonderful Assyrian antiquities which were then arriving at the Museum and 'wished them at the bottom of the sea'.[2] He was determined, according to Vaux, that no suitable rooms should be provided for these treasures. Hamilton, like so many of his generation 'would not see with anything but Greek eyes',[3] but the spirit of the age was against him and the growing public demand for the acquisition and proper display of non-classical antiquities, in particular prehistoric and medieval antiquities, forced both the Trustees and their staff to turn more and more to the development of such collections.

During this period of rapid growth and expansion, the Museum was well served by the staff of the Department of Antiquities. Taylor Combe, its first Keeper, and the man responsible for the successful absorption of such notable acquisitions as the Elgin and Phigalean marbles, died prematurely in 1826 and was succeeded by Edward Hawkins, a numismatist like Combe. Hawkins presided over his department for nearly forty years and saw it become one of the greatest collections of antiquities in the world. Hampered by insufficient staff, lack of money and by the perpetual shortage of space, Hawkins had also to contend with constant interference by the Trustees. As Vaux pointed out, two or three determined Trustees could defy the expert opinion of the officers and impose their ideas or that of their own 'expert', the sculptor Richard Westmacott,[4] on the arrangement of the exhibitits, to the virtual exclusion of the Keeper, Hawkins. No wonder Sir Charles Fellows,[5] the discoverer of the Lycian marbles, who

1. *Papers relating to the Enlargement of the British Museum*, p. 43. (PP, H. of C., 1857–1858, vol. XXXIII, p. 373).
2. Add. MS. 38, 984. f. 374. Madden had been told by Hamilton that, in his opinion, Layard's discoveries 'were a parcel of rubbish'. 'How well fitted,' noted Madden sardonically, 'is this man to be a Trustee.' (*Madden Journal*, 27 August 1850.)
3. Add. MS. 38,984. f. 374.
4. Sir Richard Westmacott, 1775–1856, sculptor, designed the pediment of Smirke's portico on the theme of 'The Progress of Civilisation'.
5. Sir Charles Fellows, 1799–1860, traveller and archaeologist.

Sir Frederic Madden, K.H., Keeper of Manuscripts (1837–1866).

Austen Layard superintends the removal of the Bull of Nineveh from its original site.

Reception of the Nineveh sculptures at the British Museum.

had likewise suffered at the hands of the Trustees, detected a 'want of power'[1] in the Antiquities department.

Nevertheless, slowly and quietly, Hawkins succeeded in guiding his department towards a new conception of a museum of antiquities. Though primarily a numismatist, he kept abreast of the latest developments in this expanding field and turned his department from a cabinet of curios into the nucleus of the highly specialised departments of today.

To assist him, he had such scholars as Samuel Birch, Charles Newton, Augustus Franks, Edmund Oldfield and William Vaux.[2] Birch was a distinguished Egyptologist and orientalist, who did much to further the decipherment of hieroglyphic script and, later, of the cuneiform inscriptions of Assyria and Babylonia, and to make more widely known the discoveries of such scholars as Hincks and Rawlinson.[3] In 1844, he became Assistant Keeper. Newton entered the department as a young assistant in 1840 and was responsible for the classical antiquities until 1852. In that year he resigned from the Museum to join the Foreign Service as vice-consul at Mytilene. In this and in subsequent posts in the Near East, he explored and excavated numerous classical sites. It was he who secured for the Museum the major part of the remains of the Mausoleum at Halicarnassus and other notable examples of the art of Greece. He at length returned, on Hawkins' retirement in 1861, to head the newly created department of Greek and Roman Antiquities.

His successor as the assistant in charge of Greek and Roman Antiquities was Edmund Oldfield, a hard-working, conscientious man who was to fall foul of Panizzi and thus to see his chances of promotion vanish. Having unsuccessfully attempted in 1861 to succeed Hawkins

1. *Royal Commission, Minutes*, para. 1686.
2. Samuel Birch, 1813–1885, Egyptologist and grandson of Samuel Birch, the dramatist who, from being a pastry cook in Cornhill, had risen to be Lord Mayor of London.
Sir Charles Thomas Newton, 1816–1894, archaeologist.
Sir Augustus Wollaston Franks, KCB, 1826–1897, antiquary, FSA.
Edmund Oldfield, appointed as assistant in the Department of Antiquities in September 1848. Though conscientious and able, he was opinionated. He first angered Panizzi through criticising the bequest left to the Museum by the latter's friend, Sir William Temple, British Minister at Naples.
William Sandys Wright Vaux, 1818–1885, antiquary, who entered the Museum in 1841.
3. Rev. Edward Hincks, 1792–1866, orientalist. Simultaneously with Rawlinson, he discovered Persian cuneiform. He also did much to decipher Egyptian hieroglyphics. He was Rector of Killeyleagh, Sir Hans Sloane's birthplace.
Sir Henry Creswicke Rawlinson, Bt, KCB, 1810–1895, Assyriologist and soldier.

as Keeper, he was at length forced to resign by the implacable Principal Librarian.

Perhaps the greatest of all these men was Augustus Wollaston Franks, who had been appointed in 1851 as the first assistant specifically to take charge of British and Medieval Antiquities. Franks had an outstanding career at the Museum, being the virtual creator of the collections from which the Department of British and Medieval Antiquities eventually grew, and, moreover, one of its greatest bene- factors in the later nineteenth century. Already, though barely twenty- five, he had acquired an enviable reputation as a medievalist. At Cambridge he had laid the foundation of his great knowledge of medieval art and had subsequently staged an exhibition for the Royal Archaeological Institute in the rooms of the Society of Arts. It was this which led to his appointment to the Museum. Once there, he took a leading part in laying the foundations of the British and Medieval collections, managing with great skill the important Bernal sale for which the government had, perhaps reluctantly, granted the sum of £4,000. Franks was now recognised as one of the coming men at the Museum.

At the beginning of this period, the Department was housed in old Montagu House and in the Towneley Galleries. The Elgin marbles were still in their shed in the grounds and there was no possibility of any adequate display of the greater part of the new acquisitions. As these grew rapidly during the second decade of the century, and the proportion of large and bulky objects continued to increase, it was obvious that new accommodation was necessary. On 10 February 1821, the Trustees resolved to present a memorial to the government request- ing the early construction of additional buildings for the 'Collections of Manuscripts' and for the 'ancient Marbles'.[1] By March 1823, Smirke had produced plans for continuing the Towneley Gallery north- wards and for the construction of a northeast wing.

Thus parallel with the King's Library, another gallery would be built, forming the western side of the projected quadrilateral range of buildings which would gradually replace both the Towneley Gallery and old Montagu House to the south. In 1828 plans were drawn up for a new gallery to house the Elgin marbles, to be located in this west wing, with ultimate extensions both to the south and to the west of the main gallery. Arrangements were also made for the rooms above to be prepared for the reception of various antiquities.

1. *General Meetings, Minutes,* vol. 5, p. 1180, 10 February 1821.

By the end of that year the northern part of this wing was ready. In the meantime, Prints, still included in the Department of Antiquities, went to temporary accommodation at the southern end of the upper floor of the east wing, until their permanent quarters at the northern end were ready.

Smirke had been instructed to give priority to the erection of a new north wing to contain the library and reading rooms, and work on this section delayed for some years the extension of the Antiquities galleries.

At this time the future of that Department was in jeopardy. The perennial question was raised, of whether to send away all or part of the antiquities collections. In 1824 it was suggested that the 'marbles', to contemporary eyes representative of the highest forms of art, should be sent to join the newly created national collection of pictures, so that the national collections, both of painting and of sculpture, should be together under one roof. This scheme was abandoned for two reasons: first, because of the expense and because valuable sculptures might be damaged during the move; and secondly, that it would probably be necessary to provide 'a new repository' for the natural history collections also, since there would be no point in leaving them at Bloomsbury, alongside the national library, if the monuments of antiquity were removed.[1]

The Trustees were now anxious to provide more space for antiquities, to rebut criticism of deteriorating conditions at the Museum. Smirke had constructed a new door through the west wall of the Towneley Gallery to connect it with the recently finished western gallery, and now came the question of properly housing the Elgin marbles. On 12 March 1831, the Trustees minuted that the shed which still contained the marbles had already stood for twice the number of years for which 'its durability was calculated'.[2] They were deeply concerned at the possibility of damage to the statues and considered that it was absolutely necessary to have a new gallery as soon as possible.

There was the question of warming the galleries for the proper conservation of the marbles. Those already erected were reported as being very cold and the matter was causing concern. Smirke reassured them that the temperature was sufficiently high for the sculptures not to be harmed and a thermometer had been placed in every new gallery. In fact, the temperature was equal to and often higher than that of the old Towneley Gallery. Though there was still some dampness in the

1. Add. MS. 43, 231. ff. 135–8.
2. *Committee Minutes*, vol. 12, p. 3330, 12 March 1831.

new gallery destined for the Egyptian sculptures, it would be quite safe to place the sculptures there and, if necessary, to provide additional stoves.

Before these massive Egyptian sculptures could be brought from their old home in the Towneley Gallery, the floor of the passage connecting it to the new wing had to be strengthened. Heavy tackle, capable of lifting 16 tons, was borrowed from the Master General of the Ordnance, together with a detachment of gunners to manhandle the huge masses of sculpture into their new positions. In May 1834, the move took place with surprising ease. Hawkins praised the 'zeal and skill' of the troops in moving the sculptures, no easy task with the comparatively primitive equipment.[1]

Once the Egyptian sculptures had left the Towneley Gallery the remaining collections were re-arranged, for it was clear that the demolition of the gallery itself would not take place for some time. Sir Richard Westmacott's ideas for this were distinctly 'artistic'.[2] In August 1834 he asked the Trustees' permission 'to intermix with the Townley Collection such other objects as might produce a suitable harmony of arrangement.'[3] Hawkins, though having strong views on the matter, was not consulted and Westmacott's request was granted.

Gradually, additional galleries were added to accommodate the growing collections. Between 1834 and 1851, the space devoted to Egyptian Antiquities increased from 1773 square feet to 9,044; the Assyrian from 218 to 2,736, with other objects from Mesopotamia still pouring in; the area set aside for the classical collections was likewise more than doubled. As for the British collections, in 1834 there were none; seventeen years later they needed 4,240 feet and were increasing rapidly. Hawkins complained of the overcrowding, 'It is almost impossible to attempt correct classification, or satisfactory arrangement, which shall be instructive to visitors, or to isolate in any degree those objects to which it is desirable to direct particular attention.'[4] The buildings, even when completed, were seldom satisfactory. As Hawkins again wrote: 'Although the building is not yet finished,

1. *Committee Minutes*, vol.13, p. 3820, 14 June 1834.
2. *The Quarterly Review* is sarcastic about Sir Richard, who had long done the 'fixing and repairing of antiquities' for the Trustees and seems to have been something of an odd-job man for them. (*Quarterly Review*, CLXXV, p. 154.)
3. *Committee Minutes*, vol. 13, p. 3857, 1 August 1834. Westmacott also wanted to put 'statues of heroic size' in front of the pilasters in the Front Hall.
4. *Communications relating to the Enlargement of the British Museum*, p. 13. (PP, H. of C., 1852, vol. XXVIII, p. 201.)

scarcely a room remains as it was originally constructed, great alterations have been found necessary in almost all; the building is surrounded by inconvenient and unsightly excrescences, and it may be
asserted with truth, that Europe cannot show any building so ill adapted
for its intended purpose as the British Museum',[1] as the Royal Commission had already noted.[2]

The rebuilding of the Museum, spread over so many years, was now
virtually complete. On 19 February 1842, Smirke had reported that he
would start demolishing the northern part of old Montagu House as
soon as he had the necessary authority. Efforts were made to save the
paintings on the walls and ceilings of the great staircase, but for all
the good intentions expressed, little or nothing was done to preserve the
'begrimed, painted staircase', which had excited the admiration of
generations of visitors. In February 1845 a Mr Russell had asked permission to take down the paintings from the walls and ceilings. The
Trustees were not unsympathetic, but time was short. Though Russell
said it would take him no more than fourteen days, Smirke pointed out
that to remove the paintings as the roofs and walls were being demolished would be a difficult undertaking. Russell continued to be interested,
but it was apparently not he who finally managed to get hold of the
paintings. According to the attendant, John Saunders, the painted
ceilings and wall decorations were bought by the lodge keeper, a shrewd
old man named Sivier, who had been butler to Lord Lyndhurst. Sivier
then sold them and made a considerable profit on the transaction. Who
he sold them to is not known.[3] Madden bitterly complained of it all.
The Museum was 'in the most horrible state of noise, dirt and dust'.
He could not, however, refrain from being moved, when, in February
1849, his old house was at last pulled down, the house where his
children were born and two had died.[4]

On 11 July 1846 Sir Robert Smirke, whose relations with the
officers, and especially with Hawkins, had become increasingly strained,
resigned from the position of architect to the Trustees owing to ill
health, and was succeeded by his brother Sydney.[5] The Towneley
Gallery was now about to be demolished. Within the next few months,

1. op. cit., p. 15.
2. Royal Commission, Report, p. 32.
3. History of the Collections contained in the Natural History Departments, vol. 2, p. 81.
4. Madden Journal, 21 August 1845, 15 February 1849.
5. Sydney Smirke, 1798–1877, architect. He restored the Savoy Chapel and completed Burlington House exhibition galleries.

additional galleries were erected over its site, extending the Elgin Room southward and communicating with the southern wing and the new front hall. Insufficient as the room still was, this for the moment was all that would be made available.

The first notable expansion in the Department of Antiquities was in Egyptian acquisitions. Almost from the beginning the Museum had contained some specimens and these had been greatly reinforced by the objects captured by the army from the French. With the coming of peace and more settled conditions in Egypt under the firm rule of Mehemet Ali,[1] a renewed interest arose in Egyptian remains, heightened by the fashionable use of Egyptian motifs in both architecture and furniture.

In 1815 Henry Salt,[2] who had first made his name as a traveller in Abyssinia, then incredibly remote, was appointed British Consul-General in Egypt. Salt was on friendly terms with W. R. Hamilton, who had written the standard work on Egyptian antiquities. He excited Salt's interest in Egyptian remains and, as a result, the latter had been asked by his patron Lord Mountnorris[3] to collect objects for that nobleman's own private museum before taking up his new post. Salt also considered 'as had Elgin' that part of his duty as the representative of Western civilisation in a barbarous land was to rescue whatever remains of the past he could and ensure their safety by transporting them back to England. So Salt was delighted when he was approached by Joseph Banks with a request to form a collection of Egyptian antiquities on behalf of the Museum. He settled in Cairo and set about the task energetically, spending large sums of money out of his own pocket. There can be little doubt that Salt believed he had been officially authorised and that anything he collected would be accepted without question by the Trustees. This turned out to be a misapprehension that was to embarrass Salt considerably.

For the practical work of excavation, Salt engaged an Italian, Giovanni Belzoni,[4] who, after a varied career (which included appearing as the 'Patagonian Samson' at Sadler's Wells, and as a strong man at Bartholomew Fair), had found his way to Egypt and had there attempted

1. Mehemet or Mohammed Ali, 1769–1849. Mehemet is the Turkish form.
2. Henry Salt, 1780–1827, traveller and antiquary.
3. George, Earl of Mountnorris, 1771–1844, styled Viscount Valentia, 1793–1816, FRS, FSA.
4. Giovanni Belzoni, 1778–1823, engineer, actor and explorer.

unsuccessfully to construct irrigation machinery for the gardens of the all-powerful Mehemet Ali. Belzoni, a giant of a man, developed a flair as an excavator and from his knowledge of engineering, was able to move the huge masses of stone which the exploitation of his discoveries usually involved.

The first object which Salt authorised Belzoni to move was the colossal head of Ramesses II, known to contemporary antiquaries as the Young Memnon. In 1816 Belzoni succeeded in transporting the enormous object, weighing many tons, from its resting place near Luxor down to the banks of the Nile and thence by boat to Alexandria. There the head, with numerous other antiquities which Belzoni and others had collected for Salt, was stored at the consulate, awaiting shipment to England.

Salt now engaged in a somewhat acrimonious correspondence with the Museum. Banks, despite his request to Salt, had concluded that it would be unwise for the Museum to accept any more Egyptian antiquities and had, moreover, become prejudiced against Salt himself. In the opinion of many, Egyptian antiquities were not 'Fine Art', and were not fit to be placed amongst 'the grand works of the Towneley Gallery', as Banks told Salt in a somewhat unkind letter.[1]

Nevertheless, in May 1819 Salt offered the whole of his collection to the Museum, hoping to be reimbursed for his considerable expenses. Piece by piece, these precious relics were brought to England and again offered to the Trustees. Meanwhile, in Egypt Belzoni was still discovering remarkable remains, amongst them the fine seated statue in black granite of Amenophis III (now in the main Egyptian Gallery of the Museum), on which he carved his name. Belzoni's request to the Trustees to be allowed to collect antiquities specifically for the Museum was turned down, even though the Trustees had made the first approaches to the explorer.

On Belzoni's return to England in 1820, many of the antiquities which he had discovered and brought back from Egypt were exhibited in the Egyptian Hall in Piccadilly, which had been given an 'Egyptian' façade when built in 1812. Here Belzoni's discoveries were shown to admiring crowds for some months. Salt, back in Cairo, seemed to be forgotten. Despite his flair for publicity and his gifts as a showman, Belzoni's real contribution to the nascent science of Egyptology must not be underestimated. His book *Narrative of the Operations and Recent*

1. Banks to Salt, 14 February 1819. Quoted in Salt, vol. 2, p. 303 and in Banks, p. 731.

Discoveries within the Pyramids, Temples, Tombs, and Excavations in Egypt and Nubia was a great and deserved success. As the *Quarterly Review* pointed out, it was a valuable contribution to the study of ancient remains. 'We may implicitly trust his pen and his pencil in what he has described and delineated.'[1] Though he was no scholar, he is justly considered as a pioneer of subsequent antiquarian research. His keen inquiring mind, allied to assiduous and meticulous field work, laid the foundations or greater work.

Throughout the years 1820 and 1821 successive batches of antiquities arrived at Bloomsbury, most of them extremely valuable. Salt's London agent had instructions to deposit them at the Museum, pending their sale to the Trustees. But the reception given to these priceless antiquities, including the head of the Young Memnon, was lukewarm. It was even decided at one time to put the head, one of the masterpieces of ancient art, out into the courtyard of Montagu House, despite the disastrous effects the atmosphere might have on it.

Salt, greatly perturbed at the expenses he had incurred, wished to offer the whole of his collection to the Museum, except for the statues, which he hoped would go to the Royal Academy. The price he put on the collection was £8,000, a figure, as he admitted to W. R. Hamilton, which was mere guesswork. Hamilton, rather rashly, showed Salt's valuation to Banks. The old man exploded with anger, under the impression that Salt was trying to make a fortune out of his discoveries and to swindle the Trustees by unloading on them worthless trash. The recent acquisition of the Elgin marbles had seemed to the unthinking a very costly business – 'a parcel of old rubbish for which ten thousand pounds would be an exorbitant price'[2] – and here was another greedy collector trying to make a fortune from the public. And these statues were not even Greek! Salt in desperation, decided to accept any sum that the Museum might care to offer. He would be satisfied, he said, with a mere £4,000 for the lot. Ellis wrote to his friend Bliss in January 1823 l5,000 does not seem too much considering the loss of Interest and risques he has sustained.[3] Hamilton and the more friendly Trustees succeeded in smoothing things over. Charles Yorke told Banks it would be an 'indelible disgrace'[4] if the collection were

1. *Quarterly Review*, XLVII, p. 140.
2. Salt, vol. 2, p. 302.
3. Add. MS. 34, 568. f. 521.
4. Quoted in Mayes, p. 268. Charles Philip Yorke, 1764–1834, politician, half-brother to Philip Yorke, third Earl of Hardwicke.

permitted to go to some foreign power. Yet Salt's treasures were still piling up at the Museum, whilst the Trustees did nothing and his offer was almost forgotten. Salt's agent in London wrote to him: 'So much has been said of *economy*, and so little in *approbation* of Egyptian antiquities, that I was almost afraid you would be left in *the lurch* entirely' and he bitterly condemned the Trustees' 'want of interest in Egyptian antiquities'.[1]

In August 1821 the alabaster sarcophagus of Sethos I arrived in England. Belzoni, who had discovered it in the Second Pyramid, now claimed to be a part-owner and produced an alleged agreement with Salt to support his claim. He asked the latter's agent not to deliver the sarcophagus to the Museum, as he wished to exhibit it with his other discoveries at the Egyptian Hall before depositing it at the Museum. On 8 December 1821, the Trustees wrote to Salt 'requesting him to specify the Persons to whom any article in the Collection not intended for the Museum may belong',[2] and to value such part of the collection as he proposed to offer for purchase. Belzoni's request was likewise turned down and the sarcophagus was duly delivered to the Museum. The controversy continued, both Belzoni and Salt being worried about their discovery's eventual fate. On 11 May 1822 the Trustees decided not to keep it 'on account of the very high value put upon it by Mr Belzoni',[3] but tentatively accepted the remainder of Salt's collection. A few weeks later they offered £2,000 for this, accepting without question Belzoni's valuation of the sarcophagus as alone worth £3,000. Salt's agent reluctantly accepted the offer, and Belzoni was informed that the sarcophagus could now be removed whenever he wished. It might, however, continue to remain at the Museum 'as a deposit'. But Belzoni had gone off to West Africa to explore the upper reaches of the Niger, and there, on 3 December 1823, he died.

After the Museum had been given a final chance, the sarcophagus of Sethos I was sold to the architect and collector, Sir John Soane, whose museum in Lincoln's Inn Fields it still adorns.

Eventually, Salt got his £2,000, but he remained, with good reason, embittered by these lengthy controversies. However, thanks to the efforts of Salt and Belzoni, the galleries of the Museum now had many fine pieces of statuary that might otherwise have perished unseen on the banks of the Nile. Besides the head of the 'Young Memnon', which

1. Bingham Richards to Salt, 22 February 1823. Salt, p. 355.
2. *General Meetings, Minutes*, vol. 5, p. 1187, 8 December 1821.
3. *op. cit.*, vol. 5, p. 1196, 11 May 1822.

Salt and Burckhardt[1] had jointly presented in 1817, the statues of the queens from Abu Simbel, the granite figures of Sekhmet, the colossal head and arm of Tuthmosis III, were brought to the Museum by the efforts of these two indefatigable collectors.

These events have been dealt with at length since they typify the difficulties nineteenth-century collectors in the field faced when dealing with an institution such as the British Museum. Most of the Trustees of the day were enlightened and highly educated men, with a proper idea of the duties which they owed both to scholarship and to the general public. Nevertheless, they were often inflexible in dealing with the many demands which the expanding science of archaeology was to make on their limited resources. Today it was Salt and his Egyptian antiquities; tomorrow Layard and the wonders of Assyria; then the prehistoric and medieval acquisitions of the latter part of the century. The Trustees, reared in the strict Graeco-Roman classical tradition of the eighteenth century, were not always capable of appreciating the merits of the collections now being offered to them with bewildering frequency. That the Museum acquired so much is a tribute to the patience and public spiritedness of so many who worked in the field on its behalf and the devotion of the Museum's staff, of whose special knowledge and experience the Trustees were only too often reluctant to avail themselves.

The next name in the field of Eastern exploration with which the Museum is connected is that of Claudius Rich.[2] Rich possessed an astonishing facility for learning difficult and obscure languages, in particular oriental ones. After obtaining a cadetship in the East India Company in 1814, he set out for India, but never reached it. Instead he travelled through the lands of the Near East, perfecting his knowledge of Turkish, Arabic and other local languages. At the age of twenty-four he was appointed Resident in Baghdad. Whilst there, he began his

1. Johann Ludwig Burckhardt, 1784–1817, explorer and orientalist, born in Lausanne, Switzerland. He travelled under the auspices of Banks and the African Association, and succeeded in making the pilgrimage to Mecca. He died in Cairo in 1817, leaving his collection of Arabic manuscripts to Cambridge University.
2. Claudius James Rich, 1787–1820, traveller. His death from cholera was due to his courageous decision not to leave Shiraz, where he had gone to study the ancient remains in the neighbourhood, and where a violent epidemic was then raging. He 'continued nobly to exert himself to quiet the alarm of the inhabitants, and to assist the sick and dying'. On 4 October 1820, he himself fell a victim to the disease and died the following day. (*Narrative of a Residence in Koordistan*, vol. 1, p. XXX.)

collection of oriental manuscripts, for which he was most remembered in his own day, and, more important, an impressive collection of medals, coins, gems and engraved tablets found at Babylon and other sites in Mesopotamia.

It was Rich who first realised that the mounds which litter the flat plains of the Tigris and the Euphrates probably concealed the remains of cities dating back to the remotest antiquity.

At first he, like other travellers before him, had considered the mounds to be of a much later period, assuming them to mark the places where the ancient Persians had exposed their dead. The 'small silver ornaments' discovered on or near the mounds, which he rightly took to be artificial, seemed to him to be of comparatively late date, Sassanian or a little earlier. Shortly before his early death from cholera in 1820, he visited Mosul and explored the great mounds close by at Kuyunjik and Nebi Yannus. Rich guessed correctly that these covered the site of the ancient city of Nineveh, a remarkable guess on such little evidence, considering that later explorers with far greater knowledge, such as Botta and Layard seem to have located it elsewhere.

As he explored the ruins and was shown or told of huge inscribed slabs found there by the natives and then mutilated and destroyed as 'devils', Rich became convinced that large buildings, in all likelihood the palaces of ancient kings, lay buried beneath the mounds. By good fortune many of the inscribed bricks, cylinders and other small objects now gathered by Rich came to the Museum, along with his fine collection of manuscripts and were the virtual foundation of the Museum's collection of Babylonian and Assyrian antiquities.[1]

For it must not be forgotten that until the 1840s almost nothing was known of the great civilisations of the ancient east, save for brief and often highly inaccurate references to them in the works of the classical writers and in Holy Scripture. Work was slowly progressing on the decipherment of the hieroglyphic script of Ancient Egypt, thanks largely to the identical inscription in Greek and in Egyptian on the Museum's Rosetta Stone, but almost nothing was yet known of the cuneiform script in which the records of the peoples of Babylon, Assyria, Sumer and other civilisations of antiquity, unguessed at in early nineteenth-century Europe, were written. This was to be the work of the next generation of scholars and explorers: Botta, Layard, Rawlinson,

---

1. In May 1825 the Trustees ordered that 'Mr Rich's smaller Babylonian antiquities' were to be housed in a 'Table Case'. At that date this was virtually the whole extent of the collection. (*Committee Minutes*, vol. 10, p. 296, 14 May 1825.)

Hincks, Rassam and others. In this unveiling of hitherto unsuspected civilisations, the Museum played a dominant role.

In the words of Sir Wallis Budge, for long the Keeper of the Museum's Department of Egyptian and Assyrian Antiquities, 'The science of Assyriology was founded by Englishmen and developed entirely by the Trustees of the British Museum and their staff. The English built the main edifice of Assyriology, and other nations constructed the outlying buildings. The Trustees took over the task of excavating the ruins of the great cities of Assyria from Stratford Canning, and built the galleries that now hold the collection of sculptures and other antiquities which were acquired by Layard, Loftus, Ross, Rassam, George Smith and later workers'.[1] This eulogy, while manifestly unfair to the pioneering work of the great French explorer, Botta, and perhaps to Layard himself, emphasises the predominant share which the British Museum, through its Department of Antiquities, took in the discovery and popularisation of the antiques of the ancient Middle East.

Rich's work had largely been mere curio hunting. What brought about a revolution in the whole conception of the history of the ancient world was excavation on a large and sustained scale and the decipherment of the languages in which the tablets, seals and inscriptions, found now in increasing numbers, were written. By identifying the kings and rulers, the peoples and the nations, whose palaces and temples were being unearthed from the desert sands, it was possible to write a new and unsuspected chapter in the history of mankind. This was to be the work of Henry Austin Layard[2] and of Henry Rawlinson, assisted by many other explorers and scholars, both within and outside the Museum.

Although the Trustees had now secured, at a very favourable rate, Salt's great collection, 'at no time', it had seemed to the disappointed Salt, had they 'evinced any great desire to possess the Collection nor to act with the slightest degree of liberality, their proceedings uniformly bearing a much stronger affinity to the trading spirit of a retail dealer than to the broad and enlightened views that ought to influence the managers of a splendid national institution'.[3]

During the next few years further valuable antiquities, mostly papyri and small objects (in particular the Sams collection and a second Salt collection which the Trustees purchased at Sotheby's on Hawkins'

1. Budge, p. ix.
2. Sir Austen Henry Layard, 1817–1894, explorer, diplomatist and politician.
3. Salt, vol. 2, p. 273.

earnest recommendation for £4,800), were secured. One of the few large specimens destined for the Museum, a finely carved stone sarcophagus found by Colonel Howard Vyse in the Pyramid of Mycerinus, was lost at sea in 1838 on its way to England, whilst a sphinx, obtained for the Museum in Egypt, was destroyed in a fire at Plymouth docks, its arrival, by some oversight, never having been reported to the Trustees. Two magnificent granite lions from the temple of Amenophis III at Soleb in Nubia were, however, presented by Lord Prudhoe in 1835 and form one of the main attractions of the Egyptian sculpture gallery.

Now further attempts were made to rationalise the custody of the various collections. In September 1836, Prints, nominally under Hawkins' charge, but with its own Keeper, was made a separate department. In July 1836 the Ethnographical collections and 'artificial curiosities', part of the Natural History Department, were transferred to the Department of Antiquities where they remained for many years. Egyptian papyri, of which there were now some outstanding specimens, notably from the Sams and second Salt collections, still formed part of the Department of Manuscripts.

In December 1838 Madden began a catalogue of all the papyri then in the Museum, part of his energetic policy of knowing exactly what was in his department. As usual, though, Madden had much to complain of. In May 1839 he read in the *Gentleman's Magazine* that a month before the Trustees had been authorised by the government to purchase some valuable papyri. Sir Frederic was extremely angry. 'This is a deplorable proof of the non-intercourse between the Trustees and their officers! I think, in common courtesy, the Secretary might have mentioned it . . . I wish I was at liberty to give the public a *statement* how affairs are *managed* in this Museum.'[1]

However, Madden was soon to be rid of this particular worry. In December 1839 the Trustees had 'felt some doubt as to the Department to which the Papyri may most conveniently and properly be attached'. Ellis was ordered to consult both Madden and Hawkins about what to do with them. The following May on the grounds that there was insufficient room to display them in his Department, Madden was induced to hand over to Hawkins' assistant, Samuel Birch, the whole of the Hieroglyphic, Hieratic and Demotic Papyri. 'They are therefore,' he noted, 'henceforth bona fidé part of the Department of Antiquities.'[2]

1. *Madden Journal*, 31 May 1839.
2. *Madden Journal*, 8 May 1840. *Committee Minutes*, vol.18, pp. 5254, 5393, 14 December 1839, 13 June 1840.

Greek papyri were retained and to this day form part of the collections of the Department of Manuscripts.

Much else in various branches of the department's activities was now acquired. Perhaps the most outstanding was the collection of vases and similar objects formed by Lucien Bonaparte, Prince of Canino. This magnificent collection was reported on by Hawkins in the most enthusiastic terms: 'The more he examined them,' he wrote, 'the more their value appeared to increase.'[1] The Trustees forthwith asked the Treasury for £12,000 to buy the whole, but met with a firm refusal. No more than £2,000 would be granted to purchase a few of the finest specimens. Hawkins was told to buy what he could at the forthcoming Canino sale in Paris.

Two years later Hawkins reported that the Canino vases were still available. In his opinion it was a unique opportunity to acquire an unrivalled collection. The Trustees asked for £7,000, but the Treasury were still adamant. However, in March 1843 a considerable number of vases and other valuable objects were obtained from the Princesse de Canino for £1,515.

The Greek collections now added the so-called Lycian marbles, discovered at Xanthos in Asia Minor by Charles Fellows[2] and consisting mostly of tombs and other memorials of the kings of Lycia. In March 1839 Hawkins showed the Trustees engravings of sculptures and inscriptions discovered by Fellows and said that immediate steps could be taken by the Navy to transport them to England. The necessary *firman* or official permission obtained from the Turkish government, the marbles were to embark for Malta with the cooperation of the Mediterranean Fleet.

Hawkins, in his eagerness had written privately to the Treasury to enlist their aid. The Trustees were horrified at this unwelcome initiative, and Hawkins was reprimanded. At all events the Treasury refused to advance any money and all that was available was about £400 promised by the Trustees. In December 1842 Hawkins urged that the ruins and rubbish round the Temple be searched for the many other objects which it was confidently believed were there and reported that the

1. *Committee Minutes*, vol.15, p. 4507, 25 April 1837. Hawkins succeeded in obtaining some very fine specimens at £1,103. 5s. A few more may have come in subsequent collections.
2. Sir Charles Fellows had led four expeditions to Asia Minor to secure the sculptures and other remains from the ancient city of Xanthos, the capital of Lycia, which he had first discovered in 1838.

Xanthian Marbles had at last arrived in England. Now came a bitter controversy between Fellows and the Trustees and their artistic adviser, Richard Westmacott. Fellows, as he was the only one who had seen the Lycian sculptures *in situ* and afterwards excavated them, claimed that he knew considerably more about their arrangement than did Sir Richard. An acrimonious correspondence ensued, in which Fellows declared that Westmacott's arrangement was a 'misrepresentation', that unrelated objects were gathered together pell-mell, and that Westmacott was 'about to pile together the monuments in some instances and to separate them in others, without any knowledge of my object in selecting them'.[1] The Trustees supported Westmacott; Hawkins, whose son Rohde Hawkins,[2] had accompanied Fellows as draughtsman on the expedition, discreetly backed Fellows. The matter dragged on for several years and was one of the subjects investigated by the Royal Commission. Most informed opinion considered that Westmacott had made a mess of the arrangement, and in addition that it was unfair to the staff that important acquisitions should be arranged without any reference to them.[3]

The Antiquities Department was now to suffer what for a time seemed an irreparable loss. On 7 February 1845, a young man named William Lloyd, for no discoverable purpose, picked up what Madden described as 'one of the large Babylonian sculptured stones' and brought it down on the glass case containing the Portland Vase 'and dashed the Vase, together with the glass cover over it to atoms'. 'This,' Madden went on, 'is the result of exhibiting such valuable and unique specimens of art to the mob.' In his opinion a facsimile should have been on view. After all, 'the mob of visitors' took no real notice of it and would probably have prefereed the Babylonian stone which smashed it. 'It is really monstrous to witness such monstrous destruction.'[4] A correspondent, the Rev. William Shepherd, wrote to Panizzi in a similar strain. 'I warrant you swore lustily at the smasher of the Portland Vase. I wish you had throttled the rascal. Can the vase be repaired?'[5] Luckily it could and was. The culprit had been arrested and

1. Letter from Fellows to the Trustees, 1 August 1845. *Royal Commission, Appendix* p. 405.
2. Major Rohde Hawkins, 1820–1884, third son of Edward Hawkins, architect.
3. *Quarterly Review*, CLXXV, pp. 154, 155.
4. *Madden Journal*, 7 February 1845.
5. Rev. William Shepherd, 1768–1847. Shepherd to Panizzi, 26 February 1845. (Add. MS. 36,715. f. 217.)

taken before the Bow Street magistrate, Mr Jardine, where it was found that there was no law under which he might be charged for the destruction. In consequence, he was fined £3 for the glass case, or in default of payment, two months' hard labour. As the miscreant was penniless, he was immediately dispatched to the house of correction. Two days later, however, a friend paid the fine and he was set free. The embarrassment of the Trustees was great. The Vase was, of course, not even their property, but on permanent loan from the Duke of Portland. It had been broken into more than two hundred pieces and to repair such a fragile object seemed hopeless. Nevertheless, the skill and patience of the Museum repairer Doubleday triumphed, and by March 1846 it was back on exhibition. Madden noted 'He has certainly restored it very wonderfully & really deserves the 25£ the Trustees presented to him.'[1]

The safety of the collections was always a nightmare, and the gravest danger that of a widespread fire. One of the witnesses before the Select Committee of 1836, Henry Petrie, Keeper of the Records in Tower, declared, 'If I were one of the persons in charge of the Museum, I should never go to bed without trembling.'[2] These fears became all the greater during the 1840s when violence was daily expected from the Chartists. A fire at the Tower of London was widely suspected to be due to arson and extra precautions were taken to protect the Museum collections. Sir Henry Ellis, for once, was sceptical. 'I really see no motive for incendiaries to attack this place,' he commented. The fire at the Tower was, in his opinion, much more likely to be due to an overheated flue than to arson and the precautions against fire which had been taken in the new buildings were likely to be entirely adequate.[3] The Trustees, however, were still worried and were not really satisfied until they had at length obtained their own fireman, complete with brass helmet, to watch over their belongings.

The Department of Antiquities continued acquiring both Egyptian and Greek antiquities, despite the strict prohibition in 1835 by the Greek government of the export of classical antiquities. In addition to the Lycian Marbles, the Department had received in September

1. *Madden Journal*, 24 March 1846. The vase was nominally valued at £1,000. The culprit stated that he 'was suffering from a kind of nervous excitement – a continual fear of everything I saw'. The name he gave was probably false. A former student of Trinity College, Dublin, he was at this time living at a coffee-house in Long Acre and earning a living as a scene painter.
2. *Select Committee*, 1836, *Minutes*, para. 4979. Henry Petrie, 1768–1842, antiquary. He was made Keeper of the Records in the Tower of London in 1819.
3. Add. MS. 34,574. f. 345.

through the good offices of Stratford Canning, Ambassador to the Sublime Porte,[1] the first sculptures to be recovered from Bodrum, in Asia Minor, the ancient Halicarnassus, a site from which further treasures were to be obtained for the Museum by Charles Newton during the next twenty years.

Small but valuable acquisitions of coins and medals, still perhaps the staple diet of the department, were obtained throughout this period. Coins, moved to a new Medal Room from their old quarters in Montagu House (in 1845), were under William Vaux, later the first Keeper of the separate department.

Little has been said so far of the numismatic collections which by the 1840s were on their way to achieving the outstanding position they now hold. To the founding collections of Cotton and Sloane were added the collection of Roman and other coins bequeathed by Cracherode in 1799, the coins and medals given in 1818 by Miss Banks and her sister-in-law, Lady Dorothea Banks, wife of Sir Joseph, and the magnificent collection of Greek coins given to the Museum in 1824 by Richard Payne Knight. To these were added the royal collection of coins and medals which came with the King's Library and was deposited in the Museum on 28 May 1825, and a fine series of oriental coins presented in 1834 by Dr William Marsden. Amongst the collections purchased in the first half of the nineteenth century was that of Barré Charles Roberts, mostly Anglo-Gallic coins, that of Charles Towneley, acquired in 1814 after the purchase of his marbles, and that of Claudius Rich, whose oriental coins were obtained in 1825.

Coins, classical antiquities and those of ancient Egypt were thus well represented by the middle of the century. This was not so with the class of antiquities losely known as 'British Antiquities' – relics of the prehistoric past, Roman Britain and post-Roman and medieval times in this country and Western Europe generally. These were on the whole despised by the older generation, and it must not be forgotten that little was known of the prehistoric ages. Although the system of the 'Three Ages' was being developed in Denmark[2] and the foundations of modern prehistoric archaeology firmly laid, ignorance on the subject was

1. Stratford Canning, Viscount Stratford de Redcliffe, 1786–1880, a cousin of George Canning, the Prime Minister. For the greater part of his official life he was the all-powerful envoy of Great Britain to the Turkish Government.
2. The system of the successive 'Ages', Stone, Bronze and Iron, had been worked out by Danish archaeologists during the first half of the nineteenth century and had revolutionised the study of prehistory.

still widespread, and all pre-Roman remains confounded together as the work of the 'Ancient Britons'.

But pressure was building up on a reluctant Board of Trustees to take a greater interest in the antiquities of their own and other lands, till now scarcely represented at the Museum. A few such had come with the earlier collections. The chance of acquiring others had been frequently turned down, for instance an offer of Scandinavian antiquities in December 1834, or of the splendid silver-gilt salver said to be the work of Cellini offered for £2,000 and refused by the Trustees in 1832. Years later, according to Vaux, the opportunity to obtain a valuable collection of early medieval antiquities was lost because a Trustee, Dundas, 'did not want a heap of Saxon antiquities in the Museum',[1] whilst in November 1836, despite the remonstrances of Hawkins, they had refused to buy a fine collection of Oriental antiquities. It was still the 'artificial curiosities' of the past rather than the fruits of scientific exploration which aroused popular interest and were likely to find their way into the Museum. Thus, the Trustees were offered in December 1835 the sedan chair of the Grand Master of the Knights of Malta, which they refused and George III's coronation anointing cap and gloves which they accepted, possibly recollecting all that monarch had done for the Museum.

Some very strange objects certainly did come. In December 1842 Madden noted that a mediaeval German 'chastity belt' was being presented to the Museum by the extremely puritanical Earl of Aberdeen. 'How very odd', thought Madden, that such an 'unbending person' as Lord Aberdeen should be giving such a curious object.[2]

But things were changing slowly. On 15 July 1837 the Trustees were informed that a collection of English antiquities would be presented if a special room were available for them. They welcomed the proposal – the Commons Committee of 1836 had emphasised the need for such a collection, which the Trustees admitted was practically non-existent – and instructed Hawkins to find a suitable room. Hawkins reported in November that he had found somewhere, the old Mummy Room, empty once the Egyptian antiquities could be moved from it to their new galleries.

1. This was the Faussett collection of late Roman and early Saxon coins and other objects from Kent. Despite strong appeals from prominent archaeologists, the Trustees refused the extra £500 necessary. (Vaux to Layard, ? April 1856. Add. MS. 38,984. f. 374.)
2. *Madden Journal*, 1 December 1842.

But room to display further collections was lacking. In November 1842 the Trustees refused to accept a display of Gothic architecture, for the most part English, from the earliest to the latest periods, unless they were given new buildings in which to exhibit it. One cannot help feeling also that they considered it was none of their business. Hawkins was all the while pressing them to form a worthwhile collection of British antiquities and suggested that the extensive excavations then taking place for new railway lines presented a favourable opportunity. Two large rooms should in his opinion be exclusively devoted to such antiquities. The Trustees were not so sure, but they decided to accept further collections now being offered by Lord Prudhoe.[1]

There was still very little on show. A description of the Museum published as late as 1850 recounts that all the antiquities of ancient Britain and Gaul were contained in four cases in one room, whilst a further thirteen cases displayed 'various British and Medieval Antiquities temporarily deposited in this room'. The writer regrets that the collection was not yet rich enough to fill an apartment of its own. On the floor in the middle of the room were 'models of various British cromlechs', reluctantly accepted by the Trustees some years before, together with a model of the churches of the Holy Sepulchre and of the Nativity, a Chinese bell, a model of an Indian temple, one of HMS *Victory*, together with a piece of that ship's timber with a 40-pound shot in it, and a plaster cast by Flaxman of the shield of Achilles.[2]

But such displays were almost a thing of the past. Criticism of the Trustees' offhand way with British antiquities was mounting. Two of the Trustees, W. R. Hamilton and Lord Mahon,[3] were cross-examined by the Royal Commission on the subject. They evinced little interest. Hamilton, for instance, when asked whether he had ever turned his attention to the question of extending and improving the collection of British antiquities in the Museum, replied succinctly, 'I have not.' He continued by saying that such a collection 'ought to be rather for the improvement of the fine arts than merely as a historical collection of

1. *Committee Minutes*, vol. 22, p. 6827, 13 December 1845.
Algernon Percy, Baron Prudhoe, 1792–1865, Rear-Admiral, FSA, President of the Royal Institute. He succeeded his brother as Duke of Northumberland in 1847.
2. D. Masson, *The British Museum, Historical and Descriptive*, pp. 43, 48, 49.
3. Philip Henry, fifth Earl Stanhope, 1805–1875, known as Lord Mahon until succeeding to the title on the death of his father in 1855. He was a distinguished historian and principal founder of the National Portrait Gallery.

objects', the outlook of the connoisseur rather than that of the archaeologist. He agreed it would be desirable to form a collection of British antiquities 'if there were a room in the Museum and an appropriate place' for such a collection, but proposed to do little about it himself.[1] His fellow Trustee, Lord Mahon, President of the Society of Antiquaries, was equally evasive. 'No,' he replied, 'I have never turned my attention to it in any practical or detailed form, beyond having a general belief and impression that such an arrangement might be very desirable; but into the questions of space, of expense, or of arrangements, I have never had occasion to enter.'[2]

Such polite avoidance of the question would no longer be sufficient. Interest in non-classical antiquities, in particular prehistoric ones, was growing ever stronger. Although not prepared to go as far as an eminent Danish antiquarian, that not one or two but twenty rooms should be devoted to British antiquities, the Commissioners were clearly of the opinion that more must be done.[3] They agreed with Hawkins that an additional department, with an officer of its own and a supporting staff, was necessary to do justice to such a collection. They agreed with various expert witnesses that there was virtually no collection of national antiquities in the Museum, 'nor can we doubt but that great accessions would flow in if such were invited for the avowed purpose of forming a connected series of relics to illustrate the arts and manners of the various races which have occupied our soil. We can do no other than speak of such an object as one to which the liberality of Government might be directed with unquestionable advantage'.[4]

The Trustees, in their report on the Royal Commission's recommendations do not even mention British antiquities, though they claimed to have noticed and commented on 'all the main observations and suggestions'[5] of the Commissioners. However, things were soon to change. In 1851 Hawkins decided that a proper room in the new building must be set aside for the exhibition of British antiquities. As a distinguished numismatist, he recognised the interest and value of pre-Roman British coins, but he needed someone specifically to look after this branch of the varied collections under his charge, and having a

1. *Royal Commission, Minutes*, para. 10564, 10574.
2. *op. cit.*, para. 10833.
3. *Report*, p. 38.
4. *op. cit.*, p. 39.
5. *Communications addressed to the Treasury by the Trustees*, p. 8. (PP, H. of C., 1850, vol. XXXIII, p. 247.)

vacancy for an assistant engaged a young man of twenty-five, Augustus Wollaston Franks, one of the most remarkable men who have ever served the Museum. In the fifteen years before the establishment of a separate Department of British and Mediaeval Antiquities in 1866, of which he was the first Keeper, Franks did much for that collection. A man of considerable wealth and knowledge, with great powers of connoisseurship, he acquired for the infant collection many objects of outstanding importance.

To many people the outstanding excavations of the 1840s were the discoveries of Layard and of his successors in Mesopotamia. Rich had discovered tablets and other small objects of great antiquity in the mounds near Mosul and, but for his death, would undoubtedly have discovered more. His collection – much of it purchased from the native discoverers – contained clay cylinders, tablets, a sculptured stele with the curiously attired figure of a king, all inscribed in cuneiform characters, an inscribed boundary stone, and small miscellaneous objects.[1] These, in two 'glass tables' and on certain low shelves, were the foundations of the great collection of Assyrian and Babylonian remains which the Museum now possesses.[2]

The man who was to make the British Museum supreme throughout the world for its collections of the art of the ancient peoples of Mesopotamia, was Henry Austen Layard. Together with Henry Rawlinson, a decipherer of cuneiform script and an archaeologist in his own right, Layard laid the foundations of the new science of Assyriology. Besides he conveyed by his popular writings a widespread knowledge of the East and a realisation of the antiquity and complexity of its history. Layard's methods of excavation may be questioned, as may those of other pioneers, but it was his flair for discovery, his enthusiasm and courage, that saved so many relics of the great civilisations of Babylon and Assyria, which would otherwise have perished.

Layard was born at Paris in 1817 and educated for the most part in France and Italy. After studying for the law, he decided to set out for Ceylon overland, travelling through the wild countries of the Levant, Mesopotamia and Persia. It was on this journey that he first caught

1. A few small objects had been received prior to the arrival of the Rich Collection. Thus, as early as February 1801, Mr Penneck, Keeper of the Reading Room, had presented 'a Brick with an Inscription on it, from the banks of the Euphrates'. (*Committee Minutes*, vol. 8, p. 2205, 14 February 1801.) A few Archaemenid sculptures had been presented by Sir Gore Ouseley and Lord Aberdeen in 1825.
2. Layard, *Nineveh and its Remains*, p. 3.

sight of those mysterious mounds which, it was increasingly realised, must cover the remains of the vanished civilisations of the Assyrians and Babylonians, of whom almost nothing was known. As Layard said, traces of these peoples had been largely lost. 'A deep mystery hangs over Assyria, Babylonia, and Chaldaea. With these names are linked great nations and great cities dimly shadowed forth in history; mighty ruins in the midst of deserts.'[1] It was Layard's destiny to lift the veil from these 'mighty ruins' and bring forth a multitude of treasures which would dispel for ever the ignorance in which this portion of human history had hitherto been wrapped.

After numerous romantic adventures, Layard obtained a post under Sir Stratford Canning, the all-powerful British Ambassador at Constantinople. In 1845 he learned of the remarkable discoveries being made by Paul Botta,[2] the French vice-consul at Mosul, on the mound at Khorsabad, ten miles from that city. Botta, who had arrived at Mosul in 1840 with instructions from the French government to collect manuscripts and antiquities, had first attempted to excavate Kuyunjik, the mound opposite Mosul. Having found nothing, he turned his attention to Khorsabad, and within a few weeks had uncovered the ruins of the magnificent palace of Sargon II, King of Assyria. Hundreds of yards of sculptured slabs, colossal winged man-headed bulls and other marvels now stood revealed.

Layard had been informed of Botta's discoveries and remembered his previous visits to these mysterious mounds. He urged Stratford Canning to let him go to Mosul and start excavations there before all the treasures had been carried off by the French. In October 1845 Layard at length persuaded the Ambassador to let him go to Mosul to carry out an investigation that was not to take longer than two months. With strict instructions to avoid all trouble, Layard went as agent of Canning who paid all the costs of the expedition. As Budge pointed out, 'but for the promptitude of Stratford Canning and his public-spirited behaviour on this occasion, the splendid collection of Ashurnasirpal's sculptures which adorn the British Museum would now be filling a gallery in the Louvre'.[3]

On 8 November 1845, Layard reached Khorsabad and found shelter for the night in an Arab village. After a troubled sleep, during which he dreamed of 'palaces underground, of gigantic monsters, of sculptured

1. Layard, *Nineveh and its Remasns*, p. 3.
2. Paul Emile Botta, 1802–1870, archaeologist and diplomat.
3. Budge, p. 68.

figures, and endless inscriptions',[1] he awoke to find that his host had returned with six helpers. The mound of Nimrud rose before him through the morning mists and the great adventure could begin. Although Layard and his contemporaries did not realize it, the mound was really the remains of a ziggurat or artificial hill, on which a temple had been constructed. It was not Nineveh whose remains they were now to explore, as both Botta and Layard had first thought, but Kalhu, the Biblical Calah, an earlier capital of the Assyrians.

On the very first day Layard came upon a chamber twenty-five feet long and fourteen feet broad, formed of marble slabs covered with inscriptions in cuneiform characters; although as yet he did not know it, this was part of the North-West Palace from which so many treasures were in due course to be obtained. Within a few days he had discovered further remains, and among rubbish at the bottom of the chamber of the North-West Palace, beautiful ivory figures, which now form part of the great Nimrud collection of ivories. Canning, and Rawlinson in Baghdad, were overjoyed at Layard's success. The latter did not think many large sculptured slabs would be found at Khorsabad, since it was too far from the mountains in which the stone for them was quarried. However, he expected – and this to him was far more important than any sculptured slabs or figures, however fine – that numerous inscriptions would undoubtedly be found there. Rawlinson was convinced he would soon have the key to these inscriptions and the more of them that could be revealed the better.

On 28 November Layard discovered some wall tablets representing a siege, a chariot fight, and other stirring and finely executed scenes. 'The marbles which I have hitherto uncovered,' he reported to his uncle, Benjamin Austen, 'are beautiful, full of life and *mouvement*, and, in the opinion of those who have seen them, superior to those uncovered by Botta.'[1]

In February 1846 he was to make his greatest discovery. Having spent a fruitful winter discussing antiquities and ancient languages with Rawlinson at Baghdad, as well as enjoying the favours of the local ladies, Layard was continuing his excavations at Nimrud, having found amongst other relics a magnificent winged bull, of which un-fortunately the head and wings had been destroyed. On 20 February he was hastily summoned by two of his Arabs who approached at full

1. *Nineveh and its Remains*, Vol. 1, p. 25.
2. Quoted in Gordon Waterfield, *Layard of Nineveh*, p. 124.

gallop, with the cry, 'Hasten O Bey! for they have found Nimrod himself.' Layard at once went to the diggings and found that a huge head, as tall as a man, forming part of a great winged bull, had been uncovered. 'I shall not myself easily forget this enormous head appearing from the earth . . . like some giant arising from the lower regions.'[1] Other marvels were obviously there, only awaiting thorough excavation. The local Turkish authorities now started to be difficult and Layard could do little more without a *firman* giving permission to excavate. Canning was busy transporting the sculptures from Bodrum to the Museum and hesitated to ask so soon for another *firman*. At last the long desired permission arrived and Layard could continue his work without further molestation.

More and more treasures continued to be unearthed daily, but funds were getting low. The excavations could not go on much longer if they were to depend merely on the private generosity of the Ambassador. Canning, who was now in London, approached the Museum. There was still almost no art of the ancient East except that of Egypt at Bloomsbury, or indeed anywhere else. A collection of Babylonian signets and cylinders had been purchased for 50 guineas in May 1835, and a few objects from the Euphrates expedition came to the Museum two years later, but this was a handful to put against what had been brought to Paris by Botta or against what Layard was now busy unearthing. But as with the Egyptian or British antiquities, men bred exclusively in the classical tradition could see hardly any artistic value or importance in these sculptures. Even Rawlinson though little of them as objects of art. In April 1845 Christian Rassam,[2] British vice-consul at Mosul, wrote to the Trustees drawing attention to the discoveries made there by Botta and suggesting that he should continue the excavations in the mound at Nimrod, begun by Rich in 1819. Such excavations would not, in his opinion, cost more than £100. The Trustees declined his offer. Canning, backed by his enormous prestige as Ambassador and the donor of the 'Canning Marbles' from Halicarnassus, was fortunately more successful.

In August and September 1846 Canning wrote to Layard to tell him that all was well and that the Museum would henceforth take charge of the excavations. 'The British Museum undertakes Nimrud in my stead. The Treasury allows £2,000. You are the agent . . . A sum between £1,000 and £1,100 will be applicable to the continuation of your

1. *Nineveh and its Remains*, p. 65.
2. Christian Rassam, elder brother of Hormuzd Rassam, Layard's collaborator, was the first English consul at Mosul.

works including the embarkation of the spoils. You are to finish all by the end of next June.'[1]

Shortly afterwards, Layard received a letter from Forshall, laying down the terms of the contract. Already annoyed by the comparative smallness of the sums offered, he was infuriated by the tone of much of the Secretary's letter. Forshall wrote that since the excavations would now be on a greater scale than hitherto, there were greater chances of disputes with the local population. Layard was enjoined 'not to relax in his caution, but rather, if possible, to be more guarded and circumspect than heretofore. The Trustees wish that every cause of offence should be avoided as well to the authorities as to the population', and the letter concluded with the pious injunction: 'It will be very gratifying to the Trustees to find when the operations on which Mr Layard is engaged are concluded, that his prudence and good feeling have enabled him to leave in Kurdistan, an impression entirely favourable to the British character.'[2]

Alarmed at the inadequate funds offered and hurt by the tone of the Trustees' instructions, Layard carried on, asking for an artist to record the new discoveries he was making almost daily. It was time too, to consider getting the treasures back to England and lodging them safely in the Museum.

Arrangements were being made for the smaller objects to be taken to Baghdad and shipped from there via Bombay to London. But what about the great bulls and the other massive sculptures, which were among the chief of Layard's discoveries? He was somewhat mollified to receive several flattering and encouraging letters from the British Museum. Thus on 11 November 1848 Forshall wrote conveying the Trustees' thanks for his 'zealous and well directed exertions in the East to which the Trustees owed the important collection of antiquities'.[3]

Before this, however, in March 1847, Layard had decided to try and move one of the Khorsabad bulls, a block of solid marble weighing over ten tons, down to the Tigris. The Trustees had written to agree to his making the attempt, but were reluctant to have any of the sculptures cut in pieces, as Botta had had to do with some of the sculptures he had discovered. Pulled by enthusiastic gangs of Arab workers, the great bull, mounted on wooden rollers, started on its journey to Bloomsbury much

1. Quoted in *Layard of Nineveh*, p. 156.
2. Add. MS. 39,077. f. 17. Forshall to Layard, 21 September 1846.
3. Add. MS. 38,978. f. 210.

in the manner in which it had originally been brought to the site. Together with one of the gigantic stone lions which Layard had also discovered, the bull at length reached the river and both were successfully embarked on to the waiting rafts.

Layard himself had now returned home, to be welcomed and feted as a national hero. The Trustees, delighted with what he had achieved and anxious for his drawings and inscriptions to be published, asked the Treasury for £4,000 for the purpose. Birch advised Layard to get as much publicity as he could for his discoveries, 'for English authorities are influenced more from without than from within'.[1] The Treasury refused to comply, so Layard decided to undertake his own publicity. The result was the famous *Nineveh and its Remains*, described by *The Times* as 'the most extraordinary work of the present age',[2] which appeared early in 1849 and took the country by storm. Henceforth, Layard had all the publicity he needed. All he now lacked was the money with which to continue his excavations.

The arrival of his discoveries was now eagerly awaited. There had been endless difficulties and delays and the Admiralty was not cooperative. Birch wrote to Layard on 23 March 1849 that Hawkins and others had gone to the Admiralty to make final arrangements, as they had heard that the vessels with the antiquities aboard were nearing England. Those already at the Museum were proving a great attraction. The Prince Consort and most of the Cabinet had been, and Layard was informed that he was a 'prodigious favourite' with the Trustees. The Nineveh room, where the antiquities were shown, was always crowded and the papers and the public generally were full of his praise.

When fifty cases from Nimrud had arrived at the Museum the previous October, it was found that the objects had been tampered with and some stolen as they lay on the wharf at Bombay. The East India Company were apologetic and henceforth more helpful than the Admiralty. Layard had now gone back to Mesopotamia where he continued to find Assyrian remains. The principal difficulty was getting them back intact. Layard frequently voiced his concern about this to Ellis. To Hawkins he wrote that he was sending boxes of

1. Quoted in *Layard of Nineveh*, p.180.
2. *The Times*, 9 February 1849. Hawkins wrote to Layard on 18 September 1849: 'It is your own book which has done everything for you, the greatest assistance I have been to you was instigating you to write it'. (Add. MS. 38,979. f. 46.) Hawkins to Layard 18 September 1849.)

objects 'of the highest archaeological interest' to England, but was reluctant to dispatch them without specific instructions.[1] The bull and the lion had reached London safely after a long and arduous journey and were now lodged in temporary quarters in the Museum, where they drew vast crowds.

Room to exhibit all these marvels properly was now the most urgent problem. Hawkins wrote in 1851: 'The Assyrian researches have poured into the Museum a collection of interesting objects, requiring a large extent of space, from a district to which no one looked for such accessions; and from other districts in the same country further acquisitions may be expected . . . For the Assyrian sculptures it can scarcely be said that any accommodation is provided. The small, narrow galleries into which at present it is proposed to thrust them are too small even to receive those at present in the Museum, and utterly inadequate for the reception of those now on their passage. As to arrangement and proper explanation of them, it is quite out of the question'.[2] Plans for the best arrangement under these difficult conditions were drawn up by Hawkins and his assistant, Edmund Oldfield, but little could be done in the existing cramped quarters. Further building was proposed, but would take time. As it was, most of these wonderful relics of a distant and hitherto unknown past had to be stored in small and inaccessible basement rooms.

There were two obvious means of increasing the space available. One was to provide new buildings; the other to clear out some of the existing collections. Most favoured a judicious mixture of the two. The situation became more desperate as more cases of Assyrian sculptures arrived. Hawkins wrote in 1855 that 'for the exhibition of these no accommodation has even been suggested, and for even the unpacking of them there is not any convenient place'.[3] A small area was provided by roofing over the narrow corridor between the Elgin room and the main gallery at a cost of about £4,500. These galleries still contain many of the reliefs discovered by Layard, though described at the time by Hawkins as 'only an expedient and not a very good one'.[4]

Detailed proposals were drawn up by Oldfield and suggestions were

1. Add. MS. 38,942. f. 12. Layard to Hawkins, 21 January 1850.
2. Report from Hawkins, 3 July 1851. *Communications relating to the Enlargement of the British Museum*, p. 13. (PP, H. of C., 1852, vol. XXVIII, p. 201.)
3. Report from Hawkins, 6 July 1853. *Papers relating to the Enlargement of the British Museum*, p. 7. (PP, H. of C., 1857–58, vol. XXXIII, p. 373.)
4. Report from Hawkins, 9 January 1856. *op. cit.*, p. 9.

made by Vaux and others. Hawkins firmly maintained that 'if the Department of Antiquities is to remain in Bloomsbury, it will be necessary to secure the whole of the ground lying to the west and south-west of the Museum'.[1] But how was this to be done? The most popular scheme for making more room, at least amongst the non-scientific members of the staff, was to get rid of the natural history collections. Panizzi had for many years advocated their removal. He had done so to the Select Committee of 1836 and had never subsequently changed his mind. Lord Cawdor in 1847 wrote half jestingly to Madden that he had long known Panizzi wanted to get rid of the 'birds and the beasts',[2] and his subsequent evidence before the Royal Commission and other parliamentary investigations into the question made his opinion plain to all. As Macaulay said, Panizzi would 'at any time give three mammoths for an Aldus',[3] but it was not merely the scientific collections that he and others wished to get rid of. It was even more the unwelcome and fast-growing prehistoric and mediaeval collections and the ethnographical collections whose removal he now urged with all the authority of his position as Principal Librarian.

The suggestion made for moving out the classical antiquities, discussed some thirty years before, had come to naught. Smirke's new galleries had seemed adequate for a time, but with the great increases of the middle of the century, the possibility was again raised.

Oldfield, and Hawkins too, were seriously reconsidering such a move. In a letter to Layard of 25 May 1862 the former urged the establishment of a 'Museum of Ancient Art . . . superior in arrangement, (as it already is in its contents) to any in Europe'. Such a Museum should be built on a new site and be quite independent of the British Museum, or, if that should prove impossible, it should become an entirely separate branch of the Museum under its own Director and with buildings isolated as far as possible from the present ones. There should be no more 'botching and tinkering of the old Building; no patching up and appropriating to ourselves the cast off clothes' of other departments; no reburying of the Assyrian collection (so unpopular with the officials) in underground vaults. Oldfield further suggested that these new buildings should be erected on a site of one and a half acres to the west of the Museum. Sufficient room might be left there for the Natural History collections, unless it would be

1. *op. cit.*, p. 9.
2. *Madden Journal*, 27 June 1847.
3. Macaulay to Lansdowne, February 1856. (Fagan II, p.15.)

thought preferable for them to expand on another site to the north-east.[4]

Such schemes, and there were others, for making a complex of quasi-independent Museums on adjacent sites came to nothing. In the Treasury's view the cost was prohibitive.

One part of the antiquities collections has so far been barely mentioned. This is the Ethnographical collection, which, as 'artificial curiosities', ranked high in the earliest days of the Museum. Since then it had been undeservedly neglected. The basis of the collection was still those objects bequeathed to the Museum by Cook, Menzies, Banks and other eighteenth-century travellers and explorers, together with the material transferred from the Royal Society in 1782.

The South Sea Room or Otaheite Room was always a popular attraction. In June 1808 it was ordered that it be used for a display 'to illustrate particular Customs of different Nations; their Religion, their Government, their Commerce, Manufacturers or Trades'.[2] This admirable purpose could only be secured by transferring the relevant objects from the second or mummy room to the South Sea Room. In consequence the 'South Seas' exhibits themselves would have to be restricted to sixteen of the twenty cases available. All continents seem to have been covered. Europe – British and Medieval collections – Asia, Africa and America, with the South Seas cases subdivided according to particular nations. Gifts were constantly arriving, brought home by various travellers. In 1825 Captain Marryat the novelist[3] gave a colossal figure of 'Gaudma, a Burmese deity' and other small collections were secured from Africa, Mexico, Australia and the Arctic. A canoe, for instance, received in 1838 was ordered to be placed under the colonnade on pedestals surrounded by an iron railing.

After they were transferred to his department in 1836, Hawkins paid more attention than the naturalists had to these often unwanted objects, but even he was unsuccessful in persuading the Trustees to purchase any oriental antiquities. To spend good money on anything but classical statuary was still anathema to many of the Board, though they did in February 1842 authorise the expenditure of a small sum

1. Add. MS. 38,988. f. 145.
2. *Committee Minutes*, vol. 9, p. 2391, 29 June 1808.
3. Frederick Marryat, 1792–1848, naval officer and novelist. Senior naval officer at Rangoon during First Burma War, 1824.

on a plan to make drawings and casts of the newly discovered Mayan ruins in Central America.

A description of the Ethnographical collection as it then was appears in *The British Museum, Historical and Descriptive* of 1850. 'The Ethnographical room [is] an oblong appartment of considerable size, though much too small for its purpose, which is the collection of articles illustrative of the manners and customs of nations lying at a distance from our own, as well as of rude ancient races.' The author, David Masson, who shows scarcely any of the prejudices common at that date, speaks witheringly of the 'five paltry cases' deemed sufficient to contain examples of all the arts and crafts of the ancient civilisations of China and Japan. In his opinion there should have been separate rooms for the display of the antiquities of China, India and Japan and another for the arts and crafts of more primitive peoples.[1] Despite the fact that the Ethnographical collections had now been increased by several fine bequests, including its first gift from the Queen in 1841, 'a collection of curious objects from the South Sea Islands', including an imitation of a lady's poke bonnet made from thin plates of turtle shell,[2] the general view among the senior officers and Trustees was that expressed by Panizzi:

You have, also, I imagine Byzantine, Oriental, Mexican and Peruvian Antiquities stowed away in the basement? – Yes, a few of them; and I may add, that I do not think it is any great loss that they are not better placed than they are.

Is it your opinion that the ethnographical collections ought to be retained in the Museum? – I think not; I think there ought to be a separate repository for them . . . if it is to be kept up as it ought to be kept up, it would take the whole of the space that is now occupied by the antiquities on the upper floor of the British Museum.[3]

They were never increased by purchase. The Principal Librarian would agree reluctantly that these collections were of some importance, but he was equally sure he did not want them in *his* Museum. Even Hawkins, whose opinion in these matters was comparatively liberal, bluntly said that he had no wish to retain the Mexican antiquities and though he knew of no other place for them, was prepared to let them go. He did, however, add: 'but I think that a collection of that sort ought to be had somewhere or other'.[4]

1. *The British Museum, Historical and Descriptive*, p. 22.
2. *BMQ*, vol. XVIII, no.3, p. 91.
3. *Select Committee on the British Museum*, 1860, para. 18; 272. (PP, H. of C. 1860, vol. XVI, p. 173.)
4. *op.cit.*, para. 1577.

It was not until these collections came a few years later under the wise rule of Franks that this hostility or indifference gave way to a better appreciation and understanding of their real value.

So the Department of Antiquities came to the end of its fourth decade as an independent department, grossly overcrowded, but with new and exciting acquisitions still coming in almost daily; a department swollen out of recognition from the comparatively few antiquities over which young Mr Combe had presided early in the century; above all, a department eager for change.

At the end of 1860 Edward Hawkins, now aged eighty-one, submitted his resignation. Who was to succeed him, and what would happen to the department over which he had presided for so long? These were questions which the next few months were to answer.

CHAPTER NINE

The Natural History Collections
[1812–1880]

IN September 1813, Charles König became Keeper of the Department of Natural History and Modern Curiosities (to give that department its full title). König had been born in Brunswick and educated at the famous Hanoverian university of Göttingen, where he was a contemporary of Queen Victoria's uncle, the Duke of Sussex. He had come to England in 1800 to arrange the collections of Queen Charlotte, consort to George III. He had then been engaged as Assistant to Dryander,[1] Banks' librarian, and finally, in 1807, had come to the Museum as Assistant Keeper in the Natural History Department.

Originally a botanist, he subsequently specialised in mineralogy and fossils, and became an acknowledged expert in that field. He was a difficult man, and his relations with J. E. Gray and Sir Robert Smirke were soon to be almost as bad as those between Panizzi and Madden. Nevertheless, König's rule, both over the undivided department of Natural History and then over the Mineralogical Branch from 1837 to his death in September 1851, was a distinguished one. His reputation and that of his department steadily grew and the evidence he gave before the various investigating committees and commissions was cogent and to the point.

At König's accession, minerals and fossils were by far the most important exhibits in his department. Among the mammalia were a few specimens from Sloane's original collection, and some even older specimens from the Royal Society's collection which had been transferred to the Museum in 1781. The same applied to the birds, some of which were said to have been secured during the three voyages of Captain Cook.[2] Insufficient attention was paid then and for long after

---

1. Jonas Dryander, 1748–1810, botanist.
2. At the beginning of the twentieth century one relic survived of the birds obtained by Cook, a Tree Starling, 'which has persisted in a kind of mummified state . . . after having been mounted and exposed to the dust and light of the old British Museum for nearly a century'. (*History of Natural History Departments*, vol. 2, p. 79.)

to preserving the specimens. It was deemed essential that everything must be mounted and put on display, and deterioration sooner or later set in. Sloane's collection, once said to contain 5,394 insects, was now considerably smaller. Accessions were few and the rate of wastage, even without Dr Shaw's bonfires, was very high.

The natural history collections were still housed in rooms on the upper floor of Montagu House. The central saloon, its floor suitably strengthened, was devoted to the minerals; room VIII contained additional mineral exhibitions; room IX was for geology, that is fossils, and for the invertebrata, with a fine specimen of the skull and horns of the giant Irish elk; room X contained the bird collection, the insects and similar specimens; room XI held the quadrupeds, including two examples of the then almost unknown ourang-outang; and room XII contained a collection of specimens in spirit. It was a varied collection, always popular with the general public, but behind the great contemporary foreign collections.

The condition of the specimens was already arousing anxiety. A sub-committee of the Trustees was appointed in February 1820 to investigate the state of the many specimens still not properly preserved and to ensure that such were in future adequately dealt with. In 1817 a start had been made on re-arranging the collections, beginning with the birds, on more up-to-date and scientific lines. The influence of König was being felt. In 1816, the Montagu collection of British birds was purchased, then the finest and most complete series in existence, though, owing to the defective preparation of the specimens, the majority have long since fallen into pieces. The following year the collection of the great traveller, William Burchell, was acquired, and in 1816 the Moll collection of minerals, together with its herbarium.

At this time the botanical collections consisted for the most part of Sloane's original herbarium which, despite statements to the contrary in anti-Museum journals, such as the *Edinburgh Review*, was still in excellent state of preservation. Robert Brown, then Keeper of the Botanical Branch, told the Committee of 1835 that 'the preservation of the collection was such as it probably must have been 50 or I would even say 100 years ago; it is in the nature of such collections, unless they are exposed to damp and to the attacks of insects, that they are not likely to suffer'.[1] To this were added Moll's recently acquired herbarium, and the collection of Chelsea garden plants, donated from 1721 to 1769, first to Sloane himself and then to the Museum. Besides these

1. *Select Committee, 1835. Minutes*, para. 3648.

H

three herbaria, there were also at Bloomsbury collections of fruits and
seeds, roots and other parts of vegetables.

Then, shortly before his death in 1820, Sir Joseph Banks bequeathed
his magnificent herbarium and library to his old friend and librarian,
Robert Brown,[1] who had served him first as Assistant to Dryander and
from 1810 in sole charge. The collections were bequeathed to Brown
for his life, but a codicil to Banks' will directed that both collections
and library should be transferred to the Museum after Brown's death.
Subject to Brown's consent, the collections might, however, pass to
the Trustees immediately or at any subsequent date.

In February 1823, the Trustees opened negotiations with Brown for
the acquisition of the Banksian library and collections. It was not until
1827 that the negotiations were completed and the great collection
with its keeper came under the care of the Trustees. Brown was to have
the rank of under-librarian or keeper of a department and to be
entitled Keeper of the Banksian Botanical Collections. Owing to the
fact that it was impossible to provide him with a residence, and the
Trustees were unwilling to give him a higher salary in lieu, it was
agreed that Brown should work only two days a week, and his assistant
J. J. Bennett[2] act for him the rest of the time. The printed books of the
Banksian library were transferred to the Library, but the very valuable
collections of manuscripts, drawings, and engraved copperplates
remained under the care of the Keeper of the Botanical Collections.

At the time of its acquisition the Banksian herbarium was one of the
largest, comprising 23,400 specimens, as well as one of the most
important in existence. It contained the invaluable collections made by
Banks himself and Solander on their voyage round the world with Cook
in 1768–1771, and the plants collected by Banks in Great Britain at
various dates, in Newfoundland and Labrador in 1766, as well as those
obtained on his journey to Iceland in 1772. He had subsequently
imported numerous other collections from all over the world, including
those made during Cook's second and third voyages and on Bligh's
voyage to Tahiti in 1791–1793.

One of the reasons given for the delay in transferring the Banksian
herbarium was that there was as yet insufficient room to receive it.
When Smirke's plans for new galleries were well underway, a transfer

1. Robert Brown, 1773–1858. He had been Flinders' naturalist on the Australasian
expedition of 1801–1805.
2. John Joseph Bennett, 1801–1876, naturalist. He succeeded Brown as Keeper of
the Department of Botany in 1858.

of a collection of this size and importance could be reasonably contemplated. From the start there was ill-feeling between Brown and König, who resented the former's quasi-independent position and, as Keeper of the natural history collections, regarded the interloper with a suspicious eye. König had a high opinion of Brown none the less, both as a botanist and as a man, as he made plain to the House of Commons Committee of 1835.[1] Nevertheless the situation was made worse in 1834 when the Trustees at last rightly came to the conclusion that all the various botanical collections at Bloomsbury should be placed under Brown's care, a transfer eventually accomplished in 1836. Brown reported on the new position to the Board. All the 23,400 specimens in the Banksian herbarium were now in order and of the older collections, the flowers and fruits of rare and succulent plants, preserved in 326 bottles, and the 67 large specimens of fronds of palms and ferns were being scientifically arranged. Out of the 46,000 known varieties, Brown informed the Trustees, the Museum contained some 26,000. Fine as it was, it was still an inferior to that of the Jardin des Plantes in Paris and the Keeper asked for £100 a year to augment the collection.

The other Keepers of the natural history collections also reported. The mineral collection, König now reported, was probably 'the most extensive any where exhibited to public view'. He said it contained a great number of valuable specimens, but also some worthless ones, 'which ought to be exchanged'. On the other hand, there was merely the 'basis of a respectable geological collection'.[2] Much of his energy over the next years would be spent in rectifying this want and coping with increasing public interest in this subject.

The zoological collections, then under J. G. Children,[3] were in a less satisfactory state. John Edward Gray,[4] who had recently joined the Museum as a temporary assistant in December 1824 was to recreate this division of the natural history collections. His long and distinguished keepership, marred only by his violent antipathy to Panizzi and to others of his colleagues, was to lead his department to the threshold of a new age.

1. 'The greatest botanist in the world.' (*Select Committee, 1835. Minutes,* para. 2854.)
2. *Committee Minutes,* vol.13, pp. 3848, 3849. 12 July 1834.
3. John George Children, 1777–1852, secretary to the Royal Society. Originally a man of considerable wealth, he was forced by his father's financial disasters to seek employment at the British Museum in 1816. He resigned on the death of his second wife in 1840.
4. John Edward Gray, 1800–1875, Keeper of the Zoological Department, 1840–1875.

Children reported to the Trustees that 330 of the 940 species of mammals known were in the British Museum collections, and of 4,109 known species of birds, 1,831 were in the Museum. All other collections under his care – the insects and so on – were, in his opinion, now properly arranged. Nevertheless the zoological collections were far from perfect, and much would have to be done before they could be compared with similar collections abroad.

Within a few weeks of these reports, the Trustees approved the purchase of the valuable collection of fossils made by Thomas Hawkins for £1,310 5s. od., which improved that section greatly, though the setting up of the specimens gave some trouble. A committee of the Trustees ordered that all plaster restorations should be clearly distinguished from those parts of the skeletons which were really 'osseous', by being lighter in colour. They were, however, to be sufficiently dark as to form a contrast with the lias in which the fossils were embedded.

The natural history collections were now moving from old Montagu House to Smirke's new building. The new quarters were the long gallery over the King's Library, originally intended for the national collection of paintings, and rooms in the north wing above the Department of Printed Books.

In 1829 the minerals and zoological specimens went into the upper gallery of the new wing and the skylights in it were made movable. The next year fossils went temporarily into the long gallery above the King's Library, and the rest of the collection awaited the completion of the remaining rooms to the north.

König was now almost continually at loggerheads with Smirke over the arrangement of the new galleries and complained to the Trustees of gross 'mismanagement' on the part of their architect. The fitting up of the cases in the long gallery, he grumbled, had now been going on for weeks and his continued remonstrances seemed to be of no avail. Even more urgent work at the Houses of Parliament had delayed matters, but König was far from satisfied. Smirke, before the Select Committee of 1836, denied that he had at any time failed to consult the officers of the Natural History Department or indeed of any other, and this seems, as far as can now be judged, to have been true.

König admitted to the Select Committee of 1835 that most of his attention had perforce been given to the minerals alone and that he had had to rely on his assistants for information concerning the other parts of the natural history collections. The immense labour of re-arranging the minerals and fossils, for example, into their 'present beautiful arrangement' had, he said, been done entirely by himself, apart from two men to line the trays with cotton.[1] Yet he still insisted that it was quite possible for him to supervise effectively the whole of the collections, provided he had good assistants. The Committee seemed dubious as to both the correctness and the desirability of this. König was dissatisfied with much of the zoological collection; 'a very miserable collection' he had publicly called it shortly before. Not more than £10 a year, for instance, was spent on acquiring entomological specimens, and other sections had for long fared almost as badly. With such resources, little could as yet be done to build up a worthwhile national collection.

Similar evidence was given by Children and Gray. They had neither the time nor the staff to arrange their collections properly nor to publish the necessary catalogues. They had neither laboratories nor workrooms and no equipment, not even a watch glass. The lack of trained lower staff was particularly galling. As Gray said, the attendants were quite suitable for cleaning and guarding 'and acting in the capacity of servants',[2] but not to provide the skilled assistance which was so desperately needed. Gray thought the Natural History collections should be now divided, Zoology and Mineralogy becoming, like Botany, distinct departments under their own keepers. He also condemned the inclusion of fossil remains of animals in the mineralogical division, so that if any scientist wanted to compare recent and fossil specimens, he had to apply to Children or to himself for one and to König for the other, a cause of obvious muddle and annoyance.

Like König, Gray thought that the government ought to be much more helpful and sympathetic towards the national collections. 'When collections were made by expeditions sent out by the government, I think that the specimens brought home should be sent to the Museum, but this has rarely been done.'[3] Gray refers to a large collection of American birds which came into the hands of the Colonial Office: 'Not a single specimen collected in that expedition has been sent to the British Museum, although most, if not all, the specimens, would have been desirable for the collection.' Some were sent to the Zoological Society, others to the University of Edinburgh, even to Plymouth Museum – to the British Museum, nothing.[4] Likewise neither the

1. *Select Committee, 1835. Minutes*, para. 2589.
2. *op. cit.*, para. 3251.
3. *op. cit.*, para. 3758.
4. *op. cit.*, para. 3358.

Foreign Office nor the Admiralty helped the national collections obtain specimens from abroad, even when the various consuls and naval officers were eager to be of assistance. This complete ignoring of the just claims of the Museum was a bitter pill to swallow, when it was being attacked for its failure to secure the very specimens that were being given away to other institutions.

As elsewhere in the Museum, much was wrong with the administration of the scientific departments. The staff were capable and eager to set things right, but, as Children said, 'It is impossible with the strength we have now ever to get it into that state it ought to be in.'[1] The same cry was to echo from every department throughout the nineteenth century and beyond: insufficient staff, insufficient money and, above all, insufficient space.

On 26 January 1837 the Trustees at last resolved that the Department of Natural History should be divided into three branches – the Mineralogical (including the fossil remains), the Zoological, and the Botanical. König, to his extreme anger, was, in his own words, 'degraded' from his position as the head of the whole department of Natural History to become merely the head of one of its branches, a degradation 'not in the title, but in the rank formerly held by the head of the Department of Natural History'.[2]

It was a sensible division, but one which was naturally going to cause difficulties. König still retained a vague and ill-defined primacy over the other branches. The status of Brown was also anomalous. He was never fully integrated into the Museum hierarchy, whilst Children, and after him Gray, though called Keepers, were paid at a lower rate than their colleagues, £450 a year compared with £600.

The Natural History Departments seem at this time to have worked under greater pressure than the rest of the Museum. They were grossly understaffed and subject more than any other part, save for the perennially unpopular Printed Books, to malicious and uninformed criticism. The strain on the staff began to show. George Gray,[3] J. E. Gray's younger brother, had a nervous breakdown, due to overwork and the anxiety created by the low rate of pay. The Trustees did, however, grant him three months paid sick leave.

Pay was indeed wretched, at a daily rate, for all below the rank of

1. op. cit., para. 3433.
2. Royal Commission, Minutes, para. 3148.
3. George Robert Gray, 1808–1872, zoologist. Entered the Museum as an Assistant in 1831. Assistant Keeper of the Department of Zoology, 1869.

assistant keeper, only granted when the Museum was open, and often paid in what was considered by most to be a humiliating manner. It was no wonder that the weaker ones succumbed. Such was the unfortunate George Samouelle,[1] in charge of the insect collection under Children. Increasingly reported as being incompetent, he seems to have taken to drink and neglected his duties. Frequently absent, Samouelle's claims of ill-health were not believed and in 1838 the Trustees resolved that he should cease to be employed. However, he seems to have been forgiven, as in October of the following year it was reported that he had deliberately taken off the registration numbers affixed to the various insects by Adam White,[2] his colleague, and that, in consequence, it was now impossible to identify any of them and the whole collection was in a state of confusion. The wretched man was thereupon suspended for the rest of the month. In 1841 poor George Samouelle was eventually sacked, after complaints had been received of further irregularities and of insulting language to his superiors.

Such minor tragedies were not uncommon. J. E. Gray was bitter about it, as indeed were Panizzi and most of the more thoughtful officers. Gray had told the Royal Commission: '[The want of retiring pensions] has a very injurious effect on the minds and health of the officers and assistants; that is they always feel subject to the danger of want. I need only refer to the fact of the deplorable state of mental disease which has existed among several of the officers.'[3] Such conditions continued for much of the nineteenth century. Successive Principal Librarians, especially Panizzi, warmly espoused the cause of their junior colleagues. Petition after petition from the assistants, endorsed by Keepers, was forwarded to the Treasury, with little result. That department was still resolved to obtain the services of hard-working scholars on the cheap. It was not for many years that conditions for most of the staff became reasonably tolerable.

All through the 1830s and early 40s the natural history collections were being moved from the fast-decaying Montagu House into Smirke's

1. George Samouelle. Appointed to the Natural History Department as an Assistant in 1821. In October 1838 Madden noted that 'he has contrived to get himself into the King's Bench'. At Children's request, Madden contributed to a fund set up to assist his unfortunate family. (*Madden Journal*, 15 Octtober 1838.)
2. Adam White, appointed Assistant in 1835. Died 1863. Until 1842 he was responsible for arranging the greater part of the insect collections.
3. *Royal Commission, Minutes*, para. 8689.

buildings, although these had already been widely condemned as inadequate and unsuitable. In 1837 the mineral collections were moved to the north wing above Printed Books, and for once König seems to have been pleased with the change, declaring that the rooms were well adopted for their purpose, light and, at the moment, with plenty of room for additions. In November 1839, the zoological collections started their move, though very slowly, for it was reported to be still proceeding as late as May 1842.

The various natural history collections were at last steadily growing. In 1837 instructions as how to collect natural history specimens were drawn up by the officers of these departments. Five hundred were printed, of which 300 were sent to the Colonial Office to be distributed to the various colonial administrations, together with a note appealing for their assistance in improving and extending the collection.

Until the new rooms were ready few large zoological specimens could be accepted and it was agreed to concentrate on rare ones. In April 1841, through the good offices of Gray, the Trustees received an offer from the Zoological Society of London to transfer to the Museum the many valuable specimens from their own Museum then in Leicester Square. This building was in a dangerous condition and a move was therefore necessary. The Society were not satisfied with the way their specimens would be housed at the Museum, and scientists at that time had a poor opinion of the Natural History Departments, an opinion which Gray and his younger colleagues were soon to alter completely. The negotiations collapsed and the Society's Museum moved first to a warehouse near Golden Square and then to the old Carnivora House in the Society's Gardens.

By 1850 the Society realised that things at the British Museum had changed and decided that now it would be better to transfer the bulk of their collections to the national Museum. In 1853 certain specimens were handed over and in 1855, the Council 'having long been impressed with the conviction that the remarkable development of the Natural History Department in the British Museum has for some years past entirely superseded the necessity of maintaining a second Zoological Museum in London . . . the Council entered into a negotiation with the Trustees of the British Museum for the transfer of such other portions of the collection by sale as were desirable for filling up desiderata in the National Museum. The series so selected by the Keeper of the Zoological Department was accepted by the Trustees at an agreed price of £500.' So this great collection finally came to the Museum. No longer could the Natural History collection be passed over to enrich the museum of a private society.[1]

On 24 March 1840 Children resigned as Keeper of Zoology. Ellis wrote to his friend Bliss that the post was to be filled immediately and that Gray would have it. In Sir Henry's opinion there was no possible rival.[2] On 11 April Gray was appointed. He was to have a distinguished career and completely to reorganise his department on modern scientific lines.

Gray was a born rebel and often sided with his junior colleagues against authority. Almost alone amongst the senior staff at that time he realised the importance of what the army terms 'man management' or the navy 'a happy ship', seeing that all pull their weight and all are treated fairly without favouritism. Gray constantly emphasised the low salaries and the poor conditions under which the staff suffered, 'the maximum salary of the Museum assistants not exceeding that frequently paid to clerks in some of those [other Government] offices when they . . . have even just entered on their duties'. Yet the Museum assistants were expected to be – and frequently were – 'living and continually progressing encyclopedias, which are incessantly consulted and seldom consulted in vain'.[3]

Determined to make his Branch a model, Gray at once overhauled the zoological collections. One of his first needs was a trained entomologist to take Samouelle's place.[4]

In May 1843 the Trustees decided to issue cheap synopses of the contents of the 'four great departments' then open to visitors, the Mineralogical and Geological Branch, the Zoological Branch, the Egyptian Antiquities, and the Greek and Roman Antiquities. The idea for these synopses first seems to have come from Sir Robert Peel. In April 1843 he wrote to Forshall: 'There is a very favourable disposition in the House of Commons towards the Museum and it is very desirable to maintain and confirm it by ready attention to suggestions offered in the House when these suggestions can be acted on with advantage or

1. *Committee Minutes*, vol. 19, pp. 5605, 5621, 5637; 3 April, 1 May, 8 May 1841. *Annual Report of the Zoological Society for 1855*, quoted in P. Chalmers Mitchell, *Centenary History of the Zoological Society of London*, pp. 59, 102, 103.

2. Add. MS. 34,573. f. 413.

3. Letters from Gray of 23 and 25 November 1859. (*Papers Relating to the Salaries of Persons employed in the British Museum*, p. 20, PP, H. of C., 1860, XXXIX A, p. 209.)

4. Samouelle's successor was Edward Doubleday, 1811–1849, a brilliant entomologist, who took over the Lepidoptera from Adam White.

without inconvenience', and urged that one such suggestion, the printing of very cheap descriptions of certain parts of the collection, might well be adopted. 'It will,' the Prime Minister went on, 'enable those who visit the collection to derive increased amusement and improvement from the visit. The smaller the sum charged the more general will be the advantage.'[1] Peel was gratified at the speedy adoption of his suggestion. A list of mammals in the Zoological Department was the first to be produced. A copy was sent to Peel for his approval. It was the first of a series of catalogues intended primarily for the scientific visitor to the Museum, a class of visitor it was increasingly urgent to cultivate. The great man was delighted with it. It 'seems very complete', he wrote, and 'I rejoice in its publication'.[2]

Not all the Museum's publications on the Natural History Departments were quite so successful. In May 1840 the official synopsis of the contents of the Museum was found to be in error. The long gallery was still described in it as being devoted to the mineral collection, 'whereas in point of fact the Mineralogical Collections had been removed upwards of a year'. There were other mistakes. The Trustees were furious with poor Sir Henry, who, as Principal Librarian, was responsible. It was most discreditable, they minuted, that 'a book published under the editorship of the Principal Librarian be so completely at variance with the facts'.[3] Ellis must in future be more careful.

The various natural history collections were now threatened by something more serious than the vagaries of the Principal Librarian. Many, both inside and outside the Museum, had long felt that the only solution to the space question was the removal of the scientific collections from their incongruous association with the rest of the Museum. In 1846 Lord Francis Egerton, afterwards Chairman of the Royal Commission on the Museum, wrote to Peel suggesting that the collection of fossils and similar objects should be transferred to the College of Surgeons, where they could be properly supervised. There they would come under the care of the distinguished naturalist, Professor Owen,[4] who was himself to come to the Museum within a few years as the first and only Superintendent of the Natural History

1. Add. MS. 40,527. f. 185.
2. Peel to Forshall, 1 January 1843. Add. MS. 40,529. f. 154.
3. *Committee Minutes*, vol. 18, pp. 5366, 5367. 9 May 1840.
4. Sir Richard Owen, 1804–1892, naturalist, who first qualified as a surgeon. He was Hunterian Professor of Comparative Anatomy and Physiology at the Royal College of Surgeons.

Departments. Egerton stressed the advantages of having 'two unrivalled collections . . . under one roof and under the inspection of one master-mind'. The Museum should, in his opinion, 'be relieved from the burden of natural history in all its branches'.[1] Egerton was a distinguished man and his opinion carried weight.

Peel, who despite his many cares as Prime Minister, was an active and zealous Trustee, replied, giving modified approval to Egerton's suggestion. 'If the Museum resolve to defend their Bones, I shall put Inglis in the front of the battle . . . if the bones go, I hope the stuffed birds and beasts will go with them.' The Museum was, he went on, 'speechless with delight' at the expected arrival of the marbles from Halicarnassus, sent there through the good offices of Stratford Canning, 'so that the time for agitating the Bone Question may not be an un-priopitious one'.[2] Owen also seems to have raised the question with Peel on a visit to Drayton Manor, the Prime Minister's country seat.

Sir Robert Inglis, perhaps at this time the most influential of the Trustees, was of quite another opinion. His prim mind was shocked at the very thought of sending the natural history collections to join the Hunterian Museum in Lincoln's Inn Fields. It would be quite impossible, he considered, 'for mothers and daughters to walk round the upper galleries of Professor Owen's museum' and it must be remembered that many of the keenest students of fossils in Victorian times were ladies. Even though, Inglis went on, it might have been wrong originally 'to unite the books of Sir Robert Cotton to the birds of Sir Hans Sloane or to add to them the Towneley, Elgin and Egyptian Antiquities', it was now much too late to unscramble that particular egg. The medical exhibits in the Hunterian Museum of the College of Surgeons were not at all suitable for *virginibus puerisque*. Scientists must just go from Lincoln's Inn Fields to Bloomsbury or vice versa. That was far easier than moving the collections themselves. To hive off the scientific collections would also mean the dispersal of the *books* on natural history. Inglis had no objection to creating an additional independent natural history museum under Owen's direction, but not at the expense of the British Museum. It would be disastrous to break up 'this magnificent fabric and magnificent collections' for the benefit of the *esoteric Museum* in Lincoln's Inn Fields.[3]

1. Add. MS. 40,586. f. 248.
2. Add. MS. 40,586. f. 250. Peel starts his letter, 'I do not mean to resign on the Big Bone Question', a reference to his increasing political difficulties.
3. Add. MS. 40,586. f. 254.

All these schemes and suggestions, however, seriously alarmed the scientists, already a powerful lobby. These were for the most part no friends to the Museum, which they thought neglected the scientific departments in favour of the antiquities and library. They were particularly incensed when Macaulay was elected a Trustee in 1847, rather than their man, the geologist Dean Buckland. Buckland was elected to the Board later in the same year, so honours were even.

This general and widespread dissatisfaction with the Museum amongst the majority of scientists culminated in a memorandum addressed to the new Prime Minister, Lord John Russell, in 1847 by members of the British Association for the Advancement of Science and of other scientific societies. In their opinion 'the promotion of the science of Natural History is very inadequately provided for by the present constitution of the Board of Trustees of the British Museum'. The Trustees, however distinguished, were 'unable adequately to direct the vast and rapidly increasing Natural History departments of the Museum'. They suggested that 'steps should be taken to effect such an improvement into the constitution of the Trust, as shall render the management of the Natural History departments of the British Museum as far as possible independent of the other divisions', though they did not desire the physical separation of the collections and the building of a completely separate Museum of Natural History.[1]

Lord John made soothing noises in Parliament, but the agitation was not to be stilled and was, as we have seen, one of the causes for the appointment of the Royal Commission to investigate the Museum. König, Gray and Brown all gave evidence, and that of Gray was especially valuable, at least when dealing with subjects on which he was an authority. Amongst his suggestions were that the whole of the palaeontological collection should be associated with the zoological collections and not with minerals, a reform he considered long overdue. His £1,000 per year, recently increased to £1,250, did not go very far in making purchases, especially of the larger and more valuable mammals, but it was better than nothing. His department was now increasing rapidly, too rapidly for his inadequate staff and lack of space.

König's evidence, though spiced with dislike and envy of Gray, covered much the same ground. In respect of assistance, he was even worse off, since Waterhouse, his second in command, was a palaentologist, as was the other senior member of his staff, Samuel Woodward,

1. *Memorial to the First Lord of the Treasury.* (PP, H. of C., 1847, vol. XXIV, p. 253.)

leaving the Keeper himself as the only one able to deal with minerals. Brown was now very old, yet gave a clear and concise account of the history of the collections under his charge. He warmly advocated the establishment of small departmental libraries, but deplored the various proposed changes which were due to be made in his department after his own death, that is, the reduction of the Keeper's salary to £350 and the abolition of the post of Assistant Keeper. Such an establishment, he complained, was utterly inadequate for the care and maintenance of what was now one of the finest botanical collections in Europe, and compared most unfavourably with the staffing of similar institutions abroad.

In their Report the Commissioners had comparatively little to say on the Natural History Departments, though in some respects it was they who had brought about the setting up of the Royal Commission. They endorsed the Botanical Department's plea for more money and staff. 'There is some ground to fear,' they remarked, 'that the greater popular attraction of other collections may divert the attention of the governing body to an undue extent from the less obtrusive exigences'[1] of that Department and welcomed the proposal that the botanical collections should shortly be thrown open to the general public. They concluded that 'the great bulk of the geological collections should be retained in the Mineralogical Department',[2] except that all fossil vegetables should go to the Botanical Department and such fossil vertebrata or invertebrata as might help to explain the specimens of living creatures in the Zoological Department should be transferred there. They deplored the rivalry between König and Gray. 'We are, at the same time, bound to remark that the interests of science have suffered more detriment than would otherwise have resulted had a more cordial spirit been manifested between the heads of the mineralogical and zoological departments and had they entertained a mutual desire to sink all jealousies and co-operate for the general good'.[3] The Commissioners, however, were able to record that 'the Natural History Collections are, as a whole, equal, if not superior, to any in the world'.[4]

Space was still the dominant question. In July 1851 the zoological collection was ten times more numerous than in 1836 and three

1. *Royal Commission*, Report, p. 41.
2. *op. cit.*, p. 43.
3. *op. cit.*, p. 41.
4. *op. cit.*, p. 44.

times as much space was devoted to its display and arrangement. Half the additional specimens had to be kept in rooms in the basement, only accessible by special permission and dangerously damp.

In 1851, old König died, having been a Keeper since 1813, and in 1858 he was followed by Brown, another relic of the past. König was succeeded by his able assistant, G. R. Waterhouse,[1] who had been in the service of the Trustees since 1843. In 1857 the department of Geology and Mineralogy was split into two separate departments, Geology continuing under Waterhouse, whilst Minerals was placed under M. H. N. Story-Maskelyne, Professor of Mineralogy at Oxford.[2] The reasons for the division are clear. Not only was the former situation confusing but, since the death of König, there had been no mineralogist on the staff of the Museum. Maskelyne remained Keeper until 1880, when he resigned on becoming a candidate for Parliament. Brown was succeeded by his assistant, J. J. Bennett, who had been with him since both had first come to the Museum in 1827, and to whom Brown left his valuable herbarium. This consisted of the important collection of nearly 3,900 species made during his voyage with Flinders off the coasts of New Holland and Van Diemen's Land in 1802–5. Bennett kept this herbarium at the Museum, permitting students use it, and on his death in 1876 he bequeathed it.

Long before this, in May 1847, Madden had gone with his children to the Botanical Department in search of specimens of sea-weed. Characteristically, he was extremely angry that there was none in the Museum collections, only in those of Brown himself. Such 'might easily be purchased', Bennett told him. 'Is this not gross neglect,' the Keeper of Manuscripts went on, 'not to procure the specimens of our own shores when they can be obtained so easily?' He might have been mollified if he had known that one day, after his own death, Brown's specimens would themselves come to the Museum. Madden considered that the botanical collections, as a whole, were being neglected. 'I think reform is wanting here,' he sourly noted.[3]

1. George Robert Waterhouse, 1810–1888, naturalist. He was originally trained as an architect, then specialised in entomology and only turned to geology on coming to the Museum in 1843. He was Keeper of the Department of Geology, 1857–1880.
2. Mervyn Herbert Nevil Story–Maskelyne, 1823–1911, mineralogist, grandson of Nevil Maskelyne, the eighteenth-century Astronomer Royal. He was Professor of Mineralogy at Oxford, 1856–1895; Keeper of Minerals, 1857–1880; and MP for Cricklade, 1880–1892.
3. *Madden Journal*, 18 May 1847.

As a gesture towards pacifying the persistent critics of the scientific departments, the Trustees, in 1856, decided to create the office of Superintendent of the Natural History Departments, much to the alarm of the newly appointed Principal Librarian, Antonio Panizzi, who feared lest the creation of this new post might lead to some diminution of his own authority. He was assured by the Trustees that this would not be so. He would still be Principal Librarian, with full authority over the whole Museum. The new post was designed primarily to serve as a link between the Principal Librarian and the various natural history departments to ensure that their just claims were not forgotten and advising him on scientific affairs. At the same time the three 'Branches' into which the Natural History Department had been divided were renamed 'Departments'. The Trustees offered this new position to Professor Richard Owen, Conservator of the Hunterian Museum at the Royal College of Surgeons in Lincoln's Inn Fields. Owen was discontented there and resented being required to perform what he considered to be unsuitable duties. He accepted the Trustees' offer and took up his new position in May 1856.

It was not, from his point of view, an altogether happy decision. His functions were ill-defined and the way he had been placed over their heads was bitterly resented by the Keepers of the natural history departments, in particular by Gray. They not unnaturally preferred to exercise the liberty and the right of access to the Trustees which they hitherto had enjoyed, and regarded Owen as unnecessary and his appointment as an insult to themselves. On the whole, Owen's relations with Panizzi were surprisingly cordial. Both were men of outstanding personality with firm views of their own, yet it would seem both had more or less agreed not to differ, at least in public. It was lucky too that on the main controversial point of the decade, the space question, Panizzi and Owen were agreed on the urgent necessity of moving the scientific collections from Bloomsbury to a new site, preferably at South Kensington.

As early as 10 February 1859, Owen had submitted an urgent report to the Trustees on this question, together with a plan for a new arrangement of the galleries under his charge. His report discloses in detail the lack of room at Bloomsbury, particularly for exhibiting the birds and larger mammals, both living and extinct. The largest space allotted to any one class of animals was still the birds – the long gallery above the King's Library. Yet, even here, as Owen emphasised, 'there now stands, more or less crowded, a part only of the collection of birds, the rest being preserved, as unstuffed skins, in boxes or drawers'.[1] The collection, fine as it was, represented only about half of the known species of birds. More new species were constantly being discovered, and specimens of these, too, would eventually come to the Museum. There ought to be on exhibition at least one full-sized whale and elephant. The need for new and larger premises for the growing collections was evident. In an accompanying note, Panizzi recommended his colleague's report to the Trustees' attention and the Board at once decided to forward Owen's proposals to the Treasury.

The scientific community, however, had already taken alarm. If anything were to go, why the natural history departments? Why not the British and Medieval antiquities, the despised ethnographical collections or even the library? In the previous July the 'Promoters and Cultivators of Science' had addressed a memorial to the government objecting strongly to the removal of the scientific collections from Bloomsbury, either bodily or by being broken up amongst various other scientific institutions. All should be preserved under the one roof in close proximity to the national library, and if more room were needed, then further extensions to the present museum should be made to the north. In addition, in their opinion, there was the great disadvantage to visitors of moving the collection from a central site to a distant suburb, 'it being a well known fact that by far the great number of visitors . . . consists of those who frequent the halls containing the Natural History collection'. The memorial concluded, 'For these reasons, as based on scientific advantages, the convenience and instruction of the people, and the saving of a large sum to the nation, we earnestly hope that the Natural History collections may not be interfered with, but be allowed to remain associated with the many other branches of human knowledge which are so admirably represented in this great national establishment.'[2]

All the principal scientists of the day signed this appeal, including several of the Trustees and, to Panizzi's extreme annoyance, Owen and all three keepers of the scientific departments. Owen, however, quickly changed his mind. What he now considered was needed was a new, large, and splendid museum where the maximum number of specimens could be on public exhibition. The Trustees, too, were coming round to this position. Others, however, were not sure. All through the early

1. *Papers relating to the Enlargement of the British Museum*, p. 22. (PP, H. of C., 1859, vol. XIV, p. 51.)
2. *Memorial*, p. 3. (PP, H. of C., 1857–8, vol. XXXIII, p. 499.)

sixties, the correspondence, at times acrimonious, between the Trustees and the Treasury went on. In April 1860 a Select Committee of the House of Commons was appointed to go into the question of the space available for the various collections at the Museum. In their report, they came down heavily in favour of leaving the scientific collections at Bloomsbury. It was clear that the natural history collections were still by far the most popular. Figures of the number of visitors showed an excess of 220 per cent over those to the King's Library and Manuscript Rooms and of 33 per cent over those that went to the much larger Antiquities galleries. On all grounds, popularity, accessibility, cost and proximity to the national library, the committee were firmly of the opinion that the natural history collections must stay at Bloomsbury. More ground should be acquired to the west and north. Ethnography should go as soon as possible; the drawings, as soon as suitable accommodation could be found for them, preferably to the National Gallery, with the few portraits left in the Museum. Absolutely nothing else. 'Sufficient reason has not been assigned for the removal of any part of the valuable collections now in the Museum, except that of Ethnography, and the portraits and drawings', was their considered decision.[1]

Panizzi, however, was not discouraged. He was quite clear what he wanted. He did not believe that more people came to see the Natural History collections than any others. They just wandered through the galleries more or less blindly. Then there were the children who shouted and scampered about in a very improper manner, annoying their elders by eating oranges and throwing the peel about. 'I think it would be a great deal better for the Museum . . . that the collection of natural history should not be there; for the fewer persons of this class are attracted as visitors the better.'[2] He was determined at all cost to remove such a temptation to young visitors.

So the struggle went on, with Panizzi and Owen's determination gradually swaying more and more of the Trustees towards the solution which they now jointly advocated, the transfer of the collections to a new site on the exhibition grounds at South Kensington. Other sites were also considered; one near Victoria Station, another, the Embankment, and even the Crystal Palace, as well as the area immediately to the south of the Museum. All had their advocates, but South Kensington remained the most favoured, largely on account of its comparative

1. *Select Committee on the British Museum*, 1860, Report, p. xiii. (PP, H. of C., 1860, vol. XVI, p. 173.)
2. *op. cit.*, Minutes, para. 218.

cheapness. All these schemes, however, fell through; a bill to permit the transfer was rejected in 1862; the opposition, for the moment, was too heavy.

Owen persevered; in the same year he published a paper *On the Extent and Aims of a National Museum of Natural History*,[1] which set forth his decided views on the matter. It was clear that it was merely a question of time. The Keeper of Mineralogy, Maskelyne, complained that he had no room for a laboratory. An attempt to provide him with one in Torrington Street was turned down by the Trustees. In 1864 Owen tried to short circuit matters by getting in touch directly with the Office of Works on the proposed South Kensington site, and was reprimanded by the Trustees for his pains.[2] Gradually opposition ceased. It was increasingly clear that transfer to the South Kensington site which had now been set aside for the new Museum was the only possible solution. In Bloomsbury, an area of the size deemed necessary by Owen would cost £458,000, as compared with £40,000 in South Kensington. Architects' plans were drawn up and, despite adverse criticism the new buildings gradually took shape.

Like Owen, some of the scientists were having second thoughts. In May 1866 another memorial was drawn up by leading scientists. 'We are of the opinion,' they wrote, 'that it is of fundamental importance to the progress of the Natural Science collections in this country that the administration of the National Natural History Collections should be separated from that of the Library and Art collections and placed under one officer who should be immediately responsible to one of the Queen's ministers.'[3] There would be no Trustees and no Principal Librarian. The exact location of the proposed natural history museum was, in their opinion, of comparatively minor importance, provided it was accessible and within the metropolitan district.

In 1869 it seemed as if it would after all be the Embankment, rather than South Kensington. In January 1869 Richard Owen wrote to Henry Layard, First Commissioner of Works, giving details of what he

1. *On the Extent and Aims of a National Museum of Natural History, Including the substance of a discourse on that subject, delivered at the Royal Institution . . . April 26, 1861.* London, 1862.

2. Panizzi wrote to Layard, then First Commissioner of Works, about this incident. In his letter he stresses the 'inconvenience' caused by heads of departments writing directly to other government departments. 'The Trustees have severely reprimanded one or two officers who have disregarded this.' (Panizzi to Layard, November 29, 1864. Add. MS. 39,112. f. 220.)

3. Add. MS. 38,996. f. 114.

considered to be necessary. After careful consultation with the Trustees' architect, he thought a site of two and a half acres sufficient for present needs. There should be no modification in the plans for the public exhibition galleries, and there should be in addition ample accommodation for both students and scientific visitors.[1] The architect told Layard that the cost of the proposed buildings would be about £1,895,000, and that he considered that brick and terra cotta would be the most suitable materials to use.

In July 1869 Layard informed the Archbishop of Canterbury, as Principal Trustee, that the government wanted to come to an immediate and final decision on the whole matter and asked that full details of the proposed plans be forwarded to him in order that he might lay them before the Cabinet. By this time Owen was demanding a building covering five acres, whilst the Trustees considered two and three-quarters to be quite sufficient. The Embankment site was now a hot favourite. If the Museum were to be put anywhere else, it would indeed be cheaper. As Alfred Waterhouse, the Trustees' architect, wrote to Oldfield, Hawkins' former second in command in the Department of Antiquities, on 16 July 1869, 'I should like Mr Layard to understand that if it had been anywhere else than on the Embankment, my Estimate would hardly have exceeded the 1,500,000.' He goes on: 'The site seems to me to demand a magnificent building.' If however the government and the Trustees were 'willing to forgo magnificence and be content with a *respectable* building . . . the accommodation described could all be secured for the Half million'.[2]

Nevertheless, the South Kensington site, the only one ever seriously considered by the Trustees and the Treasury, as being by far the cheapest, was finally decided on, and the present Natural History Museum building erected there.

By 1878 the natural history departments were preparing for their move to South Kensington. In 1880, at long last, the transfer started. The mineralogical collection was the first to go, followed by the geological and botanical ones. By September 1880 they had all gone and the Trustees announced that it was hoped to open them to the public in their new home on 18 April 1881. To move the Zoological Department, with its numerous and far more fragile specimens, was a considerably more complex undertaking. In 1882 they were still at

1. Add. MS. 38,996. f. 13.
2. Add. MS. 38,996. f. 333b. Alfred Waterhouse, the architect, to Edmund Oldfield, 16 July 1869.

Bloomsbury, awaiting the construction of the larger number of cases which were needed for them at South Kensington. It was unlikely that they could be moved before the spring of 1883, at the earliest. It was pointed out that the zoological collections were equal to all those others which had been transferred in 1880 and that their move must of necessity be a far slower affair. At last, however, in 1883 it was completed and all the natural history collections had finally left Bloomsbury.

Owen, though now almost eighty, was still in nominal charge, but each of the four Keepers was allowed such independence that the new museum for long showed the effects of the lack of overall planning. In 1883, the year of the final move, Owen retired and the post of Superintendent was abolished. All the older Keepers of the Bloomsbury days had now gone, Gray in 1874, Waterhouse and Maskelyne in 1880. New men would create the new Museum at South Kensington, though for many years the link with Bloomsbury was to be maintained and has perhaps never entirely been broken.

The collections that went to South Kensington were far finer and far more numerous than would have seemed possible earlier in the century. During the last years at Bloomsbury were acquired the herbarium of R. J. Shuttleworth, many valuable fossils of both plants and animals, including human remains and various collections of insects, minerals, and so on, the fruits of generations of scholars working in deplorable conditions, who had yet raised the scientific departments of the Museum to a position of real authority within the scientific world.

With their later history at South Kensington we are not concerned. The Museum at Bloomsbury, once considered primarily a natural history one, was now purged of all its scientific departments and devoted, as Panizzi had always wished, to antiquities and to the several library departments.

CHAPTER TEN

The Quiet Years: Consolidation and Retrenchment

O N 15 March 1856 Antonio Panizzi, Keeper of Printed Books since 1837, became the sixth Principal Librarian, to the delight of his many friends and the baffled rage of his equally numerous enemies, both inside and outside the Museum. Madden was perhaps most bitter of all. His rival, 'the blackguard Italian', had achieved the position he himself had so long coveted. For many years he had been suspicious of the machiavellian plans of 'that impudent scoundrel to overthrow Ellis and Forshall'.[1] Hawkins, another disappointed candidate, had confided his fears to Madden over the dinner-table as long ago as March 1848: 'Hawkins spoke out very plainly,' wrote Madden, 'as to Panizzi's design and said he wanted to make himself *Principal Librarian*, Secretary, *Trustee*, Director, and everything else in his own person.'[2] And now, eight years later, the incredible had happened and that 'unscrupulous, lying blackguard' Panizzi, was indeed Principal Librarian and Secretary, at the handsome salary of £1,200 a year. The wretched Madden remained a mere Keeper, burdened by the expenses of his children's education and the maintenance of a standard of living far beyond his narrow means. 'I feel quite ill and sick at the prospect before me', he says and piteously complaining that his rival's appointment 'embitters every hour of my life'.[3]

But it was now a losing battle. Panizzi was determined to exert a discipline amongst his subordinates, which Ellis had singularly failed to achieve. His first act as Principal Librarian was to send a letter formally telling the Keepers of his appointment and requesting their cooperation in the tasks which lay ahead. He politely but firmly demanded from them 'that efficient assistance which is absolutely necessary for the good of the service'.[4] One by one, the Keepers replied,

1. *Madden Journal*, 22 Feb. 1848.
2. *op. cit.*, 6 March 1848.
3. *op. cit.*, 24 March 1856, 31 December 1856.
4. Add. MS. 36,717. f. 425.

even Gray, assuring their new chief of their complete support. Only Madden absolutely declined to answer,[1] his Assistant Keeper, Bond, replying in his stead.

Panizzi was having no more of Sir Frederic's nonsense. He had put up with his tantrums for years and would do so no longer. He complained immediately to the Archbishop, as Chairman of the Trustees, concerning the Keeper of Manuscripts' boorish conduct. 'It is,' he wrote, 'unhappily too true that Sir F. Madden will not speak to me.' Panizzi continues, with that pained air of offended virtue which must have particularly infuriated his enemies, 'I never intentionally by airs or words gave offence to Sir F. Madden and I am at a loss to conceive the ground of his conduct . . . Such personal antipathies should cease . . . I mean to do my duty conscientiously with all due regard to other people's feelings but firmly',[2] and that meant not allowing this discourtesy. Madden had no intention of replying to the Principal Librarian's note. 'Mr. Hawkins asked me if I had answered Mr. Panizzi's letter & on my replying in the negative (with some surprise at the question) he said every other Head of a Department had done so, and he advised me as a friend to do so too, to avoid being placed in an antagonistic position. I should never have thought even of replying to such a letter & I am quite astonished that Hawkins & Gray should have done so! Curse this fellow! He had succeeded too well in placing his foot on our necks'.[3] But nevertheless, on 3 April, a short note was at last received from him by the Principal Librarian and so honour was satisfied.[4]

After the storms of the previous twenty years the ten years of Panizzi's Principal Librarianship were comparatively peaceful. His relationships with his Keepers were on the whole good. Of the two most difficult, Madden, in disgust with 'that devil who never ceases to harass every one around him',[5] now left things more and more to Bond, who had always got on well with Panizzi, and the introduction of the post of Superintendent of the Natural History Departments meant

1. Madden's reaction to the letter was one of stupefied rage. 'I regard this letter as a thorough piece of humbug and the real scope of it only to let us know he is our Master.' (*Madden Journal*, 24 March 1856.)
2. Add. MS. 36,717. f. 445.
3. *Madden Journal*, 2 April 1856.
4. 'I also wrote (in compliance with the advice of Mr Hawkins and Dr Gray), although sorely against my will to Mr Panizzi.' (*op. cit.*, 3 April 1856.)
5. *op. cit.*, 1 August 1856.

that the Principal Librarian dealt with Owen, rather than directly with the prickly Keeper of Zoology Gray.

The division of the Department of Antiquities in 1861 into a number of successor departments ensured that Panizzi had under him a team of friendly younger men, rather than the aged Hawkins, jealous of his rival's success. It is also true that Panizzi, conscious of the harm that Forshall had done by preventing any close relationship between the Trustees and their senior staff, now ensured that relations between the Board and their officers were as free and amicable as conditions permitted. The policy of some Trustees in having as little as possible to do with their departmental heads, and deliberately ignoring their professional advice, had done much to lower morale. For as William Vaux, soon to be the first Keeper of Coins and Medals, said in a letter to Henry Layard, much of the troubles of the past years had been due to both these inescapable facts. 'Another great evil has been the refusal on the part of the 5 or 6 [of the Trustees] who attended . . . to have any personal Communication with the officers – I say that on this the whole real efficiency of the Museum depends – I have some hope that this may be amended by Panizzi, but the amendment sh^d not rest on the chance of who may be *pro tempore* Princ. Librarian . . . Had there been that free and unreserved communication between Trustees and officers which even the last Commission recommended . . . Madden would not have thought Panizzi rapacious, nor Panizzi have quarrelled with Gray'; if there had been a 'board of officers', 'each man would have heard what the other had to say – and if there was one more obstinate than the other he w^d have been swayed or his views modified by the combined influence of the others'.[1]

Whether such an institution would, in the bitter atmosphere of these years, have been quite as effective as Vaux seems to have thought is a matter of speculation, but the situation was now better and Panizzi resolved to keep it that way.

Of the first of his two major problems, the abiding one of space, much has already been said. The second, the need for a proper salary structure, increased chances of promotion and adequate pension arrangements, involved the new Principal Librarian in a long and exhausting battle with the Treasury in which he was at last to emerge triumphant. The struggle was, needless to say, to continue under his successors, but Panizzi had the satisfaction of knowing when he retired in 1866 that the foundations of a rational staff structure had been laid and that he

1. Vaux to Layard, ? April 1856. Add. MS. 38,984. ff. 374, 375.

had secured what had been long vainly urged, adequate pensions for all the staff as a right, and not as a rarely granted concession to a favoured few.

The question of superannuation had long been a vexed one. Almost alone amongst government servants, the staff of the Museum had to work, unless blessed with private incomes, literally until they died. As Winter Jones, then Keeper of Printed Books, wrote in January 1860, 'Under the existing regulations, no person in the service of the Trustees has any claim to a retiring allowance. However enfeebled he may have become by advanced age, or bodily or mental infirmity, he has no *right* to ask to be relieved from the performance of his duties – nor have the Trustees the power to award to him the smallest pension.'[1] The fear of poverty and of being unable to provide for his family lay behind much of Madden's jealousy and cantankerousness, and the same could be said of many of the other officers. As early as March 1836, the Trustees had approached the Treasury on this question. They said they were unwilling to dismiss aged or infirm servants, yet they were, as a result, burdened with staff clearly long past their best. But the Chancellor of the Exchequer 'did not apprehend it would be expedient to introduce the principle of superannuation into the Museum, but that it would be better to select carefully and to trust to the prudential habits of the persons employed'.[2] Cold comfort for the underpaid attendants, and even for the assistants, struggling to maintain their gentility on a few hundred pounds a year.

We know what John Gray thought of this cruel system: men staying on till death released them; six carried off by mental illness within a few years, and the bitter personal tragedies of drunkenness, debt, and despair that Panizzi had often to relieve out of his own pocket. With a Board of Trustees willing to listen to him, Panizzi resolved that he would do what he could. At his insistence, an investigation was carried out in June 1857 by two Treasury experts into 'the nature of the duties performed by the different classes of officers and servants in the British Museum'.[3] They concluded that normal Civil Service regulations with some modifications, should henceforth apply to the Museum staff, and pensions be granted as in other public offices.

The Treasury insisted that in return all appointments at the Museum

1. *Printed Books, Draft Departmental Minutes*, 23 January 1860.
2. *Committee Minutes*, vol. 15, pp. 4205, 4232, 12 March, 16 April 1836.
3. Add. MS. 36,728. f. 316. The two experts were Sir Charles Trevelyan and George Arbuthnot.

would have to be by examination, and that such examinations would be conducted by the Civil Service Commissioners. This at once led to difficulties. The normal system of examination was too inelastic for the needs of the Museum. Candidates without any real knowledge of the subjects in which they were supposed to have been examined were granted certificates of appointment, whilst others, of the sort that the Museum most needed, with the warmest recommendations from the heads of their departments, were failed on technicalities. Panizzi proposed that to avoid such mistakes, an officer of the Museum should assist in setting the papers and be present when the candidates were interviewed. 'By some such arrangement the practical result of the examinations would prove more uniformly beneficial to the peculiar service of the British Museum,' he wrote.[1] But the Commissioners would have none of it, and a long and angry controversy ensued, the sort of struggle which the artful old man still loved. Floored by Panizzi's arguments and feeling that they were being made fools of, the Commissioners retaliated by not appointing anyone at all to successive Museum vacancies, deliberately failing even the most qualified candidates. These 'constant and unexpected rejections', on which Panizzi sardonically reported to the Trustees, showed that 'the system of Civil Service Examinations as at present conducted, certainly works very ill for the Museum and appears to have done much more harm than good. It failed to keep out a Gemmer, and since the consideration of this failure . . . its sole effect has been to perpetuate vacancies'.[2] Panizzi is here referring to events which occurred during the final years of his Principal Librarianship. In March 1864 Frederic Gemmer had been appointed to an Assistantship in the Department of Manuscripts. He proved to be incompetent, lacking even basic knowledge of Latin and French, subjects in which he was supposed to have been examined by the Commissioners. With Panizzi and Madden for once in complete agreement, he was induced to resign after only fifteen weeks in the Museum. A bitter public controversy followed with open letters published on both sides.[3]

A compromise was eventually reached between the Museum and the Commissioners and appointments were made without further

1. *Correspondence relative to Examination of Candidates for Situations in the B.M.*, p. 9. (PP, H. of C., 1866, vol. XXXIX, p. 241.)
2. *op. cit.*, p. 42.
3. Much of the correspondence is contained in the Appendix to PP, H. of C., 1866, vol. XXXIX, p. 241.

trouble. But in the peculiar circumstances of the Museum the Civil Service examination system never really worked and it was ultimately abandoned in favour of appointment by interviews alone.

It was not only the appointment and the superannuation of his staff which Panizzi regarded as of prime importance. He wanted to provide a secure and well-paid career which would attract the best men and keep them at the Museum. Salaries must be raised, so that men would no longer half kill themselves by undertaking outside work for the sake of a few extra pounds, as Sir Frederic Madden and many others had done, devoting to such work time and energy better spent in the performance of their official duties.

All through the 1850s and '60s, with the cost of living still rising, the various grades of the Museum staff backed by their Principal Librarian, petitioned for increases in salaries. A few improvements were granted by a reluctant Treasury, but the general position still remained far from satisfactory, and Panizzi's successor Winter Jones was likewise to be continually occupied by this intractable problem.

Panizzi was now old and ailing. In December 1862 he had had a serious breakdown and was granted leave of absence to recuperate in Naples until the following May. During this time John Winter Jones, though not the senior Keeper, was appointed Deputy Principal Librarian and was obviously being considered his old chief's successor. On 24 June 1865 Panizzi, crippled with rheumatism, tendered his resignation, which was reluctantly accepted. He was persuaded to stay on for a further period, and was granted a pension equal to his salary and emoluments. Flattered by the request, the old man agreed to remain in office, though increasingly hampered by illness and old age. 'I am still in harness,' he wrote to a friend, 'and see no prospect of being released.'[1] Tired and weary he once more tendered his resignation on 5 June 1866.[2]

There was now the problem of his successor. Changes in the administration of the Museum were again being contemplated by the

1. Add. MS. 36,723. f. 425. Panizzi to Fox Maule, 11th Earl of Dalhousie, formerly Lord Panmure, 1801–1874, Secretary of State for War, 1855–1858, and an old friend of Panizzi's. He succeeded his cousin as Earl of Dalhousie in 1860. What particularly annoyed Panizzi was the fact that, as he had already been granted a pension he was now working at the Museum for nothing. He angrily quoted precedents where government servants in similar positions had been allowed large additional fees.

2. In a letter to Sir George Grey, the Home Secretary, reiterating his desire to hand over the Principal Librarianship to a successor, Panizzi wrote 'I must trifle with my health no longer'. (Add. MS. 36,723. f. 436.) Committee Minutes, vol. 31, p. 11,022. 5 June 1866.

government and it seemed quite possible that the powers of the Principal Librarian might be curtailed or the post abolished. On 22 June Panizzi wrote to his old friend Jones, asking him whether he would be prepared to accept the position in such circumstances. Jones replied that he would.[1] The two names submitted for the customary Royal approval were those of Jones and Newton. But Charles Newton, who would have been a very popular choice, was by no means anxious to become Principal Librarian, and preferred his departmental work, as he now made plain.[2]

On 14 July 1866, Panizzi laid his successor's appointment before the Board. Also before the Board was Madden's letter of resignation, timed to the very day with that of his rival. To Sir Frederic's great chagrin, he failed to get his whole salary as pension, and was forced to be content with £600 a year. To the end the 'scoundrel Italian' had got the better of him.[3]

1. Add. MS. 36,723. ff. 459, 460. *Committee Minutes*, vol. 31, p. 11,035. 14 July 1866.
2. Newton wrote to Panizzi: 'I should not have accepted the office . . . Best where I am.' (10 July 1866. Add. MS. 36,723. f. 485.)
3. On 12 July 1866, Madden sent the Board a memorial giving details of his services since 1826. 'I am now in the 66th year of my age,' he wrote, 'and have completed forty years service in the British Museum.' He continues '*I am the only officer in the Museum whose Salary has been actually stationary since 1837.*' He therefore petitioned the Trustees to ask the Treasury 'that I should be allowed to retain my full salary and emoluments amounting to £800'. Two days later, Madden anxiously awaited the result of the Trustees' deliberations. 'It proved just as I feared that by Mr. Panizzi's tactics, my case was put before the *Standing Committee*' (whom Madden regarded as being packed by his rival's supporters) 'and a resolution was passed, accepting my resignation & ordering a letter to be sent to the Treasury without any reference whatever to the General Committee.' The matter was then adjourned at the request of Madden's supporters on the General Committee for a further week. 'And this is the treatment I receive after all my hard work of fifty years . . . Mr Jones, the *sneak* was in the Committee Room all the time but of course, did not open his lips. Mr. P. on a vote of thanks being passed for his services (in addition to his pension of £1400) was *so affected* he could not read an official paper!!! The infernal humbug of this man passes all understanding!' Page after page of Madden's journal is filled with vituperation against the man he hated, cursing him 'for all he has done to make my life wretched for so many years'. On the 21st the anxious Madden heard that the Trustees had accepted his resignation, but would only recommend that he should receive £600 a year retiring allowance. 'Not a word of regret at the loss of my services . . . they think that I probably sign a few letters and read the newspapers as Mr Panizzi has done.' Despite further angry letters to the new Principal Librarian, Winter Jones, a larger pension would not be granted and his services were ordered to be terminated from 1 October 1866. 'The Italian villain has kept his foot on me to the last moment,' groaned Sir Frederic, 'may God or rather the devil requite him for it.' (*Madden Journal*, 12, 16, 21,

Winter Jones was of a very different character from Panizzi. As Richard Garnett wrote of him some years later, 'He was not the man to innovate or originate, but was admirably qualified for the work which actually fell to his lot – first to be the right hand of a great architect, then to consolidate the structure he had helped to erect, and prepare it for still vaster extension and more commanding proportions in the times to come.'[1]

Jones's Principal Librarianship was a time of consolidation, of a steady assimilation of the gains already made. For the rest, he undoubtedly at times displayed a timidity and unwillingness to accept changes, even when such changes were long overdue. He, like his predecessor, was greatly concerned over the question of inadequate space and was constantly engaged in the controversies over the proposed move of the natural history collections to South Kensington, the final arrangements for which were made towards the end of his period of office.

To a greater extent than Panizzi, Winter Jones was deeply interested in every aspect of the collections under his care, and made certain that the antiquities in particular were never neglected. With such brilliant keepers under him as Newton, Franks and Birch, their needs were not likely to be forgotten, but these distinguished scholars were assured at all times of their chief's generous support. His efforts to secure more funds for excavations at Benghazi, Ephesus and elsewhere were particularly appreciated.

It was, however, the apparently endless controversies with the Treasury over the salaries and conditions of his staff that engaged him most deeply and probably hastened the breakdown of his health. Under his somewhat cold exterior, he had a kind and generous heart. 'He was not emotional, but his affections were warm and deep: he was not impressionable, but kindness was with him an innate principle. If

1. R. Garnett, *The Late John Winter Jones*, p. 11.

22 July.) On 29 September Madden made a final entry 'in my Note Book of Official Business . . . which I have kept ever since 1837. My last day of official duty, thank God', and went on: 'In conclusion I quit my official duties with the most bitter sense of the ingratitude with which my services have been treated by the Trustees and with a deep curse on the unscrupulous, lying, scheming Italian villain, by whose cruelty my official life has been embittered so many years and my chances to promotion and liberal recompense frustrated and denied.' (*Madden Journal*, 29 September 1866.)

On Monday 1 October, he records, 'I rose this morning a *free man*, thank God, after a slavery of more than forty years.' On 29 September he had at last passed over to Bond the keys, papers and other documents relating to the Department. (*Madden Journal*, 1 October 1866.)

ever he seemed to act with harshness, it was from a constraining sense
of official duty, and it might easily be seen that the necessity was very
disagreeable to him.'[1] Far too many of the staff, particularly the
attendants, were still staying on till an advanced age. Nothing gave the
Principal Librarian more pain than the occasional necessity of removing
the old and incompetent, while others, scarcely more suitable, lingered
on, when a more ruthless man would undoubtedly have got rid of them.
'What seemed in him stiffness – and had all the disadvantageous effects
of stiffness – was in reality a reserve which made him appear constrained
where men of less real courtesy and kindness would have seemed facile
and genial.'[2]

The Museum staff had by this time become quite large. No less than
344 persons were now employed by the Trustees and the annual vote
was £110,000. This seemed a large number when the Colonial Office,
for example, employed a mere sixty-five civil servants and had an
annual vote of £36,210. Yet salaries and prospects for promotion were
still less than in comparable positions in Whitehall.[3] As Winter Jones
emphasised, they were little different from those of forty years before,
despite a general rise in the cost of living. And as he further pointed
out: 'The British Museum is a vast educational establishment . . . The
keepers and assistant keepers become the accomplished men they are
by the long association with and study of the collection while in subordinate capacity. Each assistant must discharge his duties as though
the usefulness of the collection depended upon his own exertions. It is,
moreover, this long and intimate practice which enables the responsible
officers to make judicious additions to the collections, to distinguish
true objects from the spurious, and to estimate the market value of such
objects as are offered to the Trustees for purchase.'[4] The Trustees and
even more the Treasury, were in no mood to listen either to the petitions
of the staff or to the remonstrances of the Principal Librarian, and
turned down all schemes of substantial reorganisation. In 1877 a
certain measure of reform was at last accepted and for a time conditions
did improve.[5]

1. *op. cit.*, p. 10.
2. *op. cit.*, p. 11.
3. 'The salaries of the staff appointments in the British Museum appear to be small
with respect to the nature and importance of the work to be discharged.' *Correspondence
relating to the Salaries*, p. 2. (PP, H. of C., 1877, vol. LXVII, p. 893.)
4. *op. cit.*, p. 20.
5. The new establishment was laid down in a Treasury letter of 10 December 1877,
backdated to the previous 21 March. *op. cit.*, p. 23.

All this worry and continual controversy, however, had proved too much for Jones and his health now began to deteriorate rapidly. In 1877 Newton was appointed Deputy Principal Librarian, to act for him during his frequent absences. In the following August, Winter Jones resigned, to die suddenly and peacefully three years later, two years after his old chief Panizzi, whose funeral he was too ill to attend.

His successor, much to the suprise of all, was not the able and popular Sir Charles Newton, who had made an excellent deputy during Jones' four months sick leave in 1877, but the almost unknown Keeper of Manuscripts, Edward Augustus Bond, whose claims were, however, warmly pressed by old Panizzi. Bond had long run his Department with outstanding success. Since Madden had withdrawn from administrative duties towards the end of his career, Bond had been in virtual charge of the Department for twenty years or so. He was to prove an equally outstanding Principal Librarian, the first of the three eminent Principal Librarians which his department gave in turn to the Museum, who, among them, governed that institution for the next fifty-three years.

Bond was not only a man who knew his own mind, but one who drew the best out of others. He had achieved the impossible by being on good terms with both Panizzi and Madden, and was liked and respected by all. As Principal Librarian he had the inestimable gift of seeing at once the merits of any reform proposed by his subordinates and then ensuring, by his own tenacity and strength of purpose, that such plans were successfully translated into fact.

Bond was liberal and farsighted and no man was ever more ready to accept new ideas. Almost his very first act as Principal Librarian was the introduction of electric light into the Reading Room. There had been gas in the officers' residences for many years, but its introduction into the Museum itself was never sanctioned.[1] The question of lighting

1. The Trustees were most alarmed to find out that gas had, in fact, been installed in the officers' residences. On 23 October 1847 Edward Hawkins had asked to have gas laid on in his house. The Trustees not only refused his request, but ordered an immediate investigation as to how and why it had been installed in the other residences. It appeared that as far back as 1818 the Trustees had written to the Treasury asking if gas lamps might be erected in the courtyard and in front of the Museum. This was the only official minute on the subject. The new gas lamps were duly put up. Planta, then Principal Librarian, had had gas carried from one of the lamps in the courtyard, quite unknown – at least officially – to the Trustees, to light the first floor and basement passages of his own house. He had, at the same time, given permission to Baber, Keeper

the Museum by gas had been gone into thoroughly in 1861. The Trustees had approached James Braidwood, the Superintendent of the London Fire Brigade, for expert advice. He was absolutely against any use of gas. In no circumstances would it be safe, for there was constant risk of fire, or even explosion. Another hazard, according to Braidwood, would be the discoloration of stone and marble by the fumes. The cost of installation would be very high, entailing considerable modifications to the floors, ceilings and walls of the existing buildings. Smirke, and subsequently the Trustees, concurred. In consequence the Board unanimously resolved that they would not be justified 'in allowing the Collections . . . to be open at any hour which would require Gaslight'.[1]

Electricity was obviously safer, even with the primitive apparatus then in use, but even so, doubts were expressed as to its advisability. A friend, W. S. Jevons, wrote to Richard Garnett voicing his concern at the introduction of this dangerous system of lighting into the old building. In his opinion, to be really safe the Museum should have been entirely rebuilt on modern lines, so as to render it absolutely fire-proof, and this step should have been taken when the Natural History collections were moved to South Kensington. Public opinion would undoubtedly soon demand the extension of electric lighting to all parts of the Museum. 'The risks . . . are said to be greater than those from gas. . . . I believe that you have simply admitted the Trojan

1. *British Museum. Lighting by Gas*, p. 3. (PP, H. of C., 1861, vol. XXXIV, p. 225.) James Braidwood, 1800–1861, Superintendent of the London Fire Brigade, was killed by a falling wall shortly after during the disastrous fire at Tooley Street, London Bridge.

of Printed Books, to have a gas jet over the fanlight above the door to his quarters. The staircase in the South West Tower leading to the apartments of Panizzi, Madden and other officers was also lit by gas. Somewhat unctuously, Ellis told the Trustees that when he himself took over from Planta, he had had the gas fittings in the Principal Librarian's residence taken out.

The first of the new residences to be built was that of J. E. Gray, who asked Sir Robert Smirke if a proper system of gas lighting might not be installed in it at his own expense. Smirke, knowing that there had been gas points in the old building for many years, saw no reason to raise any objection. Gray, therefore, had had gas installed in all the main rooms of his new residence. Hawkins, somewhat unwisely, asked the Trustees if he might do the same. The Board were horrified at the mere idea and issued stringent instructions that in future gas was not to be installed in any Museum building or residence without their express permission. (*Committee Minutes*, vol. 23, pp. 7425, 7349, 13 November 1847, 15 January 1848.)

The new Reading Room had had the necessary fittings for gas lighting put in, but they were never used.

Horse.'[1] The risk of fire had always been a real one. A bad outbreak in the binder's shop shortly before Panizzi's retirement nearly spread to the main buildings, and there had been other minor incidents.

Nevertheless, Bond was right as usual and he persevered despite difficulties and defective equipment. No longer, therefore, would the Reading Room and, indeed, the whole Museum, close on a foggy day. The service would carry on despite such hazards, and the provision of ample natural light for galleries and library would cease to be a matter of concern as it had been for Panizzi and his contemporaries.

Bond's other great contribution to the general administration of the Museum and to its enjoyment by the public was to set about removing the last of the old restrictions on entrance to the galleries. As late as 1878, the public were admitted to the Museum only on Mondays Wednesdays, Fridays and Saturdays (on Saturdays from 12 noon), the other days being reserved for students. The hours were from 10 to 4 in winter, from 10 to 5 in spring and autumn, and from 10 to 6 in summer. On Mondays and Saturdays from May to August there was, however, an extension to 8 p.m.

Bond was determined to end all this. In the next year, 1879, the first of his reports as Principal Librarian announced: 'In order to prevent the disappointment of intending visitors occasioned by the closing of the Museum to the general public on two days of the week, as has been the custom, the Trustees have ordered that henceforward the Museum shall be open daily.' Certain galleries were still to be closed on particular days. On Mondays and Saturdays the whole of the galleries were open; on Tuesday and Thursday, all except Natural History; on Wednesday and Friday, all except the antiquities on the Upper Floor and the rest of Greek and Roman Antiquities. The old prohibition forbidding babies in arms was likewise swept away.

In 1882 the traditional closing of the Museum on Ash Wednesday was done away with, as well as the 12 o'clock opening on Saturdays. 'The Museum is now thrown open every weekday (except Good Friday and Christmas Day) throughout the year from 10 o'clock in the morning', though some galleries were still restricted on certain days to students.

1. W. S. Jevons to Richard Garnett, 13, 18 December 1881. Jevons remarks on recent terrible fires in Paris and Vienna, in his opinion entirely due to recently installed electrical wiring systems. The Bodleian, too, he considered now no more than a 'mere tinder box'. (Add. MS. 43,377. ff. 123, 125.) William Stanley Jevons, 1835–1882, economist and logician.

The Reading Room hours were likewise extended every night till 8 p.m., thanks to the recently introduced electric light, and the annual 'closed periods' for cleaning were cut to the first four days in March and October instead of, as hitherto, one week in February, May and October.[1] The Museum remained shut on Sunday for a few more years, until March 1896 when a motion was passed by the House of Commons that the 'National Museums and Art Galleries in London should be open . . . on Sundays, after 2 p.m., upon condition that no officer shall be required to attend on more than Six days per week, and that any one who may have conscientious objections shall be exempt from Sunday duty.' Maunde Thompson, Bond's successor, at once had applied this to the Museum, which in consequence then opened on Sunday between the hours of 2 and 6 p.m.[2]

Perhaps as a result of this more liberal policy the rise in the number of visitors during these years was continuous, 573,317 in 1875; 655,688 five years later, and 767,402 in 1882. But the removal of the popular zoological collections produced a fall in the attendance which continued for some years.

Similar increases also took place in the number of readers both to the General Reading Room and to the Manuscripts Students' Room when the latter opened in 1885. A temporary solution to the perennial space problem was also found. Not only were the antiquities and

1. *Accounts, &c*, 1877–78, 1878–79, 1881–82. (PP, H. of C., 1878, vol. LX, p. 593; 1878–79, vol. LXVII, p. 611; 1882, vol. L, p. 867.)

2. An amendment, that the Museum should be open from '10 a.m. to 10 p.m. on at least three week-day evenings each week but that Sunday opening was neither necessary nor expedient, and is contrary to the ascertained wishes of those classes chiefly interested', was defeated by 178 votes to 93. After prolonged debate, the original resolution was passed in the early hours of the following morning, Wednesday 11 March. (CJ, vol. 151, pp. 87, 88. *Hansard*, 4, vol. 38, col. 617–657.)

A similar attempt to secure Sunday opening forty years before had met with a very different fate. In the full tide of mid-Victorian evangelical fervour, Greville records in his diary for 21 February 1856; 'Last night the Evangelical and Sabbatarian interest had a great victory in the House of Commons, routing those who endeavoured to effect the opening of the National Gallery and British Museum on Sunday. The only man of importance who sustained this unequal and imprudent contest was Lord Stanley. At this moment cant and Puritanism are in the ascendent . . . and . . . it will be very well if we escape some of the more stringent measures against Sunday occupations and amusements with which Exeter Hall and the prevailing spirit threaten us.' (Greville, vol. 2, p. 293.) Their next 'triumph' was, in fact, the prohibition of the 'innocent amusement' given on Sundays by military bands in Kensington Gardens and other London parks. *op. cit.*, p. 294.)

I

ethnographical collections able to move into the rooms now vacated by the Natural History departments, but extensive new buildings were at last erected. They comprised the White Wing, constructed from money left to the Museum as long ago as 1823, which the Trustees had not been able to make use of until 1879.[1] From this money was built not only the Mausoleum Room, to house in a fitting fashion the precious sculptures from Halicarnassus, so long hidden behind glass screens on the colonnade, but also a whole new range of rooms on the east side of the Museum for the Departments of Manuscripts and Prints and Drawings, as well as a new boiler house.

Amongst the minor but none the less important features of the closing years of Bond's term was the provision in 1887 of a more commodious room for use as a public restaurant off the Egyptian Gallery. Though a decided improvement, it was to become inadequate for the growing numbers wishing to make use of it. Its predecessor, on the upper floor at the north east corner of the main buildings, was converted into an exhibition room for the display of antiquities from America. In 1888 Bond retired, respected and admired by all his colleagues, for beneath a 'cold and reserved' exterior, he had 'a most kind heart and a truly elevated mind, far above every petty consideration, and delighting to dwell in a purely intellectual sphere', a quiet, placid man who had been an outstanding Principal Librarian.[2]

To Bond succeeded the formidable Edward Maunde Thompson,[3] Keeper of Manuscripts since 1878. As with Panizzi, stories of him, especially of his temper and ruthlessness towards his unfortunate subordinates, continued to circulate for many years after his retirement

1. Kenyon, *Buildings*, p. 7. *Accounts &c.* for 1883–1884 and 1884–1885. (PP, H. of C. 1884, vol. LXI, p. 723, 1884-5, vol. LXI, p. 651.) The White bequest had originally been made in 1823 by a Mr William White, a neighbour, who was appalled at the ruinous condition of old Montagu House. It was, however, subject to a life interest which expired only in 1879. The total amount of the bequest came to nearly £72,000, but over £16,300 had to be deducted as legacy duty. The White Wing, opened in 1885, lay to the east of the Manuscript Saloon and the Middle Room of that Department. It also covered a part of the Principal Librarian's garden, which both Panizzi and Bond had freely offered as a site for an extension of the Museum.

2. R. Garnett, *The Late Sir Edward A. Bond, KCB, Essays in Librarianship*, p. 338. Although awarded a CB whilst still Principal Librarian, Bond was only made a KCB shortly before his death.

3. Sir Maude Thompson, GCB, ISC, 1840–1929, palaeographer, born in Jamaica. He entered the Museum in 1861, as an assistant in the Principal Librarian's Office, but was soon transferred to the Department of Manuscripts. He was Assistant Keeper, 1871, Keeper, 1878, and Principal Librarian, 1888.

in 1909 and, for the most part, depicted him as a savage and vindictive tyrant.

Amongst those told of Maunde Thompson to the author nearly thirty years after Thompson's retirement was that of a certain Assistant Keeper, by the author's time a dignified elderly figure, who, in the days of his carefree youth, had been reprimanded by the irate Principal Librarian for riding a bicycle in the public streets. Another story was that the Principal Librarian had once caught an attendant asleep at his post in one of the galleries. As the men had often to work as waiters until the small hours of the morning to supplement their meagre wages, this was not altogether surprising. Maunde Thompson, however, not content with a violent rebuke, refused him any further annual increases to his already pitifully small salary, a decision reversed only when Thompson was succeeded in 1909 by the more kindly Kenyon.

Maunde Thompson like Panizzi insisted on the rule that top hats were to be worn by the senior staff in all the public galleries except the Reading Room, where, by convention, only the Superintendent might wear a top hat, even the Principal Librarian uncovering when passing through that Room. The last regular Superintendent to wear one when on duty was F. D. Sladen, whilst the last person ever to do so was the late L. C. Wharton, when acting as Deputy Superintendent. He had a very old and battered topper which he kept especially for such occasions.

As far as the writer is aware, the last Director to observe this custom was Sir John Forsdyke, some twenty-five to thirty years ago, who always wore, not indeed a top hat, but a soft one when walking through the galleries, meticulously removing it upon entering the Reading Room.

Similar stories were told of Panizzi for many years after his retirement. As late as May 1929 A. R. Dryhurst, then recently retired from the post of Assistant Secretary, remarked in a letter to G. F. Barwick, 'P. may have been a Radical in Modena. In Bloomsbury he was certainly an absolutist. I always understood that he was responsible for the custom (or perhaps its retention) that an Assistant going outside his Department, should be careful to wear his topper . . . it was almost a hanging matter for an Assistant to be caught hatless in one of the Museum galleries. What he would say of these days when toppers are few and members of a hatless brigade flaunt their high principles in the streets.' Dryhurst tells also of another who incurred the wrath of the 'great Panjandrum', who exclaimed, 'O my God, you are a damned fool.' The poor man 'rushed about the office half-demented', but resolved to prove himself by working hard in his spare time to enter Holy Orders. Once he was ordained even 'the great God Pan found it was necessary to speak civilly to a worm that had turned so successfully'.[1]

The traditional picture of Maunde Thompson is probably exaggerated, but authoritarian he undoubtedly was and, like his great predecessor Panizzi, with little patience or sympathy for those less able or less industrious than himself. It must be admitted, too, that, in the closing years of the century, idleness seems to have been prevalent amongst all grades of the staff, and Maunde Thompson's ruthlessness may often have been necessary. A fine scholar, particularly in the field of palaeography, he was also a first-class administrator and man of business. By his powerful personality and friendship with many men of influence, including King Edward VII, the new Principal Librarian did much to bring the Museum to the forefront of public life and to gain for it valuable concessions from both the Treasury and the government.

In order that they might remain open in the evening, the use of electric light was now extended to the public galleries. One hundred and twenty-eight arc lamps and 644 glow lamps were installed, and the eastern and western ranges of galleries opened on alternative evenings. The experiment, however, was not a success. Few visitors came, and it was discontinued in 1898.[2]

In the same year Maunde Thompson was largely instrumental in obtaining Treasury authority to purchase for £200,000 all the houses and gardens to the east, north, and west of the Museum, thus securing the whole of the island site on which the Museum stands, with a view

1. *Barwick Papers. P.B. Departmental Archives.*
2. There had, of course, been evening opening during the summer months on certain days as late as 8 p.m. for many years. However, from 1 February 1890, with the introduction of electric light into the public galleries, the Trustees announced that 'the eastern and western galleries alternately have been opened to the public on weekday evenings from 8 to 10 p.m.'. Not more than an average of about 300 visitors seem to have come during the first few months. In the report for 1897–98 the Principal Librarian stated: 'The steady annual diminution of the number of evening visitors has satisfied the Trustees that they would not be justified in continuing to incur the expense of keeping the galleries open in the evenings.' The galleries were, however, to be kept open to 6 p.m. every weekday throughout the years. (*Accounts &c.*, 1889–90, p. 8. PP, H. of C., 1890, vol. LVI, p. 819; *Accounts &c.*, 1897–98, p. 14. PP, H. of C., 1898, vol. LXXI, p. 296.)

to providing adequate space for any subsequent enlargement.[1] Unfortunately, except to the north, hardly anything was done for many years to make use of this badly needed space, and it may indeed be said that, even today, far more use might be made of what is undoubtedly a very valuable and convenient site for a long-wanted expansion of both galleries and offices. To say this is, of course, not to blame the Trustees. Successive Chancellors of the Exchequer were more interested in the rentals to be obtained from these houses, than in giving the Museum more space.

To the north, however, plans were put in motion for a new building covering the area occupied by the houses on the south side of Montagu Place. The Trustees had at their disposal a sum of £50,000, which had been left them by a Mr Vincent Stuckey Lean 'for the improvement and extension of the Reading Room',[2] and confidently hoped to obtain additional funds from the government to carry out a building programme such as they envisaged. But now the Treasury, alarmed by the financial situation caused by the South African War, refused to grant further sums for the extension of the Museum unless the Trustees undertook to reduce the amount of their holdings. There had already been agitation with regard to this – the perennial charge of the ignorant that the Museum was housing great quantities of useless rubbish which should at once be got rid of to make room without further extensions.,

In April 1900 a Bill was introduced into the Lords by Viscount Peel, himself a Trustee, to enable the Museum to do this. After being passed by the Lords, it was introduced into the Commons by John Morley, another Trustee. Both, one would have thought, should have known better. The Bill proposed that the Trustees should be empowered to deposit with the local authorities any newspaper of that locality received since 1827 and might also, in addition, dispose of or destroy 'printed matter deposited in the British Museum, which is not of

1. Kenyon, *Buildings*, p. 8. *Accounts &c.*, 1894–95, p. 14. (PP, H. of C., 1895, vol. LXXVIII, p. 735.) This land and the houses on it had been valued at £240,000 as long ago as 1859. The action of the Duke of Bedford in disposing of them nearly forty years later for an even lesser sum was remarkably generous. As part of the arrangement the dwarf railings in front of the railings in Great Russell Street were removed and the lions by Alfred Stevens which adorned them were transferred partly to be placed round the Wellington Memorial in St Paul's Cathedral and partly to various positions around the Museum. (*A Bill to Provide for the purchase of certain Lands belonging to the Duke of Bedford by the Trustees of the British Museum.* 57 & 58 Vict. c.34. Royal Assent 17 August 1894. PP, H. of C., 1894, vol. 1, p. 105.)
2. Kenyon, *Buildings*, p. 8.

sufficient value to justify its preservation in the Museum'.[1] Widespread agitation in the columns of *The Times* and elsewhere, largely organised by Maunde Thompson, and the powerful advocacy of Sir Sidney Lee,[2] led to the dropping of this misguided piece of legislation which, if enforced, would have resulted in the loss of much valuable historical material.

The industry, accuracy and high sense of duty which Thompson had displayed in the Department of Manuscripts were even more marked on his translation to a higher office. Unlike many of his colleagues, he took but little part in the proceedings of learned societies and was by no means fond of making speeches or appearing at public meetings. His whole heart was in his Museum work and he had few outside interests. Despite his sympathy with those in real distress, he was a stern man, though in private life he could be both genial and hospitable, with a lively sense of humour. At the Museum, he was too often otherwise. Like Panizzi, he was a constant friend but a formidable adversary, and as Kenyon his successor wrote, did not easily change his opinions or his estimate of a man. To him the sole and only worthwhile test was the readiness of any member of his staff to do his job well and to serve the best interests of the Museum.

Thompson had always a strong interest in forwarding the education of the general public. He introduced radical improvements in the

1. *A Bill to authorise the Trustees of the British Museum to deposit Copies of Local Newspapers with Local Authorities, and to dispose of valueless printed matter.* (PP, H. of L., vol. IV, p. 89.) The Bill was first presented in the House of Lords on 5 April 1900 by Viscount Peel, passed and sent to the Commons on 10 May. It was there read for the first time on 14 May, came up for its second reading on 17 May, and was finally withdrawn by its sponsor, John Morley, on 2 July. (LJ, vol. CXXXII, pp. 117, 150, 155; CJ, vol. CLV, pp. 188, 204, 288.)

According to Morley, who continued to be an advocate of some such measure, it was 'framed and introduced at the request of the Treasury, and its introduction was made a condition precedent to their taking into consideration certain proposals made by the Trustees for the extension of their buildings'. However, A. J. Balfour, First Lord of the Treasury, and soon to be Prime Minister, was himself strongly opposed to the Bill and so Morley, seeing that 'it would give rise to a great deal of contention', agreed to withdraw it. (*Hansard*, 4, vol. 84, col. 1351, 1352.)

William Robert Wellesley Peel, 1st Earl and 2nd Viscount Peel, 1867–1937, statesman and a Trustee of the British Museum, 1898.

John Morley, Viscount Morley of Blackburn, 1838–1912, statesman and man of letters, author of the well-known life of Gladstone, and a Trustee of the British Museum, 1894.

2. Sir Sidney Lee, 1859–1926, Shakespearean scholar and editor of the *Dictionary of National Biography*.

exhibition and general layout of the objects in the galleries and instituted accurate and more suitable labels. He made certain that more and better popular illustrated guidebooks were available at a modest price, though he did not neglect the publication of the highly specialised catalogues on which the Museum's scholarly reputation has always largely rested.

Thompson was also instrumental in getting funds for a resumption of excavations in Egypt, Mesopotamia, Central Asia and elsewhere. Though the hard-pressed antiquities departments had obtained a little more space by the removal of the natural history departments and by the erection of the Mausoleum Room, this had merely permitted objects hitherto hidden in the cellars and basement passages of the Museum to be adequately displayed. Further room would soon be necessary to accommodate many new accessions. The Trustees had made proposals already to utilise the Stuckey Lean bequest and any additional sums which might come from a reluctant Treasury to build new accommodation to the north of the Museum. With the controversies over the British Museum Bill of 1900 at an end, and with £150,000 received from a more complaisant Treasury in 1903, it was agreed to start on the buildings. On 27 June 1907 the foundation stone was laid by King Edward VII, who permitted his name to be given to the new galleries. They were not completed until 1913, under the Directorship of Frederick Kenyon, Maunde Thompson's successor.

Despite his occasional severity towards individuals, Thompson always had the interests of his staff as a whole at heart. In 1898 he had secured the appointment of a powerful Treasury Committee to investigate the intellectual and scientific output of the Museum. As a result of this survey, considerable increases were made in the salaries of the higher staff, from 6 to 11 per cent in those above £250 per year, and from 20 to 25 per cent in those paid at a lesser rate. Maunde Thompson subsequently initiated a similar reorganization of the lower ranks, which was, however, not put into effect until after his retirement. It was as a result of these changes that the traditional title of his high office was altered and he became Director and Principal Librarian, a title borne subsequently by all his successors.

In 1909, after a term of twenty-one years, increasing ill-health forced Sir Edward to retire, to be succeeded, once again, by a Manuscripts man, Frederic Kenyon.

CHAPTER ELEVEN

The Library Departments,
1856–1909

IN April 1856 Jones succeeded Panizzi as Keeper of Printed Books. His immediate task was to complete the building and furnishing of the new Reading Room and library initiated by his predecessor. This was largely a routine matter of consolidation and of putting in the final touches, such as having the pilasters and the doors of the galleries covered with the imitation books which have so long been a prominent feature of the Reading Room. In May 1857 the new room was formally opened.

The new facilities drew more readers, which meant more work all round for the library staff.[1] At times every Attendant was needed and some of the Transcribers were brought in to help. The rest of the Department's work suffered badly.

The new Superintendent of the Reading Room was Thomas Watts. He was the first senior member of the staff to be solely in charge of the Reading Room since the death of Penneck fifty-four years before. For most of the intervening period the Superintendents had been promoted Attendants, such as Cates and Grabham,[2] men with many years of practical experience of the Reading Room and of its catalogues, but incapable of dealing with the new, more exacting readers, who demanded immediate scholarly advice and assistance.

1. On the day that the new room opened there were 442 readers. The attendance on the first and last days of the corresponding week the previous year was 213 and 179. During the last eleven days of May, 5,760 volumes had been supplied for readers in the new room: in 1856 over the same period, 3,504. (*Departmental Reports*, 3 June 1857.)
2. John Grabham, first employed as an Attendant in the Reading Room in March 1833. His predecessor John Cates had had the title of Superintendent of the Reading Room, Grabham being Second Superintendent; both ultimately became Assistants. Grabham died on 5 October 1858. According to Winter Jones, he was able to 'assist the Readers in many ways. He was constantly referred to for information respecting the catalogue and books in the Reading Room and other parts of the Library'. Jones emphasised that despite the new reforms, the post of Clerk of the Reading Room was still important. (*Departmental Reports*, 5, 7 October 1858.)

There was still a 'Clerk of the Reading Room', as a sort of nominal 'second in command', first old Grabham, till his death in October 1858, and then John Granville,[1] but, as Jones pointed out, the constant presence of the Superintendent himself was not affected by the attendance or non-attendance of the Clerk. In Watts' absence the duties of Superintendent were to be carried out by the junior Assistant Keeper, W. B. Rye, or by Jones himself. The Keeper thought that a highly educated Superintendent like Watts was absolutely necessary in the circumstances then prevailing. The readers needed expert help 'and of which they gladly and thankfully avail themselves'. Jones was also convinced that the presence of a senior officer was necessary to maintain 'proper decorum' and ensure that the Attendants carried out their duties.[2]

Watts remained Superintendent until 1866, when he succeeded Jones as Keeper.[3] His brusque manner and sharp temper made him, perhaps, a less suitable man to be in charge of the Reading Room than some of his successors, but he launched the new Room safely and surely on its way. One long overdue reform was introduced during his period of office. Owing to the constantly increasing use being made of the Room, the Trustees finally decided in 1862 to raise the age limit for readers from eighteen to twenty-one years of age.[4]

The use of the Room continued to grow. In 1861 Jones reported that in March 1857 – the last month in which the old Reading Room had

1. John Granville began as a Transcriber in 1849. 'Mr Granville . . . has received a liberal education – is extremely well-informed – is acquainted with modern languages – knows the Library well.' (*Departmental Reports*, 7 October, 8 November 1858.)

2. Jones and Watts, judging by the former's notes to W. B. Rye, did not get on very well together. Watts asked for special permission to continue to examine all accessions. Jones was against this, on the grounds that if the Superintendent of the Reading Room carried out his duties properly, he would not have sufficient time for anything else. (*Departmental Reports*, 27 July, 2 October 1857.)

3. Watts found his Reading Room duties irksome. In a letter to Panizzi of 20 February 1861 he complained, 'I am a keeper in every respect but the name and the emoluments'. (*Papers relating to the Salaries of Officers*, p. 17. PP, H. of C., 1866, vol. XXXIX, p. 199.)

4. 'Limit of age be raised from *18 to 21 years* unless in special cases, which will be laid before the Trustees at their next meeting.' (*General Meetings, Minutes*, vol. 8, p. 2280, 10 May 1862.) In November 1863 Jones reported that the prohibition of readers under twenty-one had caused a fall in numbers, but that the number of books actually being used was still increasing. (*Departmental Reports*, 10 November 1863.)

been in use – there were 5,075 readers. In the same month in 1861, there were 12,489.[1] More staff was needed and though Panizzi was against the Museum's acquiring too large an establishment, Jones at length succeeded in getting an increase at all levels.

The work of the Department was growing in every direction. Early in his Keepership, Winter Jones had reported that with the greatly enlarged space for books now available, he could once more take up the £10,000 a year purchase grant Panizzi had secured in 1846 and had then been forced, to his chagrin, to recommend should be cut, since there was no longer space for the books. Now things were different. In 1857 to 1860, for instance, the total grant was £27,000, or an average of £9,000 a year. The sum of all the grants made from 1849 to 1856 only exceeded this by £2,617. 'In other words,' wrote Jones, 'we are doing that now, under increased disadvantages, which ought to have been done ten years ago.'[2]

The results were obvious. This sudden inflow of books had to be dealt with by a staff which had been increased by merely one Assistant. To the disgust of readers, this led to many books remaining for long uncatalogued. Everywhere the Library was expanding and developing, as Panizzi's reforms bore fruit. The Transcribers were unable to cope with the rapidly growing general catalogue, formed by an amalgamation of the new and the old catalogues. By 1859 the new general catalogue numbered over a thousand volumes; three years earlier it had been just over three hundred. In the next few years the catalogue threatened to engulf the whole of the available space. The situation was becoming intolerable, but its amelioration through the decision to print both the current accessions and the catalogue itself, had to wait the arrival of a reforming Principal Librarian, E. A. Bond, in 1878. But it was not only books which were flowing into the library faster than ever. Winter Jones was determined that two neglected fields must be given greater emphasis.

The first was maps. Panizzi had always recognised their importance and had done much to lay the foundations of the map collection. It was Winter Jones, however, with greatly increased funds, who created that pre-eminence which the collection has since maintained. 'The time has arrived,' Jones wrote in October 1858, 'when a commencement should be made towards putting the geographical department on an equal

1. *Departmental Reports*, 8 April 1861.
2. *Departmental Reports*, 29 October 1859.

footing in point of completeness with the rest of the Library',[1] and he saw to it that this was done. A new section of the library was prepared in the southeast angle of the recently constructed iron library, especially for the now rapidly growing map collections. Finally, in 1867, an independent Department of Maps, Plans and Charts, comprising both printed and manuscript maps, was created under R. H. Major.[2] According to that unreliable witness, 'Stefan Poles', the idea of an independent Map Department was devised by Jones to secure promotion

1. *Departmental Reports*, 26 October 1858.
2. Richard Henry Major, 1818–1891, appointed the Assistant specifically in charge of map collections. He was Hon. Secretary to the Hakluyt Society 1849–1858, and from 1861 to 1881, Hon. Secretary, and then Vice-President, of the Royal Geographical Society. In March 1858 Winter Jones, along with the other Keepers, was asked to let Panizzi know which members of their staffs held outside appointments. Panizzi thought such practices led to inefficiency. Jones reported that only himself, Watts, Major and three others held outside appointments. Two were clergymen, the rest members of learned societies. Jones was on the Council of the Hakluyt Society, but this 'entails no duties which can interfere in any way with the business of the Museum'. 'Mr Major is Hon. Secretary of the Hakluyt Society.' Major himself wrote, 'I feel bound to admit that my time and attention have been occasionally occupied with the affairs of the Society during the hours allotted to Museum duties', but his activities for the Society 'have been similar to and often identical with those which the nature of my Museum duties required me to be acquainted with'. Jones further pointed out to Panizzi that Major had frequently given a very great deal of his own time. Nevertheless, Major felt that it would be better to give up the Secretaryship in the face of the Principal Librarian's disapproval. (*Departmental Reports*, 5 March 1858.)

At Major's retirement on 9 October 1880, it was 'resolved that the Keepership of the Department of Maps be suppressed; and the department, with its staff be placed under the Keeper of Printed Books, and the manuscript portion of the maps transferred to the Department of Manuscripts'. It was likewise resolved that application should be made to obtain Treasury sanction for the addition of a fourth Assistant Keepership in the Department of Printed Books. (*Sub-Committee Minutes*, c.15265.) On 13 November 1880, the Treasury gave its approval to these plans and the administrative arrangements for the new sub-department were drawn up. (C.15312.) R. K. Douglas was appointed Assistant Keeper in charge and E. D. Butler promoted to Assistant First Class to act as his second in command. (C.15314.) On 30 April 1881 the Department of Manuscripts reported that all the manuscript maps formerly in Major's department were now back with them. The new sub-department did however retain a certain autonomy under its first two heads Douglas and Butler.

Sir Richard Kennaway Douglas, 1838–1913. After a short spell in the China Consular service, he joined the Museum in 1865 as Assistant in charge of the Chinese Library. This distinguished orientalist was knighted in 1903 and retired in 1907.

Edward Dundas Butler had entered the Department on 7 February 1859. He began in Maps as a transcriber under Major, succeeded Douglas in May 1891, and retired in 1902.

for his favourite Major. 'Notwithstanding the strong opposition of the late Mr Watts, Mr Jones represented to the Trustees that it would be a good thing to separate the Maps from the Printed Book Department. Thus was made a keepership for "my dear Dick".'[1] No trace of any such scheme nor of the opposition of Watts can now be found.

The other division of the library to which Winter Jones gave special priority was that of official publications, a constantly increasing flow of works of every description, issued by governments from all parts of the globe. No man had realised more clearly the great importance of this class of material to the historian and to research workers in many fields than Panizzi, and, as so often, he laid the foundations on which his successors were to build. Once again, Jones was to consolidate and extend the work of his predecessor. In 1858 he urged the Trustees not to be content with a mere selection of the official publications of the various colonial governments, as the Colonial Office had suggested. 'The question of bulk is now fortunately only a secondary consideration,' he wrote, 'while it is impossible to predicate of any official or public document whether it may not prove at some time of great interest and importance. The materials for the history of a colonial government, legislature and commerce cannot be too numerous or too bulky and there is no depository in which they can be collected with so much convenience to the public as the Library of the British Museum.'[2] The same Colonial Office 'instruction' had laid it down that not only official books and documents, but official maps must be sent to the Trustees. The colony of New South Wales suggested that surely the Museum wanted only 'important' maps. Jones would have none of it. *All* maps were needed, however apparently trivial or obsolete. No one could tell whether they might prove valuable to some student or other at some time, even in the far-distant future. And all the time, Jones was steadily building up the collections of both English and foreign official publications, requesting Panizzi, for instance, to ask his friend Lord Elgin, the new Governor-General of India, to obtain for the Museum the official publications as well as other books 'printed in the East Indies'.[3]

The other important innovation which Jones introduced at this time was the holding of an exhibition in the King's and Grenville Libraries

1. Poles, *The Actual Condition of the British Museum*, p. 29.
2. W. Jones to Panizzi, *Departmental Reports*, 10 February 1858.
3. *op. cit.*, 5 February 1862.

of the history of printing and book-binding, together with documents illustrating important historical events. Such an exhibition had been put on by Panizzi in 1851, the year of the Great Exhibition, and had been a great popular success. Jones now wished to make such an exhibition permanent and to throw open these fine rooms to the general public once more. Prints would be shown alongside the printed books, since that department still had no exhibition gallery of its own. A cheap catalogue was to be made available. Jones urged on the Trustees the necessity of selling this for no more than one penny, even if it involved a slight loss, in order that the poorest visitor would be able to buy a copy.[1] Jones was always a great believer in the educative value of the Museum, a policy which would certainly have shaken Ellis and others of the old school.

Jones had his worries. In 1861 the public were admitted to the Museum between six and eight on summer evenings and had to pass through the Reading Room. This raised security problems, and Jones dreaded wilful damage to his precious new reference library. But on the whole, the decade was peaceful and when in 1866 Jones once again succeeded his old chief, this time as Principal Librarian, he handed over to Thomas Watts a fine and flourishing library.

Watts was succeeded in the Reading Room by the genial Irishman, George Bullen,[2] one of the few members of the staff who, long ago, had put up with the difficult Edward Edwards. A different type from the shy, reserved Watts, he was greatly liked by both readers and staff and helped to found the Reading Room's tradition of cheerful helpfulness, a tradition worthily carried on by Garnett and by many others of his successors. The Reading Room was still at this time without artificial light. In the dark hours of winter mornings before the readers arrived, the attendants used lamps with guttering candles to prepare the Room for the day's work. Even then fears were expressed that the constant snuffing and the hot wax, which then escaped from the lanterns,

1. *op. cit.*, 8 December 1857. On February 27 Jones forwarded to the Trustees a copy of the guide to the books exhibited in the Grenville Room and King's Library. He emphasised that the guide could be reproduced very cheaply, so as 'to be within the means of the humblest visitor to the Museum'. (*Departmental Reports*, 27 February 1858.)

2. George Bullen, CB, 1816–1894, born at Clonakilty, Co. Cork. He joined the Museum as a supernumerary assistant in January 1838, then became successively permanent assistant, 1849, Superintendent of the Reading Room and Assistant Keeper, 1866–1875 and Keeper, 1875–1890. He was also Vice-President of the Library Association.

constituted fire hazards. The virtual cessation of work whenever there
was a fog, which happened not infrequently, could not be tolerated in
an age which no longer enjoyed the leisurely existence of early Victorian
England. An article in *The Builder* of 29 July 1865 commented on the
heavy fogs which had recently occurred, uncommon even then, in
midsummer.

At such times work was suspended or gravely hampered throughout
London. In particular 'the "book-worms" who haunt the reading-room
of the British Museum, are on these occasions left without the means of
pursuing their various avocations. Many of this industrious and useful
community leave the beautiful dome, which in this light has a dim,
lurid, and somewhat ghastly appearance, and grope their way homeward;
a few, more persevering than others, having with difficulty managed
to extract the names and particulars of a few books from the catalogue,
and in the hope of the air clearing up, sit with patience until the
painstaking attendants have, in the colossal space of the King's Library,
or some of the other mighty lines of bookshelves, by the aid of lanterns,
carefully locked and strongly protected with glass or crystal, provided
the volumes wanted.' The writer also stresses the 'curious and picturesque'
effect of the fog in such places as 'the galleries of the British Museum,
in company with the Assyrian, Egyptian, and other sculptured kings of
old'.[1]

In winter the Reading Room often had to be closed early in the
afternoon and both staff and readers found their way home as best they
could. Once closed, the Room was rarely reopened, since, even if the
fog lifted, the staff took good care to be gone beyond recall.[2] Despite
continuous agitation, it was not until 1878 that the first hesitant steps
were taken through the firm leadership of Edward Bond. After a few
setbacks, the new lighting was a great success, and by its means the
Reading Room was able to keep open until 7 p.m. during the winter
months and not forced to shut at 4 p.m.

Watts, the third of that remarkable triumvirate, that had brought
such distinction to the department of Printed Books during the
previous thirty years, had only a short Keepership. Succeeding Jones in
July 1866, he held office for just over three years, dying suddenly at his

1. *Builder*, 25 July 1865.
2. According to Dr Victor Scholderer, who joined the Museum staff in June 1904,
on such days, if the staff had been sent home and the fog suddenly lifted, 'they hid . . .
behind lamp-posts and refused to come back'. (V. Scholderer, *Reminiscences*, p. 22.)

house in the Museum on 9 September 1869.[1] He was the perfect accessions officer. His ambition was clearly expressed in his famous letter to Panizzi in 1861 – a determination to make the library supreme in every language.[2] A consummate linguist, he was a tireless worker, never sparing himself or others. As Placer, responsible for the final positioning of every individual book on the shelf, he handled over 400,000 volumes. Though at times brusque and hot-tempered, he was well liked by his colleagues, who, as Garnett wrote, revelled particularly in the wit and charm of his conversation, which resembled the talk of Macaulay, perhaps the outstanding conversationalist of the age.[3]

The most important event of Watts' Keepership was undoubtedly the establishment in January 1867 of an independent Department of Maps, Charts, Plans and Topographical Drawings under R. H. Major, who for long had been regarded by both Panizzi and Jones as one of the brightest of the younger men in their department. He had first come to the Museum in January 1844 as an Assistant with the specific task of looking after the as yet relatively small collection of maps and plans. Thanks to his own zeal and energy, and to the efforts of Panizzi and later of Jones, the collection had already become one of the finest in the world, as well as one of the most numerous.

Although the experiment seems to have been a success, on Major's retirement in 1880, on the grounds of ill-health, the opportunity was taken of reuniting the Maps to their former parent department, in exchange for a fourth Assistant Keepership for Printed Books. Maps did, however, retain a certain autonomy as a separate sub-department first under R. K. Douglas and then under E. D. Butler.

Watts was followed by W. B. Rye,[4] a sound, if pedestrian, successor. Jones had some doubts of his suitability for the post, since he wrote to Panizzi, now living in retirement close by in Bloomsbury Square, to

1. Watts died as the result of an accident which occurred as he was alighting from a coach during his holiday at Bridgenorth, Shropshire in 1869. Phlebitis set in and he died some weeks later.
2. *Papers relating to the Salaries of Officers*, p. 17. (PP, H. of C., 1866. vol. XXXIX, p. 199.)
3. Article on Watts by Richard Garnett in the *DNB*, vol. XX.
4. William Brenchley Rye, 1818–1901. He was first employed in a solicitor's office, where he met his future colleague John Winter Jones. In 1838 Rye entered as a Transcriber, but was soon appointed a supernumerary assistant. In 1844 he was placed on the permanent staff. Always a favourite of Panizzi, he became Assistant Keeper in 1857, and succeeded Watts in the Keepership in 1869. He became totally blind during his last years and died on 21 December 1901.

ask him what he thought. Panizzi had always appreciated Rye's solid painstaking work, and had permitted him to superintend the Grenville library move. He therefore approved and Rye became Keeper. A shy man, he was handicapped also by grave eye trouble. Like his greater successor, Richard Garnett, Rye took a marked interest in the history of his own department and did much to bring together the scattered papers of his forerunners, which might otherwise have been thrown away.

Failing eyesight which eventually resulted in complete blindness forced him to resign in 1875, to be succeeded by George Bullen. During Bullen's Keepership the next change in the public facilities of the National Library took place. The printed edition of the catalogue, prepared by Panizzi with such determination, though much against his will, never got beyond the letter A, the first and only volume, full of mistakes, appearing in July 1841. Given the state of the library, the attempt was premature, ill-planned and deserved to fail. But by now the position was different. As a result of the work done by Panizzi, Watts and their colleagues over the previous twenty-five years, acquisitions in every field had been flowing into the library at an ever-increasing rate. When the new manuscript General Catalogue was first placed in the Reading Room in 1851, it consisted of 150 volumes. Within fifteen years it had grown to 2,000, and soon, it was calculated, would reach 3,000, once the incorporation of the general and supplementary volumes was completed. If all the swollen, oversized volumes, many of which had become so weighty as to be almost unusable, were to be broken up, it would probably come to the ludicrous total of over 9,000 volumes, or three times as many as the Reading Room could possibly contain or the public conveniently consult.[1]

In the summer of 1879, Bond proposed to the Treasury that print should be substituted for transcription in all additions henceforth to be made to the catalogue. Bond then set about carrying out the second step, the conversion of the whole of the manuscript catalogue into printed form. The Treasury was only too ready to agree to such a money-saving proposal, and granted an annual sum to be used exclusively for this purpose.[2]

The largest and most cumbersome folios were selected for treatment first and gradually, volume by volume, the whole alphabet was covered. The first volumes were published in 1881, the last in 1900. Supplements designed to contain titles of all books added between 1882 and

1. R. Garnett, On the Printing of the British Museum Catalogue, pp. 14–15.
2. op. cit., p. 7.

1899 and not included in the main work, were issued between 1900 and 1905. The editorship of this remarkable undertaking, much of which is still in use as the basis of the current British Museum Catalogue was in the hands, first of Richard Garnett,[1] who was transferred from the Reading Room in 1884 to devote himself more exclusively to the work, and then in 1890, after Garnett had succeeded Bullen as Keeper of Arthur Miller,[2] a shy man of great learning, who did much to make the catalogue the instrument of scholarship it has become.

Garnett's successor in the Reading Room, G. K. Fortescue,[3] took the next step. Fortescue was a man of great energy and sound common sense, although without much formal education, having been a sailor in his youth, and he was determined to fill a notable omission in the bibliographical resources of the Library, a comprehensive Subject Index to the accessions. In 1886 Fortescue brought out his first volume, which included all works received by the Museum between 1880 and 1885. Despite various changes and improvements, Fortescue's scheme is still basically that of the current Subject Index, issued at intervals, each covering five years, until the present day.

Once more the old problem of space presented itself. The 'iron library' which seemed at one time to contain sufficient space almost for ever was rapidly filling, despite the drastic cut in the Treasury grant made by Lord Randolph Churchill, Chancellor of the Exchequer, in 1887.[4] An ingenious solution was found, which largely solved the

1. Richard Garnett, 1835–1906. Entered Printed Books at the age of sixteen in 1851; he became Assistant Keeper in 1875 and Keeper in 1890. In 1882 he tried unsuccessfully for the post of Librarian at the Bodleian Library, Oxford.
2. Arthur William Kaye Miller, 1849–1914. Entered Printed Books as an Assistant in 1870, became Assistant Keeper in 1896 and was Keeper, 1912–1914. He died suddenly during the opening of the Edward VII Galleries in May 1914.
3. George Knottesford Fortescue, 1847–1912. Joined the Museum as an Assistant in 1870, became Assistant Keeper in 1884 and Keeper in 1890. A nephew of the Archbishop of Canterbury, Fortescue was a worthy example of the powers of patronage. When he became Superintendent of the Reading Room in 1884, although well over thirty, he looked very much younger and some discontented readers, annoyed at his brusque manner, induced two of the more popular newspapers to state 'Dr Garnett was removed from the Reading Room to make room for a beardless boy not long out of his teens, whose only known qualification for the position was great influence at headquarters'. (Quoted in Barwick, p. 133.)
4. Garnett described this as 'a great calamity'. The purchase grant was reduced by two-fifths throughout all departments. This meant that in Printed Books, for example, purchases had to be confined to new books and periodicals and little done to make good existing deficiencies. (R. Garnett, *Changes at the British Museum since 1877*, p. 1n.)

problem for the next forty years. This was the introduction of the
swinging or sliding press, designed to hang suspended on rollers from
the iron grillwork of the library floor above, in front of the fixed
presses. It could be moved easily and the books got at. Thus, at one
stroke, the amount of accommodation available was almost trebled;
despite certain inconveniences, these presses continued in use until the
gradual replacement of most of the old iron library shortly before the
Second World War. The press was invented by Henry Jenner, then
Placer, and was based on a similar scheme developed at the Bethnal
Green Library. The first batch were erected in 1887 and others were
soon fitted up in all possible places throughout the Library. Jenner was
awarded £100 by the Trustees for his idea. The disadvantages, which
gradually became apparent, were that the backs of books often became
damaged by careless handling of the swinging presses. They were also
often cumbersome and difficult to pull out, especially the great basement ones, as the author well remembers, and would have been quite
impossible to use with the largely female staff now employed. A full
'swinger' was often as much as a strong young man could move and one
often had to ask for help with the larger ones. They also dangerously
overweighted the fragile structure of the Iron Library, a fact which
only became apparent in the 1920s. A relic of them is still perpetu-
ated in the Library's press-mark system: '7000', originally meant
a wall press of that number and '07000', the swinging press in front
of it.[1]

Another step advocated since the Royal Commission of 1850 if not
before now took place. This was the amalgamation of books and
manuscripts in oriental languages into one specialist department. In
1867 it had been decided to set up a separate Department of Oriental
Manuscripts. Madden had disapproved of the idea as a diminution of
his own authority,[2] and it was left to his successor, Bond, to advocate

1. R. Garnett, *Essays in Librarianship*, pp. 264–271; *Accounts, etc.*, 1886–87, p. 9. (PP,
H. of C., 1887, vol. LXV, p. 529).
2. Madden considered that this recommendation had been put in merely to flatter
Lord Ellesmere, Chairman of the Commission, 'who pretends to a smattering of
Eastern tongues'. He also considered that the idea was not really to benefit the oriental
manuscripts nor their readers, who were rarely more than eight, but to create a separate
department for Cureton, presumably, in Madden's view, as a reward for speaking well
of Panizzi before the Commission. (*Madden Journal*, 9 September, 1849). In fact, of course,
Cureton had long resigned when the final decision was taken, and his successor Charles
Rieu was the new Department's first Keeper.

this eminently practical step. Its first Keeper was Charles Rieu,[1] who had come to the Manuscript Department in 1847 and on Cureton's resignation in 1850 had become that department's principal orientalist.

In May 1892 came the further decision to transfer to a newly created Department of Oriental Printed Books and Manuscripts, the extensive collections in oriental languages of printed books. The first Keeper of the new department was Professor Douglas, afterwards Sir Richard Douglas. He had been in charge of the Map Collection since 1880, and had also supervised the printing of the accessions to the General Library. A distinguished sinologist, he was more an orientalist than either a cartographer or a librarian, and when Charles Rieu resigned in 1891 to become Adams' Professor of Arabic at Cambridge, Maunde Thompson transferred Douglas to take charge of the new department.

The erection of the White Wing in 1884 permitted the setting up of a separate newspaper reading room in the following year, as well as a Students' Room for those using the Department of Manuscripts. Newspapers, by their size and fast rate of growth, have always presented peculiar problems.[2] During the nineteenth century, these bulky and

1. Charles Pierre Henri Rieu, 1820–1902. Supernumerary Assistant, Department of Manuscripts, 1847; Keeper of Oriental Manuscripts, 1867.

2. By the Stamp Act, 38 Geo. III, c. 78, and subsequent Acts, a copy of all newspapers published had to be deposited at the Stamp Office in Somerset House or at some branch office. In 1818 London newspapers started coming to the Museum from the Stamp Office, but not until they had been there three years. In 1822 the Trustees asked that this position might be regularised, a request that was granted by the Treasury in 1823. English provincial newspapers started coming in 1832 and, thanks to the activities of Panizzi, Scottish and Irish ones in 1848.

On 28 April 1869 Watts, as Keeper of Printed Books, reported that legislation was now going through Parliament repealing these Acts and that a Bill was likewise being introduced to amend the Copyright regulations affecting newspapers. 'The supply of newspapers to the British Museum,' he wrote, 'must instantly terminate . . . the national library, which has hitherto boasted of possessing the finest collection of newspapers in the world would be left without even a set of *The Times*.' He strongly recommended that all newspapers should in future be purchased, as it would be impossible to enforce the copyright regulations, even if upheld, against 'thousands' of newspaper proprietors. In particular, Indian and Colonial newspapers and all official publications should always be bought, as their continuity was otherwise very difficult to maintain.

Jones, not a lawyer for nothing, advised caution. He was of the opinion that the Museum, under existing legislation, had a clear right to all newspapers and that if they were to be purchased and not deposited, the legal character of the Museum copies would thereby be lost. The first Act, that to abolish the Stamp Acts, was passed; he second to amend the Copyright regulations, withdrawn. (*Departmental Reports*, 20 April 1869,

cumbersome volumes had been housed in various parts of the library. In 1899 they were put into the empty basement rooms, vacated in turn by the Natural History and by the Antiquities departments.

However, a more drastic solution to the problem was being considered. In 1902 an Act was passed enabling the Trustees to store little used newspapers and other printed matter away from Bloomsbury, but available for consultation there.[1] Land was bought in the rural area of Hendon and a repository for the storage of newspapers erected, together with a Superintendent's house. In 1905 all the provincial newspapers later than 1800 were moved there, with a few other similar classes of documents. A newspaper catalogue, listing all newspapers, both London and provincial, was produced and placed in the Reading Room. A weekly collection from Hendon was instituted, should a reader wish to consult a provincial newspaper, it being eventually delivered to him in the Newspaper Reading Room in the White Wing. Like all schemes of outhousing, this system was unsatisfactory and frustrating, both to readers and staff, but it remained the practice until the establishment of a proper newspaper library with its own reading room and ancillary services at Hendon in 1932, when all other newspapers of the nineteenth and twentieth centuries were sent to join the provincial ones.[2]

Some of the difficulties associated with newspapers is also to be found in the cataloguing and storage of official publications. Panizzi and Jones (especially the latter), had paid particular attention to this class of material and in 1887 Garnett reported to the Library Association that 'Passing to the subject of official publications, I may observe that the Museum has never at any period of its history displayed so much activity as during these latter years'.[3] This was due to the zeal of

1. 2 Edw. 7. c. 12. *An Act to enable the Trustees of the British Museum to remove certain newspapers and other printed matter from the British Museum Buildings.*
2. An almost complete set of *The Times*, duplicating the one at Colindale, together with the *London Gazette* and other official publications, remained or were gradually returned to Bloomsbury. Watts, many years before, had suggested having two sets of *The Times*. (*Departmental Reports*, 8 May 1869.)
3. R. Garnett, *Changes at the British Museum since 1877*, p. 5.

8 May 1869). *An Act to repeal certain enactments relating to Newspapers,* 32 and 33 Vict. c. 24; *Bill for amending the Law relating to Copyright so far as regards the delivery of Periodical Publications at the British Museum.* (PP, H. of C., 1868–9, vol. II, p. 1). Withdrawn 11 June 1869. (CJ, 1868–9, vol. 124, p. 243). The main purpose of the Bill was to extend the time for delivery of periodical publications, especially newspapers, to the British Museum.

Francis Campbell,[1] the Assistant in charge of this class of material, who did much to improve and diversify the Department's holdings by initiating a series of exchanges with various foreign governments.

Unfortunately the 'State Papers' as they are generally (if somewhat incorrectly) known in the Museum, were not then treated as a homogeneous whole and the English, American, foreign and colonial collections were dispersed in various parts of the department and under different subordinate administrations.[2] Thus the opportunity was lost to bring them together and create from these varied, yet related collections, a self-contained specialist division under a senior officer, on the same line as the Map and Music Rooms. After Campbell's departure in 1900, following a dispute with the authorities, they were to remain unorganised, divided and largely neglected for thirty years.

The music collections, like Maps and Official Publications, began to develop in the middle of the nineteenth century, thanks to the all-embracing accessions policy of Panizzi. Although earlier members of the library staff had paid some attention to the small music collection, it was not until Thomas Oliphant's appointment as an Assistant especially in charge of both printed and manuscript music in 1841, that it began to grow. Unfortunately Oliphant soon fell foul of Panizzi and in 1850 was forced to resign. His work was carried on by a series of distinguished successors, amongst whom the best known was William Barclay Squire,[3]

1. Francis Bunbury Fitzgerald Campbell, joined as a Second Class Assistant in 1884. He spent many years compiling an *Index-Catalogue of Indian Official Publications in the Library*, a bibliography which is used almost daily in the State Paper Room and is still valuable for readers working in this field. After a disagreement with the Trustees about whether it should be published officially, Campbell resigned in June 1900 ostensibly on medical grounds, and brought out the Index at his own expense.

2. Thus in 1893 the Indian and Colonial official documents were placed in the Banksian Library near the north end of the King's Library, 'screened from the public by a row of book-cases filled with volumes of Specifications of Patents in handsome bindings' and remained there until the creation of the modern State Paper Room in 1933. The Parliamentary Papers, Lords and Commons Journals, Hansard, the great collections of Public and Private Acts and British official publications generally were regarded as forming part of the Newspaper Library and were moved in 1887 'to a room in nearer connection with the Newspaper Reading Room, in the new White building, in which they can be conveniently consulted'. There they stayed until the Newspaper Library moved to Colindale in 1931. The American and other official foreign publications, already a vast collection, were housed inadequately in the tiny upper galleries of the Arched Room. *Accounts, &c.*, 1886–7, p. 8, PP, H. of C., 1887, vol. LXV, p. 52–; *Accounts, &c.*, 1893–3, p.21; PP, H. of C., 1894, vol. LXVIII, p. 607).

3. William Barclay Squire, 1855–1927, Deputy Keeper, 1919–20. His successors were W. A. Smith and A. H. King, the present Superintendent. The Music Room has

who was in charge of the Music Room for nearly forty years from 1883 to 1920, and did much to organise the great mass of uncatalogued music, as well as to make his division the centre for musicological research that it has remained.

Even the staid Barclay Squire would sometimes relax. Sir Henry Newbolt recalled how as a young writer working in the Reading Room in 1898 he was introduced by Lawrence Binyon to the 'Anglo-Austrians', a group composed of readers and staff. They met daily for lunch at the Vienna Café in New Oxford Street and 'talked faster and more irresponsibly than any group of equal numbers in my memory: by the noise we made, the congestion of our table . . . and the recklessness with which we shared portions with one another . . . an onlooker might have taken us for a Bohemian society of students from some romantic foreign capital. Barclay Squire alone upheld our reputation for respectability and there were times when he was the only one who was actually looking and speaking like a conventional Englishman'.

Many already famous or soon to achieve fame took part from time to time in these convivial gatherings, amongst them Samuel Butler, John Masefield, 'Baron Corvo', Edward Garnett and Roger Fry. But it was the three regular Museum members, Binyon, Squire and Streatfield to whom the young Newbolt was particularly grateful. They got him admitted to the inner recesses of the Museum, obtained permission for him to work in the King's Library during the closed weeks, 'and saved time for me again and again by taking me behind the scenes and along the vast honeycomb of shelves to pick out for myself of the volumes which would otherwise have taken half an hour to reach me in the ordinary routine'.[1]

Numbers in the Reading Room had continued to increase, until towards the end of the century a large decrease was noted.[2] This may well have been due to readers finding the room overcrowded. In 1887 it was noted in the Principal Librarian's annual report that 'literary men' were being pressed out by the 'throng of Readers for general

1. Sir Henry Newbolt, *My World as in my Time*, pp. 209, 210.
2. 1895: 194,924; 1896: 191,323; 1897: 188,628; 1898: 190,886; 1899: 188,554; 1900: 198,566.

---

probably the unique distinction of having been under only three officers for the better part of a century.

information'. The solution to this problem that was then advocated, but unfortunately never adopted, was the provision of a separate reading room 'suitably furnished with modern works' for the casual reader, a solution that might well be included in the planning of any future national library.[1]

The sudden decrease may also have been the result of the additional resources provided by the growing public library system. The time had passed when the British Museum Library was virtually the only library open in London to the general public. Various libraries, academic and otherwise, now catered for the ever greater number who needed the specialist works that an increasingly technological society now found necessary. The decline of the Reading Room was quickly reversed, and throughout the early twentieth century, numbers continued to rise with minor fluctuations.[2]

More care was paid to the comfort of readers. In 1875 the ventilation of the room was improved by the transfer of the steam pipes from the outside of the windows to the inside. The foetid atmosphere, in which the Museum flea had once grown and flourished, was now a thing of the past and though the Room could be at times, as it still is, either cold and draughty in winter or unbearably hot in the scorching summer days, particularly for anyone sitting at the Centre Desk. According to G. F. Barwick, the only person known to have been seriously affected by the atmosphere in the present Reading Room was Algernon Swinburne, who, in July 1868, after spending, as usual, many hours at his desk, was overcome by dizziness on rising from his seat and fell forward, grazing his forehead against the woodwork. Gosse gives a somewhat different version of, presumably, the same affair.[3]

In 1893, the boon of electric light was made available to individual readers, and 'incandescent electric lights' fixed to every seat. Arc lamps were retained for general lighting, but at a lower power than hitherto. At the same time 'glow lamps' were installed above the shelving round the walls, which made the selection of reference books easier.[4] Electric light had not been extended to the bookstacks, so that a secondary selection of some 20,000 volumes, thought to be those most likely to be needed by readers, were placed in the lower gallery and

1. *Accounts, &c.*, 1887–8, p. 8. (PP, H. of C., 1888, vol. LXXVIII, p. 813). Barwick p. 122.
2. 1901: 200,035; 1902: 211,244; 1903: 209,713.
3. Barwick, p. 122. Gosse, *Life and Letters*, p. 20.
4. *Accounts, &c.*, 1893–4, p. 14. (PP, H. of C., 1894, vol. LXVII. p. 607).

made freely available by ticket whenever the Reading Room was open.[1] Another improvement made at this time was the lengthening of the tables between the desks to make a considerable number of additional places. Small bookcases were provided at the end of each desk to hold bibliographies, arranged by subject roughly in accordance with the books placed on the walls of the Room in that particular area.

Percy Fitzgerald, in the periodical *Belgravia* in 1882, gives a vivid description of the Reading Room of those days. 'The visitor suddenly introduced can hardly conceal his wonder and gratification as he gazes round at the enormous chamber, so lofty, airy and vast; so still and yet so crowded, so comfortable and warm like any private library. . . . There are a few desks set apart like compartments in a railway train, "for ladies only" and one of the standing jests of the place – perfectly supported, too, by experience – is that these are left solitary and untenanted.'[2]

These 'ladies' seats' were for long a source of grievance to masculine readers, who cast envious eyes at the unoccupied places, and indeed at busy times men were permitted to occupy these seats, if no lady objected. Few did, and when the Room was closed for redecoration in 1907, these separate seats were abolished. It was then arranged that any lady who objected to sitting next to a man would be accommodated in the North Library. There is no record of the offer ever having been taken up and, in the Reading Room of today, where women in every possible variety of clothing, form between half and two-thirds of the total number, such an arrangement, if indeed it still exists, is scarcely likely to be asked for. This was the Victorian Reading Room, so familiar to Karl Marx and to other political refugees, as well as to such prominent literary figures as Leslie Stephen, Thomas Hardy and Hall Caine.

Marx, who had first become a reader on 12 June 1850 ('Dr Charles Marx, 28 Dean Street, Soho'),[3] greatly appreciated the facilities the Museum offered an almost penniless refugee. As a token of his gratitude

1. The writer vividly remembers the extremely indifferent lighting in his days as a young man in the stack area. Low-powered naked bulbs, at about ten-foot intervals, gave all the artificial light available within the old Iron Library. On a dark day or in the basement an electric torch had to be carried, so as to be sure of matching the number on the reader's application slip with that on the back of the book. Another method was to put a white card against the label on the book, to catch more readily whatever light filtered through from the glass roof in places fifty feet above.

2. Barwick, p. 131.

3. Entry in Admissions Register, Director's Office, British Museum.

he presented the Museum with a copy of the second edition of *Das Kapital* in 1873.[1] Marx was most impressed by the reports of the Inspectors of Factories and by other reports of various Committees and Commissions which he discovered among the Parliamentary Papers in the Library. In no other country, he considered, would a government publication be so permitted to give full details of the horrors of industrial conditions and of the state of the poor. Despite persistent legends to the contrary, Marx never occupied any one particular seat in the Reading Room. He usually chose a seat close to the reference shelves which held the historical works he most frequently needed.[2]

Equally apocryphal is the story of the aged attendant who, asked if he remembered Karl Marx, replied, 'Marx, Marx, was he the gentleman with the long white beard? I wonder if he ever came to anything.'[3]

Not everyone, unfortunately, had the same high opinion of the resources of the Reading Room as Marx. A writer in the *Idler* of 1896, Allen Upward, included the British Museum among 'the Horrors of London', indeed 'London's crowning horror' and claimed that the most horrible place even in the Museum was the Reading Room. 'No one who had never been to it would believe that it was possible for any Reading Room to be so horrible as this Reading Room is.' No scholar, the writer considered, would ever dream of going there. It was run 'in the interests of contributors to the snippet press'. Upward was by no means impressed by the beauties of Sidney Smirke's dome. 'The chamber in which the readers are immured is a vast round cavern not unlike a model prison, though there is a haunting suggestion of the underground railway about the atmosphere.' There were never enough reference books and one would never find them anyway and if you sent for a book you wait the better part of a day. 'Of course if they come with it while you are away, you must start after it again while the scent is fresh. If you are in luck it will then be dusk, and the Reading Room will be closed for the day'.[4]

The Reading Room was now kept open to 8 p.m., as it had been since 1882. There was considerable agitation to extend the hours to 10 p.m., but this was resisted by the Trustees. The cost in staff time and in lighting and heating would be heavy, and would not be justified by the numbers wishing to stay to that hour. Indeed, a few years later

1. *Das Kapital*, second edition, Hamburg, 1872.
2. At that time presses 2067 to 2085. Marx therefore would tend to sit at rows K to P.
3. A similar tale is told of Lenin.
4. Allen Upward, *The Horrors of London. XI, The British Museum, Idler*, vol. X, p. 798.

in 1904, it was decided to close the room at 7 p.m. throughout the year, the expense of the extension for a further hour not being justified by the number of readers then making use of the room.[1] Apart from the interruption of the First World War, these hours continued until 1939; only in recent years has the scheme for a really late opening been revived, with marked success.

G. K. Fortescue left the Reading Room in 1896 to give more time to the Subject Index and to assist the ageing Garnett in the general administration, which was already too big a burden for one man, however able.

His successor as Superintendent was W. R. Wilson,[2] a quiet, shy man, but a good administrator. Esdaile speaks of Wilson's condemnation of the brutal yet inefficient discipline lavished on the junior staff by some of their seniors in his young days and tells how very different was Wilson's conduct.[3]

G. F. Barwick[4] became the next Superintendent when Wilson was transferred to administrative duties in 1900. Barwick, a fine scholar, was in the line of great Superintendents, such as Bullen, Garnett, and Fortescue. His kindly percipient nature made him an ideal Superintendent and recollections of his gentle but firm conduct towards staff and readers were still fresh when the present writer worked in the Reading Room some thirty years ago.

In 1899 Richard Garnett retired after nearly half a century, to be succeeded by George Fortescue. As industrious as ever, despite his now pressing duties as Keeper, he continued to edit the Subject Index, and also brought out a Catalogue of the Thomason Tracts, to which he contributed a brilliant Introduction. He had already in 1898 prepared an 'analysis' of the Croker Collection of French Revolutionary Tracts and did much other good work of a bibliographical nature. This may well have contributed to his sudden death in October 1912, shortly before he was due to retire, to be succeeded as Keeper by A. W. K. Miller, the editor of the final volumes of the General Catalogue.

All this time the number of readers using the Room increased, apart

1. *Accounts, &c.*, 1904–5, p. 16. (PP, H. of C., 1905, vol. LXI, p. 715.)
2. William Robert Wilson, 1844–1928. Entered the Museum as an Assistant in 1863, Superintendent of the Reading Room, 1896, Assistant Keeper, 1899–1909, in which year he retired.
3. Esdaile, p. 149.
4. George Frederick Barwick, 1853–1931. Assistant in the Department of Printed Books, 1879; Assistant Keeper and Superintendent of the Reading Room, 1900–1914, Author of the standard history of the Reading Room.

from an occasional decline. In 1904, for instance, the figure had grown to the hitherto unheard of total of 226,323, and by 1913, the last full year before the First World War, it had reached 243,659.[1] By now, Panizzi's great new room was half a century old. It appeared to be wearing well, but it was high time that a closer look was taken at it for structural defects. It was therefore decided to close the Reading Room from 15 April to 31 October 1907 to examine the structure and at the same time to redecorate it completely.[2] The building and the 'iron library' were found to be without any sign of deterioriaton. Thus the great Reading Room, with its growing number of readers, demanding an ever greater variety of books, entered the second half of its first century. Not every book in the Library was read with equal frequency. In March 1879 a certain reader, Dr Leffing Will Jackson of Dansville, New York, took out a book by his compatriot Stephen Pearl Andrews, entitled *The Basic Outline of Universology*. He thought little of it. It had obviously never yet been read, as the pages were still uncut. After an attempt to wade through the opening chapters, Dr Jackson too left the later pages in their original state. Before returning the volume he inserted between two still uncut pages a note in a small envelope addressed to any future reader. He did not believe 'it *ever* will find one, except some student of mental excentricity . . . I fancy it has a long, easy & quiet life in store for it on the shelves of the British Museum'.

Dr Jackson's prophecy proved to be correct. In August 1891 he again looked at Andrews' masterpiece. The note was still there, hidden between the uncut pages. Obviously no one had looked at the book during the intervening years. Dr Jackson then added a further note asking anyone who should read the work after 1900 to get in touch with him.

No one ever did. The years passed by till at last in August 1971 a reader cut the pages, found the note still hidden there, and drew the attention of a member of the Reading Room staff to it. Sixty years before to the month Dr Jackson had written: 'I do not believe the pages will be cut by a curious student in a century.'

1. 1904: 226,323; 1905: 214,940; 1906: 212,997; 1907: 137,682 (6½ month closing for redecoration); 1908: 231,544; 1909: 217,975; 1910: 219,274; 1911: 223,404; 1912: 236,643; 1913: 243,659.
2. Esdaile, p. 149. *Accounts, &c.*, 1907–8, pp. 16, 17. (PP, H. of C., 1908, vol. LXXXVI, p. 1037).
    The opportunity was also then taken of weeding out obsolete reference books from the shelves of the Reading Room. (*op. cit.*), p. 71.

Among the members of the staff of the Department at this time who made names for themselves beyond the Museum walls, three are perhaps outstanding. These are Coventry Patmore, Edmund Gosse and Richard Garnett.[1]

Patmore had first come to the Museum in November 1846 as a supernumerary assistant, on the recommendation of Monckton Milnes.[2] He quickly became a valued member of the staff, though it is said that the Trustees hesitated at first to appoint him, since he knew so few languages. Richard Garnett described Patmore as he first saw him: 'When I came, a mere lad, to work in the Library of the British Museum, I was introduced to all my colleagues, with one, doubtless, accidental exception. I was some time before finding who the tall, spare, silent man was, who alone of the assistants, sat in the King's Library; who, though perfectly urbane when he did converse, seemed rather among than of the rest of the staff, and who appeared to be usually entrusted with some exceptional task . . . His diligence was certainly exemplary, though he was not considered a particularly able assistant from the librarians' point of view, and made no pretensions to extensive linguistic attainments or bibliographical lore'.[3] Another colleague, Richard Holmes, son of Madden's former second in command,[4] noted that Patmore's silence and preoccupation rather isolated him from his companions, but that his poetic reputation made him a subject of special interest, especially to his junior colleagues who were proud to know him.[5] Patmore also seems to have used his acquaintance with many persons of influence to try and improve the wretched financial lot of the Assistants and Transcribers, though with little success. In 1851, during the invasion scare following Napoleon III's *coup d'état*, he was instrumental in forming a Rifle Club, mostly from Museum staff, and then expanding it into a proper volunteer Rifle

1. Coventry Kersey Dighton Patmore, 1823–1896, poet. He entered the Museum as an Assistant in 1844.
Sir Edmund William Gosse, 1849–1928, poet and man of letters. He was appointed Librarian of the House of Lords in 1904.
2. Richard Monckton Milnes, Lord Houghton, 1809–1885, Antonio Panizzi's opponent for many years in the affairs of the Museum.
3. R. Garnett. Article in *Saturday Review*, 5 December 1896, quoted in B. Champneys, *Memoirs and Correspondence of Coventry Patmore*, vol. 1, p. 69.
4. Sir Richard Rivington Holmes, 1835–1911, librarian of Windsor Castle. Assistant in the Department of Manuscripts, 1854–70.
5. B. Champneys, *Memoirs*, vol. 1, p. 59.

Company.[1] Owing to increasingly bad health and because he wished to devote himself more and more to poetry, Patmore resigned from the Museum in 1866, his second marriage having made him financially independent.[2]

A friend of Patmore's later years and an understanding critic of his verse was Edmund Gosse. Gosse, after the rigid and pietistic upbringing which he describes in *Father and Son*, was introduced to the Museum in 1867 by the novelist Charles Kingsley as a Transcriber at a salary of £90 a year.[3] Gosse hated the Museum and seems to have been most unhappy there. He, with fifteen others of the cataloguing staff, gathered punctually at nine every morning in a basement room, 'scented with rotten morocco, and an indescribable odour familiar in foreign barracks'.[4] The Transcribers were under the iron rule of the Rev. Frederick Laughlin,[5] one of the senior Assistants, who bullied and tormented young Gosse unmercifully. However his years at the Museum do not seem to have been entirely wasted. In this 'nest of singing birds',[6] as he called the Museum, and surrounded by the books he loved and which his bigoted home life had denied him, he quickly obtained, amid a

1. *op. cit.*, vol. 1, pp. 71–6. In 1851 or probably somewhat later, Patmore helped to raise a Company of Volunteers from amongst members of the Museum staff, which he claimed was the first to be formed in the Civil Service. In 1867 its members, through Watts, then Keeper of Printed Books, petitioned the Trustees for a holiday on Easter Monday to take part in a review at Dover. The Trustees refused to grant them special leave and said that if they went it would have to be regarded as coming out of their annual leave. (*Departmental Reports*, 10, 13 April 1867.) Champneys (*op. cit.*) admits that there is some confusion in Patmore's correspondence as to the date of the formation of the Volunteers.

2. *Departmental Reports*, 21 Febuary 1866.

3. Letter from Jones to Watts, 25 January 1867. (*Departmental Reports*) Gosse is described as a 'Junior Assistant or Transcriber'. Edmund Gosse, *Life and Letters*, p. 12.

4. *op. cit.*, p. 19.
Though Gosse joined the Museum staff just too late to have any personal official knowledge of Panizzi, he seems to have picked up the views of at least some of his colleagues and describes the former Principal Librarian as a 'thorough-going tyrant'. (*Daily Graphic*, 11 October 1906. Quoted in Esdaile, p. 364.)

5. Rev. Frederick Laughlin, a formidable character, though a clergyman, entered the department in 1855. Later he became deranged and a threat to use a revolver on an offending colleague led to his removal from the Museum.

6. Gosse, *Life and Letters*, p. 13. Coventry Patmore had just left the Museum, but amongst the literary figures still there were Arthur O'Shaughnessy, 1844–1881, then an Assistant in the Department of Zoology, which he had entered in June 1861, Richard Garnett, and Théophile Marzials, a popular poet, composer and author of the day.

growing circle of literary acquaintances, a wide reputation both as a scholar and man of letters. But the poor pay and the virtual impossibility of promotion induced him to leave the Museum in 1875, on being appointed translator to the Board of Trade at the princely salary of £400 a year, more, probably, than he could ever hope to obtain from the Museum, where, as he said, 'My prospects . . . are absolutely nil.'[1] He comments on 'the extraordinary change from the unpleasant severity, the official discourtesy, the irritating surveillance of the B. M. . . . It is surely a gross mistake to treat grown-up persons of mature habits as a set of convicts, or at least, of naughty schoolboys',[2] an echo of remarks made by John Gray many years before.

This snobbish and unfriendly attitude towards the junior staff persisted for many years and indeed almost to the Second World War, if not till later.[3] One man who did as much as he was able to break down this unwholesome tradition was Richard Garnett the younger.

Garnett had come to the Museum as a boy of sixteen in the autumn of 1850, through Panizzi's kindness to his recently widowed mother. Like his father, he had already shown a faculty for acquiring languages that stood him in good stead during his years as Placer. Like many other men, he had long despaired of any improvement in the low salaries and lack of promotion in the Department. Garnett was twice passed over, first by Roy and then by Ralston,[4] and several times contemplated leaving the Museum. But he was a real Museum man, and would never have been happy far from Bloomsbury. Bishop Creighton called him 'the ideal librarian',[5] scholarly, hard working, urbane, helpful and courteous to the public; sympathetic towards his subordinates, a man who was remembered at the Museum for his kindness and humanity

1. Gosse, *Life and Letters*, p. 26.

2. *op. cit.*, p. 79.

3. Esdaile, p. 365, gives further examples of this sort of behaviour by senior members of the staff.

4. Eugene Armand Roy entered the Department as a Transcriber in 1841. He developed the idea of movable slips in Reading Room Accessions Catalogues. The same suggestion was made almost simultaneously by J. W. Croker, the essayist. Roy was made Assistant Keeper in 1871.

William Ralston-Shedden, afterwards Shedden-Ralston, 1828–1889, promoted over Garnett's head though junior to him by two years. He had first come to the Department in 1853, and was later its expert on Slavonic languages. He was something of a 'barrack-room lawyer' but this may have been the effect of increasing ill-health.

5. Quoted in the article on Garnett by Sir Sidney Lee, in the *DNB*, 20th Century, 1901–1911, p. 80.

Mandell Creighton, 1843–1901, Bishop of London, 1897.

both to readers and to fellow members of the staff. His memory was formidable. Fortescue recalled that on one occasion he reeled off the names of the Popes of the seventeenth century and all the Derby winners from 1850 to 1860, whilst Barwick relates that Garnett, when asked if he knew anything about draining Irish bogs, immediately recalled that an article on this subject had appeared in a periodical some two years before.[1] Samuel Butler,[2] a difficult man with whom Garnett got on well, dedicated to him his book *Unconscious Memory*, as a tribute to his rare power in this respect. Butler was fond of gently pulling Garnett's leg, yet was grateful to the latter for his innate kindness and generosity.

Many of the staff were still deeply discontented at conditions in the Library. The feelings of resentment and frustration which these gave rise to were to be found among every grade and led to vitriolic attacks on Panizzi and his successor Jones in the columns of *The Civil Service Gazette* and other newspapers.

In 1875 these feelings once more came to the surface. The occasion was the death in 1873 of Emanuel Deutsch,[3] the Department's distinguished Hebrew expert, who joined the Museum in 1855. Overwork and the ravages of an incurable disease brought about his early death which occurred at Alexandria, where he had gone in a vain endeavour to regain his health.

Two years later a scurrilous pamphlet by a writer calling himself Stefan Poles appeared entitled *The Actual Condition of the British Museum*,[4] In it Poles accused the Museum authorities, in particular Jones and Rye, of causing the death, not only of Deutsch, 'who was . . . slowly murdered by the studied malice, and the petty jealousy of officials'[5] but also of another Assistant, Edward Warren, who also died young. The pamphlet consists almost entirely of a spiteful and immoderate attack on the administration of Printed Books, in particular on Jones, both as Keeper and Principal Librarian, on Rye and on several other members of the staff. Behind Poles – who bore a grudge against Jones for

1. Barwick, p. 125.
2. Samuel Butler, 1835–1902, novelist and philosophical writer.
3. Emanuel Oscar Mendhem Deutsch, 1829–1873, Semitic scholar.
4. Stefan Poles, *The Actual Condition of the British Museum*, London, 1875. Poles also issued a second pamphlet, *Parson, Lawyer, and Layman, a budget of letters from various hands*, his correspondence and quarrels with Ralston and others.
According to Garnett, Poles died shortly after the publication of his pamphlets in Middlesex Hospital. (Note by Garnett in the P.B. archive copy of *The Actual Condition*.)
5. *Actual Condition*, pp. 8, 9.

refusing to act against one of the staff who had offended him – was a senior Assistant, Shedden Ralston. Ralston disliked both Jones and Rye intensely. This may have been due to the fact that on the sudden death of Watts in 1869, he had considered himself suitable for the vacant Keepership. According to Rye, Ralston wrote to Panizzi asking the former Principal Librarian to help him secure the position. Panizzi replied in a letter 'which I thought rather harsh and unforgiving'.[1] Rye was made Keeper on the recommendation of Jones and Panizzi and Ralston seems never to have forgiven either Rye or Jones.

It is now time to see what was happening in the sister Department of Manuscripts. Madden never recovered from his disappointment at Panizzi's being made Principal Librarian, and did little during the remaining ten years of his Keepership. For the twenty-nine years he had ruled over the Department of Manuscripts he had worked hard to bring new treasures to the great collections which he had inherited and, fine scholar as he was, likewise spent much time revising the manuscript catalogues and keeping them up to date. Notwithstanding his opinion to the contrary, he was no administrator and though just and kind towards subordinates he was jealous of almost all his senior colleagues. His refusal to cooperate with anyone of whom he did not approve, inside or outside the Museum, made many of his achievements sterile and left a multitude of problems.

The next keeper Bond brought the cataloguing of the Additional Manuscripts up to date, which Madden in his later years neglected. Publication of this catalogue, however, was postponed until Bond had created his Classed Catalogue. Faced, however, with the problem that the manuscripts had no general catalogue at all, but only those to the various collections, many of which were out of date, Bond decided that a classed catalogue was essential as a guide to the contents of his Department as a whole. With the assistance of Maunde Thompson, the catalogue was prepared by cutting up the older printed catalogues and arranging them under appropriate headings, further manuscript entries and notes being added at the same time. Although never printed, the classed catalogue has shown itself an indispensable tool for scholars in a number of fields.

Sir Frederic had for many years complained of the lack of room, and with the more vigorous accessions policy of his successors, the situation became acute. The completion of the White Wing in 1884 afforded some relief, in particular a Students' Room which meant that manu-

1. Letter from Rye to Garnett, 6 March 1897. (P.B. Dept. Archives.)

scripts need no longer be sent to the general Reading Room, with all the inter-departmental friction and possible damage to documents that such a practice entailed.

The departmental collections were greatly enriched at this period. Perhaps the most important accessions were the Stowe manuscripts. These valuable manuscripts had been collected by the first Duke of Buckingham and Chandos and sold by his son, the second Duke, old Thomas Grenville's great nephew, in 1849.[1] The Museum was given first refusal. In January Madden valued the collections at £8,300,[2] but the Trustees, with their usual lack of enthusiasm, delayed, and in May Madden noted that they had been bought by that voracious collector, the Earl of Ashburnham for £8,000. 'The Stowe MSS therefore will now be joined onto the mass already acquired at Ashburnham House . . . I really believe the Trustees and the Government will be glad to get rid of them.'[3] In 1879 Ashburnham died and his executors offered the whole to the Museum for £160,000, by no means an excessive sum for so fine a collection. After protracted negotiations, in 1883, the Treasury purchased for the Museum the Stowe manuscripts alone, on the grounds that they consisted primarily of manuscripts of importance in English history, whilst the manuscripts of Irish interest were deposited in the library of the Royal Irish Academy in Dublin.[4]

This was only one of the collections that through timidity or inertia the mid-nineteenth-century Trustees failed to secure for the nation. Madden was convinced, rightly or wrongly, that the culprit was Sir Robert Peel, according to Sir Frederic a man of pronounced Philistine views. He commented sarcastically: 'I do not believe that Sir R. Peel cares one button for the Museum or its contents. He has the soul of a cotton-spinner.'[5]

1. Richard Temple–Nugent–Brydges–Chandos–Grenville, 1776–1839, first Duke of Buckingham and Chandos.

Richard Plantagenet Temple–Nugent–Brydges–Chandos–Grenville, 1797–1861, Duke of Buckingham and Chandos. He died ruined, at the Great Western Hotel, Paddington, leaving only £200. The contents of his house at Stowe when sold up in 1848–49 realised only £75,526, the rest of his considerable landed property being already in the hands of his creditors. (GEC, vol. V, pp. 408–10).

2. Esdaile, p. 257.

3. *Madden Journal*, 21 May 1849.

4. *Accounts, &c.*, 1883–4, p.8. (PP, H. of C., vol. LXI, p. 723).

5. This outburst was occasioned by Madden going to look at the two fine sculptured heads from 'Khoorsabad', sent to the Museum by Peel, 'for inspection'. The Prime Minister intended these for the ornamentation of a summer house in his country

It was left to the more generous outlook of later Boards to rectify the mistakes of their predecessors, but with rising prices and increased competition from other nations, especially America, this was by no means easy.

Other important collections acquired about this time were the vast collection of the Newcastle papers,[1] an indispensable source for the political history of the middle and later eighteenth century, Warren Hastings' papers, and many others.

Bond's successor was Edward Maunde Thompson, who had come in 1861 as an Assistant in the Principal Librarian's office. Acting on Panizzi's advice, despite the opposition of Sir Frederic, he soon transferred to the Department of Manuscripts and proved himself an outstanding member of the staff. A handsome man with fine features, dark hair, light blue eyes, and an erect carriage, he dominated any company in which he found himself. In contrast with Bond, who was rather shy and reserved, he was full of high spirits and geniality, though only among those of whom he approved. Thompson, like Bond, was a conscientious scholar, who insisted on punctuality and devotion to duty, often lacking in his contemporaries.[2] Kenyon quotes a little ditty in his obituary of Sir Edward, which reflects the easy-going atmosphere of Maunde Thompson's early days at the Museum:

1. The Newcastle papers were given between 1886 and 1889 by the fourth Earl of Chichester. They consist of the papers of Thomas Pelham–Holles, Duke of Newcastle, the eighteenth-century Prime Minister, 1693–1768, and those of the first and second Earls of Chichester. They cover the period 1683 to 1826 and are contained in 537 volumes and 3,500 charters. (*Accounts, &c.*, p. 9. PP, H. of C., 1887, vol. LXV, p. 529.) Thomas Pelham, 1728–1805, was a distant relative of the father of the Prime Minister. Created Earl of Chichester in June 1801.

Thomas Pelham, 1756–1826, second Earl, son of the above, held minor posts in various administrations at the beginning of the nineteenth century. He succeeded his father as Lord Pelham of Stanmer in June 1801, and as Earl of Chichester in 1805.

2. On 11 March 1914, Maude Thompson wrote to G. F. Barwick to congratulate him on his recent appointment as Keeper of Printed Books. He emphasises to the younger man the attitude he had always adopted when running his own department or, indeed, the Museum. 'A difficult job . . . endless detail and often small thanks. Never mind, put your back into it, drive the mill without fear or favour – forget yourself and work only for others. This I know you will do.' (*Barwick Papers*, P.B. Departmental Archives.)

estate, 'with about the same love of art as prompted George IV to take away an Ancient Greek altar to place the remains on Virginia Water! Bah!' (*Madden Journal*, 1 April 1846.)

It is probable, however, that W. R. Hamilton was an even bigger obstacle to the Museum's obtaining anything but classical antiquities.

How doth the little busy –
Pass idly hour by hour
Begin to work at half-past three
And work to nearly four![1]

Thompson was always far otherwise. A brilliant scholar, especially in the field of paleography, he was also a barrister though he never practiced. His clear analytical mind was apparent in all that he undertook.[2] It was he who was responsible for initiating specialist catalogues of manuscripts in various fields, continued by his successors, and for making the resources of the department more generally available to scholars.

To the regret of many Thompson was succeeded, not by his right-hand man, George Warner,[3] but by the Assistant Keeper John Long Scott.[4] Scott was primarily an orientalist, although he had not gone, with Rieu and William Wright,[5] to the new Department of Oriental Manuscripts in 1867. It would seem probable that Bond was unable to spare a third senior member of his staff. Scott's other principal interest was charters, about which some distinguished works were published under his Keepership.

He left much of the administration of the Department to Warner, who was also responsible for editing the Additional Catalogue and for

1. The only names in the Department of Manuscripts at that period beginning with 'B', and, therefore, presumably filling the lacuna in Kenyon's rhyme, are those of an assistant W. de G. Birch and of Bond, the Keeper himself. Kenyon makes a point of saying that Bond 'was a notable exception' to the prevailing spirit of idleness and we must therefore conclude that it was Birch who was meant. (Kenyon, *Sir Edward Maunde Thompson*, pp. 3, 4. B. M. *House Lists*.)

2. A. R. Dryhurst, former Assistant Secretary, in a letter to G. F. Barwick, wrote of Maunde Thompson: 'he was a good business man & consistent in his rulings'. Dryhurst goes on to say: 'His successor [Kenyon], as we know, is also a good business man, but he never had the useful training which an Assistant gets when he becomes Keeper of a Department.' (Dryhurst to Barwick, 20 May 1929. *Barwick Papers*, P.B. Departmental Archives.)

3. Sir George Frederic Warner, 1845–1936. Entered the Department of Manuscripts as an Assistant in 1871, becoming the Assistant Keeper in 1888 and Keeper and Egerton Librarian in 1904. He retired from the Museum in 1911, in which year he also received his knighthood.

4. Edward John Long Scott, 1840–1918, had entered the Department of Manuscripts as an Assistant in 1863. He became Assistant Keeper in 1879 and Keeper in 1888. On his retirement, Scott became Keeper of Muniments at Westminster Abbey.

5. William Wright, 1830–1889, another brilliant orientalist. He stayed at the Museum only nine years, retiring in 1870 to become Adams' Professor of Arabic at Cambridge, a post in which he was later followed by Charles Rieu, his former Keeper.

the accessions policy. Junior members of the staff now turned to Warner rather than their Keeper for advice and assistance.

When at last, at the age of fifty-nine, Warner became Keeper in 1904, it only regularised a position which he had held for many years. Warner, like Thompson, was an excellent paleographer, and also took a keen interest in illuminated manuscripts. In 1907 he was responsible for an admirable series of reproductions of the finest illuminated specimens in the Museum collections, and a few years earlier had edited the Museum's first facsimiles in colour. Warner was greatly liked by his colleagues, and it occasioned surprise when the comparatively young Kenyon succeeded Maunde Thompson as Principal Librarian in 1909, and not his Keeper, Warner. It was age alone that was against him. As Kenyon himself wrote, 'I should not have been in my present place if the four senior keepers had not been too old to be taken into consideration'.[1]

During the Keeperships of Charles Rieu and of Sir Robert Douglas, the Department of Oriental Manuscripts (later the Department of Oriental Printed Books and Manuscripts) greatly increased the number and importance of its acquisitions. Douglas had for long been in charge of the Chinese and Japanese books in his Department, and in 1877 had produced a definitive catalogue of these, together with the manuscripts in the same two languages.

Douglas now had under him able assistants, among them the Semitic scholar A. G. Ellis,[2] grandson of Sir Henry; the Rev. G. Margouliath, an expert in Hebrew,[3] and Dr Lionel Barnett, who, as well as being fully acquainted with Hebrew, the classical languages and a number of modern ones, also possessed a remarkable knowledge of the many and varied tongues of India. Lionel Barnett in 1908 succeeded Douglas as Keeper and reigned over his Department for nearly thirty years until 1936.[4]

1. Kenyon to Barwick, 3 February 1914. (*Barwick Papers*, P.B. Departmental Archives.) The four senior Keepers in 1909, by date of appointment, were Sir Sidney Colvin, of Prints and Drawings, appointed in 1883; Wallis Budge, of Egyptian and Assyrian Antiquities, 1894; C. H. Read, of British and Medieval Antiquities, 1896; and G. K. Fortescue, of Printed Books, 1899. All were considerably older than Kenyon. Despite his being the oldest of them, Colvin was very much regarded outside the Museum as a possible successor to Maunde Thompson.
2. Alexander George Ellis. Entered the Department of Oriental Manuscripts in 1883.
3. Rev. George Margouliath, 1853–1924, Assistant in charge of Hebrew, Syriac and Aramaic, 1891–1914.
4. Lionel David Barnett, 1871–1960. Joined the Museum in 1899, Keeper of Oriental Printed Books and Manuscripts, 1908. After his retirement, he returned to

The other member of this brilliant band of scholars was Dr Lionel Giles,[1] who became the Department's Chinese expert on Douglas's retirement. The practice was now begun of recruiting outside experts on a temporary basis to cover languages which could not be dealt with by members of the permanent staff.

The Department of Prints and Drawings, despite the magnificent treasures which it had early acquired from the Sloane, Payne Knight and Cracherode collections, had long been somewhat of a Cinderella. Though there had been a separate Keeper of the Prints and Drawings from 1805 onwards, he had, since the appointment of J. T. Smith in 1816, ranked only as an Extra Assistant Librarian, with neither the status nor the salary of his colleagues.

At first the various collections formed part of the Department of Printed Books, then, at least as far as the drawings and engravings were concerned, of the Department of Manuscripts, until eventually they became a sub-division of the Department of Antiquities, under an Extra-Assistant Librarian, with the title of Keeper of the Prints and Drawings.[2] Set up at last as an independent Department in September 1836 on the recommendations of the Parliamentary Select Committee of that year, it for long suffered by having hardly any staff, very limited accommodation for the storage of its collections, and no exhibition space at all.[3] Josi, its first Keeper, although conscientious and hard-

1. Lionel Giles, 1875–1958. Entered the Museum in 1900 and retired in 1940.
2. Hawkins, Keeper of the Department of Antiquities, said in evidence before the 1835 Parliamentary Select Committee: 'I have a limited responsibility [over the Print Room] not easily defined.' [*Select Committee, 1835, Minutes*, para. 3476], and further said that he left all practical arrangements to its own Keeper. Hawkins strongly recommended setting up Prints and Drawings as a separate department. (*op. cit.*, para. 3487; *Report*, para. 6.)
3. *Committee Meetings*, vol. 5, p. 4351, 20 September 1836. This is the date on which Henry Josi lodged his bond for £1,000 as the first Keeper of the independent department. The succeeding Keeper, Carpenter, in his evidence to the Royal Commission, strongly deprectes the fact that he has no means of exhibiting his already fine collections to the general public. (*Royal Commission, Minutes*, para. 3565, 3566.) As late as 1857, the Keeper of Prints and Drawings was paid only £500 a year, against the £600 of the Keepers of Printed Books, Manuscripts, Antiquities and Zoology. The two other Natural History Keepers, however, also received £500.

work in his old Department as an Assistant Keeper almost up to his death. His was the last name in the Museum *House List* (as late as 1960), who had entered the Trustees' service in the nineteenth century. Lionel Barnett's son, Dr Richard Barnett, is the present Keeper of the Department of Western Asiatic Antiquities (1972).

working, had neither the academic nor the social standing of such men as Madden, Hawkins and Panizzi, and it was not until the time of W. H. Carpenter,[1] who became Keeper in 1845, that the Department commenced to build on its earlier foundations and to turn itself into the outstanding collection of prints and drawings it has become.

Henry Josi had succeeded the ailing William Ottley, Keeper of Prints from 1833, in 1836.[2] A successful print seller of Dutch extraction, he proved himself a vigorous and enterprising Keeper until his early death in 1845. It was then that a horrified Madden learnt the whole truth about his erstwhile colleague. Not only had the former Keeper's widow been left in very reduced circumstances but her husband had for years kept a ham and beef shop. 'This is the first time I ever learnt of his being so low a grade. I never thought him a gentleman. It is not pleasant however to have men appointed to situations in the Museum ostensibly on the same level as the other officers and then to find they have kept a *ham and beef* shop!'[3]

Carpenter did much to increase the collections, making important additions to the drawings by the great masters, and to the neglected British collections. He managed to secure some of the fine drawings originally collected by Sir Thomas Lawrence, which the Museum had earlier lost the opportunity of acquiring in their entirety.

In 1869 Prints and Drawings received a considerable share of the Slade Collection, of which G. W. Reid, Carpenter's successor, remarked, 'Since the Cracherode bequest . . . no acquisition of the kind approaches it in rare and choice specimens of etchings and engravings, wherein nearly every artist of distinction is represented.'[4] Another fine collection which the Department had now acquired was one of 7,000 to 8,000 satirical prints and drawings of the seventeenth to nineteenth centuries brought together by Edward Hawkins, former Keeper of Antiquities. A catalogue of this remarkable collection was commenced, and the first volume published in 1877.

1. William Hokham Carpenter, 1792–1866, Keeper of Prints and Drawings, 1845–1866, connoisseur and art historian. He had a considerable talent for drawing, and before coming to the Museum had been a publisher, both on his own and in conjunction with his father. He died, working to the last, in 1866.
2. William Young Ottley, 1771–1836. He was appointed Keeper of Prints in 1833. An amateur artist of little talent and a prolific writer on art. See the article by J. A. Gere in BMQ, vol. XVIII, no. 2, pp. 44–52.
Henry Josi, 1802–1845.
3. *Madden Journal*, 15 March 1845.
4. *Accounts, &c.*, 1868–9, p. 44. (PP, H. of C., 1868–9, vol. XXXIV, p. 137.)

It was at this time, 1878, that the Trustees decided that all portraits not directly concerned with the history of the Museum should go to the new National Portrait Gallery.[1] Gathered together on the initiative of John Gray, Keeper of Zoology, these pictures had hung most incongruously on the walls of the ornithological gallery. Now, with the approaching transfer to South Kensington, the opportunity was taken to send the pictures to a more suitable home. Thus, with a few exceptions, the only pictorial art now remaining at the Museum were the collections of the Department of Prints and Drawings.

Carpenter's successor, G. W. Reid, was that Victorian phenomenon, the entirely self-educated man who had made good.[2] He became Keeper of the Department in 1866, an unprecedented step in the acutely class-conscious world of the Museum. He proved an excellent Keeper and did much to add to the collections. Apart from the Slade and Hawkins collections, there came to the Department during Reid's tenure of office, the Crace collection of maps, plans and views of London; the Henderson bequest of watercolour drawings, including superb examples of the work of Turner, Girtin, Cozens and other artists; the collection of proofs and prints of Turner's *Liber Studiorum* and many others. Reid was also responsible for a number of valuable departmental catalogues.

On Reid's resignation in 1883 the Keepership was offered to

1. *Accounts, &c.*, 1878–9, p. 5. (PP, H. of C., 1878–9, vol. LVII, p. 611.)
2. George William Reid, 1819–1887. He was the son of a draughtsman and teacher of drawing who later became an Attendant at the Museum. Reid himself entered the Museum as an Attendant in 1842, was made an Assistant in 1865 and Keeper of Prints and Drawings in 1866. He 'possessed a most exact and comprehensive knowledge of prints and of their commercial value'. (*DNB*, vol. 16, p. 871.)

Madden was, of course, horrified. He had thought little enough of Ottley and less of Josi. Carpenter, whilst a shade better socially, was, in the snobbish Madden's opinion, scarcely a gentleman. But to have Reid as his equal, even for a few months! 'He was an *Attendant* a few years since and it will be an insult to the other Officers to put him in Carpenter's place. He knows how to clean and mount prints, but has no scholarship nor any general knowledge of Art or of Books.' (*Madden Journal*, 22 July 1866.) Robert Cowtan, a promoted Attendant now an Assistant in Printed Books, not unnaturally saw Reid's appointment in a different light. Speaking of the Department of Prints and Drawings, he writes: 'Its present Keeper is one of my oldest Museum friends' and warmly praises Reid's efforts to build up the British collections. (Cowtan *Memoirs*, p. 354, 401.) Cowtan also states that Reid's father, likewise an Attendant in Prints and Drawings, might have succeeded to the Keepership after the death of Josi but for indifferent health. (*op. cit.*, p. 354.)

Sidney Colvin, Slade professor of Fine Art at Cambridge.[1] Colvin was of course already a famous man when he came to the Museum. He had long been the friend and admirer of Robert Louis Stevenson, and did much to make his friend's work popular with the British reading public. In his later years, after Stevenson's premature death in 1894, Colvin performed a similar service for Joseph Conrad, of whom he was an early patron.

Although he was an admirer of modern literature, in art it was far otherwise. His own preference was for the Italian school, but nothing later than the sixteenth century. Though Colvin's taste was conservative, he had a sound knowledge of the art of many periods, and by his wide acquaintance with collectors and people of influence, he did much to assist the growth of the collections and to increase the appreciation of them by both the scholarly and the general public.

A tall thin man, animated and nervous, he was irritable at times, but, again like Maunde Thompson, charming towards those whom he liked. Colvin had for many years lived on the terms of the closest friendship with Mrs Sitwell, the wife of the Rev. A. H. Sitwell.[2] Their residence at the Museum was a centre for artistic and literary talent and a notable addition to the humdrum life of the Museum. In 1903 they were at last able to marry, and remained happily united until Lady Colvin's death in 1924.

The main event of the early days of Colvin's Keepership, apart from the improved arrangement and mounting of the increasing collection, was its transfer from its old cramped quarters at the northwest corner of the Museum over the former Insect Room to spacious new rooms in the White Wing. In the autumn of 1885 Colvin superintended the move. In addition to new offices and workrooms, there was a gallery of ample size, which Colvin used for a series of fine exhibitions, culminating in the Rembrandt exhibition of 1899, in which the master's etchings were for the first time shown in their correct chronological order.

1. Sir Sidney Colvin, 1845–1927. His appointment as Keeper must have been an acute disappointment to the acting Assistant Keeper, Louis Fagan, 1845–1903, Panizzi's protégé. Fagan's acting rank was never confirmed, but it was generally expected that he would be Reid's successor.
2. Fanny Sitwell had been married at seventeen to the Rev. A. H. Sitwell, a distant relative of the literary Sitwells. She had long been separated from her husband and now lived the life of a brilliant literary hostess. Colvin and she had shared what seems to have been a purely Platonic friendship for many years until her husband's death permitted them to marry.

Perhaps Colvin's greatest acquisition amongst the many which he was instrumental in securing was the Malcolm collection of drawings and engravings, for which, in 1895, he persuaded the Treasury to pay the sum of £25,000, a figure which even then was generally held to be far below its real value. Consisting of 940 drawings and 312 engravings, together with a certain number of illuminated manuscript pages, it contained numerous examples of the work of the great Italian, Flemish, French, Dutch and German masters, including Fra Angelico, Botticelli, Leonardo, Brueghel, Rubens, Van Dyck, Claude, Poussin, Watteau, Dürer, Holbein, and many others.[1]

The Department of Prints and Drawings was at this period responsible not only for the works of western artists, but also those of Asia and the Far East. During the last ten years of his Keepership, Colvin became particularly interested in this section of the collections. Between 1902 and 1909 he obtained for the Museum four important private collections of Japanese woodcuts, and in 1910 the Wegener collection of Chinese paintings, hard to match at that date outside China. In the same year, the department received the great Salting collection of drawings, 291 in all.

By the end of his Keepership, Colvin had raised his department to unprecedented heights. In 1909 he had been considered as a possible successor to Maunde Thompson. He would have made a good director, possessing considerable energy as well as administrative ability of the highest order. But by now he was too old and the Trustees chose a younger man. In 1911 he was knighted, and in 1912 at last retired.

Colvin's final years as Keeper were filled with preparations for a move, as his earliest had been. However, the new buildings at the north end of the Museum in which the Prints and Drawings had been given, at the time, ample accommodation, were not handed over to the Trustees until October 1913, and it was left to his successor, Campbell Dodgson,[2] to supervise the move to the upper floors of the King Edward Building.

In 1912, the year of Colvin's retirement, 'in view of the increasing size and importance of the collections of Oriental art',[3] a separate Sub-Department of Oriental Prints and Drawings was created. This

1. *Accounts, &c.*, 1893–4, pp. 15, 41. (PP, H. of C., vol. LXVII, p. 607.)
2. Campbell Dodgson, 1867–1948. Assistant in the Department of Prints and Drawings, 1893. Keeper, 1912. Retired 1932.
3. *Accounts, &c.*, 1912–13, p. 15. (PP, H. of C., vol. L, p. 481.)

new division was put under Laurence Binyon,[1] and became the nucleus of the later department of Oriental Antiquities. Binyon joined the Museum as an assistant in Printed Books in 1893, but transferred to Prints and Drawings two years later. In 1909 he became Assistant Keeper. Although he had published studies on western artists, in particular those of the British school, Binyon soon became a recognised authority on the art of China and Japan and did much to foster a wider appreciation of the art of these countries amongst the educated public. When the Sub-Department was created, Binyon was the natural choice to head it, and did until 1932 when, for one year, he became Keeper of his old Department, retiring finally in 1933.

1. Robert Laurence Binyon, 1869–1943, poet, translator of Dante, art historian and critic.

CHAPTER TWELVE

The Departments of Antiquities
1860–1914

I N June 1860, the Trustees learnt that the long awaited resignation of Edward Hawkins, Keeper of the Department of Antiquities, 'might now be near at hand'.[1] It is probable that the Board received the news with some relief. Hawkins, in his eightieth year, now ruled his overgrown department with an increasingly enfeebled hand, and with little reference to the wishes of the Trustees. The time had now come to break up the Department into at least some of its constituent parts. Since the distant days when the Department of Antiquities had first been created, archaeological studies had grown, both in diversity and complexity. It was now far too large and too cumbersome to be under the control of one man, however able. It was utterly illogical that Coins or Ethnography, for instance, should be under the same administration as Egyptian mummies, Greek marbles or Assyrian bulls.

In 1860 Panizzi therefore had proposed that the old Department should be broken up into three or four new departments: Greek and Roman Antiquities; Oriental Antiquities, including Egyptian and Assyrian Antiquities; and Coins and Medals. The fast-growing collections of Ethnography, British Antiquities and Medieval Antiquities might, Panizzi allowed, be considered a fourth department, but disliking such objects strongly, and hoping to get rid of them altogether, the Principal Librarian thought these collections might for the present be attached to the Greek and Roman Department.

The Trustees' Sub-Committee on Antiquities decided that it would be better to set up the four departments as Panizzi had first suggested, but this resolution was partially reversed by a General Meeting, at which it was decided, on purely economic grounds, to attach Medieval Antiquities and Ethnography to Oriental Antiquities.[2] It was agreed,

1. *Standing Committee Minutes*, 23 June 1860. (*Papers relating to the Salaries of Officers*, p. 3. PP, H. of C., 1866, vol. XXXIX, p. 199.)
2. *op. cit.*, pp. 3, 4, 8. The two senior Keepers were to have £600 a year; the two junior (eventually one) £500; the senior was also to have Hawkins' house. Birch was the senior, then Newton, and Vaux the junior.

nevertheless, to permit A. W. Franks, their brilliant custodian, to retain a measure of autonomy, though the Keeper of Oriental Antiquities would have ultimate responsibility.[1]

Who were to be the three new Keepers? Dr Samuel Birch, for many years Hawkins' right-hand man, a distinguished Egyptologist and one who had helped to lay the foundations of the science of Assyriology, was the obvious choice for Oriental Antiquities. W. S. W. Vaux, who was the old Department's specialist in numismatics, was equally clearly ordained to be the first Keeper of the Department of Coins and Medals. It was the third choice, to contemporary eyes much the most important, which was the difficult one, the Keeper of Greek and Roman Antiquities.

Panizzi urged the claims of Charles Newton, who for the last few years had been busy excavating at Halicarnassus and elsewhere in the Near East and had discovered a whole series of masterpieces which had been dispatched to Bloomsbury. Newton, who had been an Assistant in the Department of Antiquities from 1840 to 1852 before joining the Foreign Service, had recently been moved to Rome, where, if opportunities for archaeological research were limited, he had become invaluable to Panizzi as a source of political gossip from the Papal capital.

The other strong candidate for the post was Edmund Oldfield, who looked after the classical antiquities within the Department and had the backing of Hawkins. Oldfield, however, for all his virtues, was not one of the Principal Librarian's favourites. Since what the great Pan said nearly always went, Charles Newton became, in January 1861, Keeper of Greek and Roman Antiquities, while Oldfield felt that his position had become impossible and, after a few half-hearted protests, resigned.[2]

1. *op. cit.*, p. 14.
2. In February 1861, Oldfield had laid a scheme before the Trustees to sub-divide the newly formed Department of Greek and Roman Antiquities into two sections, the one under a 'senior' Keeper, Newton; the other under a 'junior' Keeper. He said he would gladly take the latter position at a nominal salary, or at none at all. The Trustees would, however, not consider any further sub-divisions of existing departments. Three would make for 'increased efficiency', but more seemed to them to be quite unnecessary. (*Committee Minutes*, vol. 29, p. 9827, 2 February 1861.)

According to Madden, Oldfield also tried for the Keepership of the Department of Prints and Drawings on Carpenter's death in 1866. 'But what does Mr Panizzi care for this. [Read's alleged incompetence.] To keep Mr Oldfield out (a scholar, an art lover and a Gentleman), Mr P. has issued a *fiat*, and Read is to have the place. It is infamous!' An angry footnote is appended: 'This found to be the fact and a most monstrous abuse of power it is.' (*Madden Journal*, 22 July 1866.)

Newton was undoubtedly a good choice, a man of boundless energy, as well as a distinguished scholar and archaeologist. He breathed fresh life into a department which had become a little moribund.

The space question was still the most pressing. Such valuable collections as the Towneley terracottas had not been exhibited for many years and were 'packed up in a kind of warehouse room'.[1] The wonderful sculptures from Halicarnassus, retrieved from the walls of a Turkish fort by Newton himself, were hidden behind glass screens on the colonnade to the west of the entrance where they would remain for many years. Another fine collection likewise had to go on the colonnade – the antiquities from the sites of Carthage and Utica in North Africa.[2]

Until something went there would be no proper display of the existing collections, let alone room for new acquisitions. In 1861 Panizzi reported to the Treasury that although 'a very large and valuable accession to the sculptures . . . may be looked for from the Cyrenaica, amounting, at present to twelve statues . . . several detached heads and other fragments', and that more were expected to be discovered on or near the same site, yet 'the Trustees have literally no space in the present buildings in which they can accommodate, still less exhibit to the public, these important remains'.[3] Newton was anxious to rearrange the Elgin Marbles, still suffering from the results of Westmacott's 'artistic' taste and 'inconveniently crowded', but could do nothing about it for want of space.[4] No wonder that the Trustees, the Principal Librarian and every Keeper kept hammering away, year after year, on the same theme. Space must be found, and such space could only be found by widespread building on or near the present site or by the removal of a substantial part of the collections.

Nevertheless, the collections went on growing. In 1864, for instance, a fine terracotta coffin from Cyprus and a collection of vases and other antiquities from Sicily were amongst the accessions received. The following year some statues from the Farnese Palace were secured,

1. *Papers relating to the Enlargement of the British Museum*, p. 26. (PP, H. of C., 1857–8, vol. XXXIII, p. 373.)
2. *Correspondence &c. relating to the British Museum*, p. 46. (PP, H. of C., 1864, vol. XXXII, p. 167.)
3. *Letter of Panizzi to the Treasury*, 28 May 1861. *Correspondence relating to the British Museum*, p. 2. (PP, H. of C., 1862, vol. XXIX, p. 169.)
4. *op. cit.*, p. 2. Newton also worried about the sculptures out on the colonnade; 'they are suffering serious injury from the want of sufficient protection and are likely to suffer still further'. (*op. cit.*, p. 2.)

together with the results of excavations taking place in the island of Rhodes. Excavations, often under the direction of the local British Consuls, were taking place continuously throughout the Near East. In 1867 the Department of Greek and Roman Antiquities reported excavations on behalf of the Museum at both Benghazi and Ephesus. Discoveries at the latter site, in particular, were outstanding, and the excavations went on for a number of years. Throughout this period, largely through Newton's influence or inspiration, many other valuable acquisitions were obtained, nearly £100,000 in special grants being secured for them from the Treasury.

The Blacas collections were outstanding even among these superlative objects. Purchased by the Museum in November 1866, they had been formed by two successive Ducs de Blacas; the father had been for many years French Ambassador at Rome and Naples; his son had devoted himself to numismatics and to the preparation of a handsome illustrated catalogue of the family collections.[1] The gems and cameos alone were of outstanding importance, but perhaps the most remarkable acquisition, at least in the field of classical antiquities, was the famous Esquiline treasure, a silver toilet service of a Roman bride, discovered in a vault in Rome in 1793 and dating from the close of the 5th century AD. These pieces are of a rare beauty and were in the finest possible condition. In addition to the Greek and Roman antiquities, there were further collections of coins, Egyptian antiquities, papyri and a few oriental antiquities.

In 1874 the sculptures from the Mausoleum were moved from their sheds on the colonnade to new quarters in the basement of the Museum, but even here the accommodation was inadequate for their display or even safety.

When the Natural History departments started their move to South Kensington in 1878 it was rightly the overcrowded Antiquities departments which were the main beneficiaries. The Greek and Roman department obtained the rooms formerly occupied by the Geological and Mineralogical collections, whilst the British and Medieval collections secured the area left empty by the Botanical collections.

In 1883 it was at last possible to display suitably the sculptures and other remains from the tomb of Mausolus at Halicarnassus, which had come to the Museum nearly twenty years before. From the White

1. A full description of the whole collection is in *Accounts, &c.*, 1866–7, pp. 29–45. (PP, H. of C., vol. XXXIX, p. 233.)

bequest a magnificent new gallery had been constructed on the open space to the north of the Hellenic Room, parallel with the main western gallery. In this Mausoleum Room, opened in 1884, these sculptures were displayed in a setting worthy of them, and the sheds on the colonnade, which had housed them for so long were removed. It was only just in time. Newton reported that many of the sculptures had suffered from their exposure to the foul air of the aptly named 'sepulchral basement' and elsewhere in the bowels of the Museum. Some were still there, including parts of the Elgin and Towneley marbles, and it was already noticeable that the surface of these statues was being adversely affected. 'The detriment to the surface of the sculptures', wrote Newton, 'will be aggravated year by year till a proper room is provided for their exhibition'.[1]

In 1886, owing to increasing ill-health, Newton retired, to be succeeded by A. S. Murray.[2] Arranging and rearranging of the collections went on year by year, and more and more use was made of the space left by the removal of the Natural History collections. An important collection, acquired in 1887, was that excavated by Flinders Petrie,[3] a name soon to be famous in other archaeological fields.

As the study of antiquities of every kind became more and more popular with the public, the need for a lecture room was felt, but for long nothing was done to provide one. Later the Assyrian basement was reconstructed to make a lecture and exhibition room. In 1888 a small extension to the department's galleries was made by the acquisition of the old Print Room at the north end of the western galleries, no longer needed by that department, since they had obtained in 1887 fine new apartments in the White Wing.

Perhaps the most noteworthy collection acquired by the Department of Greek and Roman Antiquities in the closing years of the nineteenth century was the Carlisle collection, shared between itself and the sister department of British and Medieval Antiquities. It consisted largely of engraved gems, both cameos and intaglios, the majority being of

1. *Accounts, &c.*, p. 26. (PP, H. of C., 1884, vol. LXI, p. 723.)
2. Alexander Stuart Murray, 1841–1904, Assistant in the Department of Greek and Roman Antiquities, 1867, Keeper, 1886. He died at the Museum in March 1904. His younger brother, G. R. M. Murray, was Keeper of Botany, 1895–1905, so far the only case of brothers being Keepers at the same time.
3. Sir William Matthew Flinders Petrie, 1853–1942, Egyptologist. Grandson of Matthew Flinders, the explorer.

ancient work, but with a few Renaissance specimens.[1] For the most part it was now the accumulation of numerous smaller donations and individual objects which broadened the collections, making them more representative of the art of the ancient world.

The second of the three new departments formed from the old Department of Antiquities was that of Coins and Medals. The first Keeper of the independent department was William Vaux, who had been in charge of the national collections under Hawkins. Sir Flinders Petrie haunted the department as a boy, and spoke appreciatively of 'the august figure of Vaux' and of 'the kindly help always granted in the Coin Room'.[2] This was the old Medal Room, which eventually became the Gold Ornament Room of the Department of Greek and Roman Antiquities. The Department had no exhibition gallery, and thus, like Prints and Drawings, was forced to make use of a few cases in the King's Library to show off some of its treasures, in the interests of security usually in the form of electrotype reproductions.

In 1870 Vaux retired, to be followed by Reginald Stuart Poole,[3] who was Keeper for the next twenty years. Under him were inaugurated a series of systematic Coin Catalogues, at first dealing with Greek coins, a series which has been maintained to the present day. Poole was ably supported by Barclay Vincent Head,[4] author of *Historia Numorum*, 1887, which has been termed the Bible of the Greek numismatist.

Head succeeded Poole in 1893. In January of this year the Department moved from its old quarters into a new wing on the western side of the Museum, built specially to receive it. The move involved the transfer of nearly a quarter million specimens, a formidable undertaking. The risk of losing or mislaying often unique specimens was considerable and the Department must have been greatly relieved when the move was at last safely over. Alongside the New Medal Room was an exhibition gallery, afterwards incorporated into an enlarged Medal Room. A selection of reproductions in electrotype of the finest Greek and Roman

1. The most important part of the collection was that of engraved gems formed by Henry Howard, fourth Earl of Carlisle, 1694–1758, which he had largely obtained in Rome towards the middle of the eighteenth century. The collection was purchased from the ninth Earl, 1843–1911, between 1889 and 1891. (*Accounts, &c.*, 1890–1, p. 71. PP, H. of C., vol. LXI, p. 815.)
2. F. Petrie, *Seventy Years in Archaeology*, p. 14.
3. Reginald Stuart Poole, 1832–1895, archaeologist and orientalist. Assistant, 1852, Keeper of Coins and Medals, 1870. A keen Egyptologist.
4. Barclay Vincent Head, 1844–1914, numismatist. Entered the Department in 1864, Keeper 1893, Retired 1906.

coins was also placed on exhibition in the Etruscan Saloon. A separate Exhibition Room (the old Waddesdon Room) was later fitted up near the top of what had been known from the old Natural History days as the Botanical Staircase.

The Department of Coins and Medals occupied these premises for almost a half century until their destruction by enemy action in May 1941. Its next keeper, who succeeded Head in 1906, was H. A. Greuber,[1] who remained until 1912. As a young man Greuber had been very friendly with the ageing Panizzi and was one of his executors.[2] Under him the series of scholarly catalogues of the collections continued to be issued, Roman Republican Coins, Roman Medallions, Anglo-Saxon Coins, and many more.

A word must be said of the numerous collections acquired during this period. The Greek series were enriched by the coins bequeathed by James Woodhouse, of Corfu, a bequest that almost led to legal action against one of HM Consuls,[3] whilst in the Roman series, the most outstanding donation was that of Count John William de Salis,[4] who presented his extensive collection to the Trustees in 1861 on condition that he might be allowed direct access to the coins in the department to facilitate his researches into the classification of Roman coins. Other outstanding gifts were that of the collection of Hindu coins bequeathed by Major General Sir Alexander Cunningham,[5] who had been Director-

1. Herbert Appold Grueber, 1846–1927. Assistant, 1866, Assistant Keeper 1893, Keeper 1906, retired 1912.
2. The other was Charles Cannon, from 1857 onwards Panizzi's right-hand man in the Principal Librarian's office, leaving in 1866 for a higher salary as a translator in the Foreign Office.

By the terms of Panizzi's will his estate was left to Cannon and Grueber 'to sell and to dispose of such portions as they . . . think best'. Any surplus was to be shared equally between Grueber and Louis Fagan of the Department of Prints and Drawings. (Add. MS. 36,725. f. 640).
3. The collection formed by Mr James Woodhouse, for many years Treasurer of the Ionian Islands, was bequeathed to the Museum in 1866. It consisted of extremely valuable Greek and Hellenic antiquities and coins. On Woodhouse's death the collection was impounded by HM Consul-General at Corfu, who, regardless of the protests of the Trustees, declined to furnish an inventory. Newton was of the opinion that many of the most valuable objects in the collection were quite illegally handed over by the Consul to Woodhouse's heirs. (Accounts, &c., pp. 19, 20, 1866–7. PP, H. of C., 1867, vol. XXIX, p. 233.)
4. Count John Williams de Salis, d. 1869.
5. Major General Sir Alexander Cunningham, 1814–1893, soldier and archaeologist. It was he who collected in India much of the material which Franks bought subsequently

General of the Indian Archaeological Survey after his retirement from the Army. The Department had already purchased his magnificent collection of Bactrian, Parthian, and Moghul coins in 1888, the fruits of many years of assiduous collecting in India. The collection of oriental coins was also enriched by the transfer to the Museum in 1882 of the India Office collection of coins of Bactria and the East, whilst the purchase of the Blacas collection, rich in coins as in so many other objects, added to the Roman series more than 4,000 specimens. Thus by the early years of this century the numismatic collections of the Museum were perhaps the finest in the world and a magnet to scholars from all over the globe.

The third and, for the moment, sole remaining department of antiquities was that of Oriental Antiquities, British and Medieval Antiquities, and Ethnography. This was placed under the care of Samuel Birch, since 1836 the right-hand man of old Hawkins. Birch was a remarkable scholar, who did much to further the progress both of modern Egyptology and the nascent science of Assyriology. He possessed not only a wide knowledge of Egyptian and the various Semitic languages, but also of Chinese and of numismatics. Among his many services to the Museum was his slip catalogue of the Egyptian collections, which is now bound in more than a hundred volumes, every object being described with meticulous care and the inscriptions faithfully copied and translated.

Throughout this period excavations were still being carried out at Nineveh and other sites in the Middle East, and further remarkable discoveries were constantly being made. In 1885 Birch died suddenly at the age of seventy-two, to be succeeded as Keeper by P. Le Page Renouf.[1] Long before this, in 1866, the department had shed the incongruous burden of the British, Medieval and Ethnographical collections and was restricted, as it was to be for many years, to Egyptian and Assyrian antiquities. In 1886 on the suggestion of Franks, the name of the department was changed from the increasingly ambiguous 'Oriental Antiquities', to 'Department of Egyptian and Assyrian Antiquities', which it remained for sixty-nine years.

1. Sir Peter Le Page Renouf, 1822–1897, Egyptologist, Professor of Ancient History, Catholic University of Ireland, 1855–1864; one of HM Chief Inspectors of Schools, 1866. Retired from the Museum, 1891.

and which later formed part of the 'Treasure of the Oxus'. (O. M. Dalton, *The Treasure of the Oxus*, London, 1905).

Many fine treasures continued to be obtained in both fields. In the Egyptian field the closing decades of the nineteenth century were remarkable for the Vasalli Papyri, the Abbott Papyri, and the Harris Papyri, all of which deal with an official investigation into alleged tomb robberies committed in the necropolis near Thebes during the XX dynasty, the superbly carved black granite sarcophagus of Merymes (viceroy of Nubia under the Pharaoh Amenophis III *c.* 1400 BC), the Rhind mathematical papyrus, and many other treasures.

In 1888 the Trustees decided to abandon the various sites in Mesopotamia. The main reason was the refusal of the Turkish authorities to cooperate in any way. The Turks now wished to conduct their own explorations and to secure for their own museum at Constantinople the fruits of such discoveries. The result was disastrous, involving much destruction of invaluable inscribed tablets. Bond lamented that 'the records of these ancient Empires are being scattered or altogether destroyed'.[1] The Trustees asked the British government to intervene, but nothing was apparently done. The Turks had been difficult for some time, but the Museum had been greatly helped by the fact that Henry Layard was now Ambassador at Constantinople and almost as influential there as Stratford de Redcliffe himself had been earlier in the century. Layard, who had maintained his close and friendly relations with the Museum, had done much to smooth the path of its excavators. It was due to his influence that a remarkable hoard of antiquities from Van in eastern Anatolia was acquired for the Museum, including a fine bronze winged human-headed bull. The Trustees thanked Layard for these splendid objects and 'for the great interest which you manifest at all times in the welfare of the National Collections . . . by the exercise of your powerful interest in its favour'.[2] Bond, Winter Jones' successor as Principal Librarian, also wrote to Layard in 1878 to thank him for obtaining a *firman* for Rassam to enable the excavations to continue, not only in Assyria and Babylonia, 'but in the Pashalics of Van and Aleppo', and for securing exceptional facilities for the removal of the

1. *Accounts, &c.,* 1887–8, p. 8. (PP, H. of C., 1888, vol. LXXVIII, p. 813). In a letter to Layard of 30 November 1864, Charles Newton speaks of the irreparable damage being done by the Turks at various places throughout the Near East, such as Athos [?] (the name has been altered in the manuscript from Athens), where they had quite happily demolished a temple of Augustus. Newton pleaded with Layard to force the Turkish authorities either to put such remains in a Museum of their own in Constantinople or to give them to the British Museum. 'More than this I fear we cannot do to arrest the destruction.' (Add. MS. 39,112. f. 2228.)
2. Add. MS. 39,017. f. 115, Jones to Layard 19 Dec. 1877.

antiquities discovered.[1] Layard continued to take a keen interest in the affairs of the Museum, despite the growing complexities of his political and diplomatic career.

Throughout this period, excavations, even though on a more limited scale, were being carried on at Nineveh and elsewhere in Mesopotamia. Little, however, was done to encourage similar excavations in Egypt or to collect Egyptian antiquities locally. The Museum, in this respect, was still content to rely on gifts or purchases from the private collections of returned travellers or of those long resident in Egypt. Not until the late nineteenth century was attempt made to acquire material extensively in Egypt itself. By that time it was almost too late, as various restrictions on the export of antiquities gradually came into force.

It was during Birch's Keepership of the Department of Oriental Antiquities that the Museum secured the services of one of the most remarkable men who have ever served the Trustees. This was George Smith,[2] who had been apprenticed at the age of fourteen to a firm of banknote engravers. From an early age, Smith had been devoted to the study of the Bible and everything that might throw light on the historical books of the Old Testament. The works of Layard, Rawlinson and other explorers and linguists were a revelation to him. His young mind took fire and he was determined if possible to make Biblical archaeology his life's work. During his scanty holidays, Smith was constantly at the Museum, and at every dinner hour when the Sculpture Galleries were open, studying with the utmost attention the antiquities then newly arrived from Nineveh and Babylon. About 1861, young Smith's almost continual presence at the Museum attracted the notice of Birch, who introduced him to other experts and brought the latest results of Rawlinson's pioneer researches on cuneiform inscriptions to his notice. It was soon plain to Birch that Smith had an extensive knowledge of the inscriptions on the Babylonian clay tablets in the Museum collections. He was therefore officially engaged as a 'repairer' to restore as far as possible, the various fragments of inscribed bricks to their original state. In this he was so successful that in 1870 Birch

1. 'The Trustees look forward with great interest to the result of these excavations, which they confidently hope will further enrich the splendid collection of Assyrian antiquities, for which they are already indebted to your enterprise and generosity; and by the researches at Carchemish, add a fresh series of historical monuments to the treasures of the Museum.' (Bond to Layard, 26 December 1878. Add. MS. 39,024. f. 129.)
2. George Smith, 1840–1876, Assyriologist.

proposed that he should be made an Assistant in the Department of Oriental Antiquities.

In a room over the Trustees' Board Room Smith worked away day after day without any form of artificial light, cursing the London fogs. In 1872 he discovered that a certain tablet from Nineveh contained part of an Assyrian account similar to that of the Biblical Deluge. He copied and translated the text and submitted the manuscript to Birch and Rawlinson, before reading a paper on his discovery before a distinguished audience in December 1872. It caused a tremendous sensation, and both the Trustees and the Government were urged to renew the excavations at Kuyunjik and to discover, if possible, the missing fragments of the Deluge tablet. The *Daily Telegraph* offered 1,000 guineas to finance further excavations, providing that Smith himself conducted them and also agreed to supply the paper with exclusive accounts of any discoveries that he might make. On 2 March 1873, Smith arrived at Mosul, and a few weeks later, early in May, by extraordinary good fortune, he found a further fragment, containing seventeen lines, hitherto wanting, of the deluge legend.[1]

Smith, a simple, honest man of a retiring disposition, was constantly beset by difficulties with the natives, whose ways he completely failed to understand, and many of his discoveries were seized and lost by his failure to pay the necessary bribes to the local authorities.

In 1874, and again in 1876, Smith was sent out to Mesopotamia by the Trustees on further missions. On the second of these journeys everything went wrong. There was an outbreak of cholera in the area through which he was travelling and constant fighting amongst the various tribes. Smith never seemed able to adjust himself to conditions in the East and neglected the most elementary precautions. Ill and worn out by privations, many of which, by a little forethought, he might have avoided, he was brought to Aleppo and died there of dysentery, aged thirty-six, on 19 August 1876. Smith was undoubtedly a queer character. On being handed the cleaned 'Deluge' tablet for which he had long been impatiently waiting by Robert Ready, the Department's restorer, he read a few lines which confirmed his theories, shouted 'I am the first man to read that after more than two thousand years of oblivion'. Then, placing the tablet carefully on a table, he jumped up, rushed about the room in a state of excitement and, to the astonishment of all present, started to undress!

Yet George Smith did much in his short life to put the study of

1. Budge, p. 103.

Assyriology on a sound footing. By his sensational discoveries he once more aroused popular interest in it as Layard had a generation earlier. It was by his efforts that a very considerable number of inscribed tablets were brought to the Museum for Rawlinson and other scholars to interpret, and by doing so greatly to extend the learned world's knowledge of the Ancient East.[1]

Two years before the death of Birch in 1883, another remarkable scholar arrived, who was to be as outstanding in his generation as Birch and Layard had been in theirs and who was to survive until well into the twentieth century. This was E. A. T. Wallis Budge,[2] who joined the Department of Egyptian and Assyrian Antiquities as an Assistant in April 1883 and soon, by his diligence and remarkable abilities, began to make a name for himself.

The Trustees were now worried about the situation in both Egypt and Mesopotamia, where uncontrolled native digging was doing harm to many of the most valuable of ancient monuments. Since 1877, Hormuzd Rassam[3] had once more been working on the old site at Kuyunjik, or rather supervising from a distance excavations conducted throughout the wide area granted to him under the terms of the firman secured by Layard. At Balawat, a small village fifteen miles southeast of Mosul, he now discovered a curious object 'lying on its face and spread

1. Birch was always anxious to obtain more and more tablets. Thus, writing to Layard on 22 December 1877, he states that Rassam 'should turn his attention to tablets'. (Add. MS. 39,017. f. 181.) He also hopes that a bilingual text will be found at Carchemish 'to aid in deciphering that unknown hieroglyphic writing', an allusion to the completely undeciphered Hittite script. (Birch to Layard, 15 November 1879. Add. MS. 39,023. f. 101.)

2. Sir Ernest Alfred Thompson Wallis Budge, 1857–1934. Egyptologist and Assyriologist. Like Smith, he was of comparatively humble origin. After working for eight and a half years for the firm of W. H. Smith and Son, as a 'Boy and as a Book-Collector', he was sent up to Cambridge as a result of an appeal arranged primarily by W. E. Gladstone and there did extremely well. In 1883 he entered the Museum as an Assistant in the Department of Egyptian and Assyrian Antiquities, as Gladstone had long wished him to. (See the correspondence between Gladstone and the young Budge in Gladstone Papers, Add. MS. 44,456–44,520.)

3. Hormuzd Rassam, 1826–1910. Assyriologist and explorer. A Chaldean Christian, he was for many years Layard's principal assistant. From 1852 onwards he conducted excavations independently for the Trustees, but in 1854 he accepted the post of political interpreter at Aden, leaving the work of excavation to W. K. Loftus. After exciting adventures in Abyssinia, where he was an agent of the British Government in the negotiations which led to the Abyssinian War of 1868, Rassam resumed excavations on behalf of the Trustees in Mesopotamia in 1877. He retired in 1882 and settled in England for the rest of his life.

like a gigantic hat-rack',[1] and which proved to be the famous bronze gates of Shalmaneser III, now one of the glories of the Department of Western Asiatic Antiquities. Although Rassam himself continued to make further discoveries, because of his fundamental urge to look only for the remains of massive buildings, and colossal statues, such as Layard and he had found in their youth, and because of uncontrolled digging everywhere by the native population, the situation was deteriorating dangerously. It was above all else clay tablets, inscriptions and similar objects, which scholars now needed. Whenever Rassam stopped work on the various Museum sites, as he did in July 1882, the trickle of tablets and small antiquities illegally entering the Baghdad market turned into a flood, which flowed into almost every institution in Britain and America, including even the British Museum.

In 1887 Budge, who in the previous year had made an expedition to Egypt to collect antiquities, was sent by the Trustees to Baghdad to see what he could do to stop this leakage from the Museum excavations or, if unable to do so, to secure every possible tablet for the Museum, regardless of expense. In July 1879, Rassam had considered resigning as the Trustees' Superintendent of Excavations in the East, and the Trustees were at a loss for someone to replace him. Amongst the names mentioned as possibilities for the task was that of Lieutenant Kitchener, RE,[2] afterwards to be more famous as Lord Kitchener of Khartoum, the conqueror of the Sudan. But Rassam agreed to continue to work for the Trustees for a few years more. His long association with the Museum culminated with his discovery at the end of 1880 of the famous marble tablet of King Nabu-pal-iddina, adorned with a beautiful relief of the Sun-God. In 1882, 'out of heart' at the renewed difficulties he was encountering, Rassam left Mesopotamia for the last time, after nearly forty years in the service of the Trustees.

Budge now found that men were digging openly for tablets, even by daylight on all the Museum sites, and that there was no attempt to hinder or control in any way the trade in illegal antiquities. All he could do therefore was to secure as many tablets for the Museum as

1. Rassam, *Asshur and the Land of Nimrod*, pp. 207–8. Rassam discovered the remains of two pairs of gates, the smaller dedicated by Ashurnasirpal II, builder of the palace at Imgur Enlil, the modern Balawat, the larger and better preserved being those set up by his son and successor, Shalmaneser III. In 1956 the remains of a third pair of decorated bronze gates were found on the same site.

2. Horatio Herbert, Earl Kitchener of Khartoum, 1850–1916, Field-Marshal. In 1874 Kitchener was lent to the Palestine Exploration Fund and retained a marked interest in Biblical archaeology and a sound knowledge of Arabic for the rest of his life.

could be got on the open market. In 1888 he himself received a *firman* from the Turkish government to renew the excavations at Kuyunjik, which he decided to do initially on a more modest scale, in cooperation with Nimrud Rassam, old Rassam's nephew. For the next twenty years or so, the staff of the department were busy arranging and assimilating the mass of material provided by the early explorers in Mesopotamia, and it was not until 1903 that excavations were once more resumed at Nineveh, under the direction of L. W. King,[1] an Assistant in the Department of Egyptian and Assyrian Antiquities. By this time Budge himself was Keeper, having become so in 1894. Further discoveries were made in the palaces of Sennacherib and Ashur-bani-pal, but at last, on 11 February 1905, the excavations were closed down. From 1846 to 1905 the Museum, under Layard, Rassam, Ross, Loftus, Smith, King and Thompson, had explored at Kuyunjik and elsewhere in Mesopotamia. To these men and to the constant efforts of the Trustees to sustain and support them much of our present knowledge of the ancient Middle East is due.[2]

A charming picture of the Museum as it was in the early years of this century is given in the children's tale by E. Nesbit, *The Story of the Amulet*. In it four children, transported by magic to twentieth-century London, together with the Queen of Babylon, visit the British Museum in company with a curious creature of supernatural powers, the Psammead. On seeing the Babylonian galleries, the Queen makes so much fuss at so much of 'her' former possessions being in the showcases that both she and the children are escorted out of the Museum by a crowd of angry officials. The 'nicest of the angry gentlemen . . . who was really very nice indeed, and seemed to be over all the others' is Wallis Budge, who had helped Mrs Nesbit with the background of the story and to whom she dedicated the book. The Queen in a rage then wishes 'that all those Babylonian things would come out to me here' and her wish is at once granted by the Psammead. 'Next moment there was a crash. The glass swing doors and all their frame work were smashed suddenly and completely. The crowd of angry gentlemen

1. Leonard William King, Assyriologist, joined the Department of Egyptian and Assyrian Antiquities in 1893.
2. Henry James Ross, 1820–1902, explorer and sportsman. He was Christian Rassam's business partner at Mosul.
William Kennett Loftus, 1821?–1858, archaeologist and traveller.
Reginald Campbell Thompson, 1876–1941, Assyriologist, joined the Museum staff in 1899, but left in 1905. Subsequently had a distinguished career as an archaeologist.

sprang aside . . . but the nastiest of them was not quick enough and was roughly pushed out of the way by an enormous stone bull that was floating steadily through the door . . . It was followed by more stone images, by great slabs of carved stone, bricks, helmets, seals . . . and the round long things, something like rolling pins with marks on them like the print of little bird-feet.' 'The nicest gentleman' 'stood with his hands in his pockets just as though he was quite used to seeing great stone bulls and all sorts of small Babylonish objects float out into the Museum yard. But he sent a man to close the big iron gates'.[1] As usual in Mrs Nesbit's stories, all ended happily with the aid of a little magic.

In 1860, the Trustees had placed the Ethnographical and Medieval collections somewhat awkwardly in Oriental Antiquities. A. W. Franks, the Assistant in charge of these collections, was promoted and given sole authority over them, under Birch's overall direction. In 1866 Franks emphasised to Panizzi the increasing need for an independent department. He spoke first of his ethnographical collections. 'Ethnography has assumed,' he wrote, 'such a totally different aspect within the last few years; its scientific and historical value has been so fully recognised that I feel sure that, whether the natural history collections shall be retained at the Museum or not, it will be thought desirable to keep here collections which, when properly arranged, will be highly attractive and popular.' As for the British and Medieval collections, there was, by this time, no further need to stress *their* importance, and Franks clinched his arguments with a comparison of the accessions of the Egyptian and Assyrian Antiquities and those of British and Medieval Antiquities and Ethnography. In 1861, 330 as against 242; in 1865, 170 against 917, a total in five years of 855, compared with 4,572, many of these objects (although he did not say so) having been presented to the Sub-Department by Franks himself.[2] Despite his prejudices, Panizzi realised the strength of Franks' arguments and recommended to the Trustees his subordinate's proposals for the establishment of a separate Department. On 10 March 1866, it was formally agreed that the new Department should be set up under Franks as Keeper. One of the principal reasons which induced the Trustees and, after them, the Treasury to agree to the formation of a separate Department was the acquisition of the Christy collection in December 1865. When Henry

1. E. Nesbit, *The Story of the Amulet*, pp. 185–88.
2. *Papers relating to the Salaries of Officers*, p. 33. (PP, H. of C., 1866, vol. XXXIX, p. 199.)

Christy died in 1865,[1] at the comparatively early age of fifty-five, he bequeathed his incomparable collection to four Trustees, of whom Franks was one, together with a large sum of money so that the collection might be continually added to. This he did almost entirely because of his close friendship with Franks. His Trustees were empowered to present the whole collection to a permanent institution. Within six months the Christy Trustees had offered it to the Museum, by whom it was gratefully accepted. The Christy collection consisted of prehistoric artifacts, together with the arts and crafts of primitive peoples, which Christy had collected to illustrate the close parallel between ancient primitive cultures and those of contemporary races at a similar stage of development. In addition it was extremely rich in antiquities from the civilisations of Central and South America, especially in those of the Aztecs from Mexico.

Since it was impossible to house so extensive a collection at Bloomsbury, the Trustees rented the apartments lately occupied by Christy himself at 103 Victoria Street, Westminster, and had the collection permanently arranged there (it being accessible to the public by ticket on Fridays only), the first of the Museum collections to be out-housed.

From the ample funds bequeathed by Christy, his Trustees continued to purchase valuable material in prehistory and ethnography for the Museum, a source of numerous acquisitions, especially ethnographical specimens, which the Museum would otherwise never have obtained. The Museum to this day benefits from the Christy bequest and obtains funds from it for ethnographical specimens.

Under Franks' energetic direction his collections continued to grow. A man of considerable wealth, he was continually presenting his department, and indeed other departments, with rare objects, chosen with impeccable taste. In his annual report for 1886, Bond drew attention to the extremely valuable gifts that Franks was constantly making. 'It is due to Mr Franks, not only as a judicious purchaser of antiquities on the part of the Trustees, but as a contributor from his own resources and influence with collectors, that the Museum has at this time choice and well-arranged examples of Romano-British and Medieval Antiquities, a collection of glass of all ages, representative collections of pottery, of Japanese and Chinese porcelain, of Prehistoric objects, of Hindu and Buddhist antiquities, and a gallery of Ethnographical illustration'. It was also almost entirely due to Franks, Bond went on, that the Christy collection, the Slade collection of glass, prints

1. Henry Christy, 1810–1865, banker and ethnologist.

and other works of art, the Henderson collection of pottery, glass, metalwork, oriental coins, and watercolour drawings, the Greenwell collection of prehistoric vases and flint instruments, and a host of individual objects, had come to the Museum. Bond concluded, 'The value of the various objects presented by him certainly exceeds 20,000 £, and that of the collections obtained through his influence cannot be far short of 60,000 £.'[1] Of few, if indeed of any other servant of the Trustees, can this be said – to have virtually created a whole department, through his own efforts.

Perhaps the most magnificent object which Franks was instrumental in obtaining was the Royal Gold Cup of the Kings of France and England. It had been purchased from a Spanish convent in 1883 by the French collector, Baron Jérome Pichon. In 1891 it was obtained from him by a London firm of dealers, who offered it to the Museum for the sum they had given for it. The Museum being unable to raise the money at once, the Cup was bought by Franks himself out of his own pocket. The following year it was acquired for the nation by means of a Treasury grant of £2,830 and the generous cooperation of various subscribers, including, once more, Augustus Franks. The price was £8,000, the sum which Franks had paid for it.

The Cup is a superb as well as unique relic of royal plate, an example of the finest medieval craftsmanship, the only one of its kind known to have survived the ravages of time and the greed of men. It was made towards the end of the fourteenth century for Charles V of France. It passed, via the Duke of Bedford, Regent of France for the infant Henry VI, Charles' grandson, into the possession of the Kings of England, probably about 1435. Altered under the Tudors, it was presented by James I to Juan de Velasco, Constable of Castile, chief of the Spanish mission sent to London in 1604 to negotiate peace between England and Spain. In 1610 the Constable presented it to the convent of Santa Clara near Burgos, who sold it to Baron Pichon in 1883.[2]

In 1891, having reached the age of sixty-five, Franks was retained by the Trustees for a further period of service. In 1896, now seventy, he at last retired, having been knighted in 1894. In May 1897 he died, bequeathing to the Museum large collections of maps, jewellery, drinking vessels, porcelain, Japanese ivories and sword guards, a collection of book-plates and similar cards. He also empowered the Trustees to select from his other possessions any of value to the Museum. But

1. *Accounts, &c.*, 1886–7, pp. 9, 10. (PP, H. of C., 1887, vol. LXV, p. 529.)
2. C. H. Read, *Vetusta Monumenta*, 1904; O. M. Dalton, *The Royal Gold Cup*, 1924.

the crowning of this bequest was undoubtedly the superb 'Treasure of the Oxus', gold armlets, gold and silver discs, the model of a king in his chariot in gold and many other masterpieces of the goldsmith's art.[1] This treasure was found somewhere in central Asia at or near the River Oxus in 1877. After passing through the hands of many dealers and once being carried off by bandits it was sold to General Sir Alexander Cunningham. Franks eventually bought the whole collection. Obviously much of the original find had been lost, but enough remains for it to be one of the glories of the Museum. Many of these objects were produced under the Achaemenian Persian dynasty and date therefore from the fifth to the close of the fourth century BC.

Franks' successor as Keeper was his old friend and assistant, Charles Hercules Read.[2] As a very young man Read had worked in a fairly humble position at the South Kensington Museum, now the Victoria and Albert. In 1874, at the age of seventeen, he had been put in charge of Christy's ethnographical and other collections, then still in their owner's old flat in Victoria Street. There Read remained until 1880, when Franks secured for him an Assistantship in the Department of British and Medieval Antiquities. Helped by Franks, with whom he developed a close friendship, Read became an expert in many fields of antiquarian studies, taking a particular interest in ethnography, which collections, under his guidance, started to expand rapidly. By the end of 1895, the staff of the Department had increased by two further assistants and Read himself had become an Assistant Keeper.[3] In 1896 at the age of thirty-nine, he succeeded his old chief as Keeper.

One of his first tasks was to ensure that the public were aware of the abundant material available within his Department, and he organised an impressive series of guides and catalogues to inform them of what it now contained. This work was mostly carried out by his able assistants, one of whom, O. M. Dalton, already a mature and widely travelled scholar and Read's eventual successor as Keeper, remarked, 'The work had many elements of adventure; they were novices, called upon to write as authorities'.[4] Under Read's guidance, the collections grew

1. A description of the contents of the 'Franks Bequest' will be found in *Accounts, &c.*, pp. 70–74. (PP, H. of C., 1898, vol. LXXI, p. 289.)
2. Sir Charles Hercules Read, 1857–1929, antiquary and connoisseur.
3. The two Assistants were Francis Llewellyn Griffith, appointed in 1888, who had already had archaeological experience in Egypt under Petrie. He left the Museum in 1896 to devote himself to Egyptology. The other was Ormonde Maddock Dalton.
4. Quoted in an article by A. M. Tonnachy, then Keeper of the Department of British and Medieval Antiquities. (*BMQ*, vol. XVIII, no. 3, p. 83.)

apace, expanding far more quickly than any other of the antiquities departments. By making full use of wealthy and prominent friends, Read was able to ensure that a steady stream of bequests came to the Museum or, by their influence, to obtain donations. To further these aims Read established a group of 'Friends of the British Museum' by whose aid he was able to purchase much needed antiquities in a period of rapidly rising prices. Before long the 'Friends' were merged into the National Art Collections Fund, of which Read was eventually to be Vice-Chairman. This body was to perform valuable services in obtaining objects for the Museum, which, in days of ever-recurring financial stringency, it would have been unable to obtain by any other means.

Among the many great gifts which Read secured for the Museum from his personal acquaintances was the Greenwell collection of prehistoric bronze implements and weapons, which his friend J. Pierpont Morgan,[1] the American millionaire, presented to the Department in 1909. This fine collection more or less completed the British series and filled also most of the gaps in the foreign section then exhibited in the Bronze Room. Since Canon Greenwell[2] himself had presented to the Museum his collection of Bronze Age pottery back in 1897, it was most fitting that thirty years later the rest of his great collection should come to the same department. In 1912 Read was knighted, an unusual, although not unique, honour for a serving member of the staff, other than the Director.

Read had started in Ethnography as secretary to R. H. Soden Smith, of the Victoria and Albert Museum, and then had been placed in charge of the Christy Ethnographical collections. He therefore, like his predecessor, Franks, had no trace of the prejudice against these splendid collections too often found amongst the senior staff of the Museum at this period and, indeed, until very much later. By the middle eighties, Franks could report that in his opinion it would be the Ethnographical collections which would prove the main centre of attraction to the majority of visitors now that the Natural History collections had gone, a prophecy that was borne out by his successor Read's claim twenty years later, that the Ethnographical collections were next in popular interest to the Egyptian mummies.

In the latter part of the nineteenth century, these collections more

1. John Pierpont Morgan, 1837–1913, banker.
2. William Greenwell, 1820–1918, clergyman and archaeologist, Canon of Durham, 1854–1907.

than doubled in size. In 1870 came the figures from Easter Island, which braved the worst of the London fogs out on the colonnade for years before being moved to less harmful conditions inside.

The transfer of the Natural History departments made it possible for a little while to house adequately the ever-growing Ethnographical collections, though their former room had been rearranged in a more logical and modern manner as long ago as 1873. In 1880 a large number of ancient Indian sculptures had been transferred to the Department from the Indian Museum at South Kensington. These sculptures from Amaravati were first displayed in 1883 and proved to be revelation to a public hitherto ignorant of the glories of Indian art. By 1884 the last of the Natural History collections had gone, and the Trustees were able to bring to the Museum the Christy collection of Ethnography housed in Victoria Street.

Despite the continual problem of accommodation, the Ethnographical collections continued to expand rapidly during the remainder of Franks' keepership, much of this being due to his own numerous valuable bequests. A slight enlargement of the department's limited space was secured in 1887, when a new refreshment room was opened off the Egyptian Gallery, a position it occupied for fifty-odd years. The room on the upper floor at the northeast corner of the building which had hitherto been used for this purpose was given to Ethnography, in order to display the growing collection of American antiquities. In 1896 Read took over, and even greater attention was now paid to the Ethnographical collections.

During Read's Keepership and later there was a definite change in the provenance of the ethnographical objects being received into the Department. Since the days of the great eighteenth-century explorers, they had mostly come from Oceania and the Pacific regions generally. Now Africa provided many, if not most, of the objects acquired, a reflection of the greater interest being taken in that continent by Great Britain and other powers and of the increased activities there by both colonial officials and missionaries.

Charles Read had an exceptional visual memory and great powers of observation, and an encyclopaedic knowledge both of antiquarian and ethnographical material which would be hard to match. Even if his remark 'my dear boy, what I don't know, isn't worth knowing', must not be taken too literally, his vast knowledge was cheerfully put at the disposal of his younger colleagues. Always kindly and courteous to those whom he liked, though never suffering fools gladly, his skill as a raconteur did much to enliven the little social gatherings round a marble-topped table at a nearby restaurant where, punctually at 4 p.m., he and his staff gathered daily to discuss the affairs of the department and the latest Museum gossip.[1]

Among the outstanding accessions of Read's keepership were the great bronzes from Benin, acquired in 1898. This was followed by the exceptionally rich collection of carvings, textiles and other objects from the Belgian Congo, formed during many years of travel by the explorer Emile Tarday and acquired mainly by purchase during the years 1904 to 1910. Other valuable collections were obtained at this time from Central and South America, Ceylon and elsewhere in Asia. Read was himself a constant donor of individual specimens and by the time he retired the department possessed a wide and well-balanced assemblage of ethnographical material from almost all the main regions of primitive cultures, while in certain branches its collections were unsurpassed.

In 1902 T. A. Joyce[2] was appointed to the department, the first Assistant to be specifically engaged for ethnographical duties. He was put in charge of this section of the department, whilst Dalton, who had been in charge of the section, reverted to medieval antiquities. During his early years, Joyce had the task of reorganising the American and African collections. In 1902 the northeast landing was allotted to Mexican and Mayan sculptures, and between 1903 and 1905 the American antiquities were displayed in a new suite of wall cases in the 'American Room'. In 1919 this room reverted to the Department of Egyptian Antiquities and became the 'Babylonian Room', thus separating the American antiquities at the south end of the main Ethographical gallery, from the sculptures on the Maya Landing and the collections of American ethnography.

The preparation of the *Handbook* begun by Dalton was continued by Joyce, and it was published in 1910.[3] This valuable guide made the department known to a wider public. Though hampered by lack of room, the Ethnographical collections, under enthusiastic and scholarly care of Joyce, once more grew apace. It was clear that more space would eventually have to be allotted to their display, confined as they were,

---

1. Article by H. J. Braunholtz, then Keeper of the Department of Ethnography. (*BMQ*, vol. XVIII, no. 4, p. 109.)
2. Thomas Athol Joyce, 1878–1942, entered the Department, 1902, Deputy Keeper in charge of Ethnography 1921, Sub-Keeper 1932. Retired 1938. Led many archaeological expeditions to Central America.
3. *Handbook to the Ethnographical Collections*, London, 1910.

for the most part, to the long gallery. But it was many years before
even a temporary solution to this problem could be devised.

Thus, under the wise leadership of Franks and Read, and through
the efforts of the devoted band of scholars they had assembled, the
Department of British and Medieval Antiquities, once despised,
became, as it has remained, one of the most vigorous of all the departments of antiquities, and one whose treasures are to the layman some of
the most wonderful in the Museum. Only the great knowledge,
together with the outstanding charm and personality of its Keeper,
had prevented this unwieldy department from falling apart. Some more
permanent solution would soon have to be found.

The new Reading Room (1857) at the British Museum, in course of construction.

Proposed removal of the popular Natural History collections to South Kensington (in fact not moved till the 1880s).

The main Egyptian Sculpture Gallery (mid 19th century).

CHAPTER THIRTEEN

Two World Wars and After

T HE new Director, Sir Frederic Kenyon,[1] succeeded Maunde Thompson in the spring of 1909. Kenyon sprang from an old Museum family, his mother, Mary Eliza, being the only daughter of Edward Hawkins. Kenyon was therefore the grandson of the man who had been Keeper of Antiquities for so much of the nineteenth century. His taste for scholarship, and indeed for archaeology, may well have come from this side of his family and his almost equally pronounced interest in military matters from the family of Hawkins' wife, his grandmother, a daughter of Major Rohde.

Kenyon had entered the Museum in 1889 as an Assistant in the Department of Manuscripts and soon made his name as an expert on Greek papyri. In 1898, though just thirty-five, he was promoted Assistant Keeper. He had never courted an easy popularity. Sir Idris Bell, Keeper of Manuscripts from 1929 to 1947, who knew Kenyon well for many years, comments on his taciturnity and refusal to join in light conversation with his colleagues, but emphasises that this was due far more to innate shyness than to a superior attitude.[2]

The King Edward VII Galleries, begun under Thompson, were now approaching completion. At the same time, the old Large Room at the northern extremity of Smirke's buildings was greatly altered and extended to form a link between the new wing and the older structure. A service passage was built round this new 'North Library', as it was called, to obviate the need for traffic through the room itself, disturbing the readers working there. This meant, however, that the once admired vista, stretching all the way from the Arched Room in the west to the Catalogue Room in the east, was now permanently interrupted. This North Library, of an elaborate and even fussy design characteristic of its period, was used as a special reading room for the study of rare books and of other items which needed closer supervision than was possible in the main Reading Room.

1. Sir Frederic George Kenyon, 1863–1952.
2. Sir H. I. Bell, *Sir George F. Kenyon. Proceedings of the British Academy*, 1952, vol. XXXVIII, p. 269.

The King Edward VII Building was opened by his successor, George V, on 7 May 1914.[1] It contained exhibition space, work rooms and offices for a number of departments. These fine new quarters provided much badly needed room, but were clearly only a stop-gap. Pressure on the available space, scarcely adequate even in the middle of the nineteenth century, temporarily relieved by the departure of the Natural History collections to South Kensington, was to remain a perennial problem.

On the outbreak of the First World War in August 1914, Kenyon, a keen Territorial, was in camp, and crossed to France on 9 August with the British Expeditionary Force.[2] Recalled a month later to take part in measures for the Museum's safety, he served in the Army for the rest of the war, spending about a week each month at the Museum, attending all Trustees' meetings, but leaving the day-to-day running of the institution in the hands of the Assistant Secretary, A. R. Dryhurst.[3]

It was not at first thought necessary to evacuate the Museum. Total war was then a new experience and it was widely believed that the

1. The ceremony took place in the new North Library, in which a dais had been installed for the royal party. Their Majesties arrived at the Museum at noon. The King first unveiled the bust of his father which still stands in the North Entrance Hall. Then after receiving a copy of Kenyon's *The Building of the British Museum* from the Archbishop of Canterbury as Principal Trustee, King George formally declared the building open, under the name of King Edward the Seventh's Galleries, and was presented with a silver-gilt symbolical key by the First Commissioner of Works. As Esdaile points out, by a curious coincidence the opening of the Edward VII Building by George V and that of the new buildings of the Royal Library at Berlin by Kaiser Wilhelm II, were the last state ceremonies to be performed by the respective monarchs before the outbreak of war. (Esdaile, p. 157.)

2. The Trustees now encouraged members of their staff to belong to the Territorial Army. At the outbreak of the War, the Director himself, five Assistants and twenty-four others were mobilised. When Kenyon crossed to France on 9 August 1914 on the first troop ship carrying the British Expeditionary Force, he recalled that it was 499 years to the very day since the last British Army under Henry V had similarly sailed from Southampton to Le Havre. (*The British Museum in War Time*, pp. 6, 7.)

3. Alfred Robert Dryhurst, ISO, Assistant Secretary 1908–1924. He had entered the Principal Librarian's Office as an Assistant in 1878 and had been promoted Assistant Secretary – then the virtual head of the Office – in 1908. The Director was still, as his predecessors had been since the retirement of Forshall in 1850, the titular Secretary. In 1926 owing to the greatly increased administrative work now involved, the separate post of Secretary was revived, its first holder being A. J. K. Esdaile, 1880–1956, from Printed Books. He was succeeded in 1940 by J. H. Witney, who had been Assistant Secretary since 1925 and had spent all his Museum service in the Director's Office, since entering as a Boy Clerk in 1896. Witney retired in 1946 to be succeeded by Frank Francis.

conflict would speedily be over. Strong-rooms were, however, erected in various parts of the basement and, as a precaution the most precious books, manuscripts and small antiquities placed there within special safes. Compared with the Museum's harrowing experience in the Second World War, bomb damage, as it turned out, was minimal. The nearest bomb explosion, about one hundred and fifty yards away, was in Bedford Place, the only harm caused to the Museum itself being from a fragment of spent AA shell, which entered the Iron Library and ripped the backs off two books!

In 1917 the increasing air raids necessitated the evacuation of the Museum's more valuable treasures. The Trustees therefore accepted an offer by the National Library of Wales to act as host for a large number of books, manuscripts, prints and drawings, which were moved to Aberystwyth. Some of the most valuable of the printed books were removed to the house of C. W. Dyson Perrins near Malvern, a wealthy collector and a good friend of the Museum.

But the main threat to the Museum came from the conduct of the government, not from enemy action. Swayed by false notions of economy, the government made strenuous efforts in 1916 to close down the Museum altogether. Opponents successfully argued that to shut the Reading Room and the Manuscripts Students Room would impede the war effort, but the galleries were forced to close in March 1916, thus depriving both the public and service personnel on leave of one of the few civilising influences still left available in London, at a saving, it was reckoned, of the cost of the war for $2\frac{1}{2}$ minutes![1]

Prevented from imposing a charge for the use of the Reading Room, which the Law Officers declared to be contrary to the Act of 1753, the Treasury succeeded in cutting off all grants to the Museum except for a pittance to purchase essential books and periodicals, £2,000 in 1915, £3,500 in 1916, and £3,000 in both 1917 and 1918. The Department of Manuscripts made do with the money from the Egerton and Farn-borough Funds, which were not subject even in wartime to Treasury control.

A greater threat now faced the Museum. In 1917 the recently created Air Board demanded to occupy the whole of the premises, which would have rendered the conspicuous buildings a legitimate target for enemy planes. The Trustees protested at this foolhardy proposal. The Director was permitted to attend a meeting of the War

1. *The British Museum in War Time*, pp. 16–18.

Cabinet on 20 December 1917, during which the matter was discussed. He noted 'that, with one exception, the members of the War Cabinet showed complete indifference to the interests of the Museum or the effect the proposed action would have on the good name of the country'.[1] Fortunately, the determined efforts of the learned societies and of influential individuals caused the government to pause, and with the realisation of the Air Board itself that museum premises were hardly suitable for its purposes, the proposal was dropped.

The end of the war, therefore, found the Museum intact. The evacuated material was brought back, and by April 1919 many of the exhibition galleries had re-opened and the Museum gradually began to return to normal.

G. F. Barwick had succeeded Miller as Keeper of Printed Books on the latter's death in May 1914, and guided the department through the wartime years. His successor as Superintendent of the Reading Room was R. F. Sharp,[2] who had already won fame as a translator of the plays of Ibsen, when the works of that dramatist were by no means as respectable as they are today. On Barwick's retirement in 1919, Sharp left the Reading Room to be second in command to the new Keeper, A. W. Pollard,[3] the distinguished bibliographer and the joint author with G. R. Redgrave of the well-known *Short Title Catalogue of Books Printed in Great Britain before 1640*. Pollard had a short spell as Keeper, succeeded by R. F. Sharp in 1924.

Sharp's successor in the Reading Room had been F. D. Sladen,[4] who had a reputation for being a martinet of the old school of Panizzi and Maunde Thompson, and was a stickler for the proprieties, both of

1. *op. cit.*, p. 24. The Museum was already housing the Statistical Branch of the Medical Research Committee and storing the effects of German prisoners-of-war on the north side of the King Edward Basement. In Kenyon's words 'for the remainder of the War and a considerable time afterwards, this space resembled nothing so much as the left-luggage office of a London terminus'. (*British Museum in War Time*, p. 19.) The Registry of Friendly Societies, which after the termination of hostilities proved exceptionally hard to get rid of, was also installed in part of the Egyptian gallery on the upper floor.

2. Robert Farquharson Sharp, 1864–1914. Entered the Museum as an Assistant in the Department of Printed Books in 1888. His son Mr Noel Sharp, was until recently the senior Keeper in Printed Books, and before that, Superintendent of the Reading Room.

3. Alfred William Pollard, CB, 1859–1944, bibliographer. He had entered the Museum as an Assistant in 1883, becoming Assistant Keeper in 1909. One of the most distinguished scholars the Department has ever possessed.

4. Francis Danvers Sladen, entered the Department 1889.

dress and of language. He was the last regular Superintendent of the Reading Room to wear the traditional top hat when on duty.

Sharp, like Pollard, had a comparatively short term as Keeper of Printed Books and was succeeded in 1929 by W. A. Marsden,[1] who was Keeper during those difficult years just before the Second World War. He retired in 1943 and was succeeded by Henry Thomas, who continued in office until well after the close of hostilities.[2] In 1923 to relieve some of the growing pressure, a fourth storey had been added to the southeast quadrant of the Iron Library. Plans were then drawn up and money voted for adding similar extensions to the other three quadrants. However, it was discovered that the new floor had dangerously strained the quadrant it was built on, and 'the whole structure of the iron library is too slight for the purpose for which it is used'. The increasing use of 'swinging' or 'sliding' presses to increase the capacity of the shelves was overloading the ironwork. The erection of an additional storey on the three remaining quadrants was forbidden and the removal of more than 250 'sliding' presses insisted on. Accommodation had to be found for some 88,000 books turned out from the condemned presses. The experts were also disturbed at the fire hazard which the old library presented with its open floors and galleries. 'The whole of the Reading Room and Iron Library,' they reported, 'constitutes one immense risk, without sub-division, either vertically or horizontally. A fire of even small dimensions might lead to collapse in one portion, which might progressively involve the whole structure'.[3] A great deal must soon be done about the Museum, in particular the library, if the risk of something worse than chaos was to be avoided.

In 1927 a Royal Commission[4] was set up under Viscount D'Aber-

1. Wilfred Alexander Marsden, 1878–1949. Assistant in the Department of Printed Books 1903, Deputy Keeper 1924, Keeper 1930.
2. Sir Henry Thomas, 1878–1952. He entered the Museum in 1903. Deputy Keeper, 1924–43, Keeper 1943–5 and the first Principal Keeper of the Department, 1946–7. Knighted, 1946. A great Spanish scholar and a shy, though kindly man.
3. Quoted in Sir Frederic Kenyon's *Memorandum*. Royal Commission, *Minutes*, p. 57. The evidence given by the Office of Works to the Royal Commission again strongly emphasised these points. With regard to fire risks: 'the building is far from satisfactory both as regards the means of exit and the construction from a fireproof point of view . . . The columns are essentially weak'. To the Chairman's question: 'Your general view is that the condition of the structure [the "Iron Library"] is extremely dangerous', the answer was simply 'Yes'! (*Royal Commission, Minutes*, p. 97.)
4. Royal Commission on National Museums and Galleries, 1928–9.

non,[1] to investigate affairs there, and in other national museums and art galleries. At the British Museum, the two main problems with which the Commissioners had to deal were overcrowding in the Library and in the department of Ethnography. We have seen to what straits the library was reduced, with 88,000 volumes now stacked on a basement floor, but the position of the Ethnographical collections was, if anything, worse. As Kenyon said in his evidence before the Commission: 'Here there is a long range of galleries, packed to overflowing with objects from Asia, Africa, America and Oceania, where the visitor passes in a few steps from the pottery of ancient Peru to the canoes of the Solomon Islands, the fetishes of Benin, the carvings of the Maoris, and the implements of the Esquimaux . . . The effect is simply that of a large curiosity shop.'[2]

In 1929 the Commission issued an interim report,[3] recommending the replacement of the four quadrants of Panizzi's Iron Library by modern stack rooms, four storeys high, together with annexes, each quadrant being so constructed as to carry two additional floors 'in the remote future'. Reconstructions in four floors, the Commission considered, would be sufficient to contain all additions to the library for half a century to come and with the annexes, which they also recommended, for a further fifty years.[4] As an interim measure, they urged the construction of additional floors in the Supplementary Rooms[5] and an annexe to the southeast quadrant, to accommodate the books during the reconstruction. They recommended the transfer of all the newspapers subsequent to 1800 to Hendon, and the conversion of the existing repository there into a proper newspaper library, with its own reading room and other modern facilities. The space thus evacuated would then be used by the antiquities departments as storerooms, whilst the former Newspaper Reading Room at Bloomsbury should by handed over to the Department of Oriental Printed Books.[6]

1. Sir Edgar Vincent, 1857–1941, sixteenth baronet, created Baron D'Abernon of Esher, 1914. Financier and diplomatist. Ambassador at Berlin, 1920–6, created a Viscount, 1926.
2. Kenyon, *Memorandum*, Royal Commission, *Minutes*, p. 58.
3. *Interim Report dated 1st September, 1928*. (PP, H. of C., 1828–9, vol. VIII, p. 699. Cmd. 3192.)
4. *op. cit.*, pp. 32, 33.
5. Those rooms to the west of the North Library and between it and the Arched Room. Though during the next few years the Supplementary Rooms were completely reconstructed, the proposed annexe to the South-East Quadrant was never built.
6. It is still so used by that Department. In a footnote the Commission remarks that

The Commissioners made one criticism of the Museum authorities: 'Bound by a policy too individualistic and self-centred, they have failed to represent their case for assistance coherently and convincingly either to the government or to the public',[1] a stricture, possibly just, which did not allow for the difficulties of obtaining money from the Treasury.

In their Final Report issued a year later the Commissioners urged the establishment of a separate Ethnographical Museum, if possible in close proximity to the Museum. The absence of such a museum, they remarked, 'in the capital city of the British Empire is a glaring defect'.[2] (Defect or not, nearly fifty years later no such museum is even contemplated, though temporary exhibition galleries have been opened for the ethnographical collections in the former premises of the Civil Service Commission at the rear of Burlington House in Piccadilly.) A separate Museum of Far Eastern Antiquities, on the other hand, they did not consider to be a practicable proposition at the moment. It would be better to create a separate Department of Far Eastern Antiquities at the British Museum itself.[3]

Among other recommendations was the setting up of a separate Standing Committee of the Trustees to deal exclusively with the Natural History Departments and the end of residual authority over them hitherto retained by the Bloomsbury Director. Certain minor alterations should be made in the Copyright regulations,[4] and a new edition of the General Catalogue of Printed Books undertaken. They further recommended that the annual Parliamentary grants – still at the pre-war figure despite the drastic change in the value of money – should be greatly increased, that the British Museum's long-established patronage of excavations outside England should be continued and extended, whilst – one of the comparatively few criticisms they made

1. *Interim Report,* p. 50.
2. *Royal Commission, Final Report,* part I, p. 59. (PP, H. of C., 1929–30, vol. XVI, p. 431. Cmd. 3401.)
3. *op. cit.,* p. 61.
4. *Royal Commission, Final Report,* part II, pp. 14, 15, (PP, H. of C., 1929–30, vol. XVI, p. 525. Cmd. 3463).

the authorities wish to retain at Bloomsbury the complete file of *The Times,* newspapers published before 1850 (later put back to 1800), and all English Parliamentary Papers, 'Blue Books', and so on. This was in fact done, except that the complete file of *The Times* went to Colindale, the duplicate set remaining at Bloomsbury. (*Interim Report,* p. 33, note.)

on the activities of the Museum – more should be done by the Trustees
to encourage similar excavations in Great Britain itself. The Commission rejected any suggestions that a charge be made for admission to
the museums and recommended that in cases where such a charge was
already being made it should be abolished.[1] They quote with approval
Kenyon's remarks on this subject. 'The question at issue is a very simple
one. Is it desired to encourage the use of the Museum or is it not?
There is not the smallest doubt that the imposition of fees discourages
attendances . . . The question therefore simply is whether it is worth
while to exclude the public (and especially, of course, the poorer members
of the public) for the sake of the pecuniary return to be expected from
fees . . . The nation has a very large capital interest in the Museum, and
it is better to look for the return on it of educational advantages offered
to the public than from a trivial taking of cash at the turnstiles'.[2]
Finally, they suggested that the Research Laboratory which had been
established in 1921 under Dr Alexander Scott with staff drawn from
the Department of Scientific and Industrial Research should pass from
the control of that body and henceforth form an integral part of the
Museum under the Trustees themselves.

Almost all these recommendations were eventually adopted. Despite
the financial stringency caused by repeated economic crises and the
subsequent depression, the work of reconstructing the library went on.

In 1932 the new Newspaper Library was opened at Colindale. In the
June of that year, the State Paper Room was created with its own
Reading Room, and in 1934 reconstruction began of the Northwest
Quadrant, the first portion of Panizzi's Iron Library to disappear,
whilst a few months later, the North Library was in process of being
rebuilt. By the outbreak of the Second World War, one quadrant
of the new library had been finished and the books moved into it;
a second, the northeast, was structurally complete, but lacked its
shelving; and the reconstructed North Library was once more open
to readers.

In 1930 the Trustees had decided to embark on a considerably revised
edition of the General Catalogue. It was quickly realised that this
imposed too heavy a burden on the existing senior staff. From January
1934 onwards a number of young men and women were engaged to
help with the new catalogue. Although the highest academic qualifications were demanded, they were recruited merely on a temporary basis,

1. *Final Report*, part 1, pp. 54, 55. *Interim Report*, p. 25 and note.
2. Kenyon, *Minutes*, p. 55.

with the rank of Assistant Cataloguers. The recruitment of further permanent Assistant Keepers in the Department was suspended, vacancies caused by retirement or promotion being gradually filled from the ranks of the Assistant Cataloguers. By the middle of 1946 all had been absorbed into the permanent staff as Assistant Keepers or had left the Museum.

The first volume of the new edition of the General Catalogue appeared in 1931, but by 1939 it had progressed only as far as the end of the letter 'B'. A few more volumes, down to COEN, were brought out between 1939 and 1945, but the work was falling behind schedule. The last volume appeared in 1954, after which a completely new scheme was evolved.[1]

For many years the Map Room had enjoyed a special status as a Sub-Department, but in 1902 it was brought once more fully under the control of Printed Books. Basil Soulsby,[2] who was put in charge, remained only a short time, leaving to go to the Natural History Museum. His successor was John de Villiers,[3] who had entered Printed Books in 1887. Later he had assisted the Foreign Office in arbitrations affecting Venezuela and Brazil. He was of South African extraction and spoke Dutch and Portuguese fluently. His success in the diplomatic and social worlds, as well as his scholarship, restored the Map Room to the pre-eminence enjoyed under Major and which it has never lost.

De Villiers retired in 1924 with the rank of Deputy Keeper, to be followed by Frederick Sprent,[4] who died in 1931, and was succeeded by Dr Edward Lynam,[5] who held the post until after the Second World War.

The State Paper Reading Room, opened in 1932, was now made the administrative focus for the various scattered collections of official publications, some of which had been left homeless by the departure of the bulk of the newspaper collection for Colindale.

1. Instead of continuing with the revised edition of the General Catalogue, whose ultimate completion now seemed unlikely before the middle of the twenty-first century, it was decided to publish a photolithographic edition of the existing catalogue as it stood at the end of 1955, to which supplements would be issued at regular intervals.
2. Basil C. Harrington Soulsby. Joined as an Assistant in 1892.
3. Sir John Abraham Jacob de Villiers, 1863–1931. Author of many books on geographical and related themes. Secretary, Hakluyt Society, 1909–23.
4. Frederick Puller Sprent. Entered the Museum as an Assistant in 1910.
5. Edward William Francis Lynam, 1885–1950. Entered the Museum as an Assistant in 1910. Before going to the Map Room in 1931 he had specialised in Irish and modern European languages.

During these years aquisitions included a rare Virgil of 1475; four unique Spanish incunabula from Toledo and Seville; a copy, one of only five known, of Smart's *Songs to David*, with the author's signature; T. E. Lawrence's *Seven Pillars of Wisdom*, presented by the author; *Mercator's Atlas*, 1595; several fine bindings of all periods; *The Anti-Jacobin* of 1797 and 1798, with notes by George Canning; and a set of forty-five works in fifty-six volumes printed on vellum by William Morris, given by his daughter.

Outside the Department of Printed Books – whose needs both the Trustees and Government considered to be paramount – the changes were fewer. As recommended by the Royal Commission, a Department of Oriental Antiquities was set up in 1933, by combining the Oriental prints from the Department of Prints and Drawings, the Oriental antiquities from the Department of British and Medieval Antiquities and the Indian, Far Eastern and other Asiatic collections of pottery from the new Department of Ceramics which had been set up in 1921 with R. L. Hobson as Keeper. This Department now ceased to exist, its collections of European ceramics returning once again to British and Medieval Antiquities.[1] One important recommendation of the Commission was unfortunately not adopted the government deciding it was not feasible to establish a separate Museum of Ethnography. Indeed, it was not deemed possible to create a separate department within the Museum. The plaything of administrative convenience for at least the previous seventy years, they were now placed in an uneasy partnership with Oriental Antiquities.

The Laboratory fared better. In 1931 it was made an integral department of the Museum under Dr Alexander Scott as part-time Director. In 1938 Scott, now aged eighty, retired, his successor being Dr H. J. Plenderleith.

There were other changes. At the end of 1930 Kenyon went, to be succeeded by G. F. Hill, Keeper of the Department of Coins and

1. This Department was officially known as the Department of Ceramics and Ethnography. Hobson was expert in both European and Oriental ceramics, particularly the latter. T. A. Joyce was the Deputy Keeper in charge of Ethnography. The new Department of 1933 was called the Department of Oriental Antiquities and Ethnography, but Ethnography, still with Joyce in charge, now ranked as a semi-autonomous Sub-Department.
Robert Lockhart Hobson, CB, 1872–1941. Entered British and Medieval Antiquities as an Assistant in August 1897. Deputy Keeper in charge of ceramics, March 1921; Keeper, Department of Ceramics and Ethnography August 1921; Keeper, Department of Oriental Antiquities and Ethnography, 1933. Retired, 1938.

Medals,[1] the first Director in modern times ever to be appointed from a non-Library Department,[2] so breaking the long run of Directors from the Department of Manuscripts, which had lasted since the appointment of Bond in 1879. Hill, already a comparatively elderly man, was regarded as something of a stop-gap. He nevertheless proved to be a capable Director, who did much to popularise and improve the image of the British Museum. His first major task was to organise the acquisition of Mount Sinai Manuscript of the Bible.

In the summer of 1933 it was learnt that the Russian government was interested in the disposal of this extremely valuable manuscript, long known as the Codex Sinaiticus,[3] because of the place of its discovery. In May 1844 the German scholar Konstantin Tischendorf,[4] during a visit to the ancient monastery of St Catherine on Mount Sinai, found in a waste-paper basket one hundred and twenty-nine leaves of the manuscript about to be destroyed in a furnace, in which two other basketfuls of fragments had already been consumed. He succeeded in obtaining forty-three of these leaves as a gift from the Monks and presented them to the King of Saxony. In 1857 he again visited the monastery, this time with a letter of introduction from the Tsar, Protector of the Orthodox Church throughout the Near East, and was then shown the remaining portion of the manuscript. In due course the monks were persuaded to present it to the Tsar in return for a donation of 7,000 roubles. Three hundred and ninety out of about an original seven hundred and thirty leaves passed thus into the Imperial Library at St Petersburg. In 1933 these still unbound leaves were offered for sale by the Russian government for £100,000. Owing to the Depression, America was for once out of the running and it was left to Great Britain to try to secure the Codex. The Trustees were not able to find from their own resources more than £7,000. The government

1. Sir George Francis Hill, KCB, 1867–1948. Entered the Department of Coins and Medals on the advice of the distinguished numismatist and member of staff, Percy Gardner (1846–1937) in 1883; Keeper, 1912. During the First World War, he kept his department going almost single-handed, supervising the evacuation of over 500 cabinets which he had personally packed. He became Director and Principal Librarian in January 1931.
2. Hill was the first archaeologist and the first Keeper not from a Library Department to hold that office since the second Principal Librarian, Matthew Maty, Keeper of what was afterwards the Natural History Department, appointed in 1772.
3. For a full description of this remarkable manuscript, see *The Mount Sinai Manuscript of the Bible*, published by the Trustees in 1934.
4. Lobegott Freidrich Konstantin von Tischendorf, 1815–1874, biblical scholar.

at the earnest request of the Archbishop of Canterbury, Chairman of the Trustees, and Kenyon, agreed to loan to the Museum the necessary funds. In addition, they offered to give £1 towards the cost for every £1 subscribed by the public. By an intense effort the greater part of the enormous sum was raised, the government contributing £30,000.

The Codex, the most expensive single manuscript ever bought by the library, arrived at the end of 1933 and was placed on exhibition in the Entrance Hall. Great queues formed to view this new national treasure, and large sums were received, mostly in coins of low denomination, by means of a collecting box. Further sums were raised by individual contributions and collections made in churches and similar places throughout the country. This proved one of the most successful fund-raising tasks ever undertaken, up to then by a national museum. Hill had always considered that his policy as Director of a great national museum should be to secure the big things, and that then the small things would take care of themselves. He was the main inspiration of the acquisition of the Codex Sinaiticus and a few months later, jointly with the Victoria and Albert Museum, of the Eumorfopoulos collection of Oriental Antiquities, also bought for £100,000.[1] The purchase of this collection, valued at £250,000, at the end of 1934, greatly strained the finances of the Museum, already overburdened by the efforts to raise the money for the Codex. Every fund at the Trustees' disposal was drawn upon, and a loan of £10,000 at 1 per cent interest was received from the Bank of England. This latter sum was paid off in a surprisingly short space of time.

A further problem, which disturbed much of Hill's tenure, was the question of the Duveen galleries. That great patron of the arts, Lord Duveen,[2] had donated a large amount for a new gallery to house the Elgin marbles. Unfortunately Lord Duveen's views and those of his architect were at odds with those of the Trustees and the Director. With difficulty, the original design was abandoned for one in which the Elgin marbles, and not the architecture of the building, were to be the main object of attention. Hill's successor eventually negotiated a solution to this ticklish problem.

In 1936 Hill retired, to be succeeded by the Keeper of Greek and

1. *Annual Report*, 1935, p. 13.
2. Joseph, Baron Duveen, 1869–1939, art dealer and patron of the arts. Knighted 1919; created a baronet in 1927 and elevated to the peerage as Baron Duveen of Millbank in 1933.

Roman Antiquities, E. J. Forsdyke.[1] Hill had done much to maintain the morale of the Museum during the difficult depression years, often by little touches like planting flowering almond trees in the forecourt, and having bay trees placed round the colonnade between the pillars. It was Hill, too, who opened the colonnade to the public, providing it with seats and giving permission for smoking there and elsewhere outside the building. Despite the shortness of his term of office, Sir George Hill was one of the most popular Directors the Museum has known.

By the time Forsdyke became Director the shadow of approaching war fell over the Museum. Steps were already being taken to safeguard the treasures in an emergency. The initiative for providing repositories for evacuated material was taken by the Office of Works as early as 1933, when arrangements were made with the owners of various country houses in what were considered to be safe areas, for storage in time of war. Boughton House and Drayton House, both in Northamptonshire, were chosen by the Museum authorities as suitable for this purpose. Books, manuscripts, prints and drawings would, as in the First World War, be transferred to the National Library of Wales at Aberystwyth. In 1938 the Council of that Library decided to construct a bomb-proof shelter within the rock on which the building stands, and invited the British Museum to share its cost and use. This offer was accepted and a tunnel with automatic heating and ventilation was completed in 1940. Large numbers of collapsible packing cases had been ordered and were stored at the Museum ready for immediate use. The Munich crisis served as a dress rehearsal for the evacuation, and several changes were found to be necessary.

Towards the middle of August 1939, when war with Germany seemed inevitable, arrangements were made with the railway companies for escorted container vans for the evacuated material. Late in the evening of 23 August word was received from the Home Office that the evacuation must at once begin. At 7 a.m. on Thursday the 24th the packing and dispatch commenced. By noon of the Saturday, all easily movable material of the highest importance and the whole collection of coins and medals had been sent to Aberystwyth, to the two country houses, and to the Aldwych Tube tunnel, a little used section of the London underground, which was closed for the duration

1. Sir Edgar John Forsdyke, KCB, entered the Museum as Assistant in Greek and Roman Antiquities, 1907, Keeper, 1932–6, Director and Principal Librarian, 1936–50.

of the war, and used for such material as the Parthenon and Bassae friezes which could not be easily stored elsewhere. Within a fortnight, eight days before the declaration of war, more than a hundred tons of books, manuscripts, prints and drawings had been sent safely to Aberystwyth.

In the next few months the smaller antiquities and ethnographical specimens were moved into the Aldwych tunnel, and heavy pieces of sculpture continued to be transferred there throughout the war. What had to be left at Bloomsbury was heavily sand-bagged, either in position or in vaulted basements.

With the clearing of the various galleries and the posting away of many of the warding staff, public admission to the antiquities departments came to an end. The galleries did not reopen (and then on weekdays only) until 22 February 1940 when (as the expected heavy air raids had not materialised) a small exhibition of printed books, manuscripts, prints and drawings in the Grenville Library, the Manuscripts Saloon and the Bible Room was arranged. An illustrative exhibition of the recently discovered Sutton Hoo Treasure was likewise placed in the Entrance Hall.

Meanwhile the Reading Rooms, which had been closed only for a few days during the evacuation, had been reopened and were well attended. The main Reading Room was open from 9 a.m. to 4 p.m. with a limited service only. The North Library, since the rare books normally seen there had been evacuated, remained closed. All readers were warned to bring their gas masks with them.

In the event of an air raid warning – and in the opening weeks of the war heavy raids were widely expected – the Room was to be cleared at once. Readers were to leave all Museum books at their seats, being reminded that it was an offence to take such books out of the Room, and, guided by the Superintendent and his staff, descend to the Air Raid shelter in the basement.

In September 1940, heavy air raids on London at last began. At once the Library exhibitions were withdrawn, the Manuscripts Students' Room closed, and all manuscripts still remaining at Bloomsbury sent away to a place of safety. On 23 September the King's Library was hit by a small high explosive bomb which destroyed part of the ceiling and about one hundred and fifty volumes. Three weeks later, on 16 October, the dome of the Reading Room was pierced by an oil bomb, which fortunately left its burning oil on the copper sheathing outside. Had the bomb burst inside, it would have undoubtedly destroyed the whole room. The King Edward VII Building was struck by two bombs, both of which failed to explode.[1] On 20 October, however, the storage block of the Newspaper Library at Colindale, containing 100,000 bound volumes of newspapers, was totally destroyed, and 30,000 volumes, mostly of nineteenth-century British provincial newspapers, lost irretrievably. The Duveen Gallery, still empty, was hit by a small bomb which did no structural damage but caused considerable disfigurement to the interior.

The scale and violence of these attacks, and the deteriorating war situation generally led to a drastic revision of the plans for the safety of the dispersed collections. Clearly, the two old houses, both well-timbered and in an area no longer by any means 'safe', were now a liability, and even Aberystwyth was officially designated no longer 'secure', in view of possible enemy occupation of Ireland. Safer accommodation had to be sought and was found at Compton Wynyates in Warwickshire, Haigh Hall, near Wigan in Lancashire, Northwick Park in Gloucestershire, and the medieval fortress of Skipton Castle in a remote part of Yorkshire. As air attacks grew in intensity, the greater part of the collections were moved to a series of underground air-conditioned chambers, constructed out of an old stone quarry hitherto used for mushroom culture in the West Country. The collections were moved to these galleries under ninety feet of solid rock in 1942 and 1943, and remained there unharmed until they were brought back to the Museum in 1946.

Meanwhile, the Museum itself was not faring so well. On the night of 10 May 1941 a large cluster of small incendiary bombs fell all over the roofs, causing heavy fires in many places, which were beyond the powers of the Museum night staff to extinguish. Before the Fire Service could get into action the South-West Quadrant of the old Iron Library was well alight, and despite every effort, was soon entirely destroyed, with the loss of over 250,000 volumes. Hardly any books were salvaged, those which had survived the flames being destroyed or damaged by water.

1. Both bombs came through the same hole and both failed to explode, a possibly unique phenomenon. The first, a very large one, had had its tail torn off by a girder in the roof, which it hit first. This had the effect of pulling out its lead-cased detonator which was found intact near by the following morning. The main body of the bomb had then gone down through four concrete floors until it came to rest on the sub-ground floor. Had it exploded, it would almost certainly have destroyed the entire building. The second bomb, a small one, entered by the same hole four days later, but got no further than the mezzanine floor. (E. J. Forsdyke, *The Museum in War Time*, BMQ, vol. XV, 1941–50, p. 4.)

Other parts of the Museum which perished that night were the Roman-Britain Room, the Room of Greek and Roman Life and other galleries in the Department of Greek and Roman Antiquities; the whole of the Department of Coins and Medals and the Central Saloon of the Department of British and Medieval Antiquities. The temporary exhibition of antiquities in that room was almost totally destroyed, thus justifying the remark of its Keeper, T. D. Kendrick, that it was 'a possible sacrifice to the perils of war'.[1]

Though the damage was severe, it might have been worse and after this the Museum escaped further major damage. It was fortunate not to be hit by the more destructive flying bombs or rockets of the later war years. As it was, battered and shabby, it survived, maintaining throughout a skeleton service to readers in the North Library, until on 24 April 1946 the galleries at last reopened to the public.

The history of the Antiquities departments during the inter-war years is one of a series of exciting discoveries. In 1919 R. Campbell Thompson, formerly an Assistant in the Department of Egyptian and Assyrian Antiquities and at that time an Intelligence Officer with the British Army in Mesopotamia, excavated at Eridu, the sacred city to the southwest of Ur, which the ancient Sumerians believed to be the oldest city on earth, and made soundings at Ur itself. Ur, the traditional home of Abraham, had first been identified at this spot in 1854 by J. E. Taylor,[2] the British Vice-Consul at Basra, working for the Museum, but little had been done to explore the site. Now the Museum put a regular expedition into the field under H. R. Hall,[3] who, during the winter of 1918–19 dug extensively at Ur, Eridu, and a third site, al'Ubaid. Though the work was mainly of an experimental nature, it resulted in some interesting architectural discoveries at al'Ubaid, before lack of funds brought it to a standstill. Then, in 1922, the University Museum of Pennsylvania approached the British Museum with a proposal for a joint expedition to Mesopotamia. The offer was accepted and Ur chosen as the scene of the first excavations.

1. BMQ, vol. XIV, 1939–40, p. 114.
2. Taylor had excavated extensively in Mesopotamia for the Museum following the departure of Layard. (Budge, p. 84.)
3. Harry Reginald Holland Hall, 1873–1930, Keeper, Department of Egyptian and Assyrian Antiquities. Entered the Museum in 1896 and became Deputy Keeper of his Department under Budge in 1921. He succeeded the latter as Keeper, 1924. Between 1903 and 1919 he conducted some brilliant archaeological expeditions in both Egypt and Mesopotamia.

A relatively young and unknown archaeologist, Leonard Wooley,[1] was picked to be the director of the joint expedition and work at Ur commenced, the start of twelve years of excavation which were to transform our knowledge of the ancient peoples of this area and to fill the museums concerned with treasures of outstanding interest and beauty. In 1927 Wooley and his team started to dig in the area near Ur which came to be called 'The Royal Cemetery', and immediately came upon a whole number of graves filled with the most wonderful treasures.

In each of the royal tombs, which Wooley dated in the third millenium before Christ, were revealed the bodies of guards, ladies in waiting, and other attendants, the ladies adorned with elaborate headdresses of gold, lapis lazuli and cornelian. Alongside were placed harps, bowls, gold and silver weapons and other treasures, together with remains of the chariots and other vehicles with their draught animals, which had been backed down into the tombs by the attendant grooms. All, guards, attendants, musicians, court ladies, and high officials, had apparently walked of their own free will down into the open pits above the already covered in tomb, decked in their finest clothes, and had then taken poison or some form of soporific drug before the shaft was filled in on top of them. These graves were unique for their period and an exhibition in 1928 of some of these treasures created a sensation. 'The wealth of objects in gold, silver, and copper, the personal ornaments of Queen Shubad and her attendants, the wonderful mosaics of scenes of Sumerian life in the fourth millenium BC, the skilfully restored harp and chariots, and the evidence of extensive human sacrifices as part of the funeral ceremonies of princes, all combined to form an exhibition of quite exceptional importance and of popular interest!'[2] Excavations at Ur continued under Wooley until 1934, but nothing quite so sensational afterwards came to light.

Popular interest in Egyptology was greatly increased by the discovery of Tutankhamen's tomb by the Earl of Carnarvon and Howard Carter in 1922.[3] Though the major objects from this great discovery remained in Cairo, certain small but valuable pieces were presented to the

1. Sir Charles Leonard Wooley, 1880–1960, probably the most distinguished archaeologist of his generation. His excavations at Ur and elsewhere in Southern Mesopotamia and his brilliant popularisations of his discoveries in his books, and more scholarly publications, produced a whole new concept of the history of the most ancient East.

2. *Annual Report*, 1928, p. 6.

3. *Annual Report*, 1923, p. 5.

Museum in 1923 by Lady Carnarvon. The enormous interest aroused by these discoveries was reflected in the attendance at the Museum. In 1923 it was 1,095,353, almost identical with that for 1850 (1,098,863), and only exceeded by that for 1851, at the time of the Great Exhibition. This interest, together with the great number of visitors in London for the British Empire Exhibition at Wembley, caused even this figure to be exceeded the following year, 1,181,242, the highest ever recorded, apart from the record year of 1851.[1]

A steady flow of Egyptian antiquities arrived at the Museum in the nineteen twenties and thirties, the result of the efforts of the Egyptian Exploration Fund with which Sir Wallis Budge had been associated for many years. On the whole, however, the Egyptian collections depended then, as always, on a policy of acquisition through commercial channels rather than through excavations at individual sites. The Museum now possesses the most representative collection outside Egypt, and the largest and most important library of hieratic papyri in the world.

The Department of Greek and Roman Antiquities has had in recent years no such sensational acquisitions as the nineteenth-century ones, but has grown steadily wider and deeper. One of the finest smaller acquisitions of this period is the fine marble statuette of Socrates, of about 300 BC, acquired in 1925. A significant development was the building of a new gallery for the Elgin Marbles. Although completed shortly before the war, because of war damage it lay derelict for over twenty-five years, and was not opened until 1962.

British and Medieval Antiquities was by now far the largest of the Antiquities departments, even though it had lost its ethnographical and part of its ceramic collections to the short-lived Department of Ceramics and Ethnography in 1921. Amongst its acquisitions were a fine enamelled gold Byzantine reliquary of the twelfth century and the clock made by Thomas Tompion for the first Astronomer Royal, Flamstead,[2] in 1676, which was probably the first clock to go for twelve months on a single winding. The most remarkable recent acquisition of this department came on the eve of the war, the famous Sutton Hoo treasure, an Anglo-Saxon ship burial of unparalleled richness. It was discovered in a barrow, one of a group of twelve overlooking the River Deben near Woodbridge, Suffolk, tentatively opened in May 1939.

1. *Annual Report*, 1924, p. 5.
2. John Flamstead, 1646–1719. Appointed Astronomer Royal by Charles II in 1675. Thomas Tompion, 1639–1713; 'father of English watchmaking'. Many of his clocks and watches are still in perfect working order. (*Annual Report*, 1928, p. 9.)

When it was realised by the first excavators that within this barrow lay the remains of a large ship, a halt was wisely called, and the excavation resumed after discussions with the Museum and other interested bodies.

It was then discovered that the ship, whose form could be clearly traced in the sand in which she had lain, was 84 feet long, and 14 feet in the beam. Amidships, under a collapsed wooden shelter, was the funeral deposit, the richest grave goods ever found in England. The gold and silver objects amongst them were the subject of a Coroner's inquest, at which the jury came to the conclusion that these articles were not Treasure Trove and therefore the property of the lady, Mrs Pretty, on whose land they had been discovered. With great generosity Mrs Pretty presented these incomparable treasures to the nation.

As war was imminent, the objects were quickly removed to safety and a detailed examination of the treasures postponed to a more favourable opportunity. Fortunately, some of the most precious had been sent by Mrs Pretty to the Museum as soon as they were found. The Research Laboratory was thus given a chance to clean one or two of the pieces and to strengthen the more perishable items, before they were packed and sent away. A first examination of the treasures revised hitherto accepted ideas on the art of Dark Age England. It was the grave, or possibly, since no remaining trace of a body has as yet been found, the cenotaph, of a person of great consequence, presumably a prominent member of the local East Anglian dynasty.[1]

A detailed study and restoration of these treasures had to wait for the end of the war, but such marvels as the helmet with its lifelike masked visor, the great shields, the jewellery, the silver dishes, the harp and other priceless objects were one of the central attractions in the newly reopened Edward VII gallery in 1947.

Another important acquisition of the interwar years was the Eumorfopoulos collection at the end of 1934. Its owner Mr George Eumorfopoulos,[2] a wealthy businessman of Greek descent, who had already

1. The most recent scholarly opinion is that the Ship Burial was probably the actual burial place of Redwald, King of East Anglia, who died sometime before 626 AD, one of the most powerful monarchs of his age. A nominal Christian, he set up a temple with a pagan altar on one side and a Christian one on the other. Dr Rupert Bruce–Mitford, present Keeper of Medieval and Later Antiquities, is engaged on a detailed study of the many problems to which this wonderful treasure gave rise.
2. George Eumorfopoulos, 1863–1939, collector of Chinese and of other works of art. He was Liverpool born, though his family had originally come from the Island of Chios.

made a number of valuable gifts to the Museum, offered his celebrated collection of Chinese antiquities, valued then at a quarter of a million pounds, for £100,000. It covered almost the whole of Chinese art from the earliest ritual bronze vessels, from about 1122 BC, through the more elegant bronzes and superb jades of the Han dynasty (206 BC–220 AD), the sophisticated ceramics of the T'ang and Sung periods, down to the latest products of the Ch'ing dynasty, which ended only with the fall of the monarchy in 1912. The loveliest of these objects are the Sung dynasty ceramics, which combine exquisite proportions, with a superb colouring, together with details of handle and spout which would be hard to match at any period. Equally fine are the contemporary painters well represented in the collection, in particular the studies of flowers and birds painted on silk.

The staff of the Sub-Department of Ethnography realised that they were now engaged in a race against time. The once backward races of the world were losing their primitiveness, with the result that ancient crafts, rituals and objects, were being discarded as no longer worthy of a 'civilised' people.

This tendency was to some extent redressed by the post-war spread of the Commonwealth and the renewed interest which administrators now took in the traditions and customs of the peoples still under their tutelage. The whole world, save for a few remote spots like the highlands of New Guinea, was now becoming increasingly accessible to modern means of communication. For the time being the native races of Africa and Polynesia and other areas covered by the Department were not interested, or were not encouraged to be interested, in forming museums of their own. This was to become a much later phenomenon, assisted by the world-wide rise of nationalism and the subsequent attainment of independence by people after people. In the 1920s and 30s this was still all far in the future, and in the meantime an increasing flow of valuable objects came to the Museum, from Africa, especially West and Central Africa, New Zealand, New Guinea and, indeed, from every part of the globe in which primitive cultures existed.

The Ethnographical collections continued to lack any proper exhibition space. The long gallery over the King's Library – the bird gallery of Victorian times – was still their home, and there they remained, a rag-bag of treasures from every corner of the globe. Confusion was made worse by the discovery late in the 1930s that the floor was unsound and that cases would have to be rearranged to direct the stream of visitors from the centre to the sides of the gallery. Notwithstanding such handicaps, the Ethnographical collection remained one of the most popular sections of the Museum. The war put an end to aspirations for a new home for them for another thirty or more years.

Besides the artefacts of primitive peoples, the Department was responsible for the antiquities of the ancient civilisations of Central and South America. Amongst the valuable objects which the Department acquired were a fine series of ancient Peruvian textiles from Nasca, a Maya vase in calcite and an archaeological series from San Jose, British Honduras, given by the Carnegie Institute of Washington.

Of the remaining departments, there is less to say. Prints and Drawings, under Colvin's successors, Campbell Dodgson and A. M. Hind,[1] continued on the lines which he had laid down. Acquisitions included a collection from the Albertina at Vienna, consisting of engravings and woodcuts of the early Italian and German and Netherlandish Schools turned out as duplicates and acquired in 1923 and 1924; a large paper copy of Blake's 'Songs of Innocence' and 'Songs of Experience', and a drawing by Dürer, dated 1505, of a Slavonic peasant woman. There was also a very large number of modern drawings and prints presented by the Contemporary Art Society.

Among the many notable acquisitions obtained by Oriental Printed Books and Manuscripts| during the interwar years, the most important were the fine collection of Hebrew and Samaritan manuscripts and books purchased in 1925 from Dr Moses Gaster,[2] a Rumanian Jew long resident in London, where he had been Chief Rabbi of the Portuguese and Spanish Synagogue; the Tibetan manuscripts and printed books presented in 1933 by Sir Charles Bell[3] and the Turkish manuscripts of Sir Alfred Chester Beatty.[4]

During his short Keepership of four years, from 1936 to 1940, Lionel Giles produced a catalogue of the important Backhouse collection of rare Chinese books[5] and, after his retirement, another one of the even more important Stein Collection of ancient Chinese manu-

1. Arthur Mayger Hind, 1880–1957. Entered the Department of Prints and Drawings in 1903, Keeper, 1933–45.
2. Dr Moses Gaster, 1856–1939. One of the most eminent Anglo–Jewish scholars of the period and equally distinguished in Jewish religious circles.
3. Sir Charles Alfred Bell, KCIE, 1870–1945. Indian administrator and authority on Tibet.
4. Sir Alfred Chester Beatty, 1875–1968. Mining engineer and patron of the arts.
5. Esdaile, p. 319.

scripts and printed documents.[1] These were discovered by Sir Aurel Stein,[2] the celebrated explorer, in the Gobi Desert in Eastern Turkestan. There the excessively dry climate had preserved them intact for many centuries.

Stein discovered these precious documents in the secret chamber of a cave temple, a solid mass of manuscript bundles, comprising, it is estimated, some 13,500 paper rolls. He considered that they had been brought to the cave for safety from nearby monasteries and had lain there forgotten for over nine hundred years. Stein managed to purchase a large proportion, but as he knew no Chinese it was rather a mixed collection which eventually reached the Museum. Nevertheless, it contains many extremely rare Buddhist, Taoist and a few secular manuscripts and printed books.

Apart from the Codex Sinaiticus, the Department of Manuscripts had received a number of other important accessions, especially the famous Luttrell Psalter obtained in 1929 at the same time as the Bedford Book of Hours, through Mr John Pierpont Morgan,[3] who advanced the money for these two manuscripts without interest for a year. The Luttrell Psalter was acquired from its owner for £31,500, whilst the Bedford Book of Hours was bought at auction for £33,000. A subscription succeeded in raising the money within the agreed time.[4]

The Luttrell or Louterell Psalter which had been on loan to the Museum for thirty-two years was executed in about 1340 for Sir Geoffrey Louterell of Irnham in Lincolnshire. It is particularly renowned for its marginal drawings of English mediaeval life. The Bedford Book of Hours was probably written around 1414, for John, Duke of Bedford, the third son of King Henry IV. Lavishly decorated in the manner of the period, it also contains a wonderful series of portrait heads, amongst them one of the Duke's father, Henry IV. The existence of this superb manuscript was not suspected by students until it was brought into the Museum for an opinion, but it now ranks as one of its greatest treasures.

The end of the Second World War found the Museum with many of its finest galleries partially or totally destroyed, its treasures dispersed, and its financial situation difficult. As prosperity returned the speed and

1. Lionel Giles, *Six Centuries at Tunhuang*, pp. 5, 6.
2. Sir Mark Aurel Stein, KCIE, 1862–1943, scholar, explorer and archaeologist. Responsible for numerous discoveries in Central Asia.
3. John Pierpont Morgan, 1867–1943, banker, philanthropist and connoisseur.
4. *The Luttrell Psalter and the Bedford Book of Hours.* (BMQ, vol. IV, 1929–30, p. 63.)

cheapness of modern travel ensured that far more visitors and scholars from all over the world came to the Museum than ever before. Moreover, the growth of higher education in this country, and the widespread interest in archaeology aroused by the mass media and by television meant a greater proportion of British readers and visitors. This vaster, better educated and more critical public demanded more facilities and services than had their predecessors.

In the work of restoration and rehabilitation it was decided to give urgent priority to restoring the library services, now so greatly in demand by both British and foreign scholars. An exhibition of selected objects from all the antiquities departments and certain historical documents, such as Magna Carta, from the Department of Manuscripts, was likewise put on display in the King Edward VII Gallery, to which damage had fortunately been slight.

Early in 1946 the dome of the Reading Room was repaired. On 3 June 1946 the room was reopened to the public, whilst the North Library, which had served as a general reading room for most of the war and its immediate aftermath, reverted to its proper function as a special reading room for the study of rare books.

Meantime the staff were gradually returning from the services or other war duties and new members being recruited. A sign of the times was the great increase in the number of women who now joined the Museum service at all levels. Not quite yet the flood it was later to become, it was considerable by pre-war standards, when women members of the staff, besides the traditional 'housemaids', were very much of a novelty. Within a year or two, many of the older members who, in some cases, had stayed on beyond the normal retiring age, resigned and the stage was set for a new generation to take command.

In 1950 Sir John Forsdyke, having successfully steered the Museum throughout the war and the first difficult post-war years, retired. His successor was another Antiquities man, the third in succession, Thomas (now Sir Thomas) Kendrick,[1] formerly Keeper of the British and Medieval Antiquities, who was Director for the next nine years. During his Directorship, a number of the war-damaged galleries were restored to use, although the majority still remained out of action. Though much of the planning for a new library was done under his successor, during Sir Thomas's Directorship the initial decision to build a new National Library on the nearby site was first taken.

1. Sir Thomas Downing Kendrick, KCB, Keeper of the Department of British and Medieval Antiquities, 1938–50; Director and Principal Librarian, 1950–9.

In the County of London Development Plan of 1951[1] the area immediately south of Great Russell Street had been designated as the site for such a new National Library, and the proposal was investigated at a public inquiry held in 1952. The Trustees had considered this site as an area for the future expansion of the Museum as long ago as 1860, when a Special Committee had rejected the proposal.[2] In 1955 the site was formally approved by the Minister of Housing. An outline scheme was drawn up in 1962 by two architects, Sir Leslie Martin and Mr Colin St John Wilson, for the development of the entire site, including new library buildings, which it was then envisaged would contain four of the existing departments: Printed Books, Manuscripts, Oriental Printed Books, and Prints and Drawings. The architects' scheme got tentative government approval in 1964. In October 1967, however, the Secretary of State for Education and Science, Patrick Gordon Walker, announced that the Great Russell Street site which had been designated since 1951 as the area for a new National Library, was now unacceptable to the government, and that the Library would have to be housed elsewhere.[3]

This unwelcome decision was opposed by the Trustees and by a large body of academic opinion in Great Britain and elsewhere. In February 1968 a Committee on National Libraries was set up under the chairmanship of Dr F. S. Dainton, which reported strongly in favour of the Bloomsbury site.[4] In April 1970, the government reversed itself and agreed to study the possibility 'of meeting the needs of both libraries, the National Reference Library of Science and Invention and the

1. *Administrative County of London Development Plan*, 1951. *Statement*, p. 14.
Statement as approved . . . by the Minister of Housing and Local Government, 1955, p. 14.
2. *Report of Special Committee, Papers relating to the Enlargement of the Museum*, p. 11. (PP, H. of C., 1860, vol. XXXIXA, p. 265.)
3. *Hansard*, 5th series, 1966–7, vol. 751, col.1904–7.
4. *National Libraries Committee*. Report. (Cmnd. 4028.) Sir Frederick Sydney Dainton, FRS, then Vice-Chancellor, Nottingham University.

Though the practice varied slightly under different administrations, the Museum had been under the direct control of the Treasury and the Parliamentary spokesman for questions relating to it was the Financial Secretary to the Treasury. A concise definition of the relationship between the Museum and the Treasury will be found in Hansard, 5th series, 1948–9, vol. 468, *Written Answers*, p. 178: 'Under the Act of Incorporation, responsibility for the direction of the affairs of the Museum rests with the trustees . . . In matters of finance and staffing the Museum is subject to normal Treasury control; and Treasury Ministers answer for the Museum in this House.' Mr Glanvill Hall, Financial Secretary to the Treasury, 27 October 1949. (*op. cit.*) The Museum was put under the Department of Education and Science during the financial year 1965–6.

British Museum Library, on a smaller area of the Bloomsbury site than was previously envisaged for the British Museum Library alone'.[1] This was generally held to mean that the new Library would be erected opposite the present Museum.

After the Conservative victory at the General Election of June 1970, the former Chairman of the Trustees, Viscount Eccles, was appointed Paymaster-General, with special responsibility for the Arts, including the national museums and art galleries.

It was understood that the new administration would not reverse the decision of their predecessors with regard to the site for the proposed new National Library, and that a White Paper would be issued in due course to clarify the whole situation.

The White Paper came out in January 1971.[2] This History must, of necessity, deal primarily with the past and present of the British Museum and not with its future, but a brief mention of the main proposals contained in the White Paper will be made later.

It was also clear to the Trustees that, regardless of the ultimate fate of the Library, a comprehensive survey had to be made of the existing area at their disposal, so as to see what could be done with the present buildings, both before and after the Library was removed. All departments had now become so overcrowded that, without a great deal of new building, further expansion was virtually hopeless. Mr St John Wilson, who had been partially responsible for the plans for the new Library in 1962–4, was appointed by the Ministry of Public Building and Works to carry out this survey. It is already clear that the possibilities for expansion are far greater than had formerly been imagined and, provided that the necessary funds can be obtained, it would seem certain that the Museum will at last be able to provide a greatly increased amount of space for exhibition purposes, for far better accommodation than has hitherto been possible for both staff and reserve collections, and for the provision of new and improved facilities for both general and scholarly public alike. All this of course lies still in the future, but it is reasonable to hope that Smirke's buildings, condemned as being inadequate for their purpose within a very few years of their erection, will serve as a basis for a new and greatly enlarged Museum, worthy of the twentieth or even of the twenty-first century.

·   ·   ·   ·   ·

1. *Hansard*, 5th series, 1969–70, vol. 799, col. 247–51.
2. *The British Library. Presented to Parliament by the Paymaster-General . . . January 1971.* Cmnd. 4572. It was debated first in the House of Lords on 2 March 1971.

In the immediate post-war period a greatly increased demand for supplementary services of all kinds was a marked feature. Particularly heavy was the pressure on the photographic services, which were almost as old as photography itself, but which have broken all previous records in the post-war period. In 1955, 36,720 photographic reproductions were produced; ten years later the number increased almost ten-fold and shows no signs of slackening.[1] Equally dramatic has been the demand for publications of all kinds, from postcards and simple guides (now produced in several languages), to works of scholarship, for which the Museum has always been justly renowned.[2]

The Duveen Gallery, which should have opened in 1939, had remained semi-derelict for twenty-five years. Plans were eventually approved for its reconstruction, and by early 1962 repairs to it were completed. The famous sculptures were then rehoused. Machinery for cleansing the air in the Gallery was installed at the same time, the first part of the Museum to be so equipped. As the pollution in the atmosphere of London becomes steadily worse only a complete system of modern air conditioning will suffice to protect the treasures of the Museum. On 18 June 1962, the Duveen Gallery was opened by the Archbishop of Canterbury, as the senior of the three Principal Trustees, and the Elgin Marbles had, at long last, a setting worthy of them.

The four galleries at the head of the main staircase, which had for many years contained the Prehistoric and Romano-British collections, had been very badly damaged and had now to be virtually rebuilt. The opportunity was taken, not only to provide new exhibition space of a more modern design, better equipped students' rooms, offices and storage space, but to split up the old Department again, still essentially the residue of the early nineteenth-century Department of Antiquities, on a more rational basis. In 1969, therefore, a new Department, that of Prehistoric and Romano-British Antiquities, was created, British and

1. Photographic reproductions, 1965: 340,200. The comparable figures for microfilm frames during this period are: 1955, 148,110; 1965, 2,727,110. (*Appendix I, Statistical Summary, Report of the Trustees*, 1766, p. 78.)
More recent statistics show a slight decline in the number of black and white photographs but a considerable increase in the number of electrostatic copies.

	1966	1968	1970/71
Microfilm (frames of negative)	2,872,000	3,976,000	3,351,326
Microfilm (feet of positive)	583,000	885,000	1,800,373
Photographs	47,000	54,000	51,480
Electrostatic copies	1,224,000	1,742,000	2,264,630

2. *op. cit.*, p. 78.

Medieval Antiquities being renamed, more logically, Medieval and Later Antiquities.

However, the most ambitious scheme of rebuilding so far undertaken at the Museum is the complete replanning of the ground floor rooms of the Department of Greek and Roman Antiquities, designed by Professors R. Gooden and R. W. Russell. This fine series of galleries enables both large masses of sculpture and the smaller antiquities to be displayed side by side. The exhibits have been arranged chronologically to show the development of classical art from the Bronze Age to the end of the Roman period. The partial reconstruction of the 'Treasury of Atreus' from Mycenae, the Nereid Monument and the 'Harpy Tomb' from Xanthos (over whose arrangement Westmacott and Fellows had squabbled so long ago), and the Caryatid Porch of the Erechtheum at Athens, do much to give an idea of what the buildings must have looked like. Other alterations are now being carried out or contemplated. The reconstruction, for instance, of the former Assyrian Saloon, to display better the famous lion hunt frieze and the monumental sculptures from Assyria, has been completed. This at last does justice to the discoveries of Layard, Rawlinson, Rassam and their successors. The famous Bulls now flank the entrances to fine new galleries, and look very much as they did when they guarded the palaces of the Kings of Assyria. The remodelling and improvement of the Print Room and the gallery of Oriental Art on the upper floors of the King Edward Building is likewise finished and it is hoped that an extension at the southwestern corner of the site containing new restaurants for public and staff, exhibition galleries and administrative offices, will not too long be delayed. On the site of the old Mausoleum Room, to the west of the main Egyptian gallery, a public lecture theatre has been constructed in the basement, whilst above are galleries for the display of later Greek and Roman sculpture.

In the Department of Printed Books Sir Henry Thomas, its Keeper during the latter part of the war years, retired at the end of 1947, being succeeded by C. B. Oldman. It was during the last year of Thomas's Keepership that the decision was taken to make this post a Principal Keepership, with two Departmental Keepers to assist the Principal Keeper.

The Library had suffered severely during the Second World War and had lost a great many books; in all 250,000 volumes were destroyed. These were of many different kinds: liturgies and sermons; German, Scandinavian and Slavonic works on law, some exceedingly rare together with numerous other legal treatises; medical books; books on art and architecture, cooking and other useful arts, sports and pastimes and many others. Perhaps the hardest loss to replace was of periodicals on a variety of subjects, but especially eighteenth- and nineteenth-century domestic and fashion magazines. Though many have been replaced from various sources, complete runs are hard to find and this now constitutes one of the most serious gaps in the resources of the library.[1]

A very high proportion of these destroyed books are now back in the collection, thanks to the generosity of various foreign governments, learned institutions, and private individuals. Many, too, have been replaced by purchase or from those books turned out in the various wartime salvage drives, to which the Museum was given the first claim. The work is still going on and, even now, many are replaced during the course of a year. Nevertheless, all too often a ticket is returned to a reader with the increasingly anachronistic message that the book he needs has been 'Destroyed by enemy action'.

Nevertheless several additional facilities for readers have been provided within the limited space available. A typing room, with soundproof dictating cubicles, has been constructed by the removal of a few bookstacks, and the rapid copy service in the Reading Room has been greatly improved and extended.

For the first fifteen years after the war, the Reading Room, which before 1939 had stayed open every evening until 6 p.m., and then until 7 p.m., closed at 5 p.m. From July 1960 onwards, the Reading Room, North Library and State Paper Room, but not the other public rooms, remained open on certain evenings until 9 p.m.; from July 1960 to January 1964 on two evenings a week and from February 1964 on three evenings a week.[2] Approval in principle has been given by the Trustees for an extension to five evenings a week. Financial and other considerations have so far prevented this decision from being implemented.

The main tasks of the Department have remained those of acquisition, cataloguing and conservation. The difficulties and scale of all three have grown considerably in recent years. Although the number of books

1. Details of the losses suffered by the Department of Printed Books during the war are given in the article: *The Library's Losses from Bombardment*, by A. F. Johnstone Wilson. (BMQ, vol. XV, p. 9.)
2. For a very short time the Reading Room was kept open to 9.30 p.m., on an experimental basis, but for a number of reasons it was found impracticable to continue this.

received by copyright has remained fairly constant – approximately a quarter of a million items annually – the number of books received by other means has greatly increased. From a total of 419,323 items in 1939, it has risen to 540,716 by 1959 and to 1,144,892 ten years later (1968). This last figure in fact marked a decline by 17 per cent from a record intake of 1,377,636 items in 1965, caused by devaluation and rising prices.[1]

Important acquisitions of the period include over 100 books of the fifteenth to seventeenth centuries from the Earl of Leicester's library at Holkham Hall, Norfolk, purchased in 1951, a collection of works by Rudyard Kipling presented by the author; 140 books from the library of the Duke of Devonshire at Chatsworth; the Hirsch and Royal Music Libraries and many others.

Perhaps the solution to cataloguing problems will be found to be some form of automation, and a measure of shared cataloguing with other libraries. But the most significant event of the post-war years, as far as Printed Books is concerned, was the decision in 1960, to establish a National Reference Library of Science and Invention, by combining the scientific collections of the Museum with those of the Patent Office Library. Since 1963 considerable numbers of scientific books and periodicals hitherto not taken by the Museum have been acquired. In November 1966, those members of the staff who had been located at Bloomsbury, with the primary task of building up the scientific collections, together with the large number of books obtained either by purchase or by transfer from the existing Library stocks, moved to temporary accommodation in Bayswater. In April 1966, the Patent Office Library was transferred from the Board of Trade to the British Museum but remained at its old site near Chancery Lane. But it is obviously inconvenient that the National Reference Library of Science and Invention, ultimately to be of 1,000,000 volumes, should be so divided and a new building to contain the scattered divisions is urgently required. It is proposed that the National Reference Library of Science and Invention, renamed the Science Reference Library, and the British Museum Library will now be entirely independent of each other, but will both form part of an overall organisation known as The British Library.[2]

The policy of outhousing portions of the collections, legalised by the British Museum Act of 1963, has been applied even more drastically to the collections of another division of the Department of Printed

1. *Report of the Trustees*, 1966–9, Appendix II, p. 46.
2. See *Epilogue*.

Books, the State Paper Room. Over two-thirds of that division's collection of official publications of all periods and countries has been housed at Woolwich Arsenal, where a former machine shop was fitted up in 1964. A second building is now being converted, and further portions of the general collections of the Library will be transferred there as soon as possible.

The Map Room has continued to increase at the rate of some 15,000 maps and atlases annually. As a result it is perhaps the finest carto-graphic collection in the world. Among acquisitions in recent years are the maps from the Library at Windsor Castle, presented by King George VI in 1940, the Chinese Terrestrial globe of 1623, presented in 1961 – the earliest known Chinese globe – and the sheet map collection of the Royal United Service Institution, acquired jointly with the Department of Manuscripts in 1969.

The Music Room's finest acquisitions during this period are the Hirsch Library, purchased in 1946 and consisting of 15,000 volumes of printed music and musical literature from the fifteenth century to the present, and the Royal Music Library presented by the Queen in 1957. This collection had been deposited on permanent loan by King George V in 1911 and the gift has made it an integral part of the Museum collections. It contains autograph scores of Purcell, Handel, Scarlatti and J. C. Bach.

The Division which has shown the greatest increase in the last few years is the State Paper Room, from an annual intake of 18,000 items in 1938, to 200,436 by 1958 and 934,834 by 1965.

The State Paper Room does not restrict itself to contemporary publications, but endeavours to obtain older material in its field. Amongst its recent acquisitions have been an almost complete set of Foreign Office prints, running from 1823 to 1913, the third Marquess of Salisbury's personal set of Foreign Office documents as Foreign Secretary and Prime Minister covering the last quarter of the nine-teenth century, numerous Tudor and Stuart proclamations and other sixteenth- and seventeenth-century official publications, and a collection of rare proclamations and other documents of the Napoleonic Kingdom of Italy for the period 1802–14.

The solution adopted to the problem of space at the Newspaper Library at Colindale was to microfilm all foreign newspapers or to pur-chase them where possible in microfilm form. When the programme is completed the originals of all foreign newspapers after 1850 will have been disposed of and space thus made available for United Kingdom newspapers.

The remaining division of the Department is that of Philatelic collections. The Museum has possessed extremely valuable collections of stamps for many years, beginning with the Tapling collection in 1892. Other smaller collections were subsequently acquired, but no full-time officer was appointed to look after them until 1961. Since then the collections have grown spectacularly, notably with the deposit of the Berne collection of Postage Stamps of the World by the Post Office in 1964.

After the reopening in 1946 of the Students' Room of the Manuscripts Department it was realised that the room was inadequate, and although it was enlarged in 1956, the number of students using it continues to increase.

The Department has received some remarkable acquisitions, amongst them the papers of Herbert, Viscount Gladstone; the Holland House papers, comprising letters and other documents of the great Whig family of Fox. Of particular importance are the letters of Henry Fox, third Lord Holland, the Whig statesman, and of his wife, whose salon at Holland House in Kensington, was the focus of London political social life during the first forty years of the nineteenth century. To the historian of the British Museum, the letters and papers of his son, the fourth Lord, are also of great interest. He and his wife were close friends of Antonio Panizzi, and their papers include a number of letters dealing with the affairs of the Museum. Other important manuscripts are Lewis Carroll's autograph of *Alice's Adventure Underground*, the original version of *Alice through the Looking Glass*, with illustrations by the author; the Benedictional of St Ethelwold, Bishop of Winchester, 963–4; the Lacock Abbey copy of the 1225 Magna Carta; the Hours of Elizabeth of York, daughter of Edward IV and consort of Henry VII written and illuminated about 1420 and containing the Queen's signature and forty-six manuscripts from the collection of the eminent bibliophile, Henry Yates Thompson,[1] containing amongst other treasures the Ghislieri Hours, written between 1492 and 1503 for a Bolognese senator with illuminations by Perugino and the Bolognese illuminator Aspertini.

In Oriental Printed Books and Manuscripts, the story is similar.

---

1. Henry Yates Thompson, 1838–1928, book collector. He limited his famous collection of illuminated manuscripts always to one hundred and always those of the finest quality, discarding inferior manuscripts as finer examples were obtained This collection was partially dispersed by auctions in 1919, 1920 and 1921. Thompson had already given one of his finest manuscripts, the *St Omer Psalter*, to the Museum.

Of all the literature of the countries of Asia and North Africa only official publications are excluded. These are dealt with in the State Paper Room, where a very large collection in the main oriental languages is held. As with all other departments, the rate of accessions has grown very considerably since the end of the war, and so too has the number of readers, which rose from 4,604 in 1959 to 19,504 in 1969.

During this period, despite rising costs and the increasing difficulty in obtaining manuscripts or early printed books from foreign countries, the department has obtained some remarkable things. Perhaps the finest is the magnificent Kamseh or Five Poems of the Persian poet Nizāmī, written and illuminated for the Emperor Akbar in 1595–6. It has been described as the most beautiful Indian manuscript in England, with miniatures of outstanding quality.

The Department of Prints and Drawings has also benefitted from several outstanding acquisitions, the most important of which is the Phillipps-Fenwick collection of over 1,500 drawings, for the most part Italian of the sixteenth and seventeenth centuries, presented in 1946. This fine collection was mainly acquired by the bibliophile Sir Thomas Phillipps,[1] at the dispersal of Sir Thomas Lawrence's collection in 1860. Lawrence had always wished that at his death his collection should come to the Museum, of which he was a Trustee, but through Treasury parsimony and lack of interest on the part of the Trustees, it failed to do so.[2] More recently, the César Mange de Hauke Bequest of fifteen drawings by Ingres, Gericault, Degas, Van Gogh, Toulouse-

1. Sir Thomas Phillipps, 1792–1872, antiquary and bibliophile. He amassed probably the greatest collection of rare manuscripts of all periods, countries, languages and subjects ever to be made by one man. He also acquired a large collection of printed books, including many incunabula, Sir Thomas Lawrence's collection of drawings, and further collections of coins and pictures. A working antiquary, he was a close friend of Madden, though Sir Frederic frequently abused him in the pages of his *Journal*. Phillipps was godfather to Madden's second son, George Ernest Phillipps Madden. The eccentric collector presented the baby, as a christening present, a copy of the Cottonian Manuscripts Catalogue by Joseph Planta, instead of the handsome gift expected by the child's doting parents! 'He certainly is crazy,' wrote the furious and disappointed Sir Frederic. 'What mortal ever heard of such a present before!' (*Madden Journal*, 25 July 1841.) Phillipps' immense collection has been gradually dispersed since the later part of the nineteenth century, but some of it has still not reached the sale rooms.

2. An interesting article by J. A. Gere on the Lawrence collection and its connection with W. Y. Otley, Keeper of Prints and Drawings, 1833–6, is in *BMQ*, vol. XVIII, 1953, p. 45.

Panizzi's Iron Library (c. 1860).

The British Museum Reading Room in the 1930s.

Bomb damage in the Second World War. *Above*, the South West quadrant of Panizzi's Iron Library. *Below*, the newspaper store at Colindale.

Lautrec and others has strengthened the Museum's holdings in this field.

Amongst the treasures acquired by the Greek and Roman Department during the last twenty-five years, two are of particular interest to the historian of the British Museum: the Portland Vase, purchased in 1945 after being on permanent loan since 1810, and the Elgin jewellery. This collection, formed in Greece by Lord Elgin, remained in his possession when his marbles and other antiquities were acquired for the nation in 1816. It consists of about fifty pieces of rare gold jewellery, dating for the most part from about 1,000–700 BC. These include a pair of exquisite earrings and four brooches engraved with ships, animals and swastikas, and a gold myrtle-spray from a fifth-century BC tomb near Athens. Another important acquisition is the so-called 'Chatsworth head', a bronze head of Apollo from a statue found in Cyprus in 1856. The rest of the statue was apparently broken up for scrap, but the head was preserved and came into the possession of the sixth Duke of Devonshire. Dating from about 460 BC, it is one of the very few surviving examples of bronze statuary from the greatest period of Greek art.

At the end of the war, the Department of Egyptian and Assyrian Antiquities, which had suffered little physical damage, was quickly able to return to normal. However, the increasing divergence between Egyptology and the archaeology of the other ancient races of the Near and Middle East made it imperative that a change should be now made. The opportunity was taken at the retirement of the Keeper Dr C. J. Gadd in 1955, to divide it, creating two independent departments, one of Egyptian Antiquities, the other of Western Asiatic Antiquities.

In Egyptian Antiquities particular attention has been paid to the conservation of the large collection of documents written in ink on flakes of limestone which were threatened with gradual decay. Other antiquities have also been treated by modern conservation methods, whilst the mummies have for the first time been X-rayed, revealing beneath the bandages in which the bodies are swathed, amulets, jewellery and similar objects hidden from human eyes for 2,000 or more years.

Perhaps the most outstanding objects acquired during this period are two portraits painted in wax on wooden panels, one a young man with the luxuriant hair and beard, characteristic of the second century AD, the other a young woman. Both give important information on the

M

Graeco-Roman tradition of portrait painting, of which few examples have survived.

The sister Department of Western Asiatic Antiquities now covers the antiquities of all the peoples of the ancient East, from the Black Sea to the Red Sea, and from the Bosphorus to the borders of India. Interest in this area has grown enormously since the war and the picture is now very different from what it was in the days of Layard, when Edward Hawkins could say of the newly discovered Assyrian sculptures, 'I am getting quite impatient to have objects of such immense importance . . . pour in upon us in hopes that by their means a flood of light may be poured upon those ages of which we know scarcely any thing, and of a great part of which we know absolutely nothing.'[1] Before the war the Museum collections covering this area were (with the obvious exceptions of Assyria and Babylonia) by no means representative, and so attention has been paid to acquiring objects from these scarcely known lands and peoples. The work of conservation has gone on without ceasing over the years, especially by the baking of the entire collection of some 120,000 cuneiform tablets, which at the same time are being treated to remove deleterious salts, a process which will take some twenty years to complete.

The Department of Coins and Medals suffered more than any other department from the ravages of war. For fourteen years it was without a permanent home. Nevertheless it has shared in that outburst of interest in every aspect of archaeology characteristic of the post-war years. In May 1959 the rebuilt Medal Room was at last opened. One of the most valuable, as well as one of the most time-consuming services, which the department undertakes, is the examination and appraisal of coins thought to be treasure trove. This may involve the detailed study of a large number of coins, in two cases of some 10,000 individual specimens. Yet the time is by no means wasted, as the scientific identification of coins from excavations may often provide evidence of great historical significance.

Of the recent accessions two are specially interesting to British visitors: an extremely rare gold aureus, minted at Rotomagus (the modern Rouen) of the rebel Emperor Carausius, who, in the third century AD siezed power in Britain and North Gaul and for a few years held his Empire together, principally by means of the British fleet; and another of a British ruler, some five hundred years later, a gold piece of Offa of Mercia, 757–96. This coin, after being illustrated in the 1611 edition

1. Hawkins to Layard. (No date, but before April 1849.) (Add. MS. 38,978. f.302.)

of Speed, who attributed it to Uther Pendragon, the legendary father of King Arthur, disappeared and only recently came to light again.[1]

Not until the 1960s were the war-damaged Prehistoric and Roman-British rooms once more made available. Some of the acquisitions received by the Department are amongst the most significant of any to have come to the Museum in recent years: the Mildenhall Treasure, a service of late Roman silver plate, buried by its Suffolk owners to prevent it falling into the hands of marauding Saxon pirates; the Hinton St Mary mosaic, a Roman mosaic pavement ornamented with a head of Christ from a villa of the fourth century AD which was discovered in 1963 and bought by the Museum two years later; the Snettisham Treasure of superb early Iron Age ornamental necklets of gold and silver alloy; the unique Sutton Hoo ship burial; the Lycurgus Cup, a late Roman glass vessel of the fourth century, with carved scenes of mythological subjects; and the Ilbert collection of 315 clocks and 1,778 watches and other related objects.

The Department of Oriental Antiquities was founded in 1933 to bring together collections hitherto scattered throughout no less than four Departments. Until 1946 the Sub-Department of Ethnography was also joined to Oriental Antiquities. During recent years the department has greatly benefitted from the generous bequest to it of several large private collections, either by the owners or by their heirs. As a result the Department of Oriental Antiquities now possesses one of the finest collections of oriental art to be found anywhere.

The Royal Commission on the National Museums had recommended an independent Museum of Ethnography, and provisional plans for the creation of such an institution at South Kensington had been drawn up shortly before the war. To be built between 1942 and 1946, it was never begun and the post-war years saw the Department of Ethnography more overcrowded than ever. Unlike much of the collections of the other Departments, the greater part of those of the Department of Ethnography are, without constant care and attention, highly perishable. Modern exhibition techniques rightly demand far less to be on show than was normal thirty years ago, and this means a far higher proportion

1. In the eighteenth century it was recognised from the Speed illustrations as Anglo-Saxon, but had long disappeared from the Cotton Collection. (BMQ, vol. XXVI, 1962–3, p. 72.)
John Speed, *The History of Great Britaine*, etc., London, 1611, p. 315.
An article by R. A. G. Carson on the Aureus of Carausius will be found in BMQ, vol. XXVII, 1963–4, p. 73.

of the Department's collections in reserve. Thus the number of exhibits on view before the war was about 200,000; by 1965 these had been reduced to 13,000. The Trustees in November 1967 obtained authority to display the exhibited collections, as a temporary expedient, in the rooms at Burlington House recently occupied by the Civil Service Commissioners and the British Academy. This allows the Department twice the exhibition space it had at Bloomsbury as well as offices, a students' room and some storage space. The preparatory planning for this move was under the direction of Mr Adrian Digby, Keeper of Ethnography, 1963–9, and has been concluded by the present Keeper, Mr W. B. Fagg.

These new rooms are examples of the latest exhibitions technique. To anyone used to the old galleries at Bloomsbury, they are indeed a revelation of how familiar objects, cleverly displayed, may be seen in an entirely new light. Of particular interest to the historian of the Museum is the exhibition displaying some of the objects which have survived from Sir Hans Sloane's once extensive ethnographical collections.[1]

The Research Laboratory, although an independent department under its own Keeper, is designed to serve all the other departments as well as the outside institutions from all over the world which come to it for expert assistance. In more recent years there has been a gradual change in policy with regard to the work done by this department. The day to day conservation of antiquities is done by the individual departments, subject, if necessary, to advice and assistance from the Laboratory. The Laboratory as far as possible concentrates on research into improved techniques of conservation. New methods have been developed, such as the use of polyethyline glycol wax for the consolidation of fragile antiquities, the intensive washing technique for bronzes, new electro-lytic methods for the cleaning of corroded lead objects, and many others.

Considerable work has been done since the war on the development of accurate methods of determining the age of objects by means of radio carbon dating. This has long been a special care of the Laboratory, which has done much to devise new techniques. This process, started in 1949 in cooperation with the Atomic Energy Research Establishment, was taken over ten years later by the Research Laboratory, which is

1. At his death Sloane had about 350 ethnographical specimens. By far the largest number were of North American Indian or Eskimo origin. A few specimens from Jamaica may have been acquired by Sloane himself during his stay there in 1687–8. The majority of objects listed in Sloane's catalogue remain unidentified and must be presumed to have long perished.

widely considered to be the best centre for the training of conservation experts from other institutions as well as a constant source of help for every department of the Museum in solving varied technical problems.

In 1958, Sir Thomas Kendrick retired, to be succeeded by F. C. Francis, later Sir Frank Francis.[1] Sir Frank was the first Printed Books man to become Director since Winter Jones ninety-two years earlier, and the only one besides Kenyon to achieve the Directorship without having been in charge of his own Department.

In 1963 a momentous change occurred in the administration of the British Museum. After just over two hundred years, the British Museum Act of 1753 was repealed and a new Act, the British Museum Act of 1963, passed to replace it.[2] This Act achieved what disgruntled radicals, Royal Commissions and Parliamentary Committees throughout the nineteenth century had failed to do – dissolved the old Board of Trustees and replaced it by a new Board, which, it was felt, was more in accordance with the requirements of the age. The ex-officio Trustees and the Family Trustees were abolished, although certain individuals from these two categories were invited to serve on the new Board. The three former Principal Trustees, the Archbishop of Canterbury, the Speaker and the Lord Chancellor were no longer automatically members of the Board and their place was taken by a Chairman elected by the other Trustees who would hold office for not more than five years.[3] The first Chairman of the new Board of Trustees was Lord Radcliffe, a former Lord of Appeal in Ordinary, who guided the Museum through a very difficult period. In February 1968, Lord Radcliffe resigned the Chairmanship and a few months later likewise resigned as a Trustee. He was succeeded

1. Sir Frank Charlton Francis, KCB, Director and Principal Librarian, 1959–68.
2. 'An Act to alter the composition of the Trustees of the British Museum, to provide for the separation from the British Museum of the British Museum (Natural History), to make new provision with respect to the regulation of the two Museums and their collections in place of that made by the British Museum Act 1753 and enactments amending or supplementing that Act, and for purposes connected with the matters aforesaid.' (PGA, 1963. c. 24. 10 July 1963.)
3. The Board was now to 'consist of twenty-five persons . . . (a) one appointed by Her Majesty; (b) fifteen appointed by the Prime Minister; (c) four appointed by the Treasury on the nominations of the Presidents of the Royal Society, the Royal Academy, the British Academy and the Society of Antiquaries; and five appointed by the Trustees of the British Museum'. (PGA, 1963, p. 296.)
    Though the election of a Chairman of the Board is not specifically mentioned in the Act, it is presumably covered by Section 5 to the First Schedule: 'The Trustees may make rules for regulating their proceedings and further matters relevant to the exercise of their functions'. (PGA, 1963, p. 301.)

by Lord Eccles, whose tenure of office was also comparatively brief, since he relinquished his Chairmanship in June 1970. His successor, elected by the Board in July 1970, was Lord Trevelyan, a member of a family long and honourably associated with the Museum. In October 1968 Sir Frank Francis resigned, after being Director for ten years. The present (1972) Director is Sir John Wolfenden, who has held the appointment since the beginning of 1969.

An important change made possible by the 1963 Act was that the Trustees were permitted for the first time to lend objects to outside institutions. Hitherto, except in very exceptional circumstances, such as the two World Wars, when certain books, urgently needed by government departments, were permitted to go from the Museum, a book or object might leave the Museum only if a court of law ordered it to be produced in evidence and then, only if the object were accompanied by a member of the staff, who was to never let it out of his sight. That a widespread demand for such a loan service existed, is proved by the fact that during the years 1966–9 objects with an insured value of £5,085,788, were lent to about one hundred and eighty exhibitions in fourteen countries, ranging from Afghanistan to Sweden, as well as to exhibitions large and small all over Great Britain.

The many exhibitions which have been held at the Museum since the war have dealt with numerous themes both literary and historical. The lack of a suitable permanent exhibition gallery has been a severe handicap and has made the task of mounting them at times extremely difficult.

The Trustees hope that the increased exhibition space which should be available in the near future will permit a major expansion in the Museum's services to the educational world, and that the Museum will come to play an increasing part in the cultural education of the young, a far cry, indeed, from the fears and doubts over the admission of the young expressed by Sir Henry Ellis, and even by a liberal-minded Principal Librarian like Panizzi.

In March 1969 the Dainton Committee on National Libraries recommended that the Department of Printed Books and other Library Departments – in short the National Library – should cease to form part of the British Museum and that its care should devolve from the Trustees onto a newly constituted statutory authority, which would also take certain other libraries under its control.[1]

These recommendations were modified by the Command Paper,

1. Report of the *National Libraries Committee*, p. 88.

The British Library,[1] issued in January 1971. In this the government proposed that the British Museum Library, the National Reference Library of Science and Invention, the National Central Library, the National Lending Library for Science and Invention, and the British National Bibliography, be combined into a single organisation to be known as the British Library. Within this structure the British Museum Library will retain its historic name and the National Reference Library of Science and Invention will then be known as the Science Reference Library. Both new libraries will be built on the site south of Great Russell Street.

Thus the Museum enters its third century not unmindful of its glorious past, yet facing the future with a new and assured vigour. Given the necessary financial backing, the British Museum and the British Museum Library, which will stem from it, will seek to serve, as they have always done, both scholar and the public, in ever expanding fields, aided now by all the resources of technology. Two hundred years is a brief moment in human history, and whatever changes may occur, our successors will surely remember and echo the words of the *Statutes and Rules* of 1757: 'For altho it was chiefly designed for the use of learned and studious men, both natives and foreigners, in their researches into the several parts of knowledge; yet being founded at the expence of the public, it may be judged reasonable that the advantages accruing from it shall be rendered as general, as may be consistent with the several considerations above mentioned[2].'

1. *The British Library*, Cmnd. 4572.
2. *Statutes and Rules to be observed in the management and use of the British Museum*, etc., 1757, p. 3.

The British Library

IN October 1967 the government announced that they were no longer willing for the British Museum Library to move to the site south of Great Russell Street, which for sixteen years had been designated as the area on which a new national library was to be built.

In December a departmental committee was set up under the chairmanship of Dr F. S. Dainton, Vice-Chancellor of the University of Nottingham 'to examine the functions and organisation of the British Museum Library, the National Central Library, the National Lending Library for Science and Technology and the Science Museum Library, in providing national library facilities to consider whether, in the interests of efficiency and economy, such facilities should be brought into a unified framework'. In June 1969 the Committee's report was published. It recommended the setting up of a National Libraries Authority, under which would be grouped the British Museum Library – renamed the National Reference Library – the National Reference Library for Science and Invention, the National Central Library, the National Lending Library for Science and Technology, and the British National Bibliography. A new management board would be set up to exercise general control, together with an executive committee, and advisory councils for each major library.

A number of further recommendations on the working of the proposed authority and its constituent libraries were made, including the all-important one for the Museum: 'A site immediately adjacent [to the British Museum] is most suitable for the N.R.L.'

In April 1970 the government accepted the main recommendations of the report, and reversed its decision over the Bloomsbury site for the new Library.

However, it was felt by many that the Dainton Committee had looked at the question almost solely through the eyes of scientists, and that the problems and special needs of a library such as the British Museum, which was used mostly by scholars working in the very different fields of the humanities and social sciences, had not really been understood. It was also felt that the report had displayed considerable prejudice against the British Museum, and that the Committee had failed to give due weight to the evidence submitted by its Trustees and by other friendly witnesses.

In January 1971 a White Paper, *The British Library* (Cmnd. 4572), was submitted to Parliament by the Paymaster General, Viscount Eccles, the minister responsible for the arts in the new Conservative administration and former Chairman of the Board of Trustees of the British Museum.

The government had decided to set up an organisation to be known as the British Library, which would take over the administration of the British Museum Library, the National Reference Library for Science and Invention, the National Central Library, the National Lending Library for Science and Technology, and the British National Bibliography. Within this organisation the British Museum Library would retain its historic name. Both the British Museum Library and the National Reference Library for Science and Invention would be housed in new buildings to be erected on the seven-acre site between Great Russell Street and New Oxford Street. The lending facilities of the National Lending Library at Boston Spa, Yorkshire, would likewise be expanded. There would thus be two complexes: one for reference, research and bibliographical services at Bloomsbury, the other for lending services at Boston Spa.

The British Library will be 'an independent body corporate enjoying the maximum freedom over its internal affairs . . . employing its own staff and paying for goods and services obtained from government Departments'. It will be financed by an annual grant from the Department of Education and Science. A British Libraries board is to be established consisting of a chairman, a full-time deputy chairman, three other full-time members, and a number of part-time members. Among the latter will be one appointed by the Queen with special responsibilities for the King's Library.

During the interim period until the board can take over the administration of its various libraries, a committee under the chairmanship of Lord Eccles has been set up to plan the new organisation, and to co-ordinate the planning policy with the object of ensuring that the organisation comes into being at the earliest date possible as an effective going concern.

Much other preliminary work is also being done, including the detailed planning of the new building, the architect for which is Mr Colin St John Wilson, and a libraries planning group has been formed to assist him. A planning secretariat with officers appointed from within the organisations which will eventually comprise the British Library will enable the architect's original brief to be transformed into its final version, and will provide the necessary data on the future organisational structure of the British Library. It will be necessary to make arrangements for library accommodation during the probably long interim period until the new buildings are ready.

It is impossible to foresee exactly how the British Library at Bloomsbury will develop during the years ahead. But it seems probable that it will consist ultimately of a single organisation with certain centralised functions, serving specialised reference departments which will between them cover the whole field of both arts and sciences in all languages. Such developments will involve fundamental changes in the present organisations, and the British Museum Library, as it has been known for over two hundred years, will almost certainly disappear. Its traditions, however, will remain, and in whatever form it may eventually exist, it will surely still be regarded as one of the greatest reference libraries of the world in the field of humanities and the social sciences.

The British Library will provide the apex of a national library system, an authority to which all other libraries will be able to turn for advice and assistance. For a variety of reasons the British Museum Library has never occupied the position in the library system of this country which the Library of Congress, for instance, holds in that of the United States. It has tended to stand apart – perhaps too much – from the public libraries and even from the other national and specialised libraries of the country.

Though much will undoubtedly be lost with the severance of the Library from those other departments of the Museum, which have been its companions for over two hundred years, relations between the British Museum Library and its parent institution over the road will remain, it is hoped, very close. Given good will and the benefit of the careful planning which the new organisation is undoubtedly now receiving, and drawing on the traditions and experience of the British Museum Library as well as on those of its other constituent libraries, the British Library should be able to provide a library service second to none for this country and indeed for the whole world.

The Principal Librarians and Directors of the British Museum

(From 1898 onwards Director and Principal Librarian.

1756   Gowin Knight, MD
1772   Matthew Maty, MD
1776   Charles Morton, MD
1799   Joseph Planta
1827   Henry Ellis (Sir Henry Ellis, KH)
1856   Antonio Panizzi (Sir Anthony Panizzi, KCB
1866   John Winter Jones
1873   Edward Augustus Bond (Sir Edward Bond, KCB)
1888   Edward Maunde Thompson (Sir Edward Maunde Thompson, GCB, ISO)
1909   Frederic George Kenyon (Sir Frederic Kenyon, KCB)
1931   George Francis Hill (Sir George Hill, KCB)
1936   Edgar John Forsdyke (Sir John Forsdyke, KCB)
1950   Thomas Downing Kendrick (Sir Thomas Kendrick, KCB)
1959   Frank Chalton Francis (Sir Frank Francis, KCB)
1968   John Frederick Wolfenden (Sir John Wolfenden, CBE)

The Keepers of the Departments

Department of Manuscripts

1756	Charles Morton, MD
1776	Joseph Planta
1799	Francis Douce
1812	Henry Ellis (Sir Henry Ellis, KH)
1827	Rev. Josiah Forshall
1837	Frederic Madden (Sir Frederic Madden, KH)
1866	Edward Augustus Bond (Sir Edward Bond, KCB)
1878	Edward Maunde Thompson (Sir Edward Maunde Thompson, GCB, ISO)
1888	Edward John Long Scott
1904	George Frederic Warner (Sir George Warner)
1911	Julius Parnell Gilson
1929	Harold Idris Bell (Sir Idris Bell)
1944	Eric George Millar
1947	Arthur Jeffries Collins
1956	Bertram Schofield
1961	Theodore Cressy Skeat

Department of Printed Books

1756	Matthew Maty, MD
1765	Rev. Samuel Harper
1803	Rev. William Beloe
1806	Henry Ellis (Sir Henry Ellis, KH)
1812	Rev. Henry Hervey Baber
1837	Antonio Panizzi (Sir Anthony Panizzi, KCB)
1856	John Winter Jones
1866	Thomas Watts
1869	William Brenchley Rye
1875	George Bullen
1890	Richard Garnett
1899	George Knottesford Fortescue
1912	Arthur William Kaye Miller
1914	George Frederic Barwick
1919	Alfred William Pollard
1924	Robert Farquharson Sharp
1930	Wilfred Alexander Marsden
1943	Henry Thomas (Sir Henry Thomas)

1948	Cecil Bernard Oldman
1959	Robert Andrew Wilson
1966	Arthur Hugh Chaplin
1970	Kenneth Burslem Gardner

Department of Maps, Charts, Plans and Topographical Drawings

1867–80   Richard Henry Major

Department of Natural History

(Originally known as the Department of Natural and Artificial Productions)

1756	James Empson
1765	Matthew Maty, MD
1773	Daniel Charles Solander
1782	Rev. Paul Henry Maty
1787	Edward Whittaker Gray
1806	George Shaw, MD
1813	Charles Eberhard Dietrich König

In 1836 the Botanical Branch was formed, and in 1838 the remainder of the department sub-divided into the Mineralogical and Geological Branch and the Zoological Branch.

Botanical Branch	Mineralogical and Geological Branch	Zoological Branch
1835 Robert Brown (Since 1828 Keeper of the Banksian Botanical Collection)	1838 Charles Eberhard Dietrich König. 1851 George Robert Waterhouse	1838 John George Children 1840 John Edward Gray

In 1856 Sir Richard Owen was appointed Superintendent of the Natural History Departments, and the several 'Branches' were turned into 'Departments'. In 1857 the Mineralogical and Geological Department was split into the Geological Department and the Mineralogical Department.

Department of Botany	Department of Geology	Department of Mineralogy
1856 Robert Brown 1859 John Joseph Bennett 1871 William Carruthers	1857 George Robert Waterhouse 1880 Henry Woodward	1857 Mervyn Neville Storey-Maskelyne 1880 Lazarus Fletcher (Sir Lazarus Fletcher)

Department of Zoology

| 1856 | John Edward Gray |
| 1872 | Albert Charles Lewis Gotthilf Günther. |

By 1883 the Natural History Departments had all left for South Kensington.

Department of Antiquities

1807   Taylor Combe
1826   Edward Hawkins
In 1860 the Department of Antiquities was divided into three new Departments: Oriental Antiquities, including the British, mediaeval and ethnographical collections; Greek and Roman Antiquities; Coins and Medals.

Department of Oriental Antiquities

(In 1886 renamed Department of Egyptian and Assyrian Antiquities.)
1860   Samuel Birch
1885   Peter Le Page Renouf (Sir Peter Renouf)
1894   Ernest Alfred Thompson Wallis Budge (Sir Wallis Budge)
1924   Harry Reginald Hall
1931   Sydney Smith
1948   Cyril John Gadd
In 1955 the Department of Egyptian and Assyrian Antiquities was split into the Department of Egyptian Antiquities and the Department of Western Asiatic Antiquities.

Department of Egyptian Antiquities	*Department of Western Asiatic Antiquities*
1955 Iorwerth Eiddon Stephen Edwards	1955 Richard David Barnett

Department of British and Medieval Antiquities

In 1866 the British, mediaeval and ethnographical collections were taken from the Department of Oriental Antiquities and formed into the Department of British and Medieval Antiquities.
1866   Augustus Woolaston Franks (Sir Augustus Franks)
1896   Charles Hercules Read (Sir Hercules Read)
1921   Ormonde Maddock Dalton
1928   Reginald Allender Smith
1938   Thomas Downing Kendrick (Sir Thomas Kendrick, KCB)
1954   Rupert Leo Scott Bruce–Mitford
In 1969 the Department of British and Medieval Antiquities was divided into the Department of Prehistoric and Romano–British Antiquities and the Department of Medieval and Later Antiquities.

Department of Prehistoric and Romano-British Antiquities

1969   John William Brailsford

Department of Medieval and Later Antiquities

1969   Rupert Leo Scott Bruce–Mitford

Department of Greek and Roman Antiquities

1860	Charles Newton (Sir Charles Newton)
1886	Alexander Stuart Murray
1909	Arthur Hamilton Smith
1925	Henry Beauchamp Walters
1932	Edgar John Forsdyke (Sir John Forsdyke, KCB)
1936	Frederick Norman Pryce
1939	Bernard Ashmole
1956	Denys Eyre Lankester Haynes

Department of Coins and Medals

1860	William Sandys Wright Vaux
1870	Reginald Stuart Poole
1893	Barclay Vincent Head
1906	Herbert Appold Grueber
1912	George Francis Hill (Sir George Hill, KCB)
1931	John Allan
1949	Edward Stanley Gotch Robinson
1952	John Walker
1965	Gilbert Kenneth Jenkins

Department of Prints and Drawings

Until 1836 the print collection formed part of the Department of Antiquities, although the officer in charge had the title of Keeper of Prints.

1808	William Alexander
1816	John Thomas Smith
1833	William Young Ottley
1836	Henry Josi
1845	William Hokham Carpenter
1866	George William Reid
1883	Sidney Colvin (Sir Sidney Colvin)
1912	Campbell Dodgson
1932	Robert Laurence Binyon
1933	Arthur Mayger Hind
1945	Arthur Ewart Popham
1954	Edward Frederick Croft–Murray

Department of Oriental Printed Books and Manuscripts

Until 1892 entitled Department of Oriental Manuscripts.

1867–91	Charles Rieu
1892	Robert Kennaway Douglas (Sir Robert Douglas)
1908	Lionel David Barnett

1936   Lionel Giles
1940   Alexander Strathern Fulton
1953   Jacob Leveen
1957   Kenneth Burslem Gardner
1971   Martin Lings

Department of Ceramics and Ethnography

Formed out of the ceramic and ethnographical collections of the Department of British and Medieval Antiquities.
1921–33   Robert Lockhart Hobson
In 1933 the ceramic collections were divided, the oriental ceramics going to the newly created Department of Oriental Antiquities and Ethnography; the remainder being returned to the Department of British and Medieval Antiquities.

Department of Oriental Antiquities ond Ethnography

1933–38   Robert Lockhard Hobson
1939–46   Hermann Justus Braunholtz

Sub-Department of Ethnography

1933–38   Thomas Atholl Joyce

Department of Oriental Antiquities

1946   Basil Gray
1969   Douglas Eric Barrett

Department of Ethnography

1946   Hermann Justus Braunholz
1953   Adrian Digby
1969   William Buller Fagg

The Laboratory

1931   Alexander Scott (part-time Director)
1938   Harold James Plenderleith
1959   Alfred Emil Anthony Werner

The Keepers and Superintendents of the Reading Room

1758   Peter Templeman, MD
1761   Rev. Richard Penneck

Between 1803 and 1856 the duties of the Keeper of the Reading Room were first carried out by the senior officers in rotation, and then from 1824 by an Attendant of the Room, under the direction of the Principal Librarian. In 1856 the position of Superintendent of the Reading Room was established, with the rank of Assistant, afterwards Deputy Keeper.

1857   Thomas Watts
1866   George Bullen
1875   Richard Garnett
1890   George Knottesford Fortescue
1899   William Robert Wilson
1900   George Frederick Barwick
1914   Robert Farquharson Sharp
1919   Francis Danvers Sladen
1929   Arthur Isaac Ellis
1946   Francis Geoffrey Rendall
1948   Robert Andrew Wilson
1952   Noel Farquharson Sharp
Feb. 1959   Arthur Hugh Chaplin
Oct. 1959   Richard Francis Laurence Bancroft

Abbreviations used in the Notes

Accounts, &c.	*British Museum. Accounts relating to the income and expenditure (accounts for the financial year)*, etc.
Add. MS.	*Additional Manuscripts*, Department of Manuscripts, British Museum.
Banks	*The Banks Letters. A calendar of the manuscript correspondence of Sir J. Banks.*
BMQ	*British Museum Quarterly.*
Barwick	G. F. Barwick, *The Reading Room of the British Museum.*
Boswell	J. Boswell, *The Life of Samuel Johnson. Edited by G. B. Hill.*
Budge	Sir E. Budge, *The Rise and Progress of Assyriology.*
CJ	*Journals*, House of Commons.
Cary	H. Cary, *Memoir of the Rev. F. Cary.*
Committee Minutes	Minutes of the Committee of the Board of Trustees, British Museum.
Communications	*Communications relating to the enlargement of the British Museum.*
Cowtan	R. Cowtan, *Memories of the British Museum.*
DNB	*Dictionary of National Biography.*
Departmental Reports	Miscellaneous Departmental Reports, Department of Printed Books, British Museum.
Edwards, Diary	E. Edwards, Manuscript diary, Department of Printed Books, British Museum.
Edwards, Founders	E. Edwards, *Lives of the Founders of the British Museum.*
Elgin	*Report from the Select Committee appointed to inquire into the expediency of purchasing the collection mentioned in the Earl of Elgin's Petition*, etc.
Esdaile	A. Esdaile, *The British Museum Library.*
Fagan	L. Fagan, *The Life of Sir Anthony Panizzi.*
GEC	G. E. Cokayne, *The Complete Peerage*, etc.
GM	*The Gentleman's Magazine.*
General Meetings, Minutes	Minutes of the General Meetings of the Board of Trustees, British Museum.
Gray, Correspondence	*Correspondence. Edited by P. Toynbee and L. Whitley.*
Greville	*The Greville Diary. Edited by P. W. Wilson.*
Grosley	P. J. Grosley, *A Tour to London.*
Kenyon	Sir F. Kenyon. *The Buildings of the British Museum.*
LJ	*Journals*, House of Lords.
Madden Collection	Sir F. Madden. [A collection of newspaper cuttings relating to the British Museum.]

Madden Journal	Sir F. Madden, *Journal, 1819–1866.*
Mayes	S. Mayes, *The Great Belzoni.*
Passages	A. Panizzi, *Passages in my official life.*
PGA	*Public General Acts,* 1700, etc.
PP, H. of C.	*Parliamentary Papers,* House of Commons.
PP, H. of L.	*Parliamentary Papers,* House of Lords.
Panizzi Papers	Official Papers of Antonio Panizzi, Department of Printed Books, British Museum.
Parliamentary History	W. Cobbett, *Parliamentary History of England, 1066–1803.*
Royal Commission	*Commission appointed to inquire into the constitution and government of the British Museum.*
Salt	J. J. Halls, *The Life and correspondence of Henry Salt,* etc.
Select Committee, 1835	*Select Committee to inquire into the condition, management and affairs of the British Museum.*
Select Committee, 1836	*Select Committee on the Same Subject the following Session.*
Simond	L. Simond, *Journal of a Tour and Residence in Great Britain.*
Smith	A. H. Smith, *Lord Elgin and his Collection.*
Sub-Committee Minutes	Minutes of the Sub-Committees of the Board of Trustees, British Museum.
Walpole, *Anecdotes*	H. Walpole, Earl of Orford, *Anecdotes of Painting in England.*
Walpole, *Correspondence*	H. Walpole, Earl of Orford. *Letters.* *Yale edition of H. Walpole's correspondence.*
Walpole, *Letters*	H. Walpole, Earl of Orford. *Letters. Edited by P. Cunningham.*

Bibliography

GENERAL

A. PRIMARY SOURCES

BRITISH MUSEUM
Board of Trustees. *General Meetings. Minutes* December 1753, *etc.*
Committee Minutes, January 1754, *etc.*
Sub-Committee Minutes, March 1828, *etc.*
Annual Report of the General Progress of the Museum for the year 1921 (–1938). [Earlier reports were issued as Parliamentary Papers.]
Report of the Trustees, 1966. [Covers the period since the last pre-war report.]
Report of the Trustees, 1966–69.
PARLIAMENTARY DEBATES, 1803, *etc.*
HOUSE OF LORDS.
Journals.
HOUSE OF COMMONS.
Journals.
Parliamentary Papers, 1801, *etc.* [Details of individual papers relating to the British Museum are given below in the sectional bibliographies.]
Regulations and Returns respecting Admission to the Museum – Receipts and Payments – Accounts relating to the Income and Expenditure – Annual Accounts, etc. [Issued from 1803 to 1921 under a variety of names. The later reports are more detailed and are virtually Annual Reports. From 1921 onwards issued as Non-Parliamentary Papers.]
PUBLIC GENERAL ACTS, 1700, *etc.*

B. SECONDARY SOURCES

BAZIN (GERMAIN). *Le Temps des musées.* Liége, 1967.
BARWICK, GEORGE F. *The Reading Room of the British Museum.* Benn, London, 1929.
BRITISH MUSEUM. *The British Museum Quarterly.* London, 1926, etc.
The Catalogues of the British Museum.
  I. *The Catalogues of the Printed Books.* By F. C. Francis, London, 1952.
  II. *The Catalogues of the Manuscript Collections, etc.* By T. C. Skeat. London, 1951.
  III. *The Catalogues of the Oriental Printed Books and Manuscripts.* By F. C. Francis, London, 1951.
BRITISH MUSEUM (NATURAL HISTORY). *The History of the Collections contained in the Natural History Departments, etc.* 3 vol. London, 1904–12.
COCKAYNE, GEORGE F. *The Complete Peerage of England, etc.* Edited by V. Gibbs [and others]. St Catherine's Press, London, 1910–59.

CROOK, JOSEPH M. *The British Museum.* Allen Lane, The Penguin Press, London, 1972.

EDWARDS, EDWARD. *Lives of the Founders of the British Museum, etc.* Trübner & Co., London, 1870.

EDWARDS, EDWARD. *Memoirs of Libraries, etc.* Trübner & Co., London, 1859.

ESDAILE, ARUNDELL. *The British Museum Library. A Short History and a Survey.* Allen and Unwin, London, 1946.

The Gentleman's Magazine, London, 1731–1868.

KENYON, SIR FREDERICK, *The Buildings of the British Museum, etc.* Trustees of the British Museum, London, 1914.

MADDEN, SIR FREDERIC. [A collection of newspaper cuttings, views, etc. relating to the British Museum, 1755–1870.] 4 vol.

MURRAY, DAVID. *Museums. Their history and their use, etc.* James MacLehose & Sons, Glasgow, 1904.

FROM THE EARLIEST TIMES TO THE OPENING OF THE MUSEUM, JANUARY 1759

A.   Primary Sources

BRITISH MUSEUM. DEPARTMENT OF MANUSCRIPTS.
Yorke (Philip). *1st Earl of Hardwicke.*
Letters and Papers relating to the establishment and maintenance of the British Museum 1742–1813.
[For the most part, of the period when Lord Chancellor Hardwicke was a Trustee, with a few later additions.]
Hardwicke Papers, vol. DCCCCXXI. Add. MS. 36,269.
Ellis (Sir Henry). *Diaries and memoranda.* Add. MS. 36,657.
Madden (Sir Frederic). *Material for a history of the British Museum.* Add. MS. 38,791.
COBBETT, WILLIAM. *Parliamentary History, 1066–1803.* Hansard, London, 1806–20.
HOUSE OF COMMONS. *Report from the Committee appointed to view the Cottonian Library, etc.* Reports. First series, vol. I. p. 443.
PUBLIC RECORD OFFICE. *Calendar of State Papers, Domestic,* 1649–50; 1651–52.
Calendar of Treasury Papers, 1702–07; 1714–19; 1729–30.

B.   Secondary Sources

ASHMOLE, ELIAS. *The Diary and Will of Elias Ashmole,* edited by R. T. Gunther. Oxford, 1927. [Old Ashmolean Reprints. no. 2.]

BENEZIT, EMMANUEL. *Dictionnaire critique et documentaire des peintres, etc.* 8 vol. Librarie Gründ, St-Ouen, 1948–55.

BENTLEY, RICHARD. *A Proposal for building a Royal Library, and establishing it by Act of Parliament.* London, 1697.

BLUNT, REGINALD. *By Chelsea Reach. Some riverside records.* Mills & Boon, London, [1921.]

BRITISH MUSEUM. *The Old Royal Library.* London, 1957.
Statutes and Rules to be observed in the Management and Use of the British Museum. London, 1757.

374 THAT NOBLE CABINET

Statutes and Rules, etc. London, 1758.

Statutes and Rules relating to the Inspection and Use of the British Museum, and for the better security and Preservation of the same. London, 1759.

BRITISH MUSEUM. DEPARTMENT OF MANUSCRIPTS. *A Catalogue of the Manuscripts in the Cottonian Library deposited in the British Museum.* [By J. Planta.] [London,] 1802.

Catalogue of Western Manuscripts in the Old Royal Library and King's Collection. By Sir George F. Warner and J. P. Gilson. 3 vol. London, 1921.

A Guide to a Select Exhibition of the Cottonian Manuscripts in celebration of the Tercentenary of the Death of Sir Robert Cotton, 6 May 1931. London, 1931.

BROOKS, ERIC ST J. *Sir Hans Sloane. The great collector and his circle.* Batchworth, London, 1954.

COTTON, SIR ROBERT B. *A Brief Abstract of the Question of Precedency between England, Spain. etc.* London, 1642.

COTTON, SIR ROBERT B. [Or rather by Thomas Scott.] *A Choice Narrative of Count Gondomar's Transactions, etc.* Edited by J. Rowland. London, 1659.

COTTON, SIR ROBERT B. *Cottoni Posthuma, etc.* London, 1651.

Cornhill Magazine. The Creation of the British Museum. By Sir Edward M. Thompson. New Series, vol. 19, p. 641.

CUNNINGHAM, PETER. *A Handbook for London, past and present.* 2 vol. John Murray, London, 1849.

DAVIES, RANDALL. *The Greatest House at Chelsey.* John Lane, London, [1914.]

DE BEER, SIR GAVIN R. *Sir Hans Sloane and the British Museum.* Oxford University Press, London, 1953.

D'EWES, SIR SIMONDS. *Autobiography and correspondence, etc.* R. Bentley, London, 1845.

EVANS, JOAN. *A History of the Society of Antiquaries.* University Press, London, 1956.

EVELYN, JOHN. *The Diary of John Evelyn.* Edited by E. S. De Beer. 6 vol. Clarendon Press, Oxford, 1955.

FAULKNER, THOMAS. *An Historical and Topographical Description of Chelsea, etc.* London, 1829.

Friends' Quarterly Examiner. Narrative of some occurrences in the Life of Edmund Howard. vol. 40, 1906.

HEARNE, THOMAS. *A Collection of Curious Discourses written by Eminent Antiquaries, etc.* Oxford, 1720.

KNIGHT, CHARLES. *London.* 6 vol. London, 1841–44.

JAYNE, SEARS and JOHNSON, FRANCIS R. *The Lumley Library, The Catalogue of 1609.* Trustees of the British Museum, London, 1956.

The Library. Sir Hans Sloane's Printed Books. By J. S. Finch. vol. 22, 1942.

NICHOLS, JOHN. *Literary Anecdotes of the Eighteenth Century.* 9 vol. Nichols, Son & Bentley, London, 1812–15.

SALTER, JOHN. *A Catalogue of the Rarities to be seen in Don Saltero's Coffee House in Chelsea, etc.* London, 1729.

SKELTON, RALEIGH A. *The Royal Map Collections.* [BMQ vol. 26 p. 1.]

SLOANE, SIR HANS. *A Voyage to the Islands Madera . . . and Jamaica.* 2 vol. 1707–25.

SLOANE, SIR HANS. *The Will of Sir Hans Sloane, etc.* J. Virtuoso, London, 1753.

[With MS. additions consisting of the proceedings of the Sloane Trustees and of the House of Commons in reference to the purchase by the Nation of the collection of Sir Hans Sloane.]

SLOANE, SIR HANS. *Authentic copies of the codicils belonging to the last will and testament of Sir Hans Sloane, Bart., etc.* D. Browne, London, 1753.

SLOANE, SIR HANS. *The names and numbers of the several things contain'd in the Musaeum of Sir Hans Sloan, Bart.* In: *Authentic copies, etc.* p. 33.

SMITH, JOHN T. *A Book for a Rainy Day; or recollections of . . . the last sixty years* London, 1845.

STOW, JOHN. *A Survey of the Cities of London and Westminster . . . improved and very much enlarged . . . by J. Strype, etc.* 2 vol. London, 1720.

STUKELEY, WILLIAM. *Intinerarium Curiosum; or an Account of the Antiquitys and remarkable curiositys . . . observ'd in travels thro.' Great Britain.* London, 1724.

THORESBY, RALPH. *The Diary of Ralph Thoresby.* 2 vol. London, 1830.

TRADESCANT, JOHN. *The Younger. Musaeum Tradescantianum, etc.* London, 1656.

WALCOTT, MACKENZIE E. C. *Westminster. Memorials of the city, etc.* London, 1849.

WALPOLE, HORACE. *Earl of Orford. Anecdotes of Painting in England . . . with additions, etc.* 3 vol. Swan, Sonnenschein & Co., London, 1888.

WALPOLE, HORACE. *Earl of Orford. Letters. Yale edition of Horace Walpole's correspondence.* Edited by W. S. Lewis, Oxford University Press, London, 1937, etc.

WANLEY, HUMPHREY. *The Diary of Humfrey Wanley 1715–1726.* Edited by C. E. and R. C. Wright, Bibliographical Society, London, 1966.

WHITELOCK, BULSTRODE. *The Elder. Memorials of the English Affairs . . . to the end of the reign of James I, etc.* London, 1709.

WRIGHT, CYRIL E. *Humfrey Wanley. Saxonist and Library Keeper.* [British Academy Proceedings. vol. XLVI, 1960.]

THE UNREFORMED MUSEUM

1759–1837

A. Primary Sources

BRITISH MUSEUM.
Report concerning the theft of certain prints from the Cracherode collection and the dismissal of W. Beloe.
Original Letters and Papers, vol. 2, 1785–1809.

DEPARTMENT OF MANUSCRIPTS.

CRACHERODE, REV. CLAYTON M. *Notebook giving lists of the Trustees, Officers, and of donations to the Museum, etc. 1784–1796.* Add. MS. 47,611.

ELLIS, SIR HENRY. *Correspondence etc., 1795–1866.* Add. MS. 41,312. *Correspondence portraits and miscellaneous documents for the most part relating to the British Museum.* Add. MS. 42,406.

PEEL, SIR ROBERT. *Correspondence with King George IV and others concerning the bequest of the King's Library to the British Museum.* Add. MSS. 40,300. ff. 246–252; 40,393. f. 52.

YORKE, PHILIP. Second Earl of Hardwicke. *Papers and documents on the British Museum, etc.*, 1762–1775. Add. MSS. 35, 607, 35,612.

MADDEN, SIR FREDERIC. *Journals*, 1819–1837. [A photographic reproduction of the original in the Bodleian Library, Oxford.]

Memoranda by the Superintendent of the Reading Room, 11 July 1759 to 11 December 1761. Add. MS. 45,868.

The Register of Persons admitted to the Reading Room, 12 January 1759 to 11 May 1763 (–2 March 1781 to 9 June 1795). Add. MSS. 45,867–870.

DEPARTMENT OF PRINTED BOOKS.

Collections for a history of the Department of Printed Books. [A collection of manuscript and printed material formed by W. B. Rye.]

Manuscript memorandum in the handwriting of Nicolas Carlisle, dated June 19, 1828, on the books taken out of the Royal Catalogue by George IV's command.

PARLIAMENTARY PAPERS, HOUSE OF COMMONS.

Papers respecting the mode of admission to the British Museum, and its Reading Room. [1803–04, vol. VIII, p. 647.]

Report from the Select Committee respecting the late Mr Towneley's Collection of Marbles. [1805, vol. III, p. 319.]

Report from the Select Committee . . . relative to the Lansdown MS. [1807, vol. II, p. 19.]

Report from the Select Committee . . . respecting the purchase of Mr Greville's Collection of Minerals. [1810, vol. II, p. 239.]

Report from the Select Committee . . . respecting the Towneley Collection of Medals and Coins, etc. [1813–14, vol. III, p. 109.]

Report from the Select Committee appointed to inquire into the expediency of purchasing the Collection mentioned in the Earl of Elgin's Petition to the House, etc. [1816, vol. III, p. 49.]

Estimate of Expense of a Temporary Building for the reception of the Elgin Marbles at the British Museum. [1816, vol. XII, p. 305.]

Report from the Select Committee on the . . . Propriety of purchasing the Collection of the late Dr Burney. [1818, vol. III, p. 355.]

Report from the Committee to whom the Papers relating to the Library which His Majesty has been graciously pleased to present to the British Nation, etc. [1823, vol. IV, p. 41.]

Report from the Select Committee . . . relative to Mr Rich's collection of MSS., Antiquities and Coins. [1825, vol. V, p. 107.]

Report from the Select Committee appointed to inquire into the Condition, Management and Affairs of the British Museum. [1835, vol. VII, p. 1.]

Report from the Select Committee appointed in the following Season to consider the same subject. [1836, vol. X, p. 1.]

[Details of other papers on the affairs of the Museum during this period will be found in: *General Index to the Reports of Select Committees, 1801–1852* and in *General Index to Accounts and Papers, 1801–1852.*]

B.   Secondary Sources

ASHMOLE, BERNARD. *A New Interpretation of the Portland Vase.* [Journal of Hellenic Studies, vol. LXXXVII, 1967.]

BOSWELL, JAMES. *Boswell's Life of Johnson* . . . Edited by G. B. Hill. 6 vol. Clarendon Press, Oxford, 1887.

BRANDER, GUSTAVUS. *Fossilia Hantoniensia collecta et in Musaeo Brittanico deposita, etc.* Londini, 1766.

BRITISH MUSEUM. *Acts and Votes of Parliament relating to the British Museum, with the statutes and rules therefore and the succession of officers.* London, 1805.

Acts and Votes, etc. London, 1808.

Acts and Votes of Parliament relating to the British Museum, etc. London, 1824.

Acts and Votes . . . and the succession of Trustees and officers. London, 1828.

Directions to such as apply for tickets to see the British Museum. [London, *c.* 1784.]

Directions respecting the Reading Room of the British Museum. London, 1803.

The General Contents of the British Museum: with remarks. Serving as a directory in viewing that noble cabinet. Dodsley, London, 1761.

Librorum impressorum qui Museo Brittannico adservantur catalogus. [Edited by P. H. Maty, S. Harper and S. Ayscough.] Londini, 1787.

Librorum impressorum, etc. [Edited by Sir H. Ellis and H. H. Baber.] 7 vol. Londini, 1813–19.

List of Additions made to the collections in the years 1831 (–1835). London, 1833–39.

List of Additions to the Natural History, Antiquities and Prints in the years 1836–1839. London, 1843.

Statutes and Rules relating to the Inspection and Use of the British Museum, and for the better security and preservation of the same. London, 1759.

Statutes and Rules, etc. London, 1768.

Statutes and Rules . . . as altered in consequence of the report of Committee of the Trustees, etc. London, 1833.

Synopsis of the Contents of the British Museum. [Various editions.] 1808–1856.

Department of Greek and Roman Antiquities. *An Historical Guide to the Sculptures of the Parthenon.* London, 1962.

CASANOVA DI SEINGALT, GIACOMO G. *Mémoires, etc.* 3 vol. [Paris, 1958–60.] Bibliothèque de la pléiade vol. 132, 137, 147.

CLINTON, HENRY F. *Literary remains . . . Consisting of an Autobiography, etc.* Longman, London, 1854.

COWTAN, ROBERT. *A Bibliographical sketch of Sir Anthony Panizzi, etc.* Asher & Co., London, 1873.

Memories of the British Museum. R. Bentley & Son, London. 1872 [1871.]

DAVY, JOHN. *Memoirs of the Life of Sir Humphrey Davy, etc.* Rees, Orme & Co., London, 1836.

DAWSON, WARREN R. *The Banks Letters. A calendar of the manuscript correspondence of Sir Joseph Banks preserved in the British Museum, the British Museum (Natural History) and other collections in Great Britain.* Trustees of the British Museum, London, 1958.

D'ISRAELI, ISAAC. *The Illustrator Illustrated, etc.* E. Moxon, London, 1838.

EDWARDS, EDWARD. *Remarks on the Minutes of Evidence taken before the Select Committee on the British Museum.* London, 1836.

ENGLISH REPORTS, COMMON PLEAS. *The Trustees of the British Museum v Payne and Foss, Feb. 11, 1828.* [Part of the series, Flora Graeca, held not to be a book demandable by the British Museum under 54 Geo 3. c. 156.] Vol. CXXX. Common Pleas, vol. VIII, p. 877. W. Green & Sons, Edinburgh; Stevens & Sons, London, 1912.

FAUJAS DE SAINT FOND, BARTHELEMI. *Travels in England, Scotland, and the Hebrides, etc.* 2 vol. London, 1799.

FORTESCUE, GEORGE K. *Catalogue of the Pamphlets . . . relating to the Civil War. Collected by George Thomason, 1640–1661.* 2 vol. Trustees of the British Museum, London, 1908.

FOTHERGILL, BRIAN. *Sir William Hamilton. Envoy Extraordinary.* Faber & Faber, London, 1969.

GOUGH, RICHARD. *British Topography or, an historical account of . . . the topographical antiquities of Great Britain and Ireland.* 2 vol. London, 1780.

GRAY, THOMAS. *Correspondence, etc.* Edited by P. Toynbee and L. Whibley, 3 vol. Oxford, 1935.

GREVILLE, CHARLES C. F. *The Greville Diary.* Edited by P. W. Wilson, 2 vol. Heinemann, London, 1927.

GROSLEY, PIERRE J. *A Tour of London, etc.* 2 vol. London, 1772.

HALLS, J. J. *The Life and Correspondence of Henry Salt, etc.* 2 vol. R. Bentley, London, 1834.

HAMILTON, SIR WILLIAM. *An abstract of Sir W. Hamilton's Collection of Antiquities.* [London, 1772.]

HAMILTON, SIR WILLIAM. *Collection of Etruscan, Greek and Roman Antiquities, from the cabinet of the Hon. W. Hamilton, etc.* 4 vol. Naples, 1766, 1767.

HAMILTON, SIR WILLIAM. *Observations on Mount Vesuvius, Mount Etna, and other Volcanos, etc.* London, 1772.

HAYDON, BENJAMIN R. *The Life . . . from his Autobiography and Journals.* Edited by . . . by T. Taylor, London, 1853.

HAYNES, DENYS E. L. *The Portland Vase.* Trustees of the British Museum, London, 1964.

HOLLIS, THOMAS. *Memoirs of Thomas Hollis.* 2 vol. London, 1780.

HUGHSON, DAVID. [i.e. D. PUGH.] *London; being an accurate history of the British Metropolis, etc.* 6 vol. London, 1805–09.

JONES, JOHN W. *A List of the Books of Reference in the Reading Room of the British Museum.* [Edited with a preface by J. W. Jones.] Trustees of the British Museum, London, 1859.

LOMER, GERHARD R. *Sir Henry Ellis in France. A chapter in the history of the British Museum.* In: *William Warner Bishop, a tribute, etc.* pp. 116–144. Yale University Press, New Haven, 1941.

LONDON. *London and its Environs Described, etc.* 6 vol. R. & J. Dodsley, London, 1761.

MALCOLM, JAMES P. *Londinium Redivivum; or an ancient history and modern description of London, etc.* 4 vol. London, 1802–07.

MAYES, STANLEY. *The Great Belzoni.* Putnam, London, 1959.

Mechanics Magazine, Museum Register, Journal and Gazette. 'The New Buildings at the British Museum.' By P.P.C.R. (Thomas Watts). Vol. 36, 1 October 1836–31 March 1837, p. 454.
'The British Museum and its Library.' By P.P.C.R. (Thomas Watts). Vol. 36, p. 291. A review of the report of the Select Committee of 1836.

MICHAELIS, ADOLF T. F. *Ancient Marbles in Great Britain . . . Translated by C. A. M. Fennell.* University Press, Cambridge, 1882.

MILLINGEN, JAMES V. *Ancient Unedited Monuments, etc.* 3pt. London, 1822–26.

MORRISON, ALFRED. *Catalogue of the Collection of Autograph Letters and Historical*

Documents . . . formed by A. Morrison . . . Second series. The Hamilton & Nelson Papers. 2 vol. London, 1893, 1894.

NICHOLS, JOHN. *Illustrations of the Literary History of the 18th century, etc.* 8 vol. Nichols, Son & Bentley, London, 1817–58.

Quarterly Review. Narrative of the Operations and Recent Discoveries within the Pyramids, *etc.* (A Review of Belzoni's account of his discoveries in Egypt.) Vol. 24, no. XLVII October 1820. Art. VI.

Quarterly Review. Report from the Select Committee, 1835, etc. (Review of this and subsequent Parliamentary Committees and Commissions and related documents.) Vol. 88, no. CLXXV. December 1850. Art. VI.

RICH, CLAUDIUS J. *Narrative of a Residence in Koordistan and on the site of ancient Nineveh, etc.* 2 vol. J. Duncan, London, 1836.

RYMSDYK, JAN VAN and ANDREAS VAN. *Museum Britannicum, being an exhibition of great variety of Antiquities and natural curiosities belonging to the British Museum, etc.* London, 1778.

SIMOND, LOUIS. *Journal of a Tour and Residence in Great Britain during the years 1810 and 1811.* A. Constable & Co., Edinburgh, 1815.

SMITH, ARTHUR H. *Lord Elgin and his Collection.* [London,] 1916.

SMITH, EDWARD. *The Life of Sir Joseph Banks, etc.* John Lane, London, 1911.

SMITH, JOHN T. *Nollekens and his Times.* R. Bentley & Son, London, 1894.

SOCIETY OF DILETTANTI. *Specimens of Antient Sculpture, etc.* 2 vol. London, 1809.

THOMSON, ALEXANDER. *Letters on the British Museum.* Dodsley, London, 1767.

WALPOLE, HORACE. *Earl of Orford. Letters, etc.* Edited by P. Cunningham, etc. 9 vol. R. Bentley & Son, London, 1891.

WALPOLE, HORACE. *Earl of Orford. The Yale edition of Horace Walpole's Correspondence.* Edited by W. S. Lewis. Oxford University Press, London, 1937, etc.

THE AGE OF PANIZZI

1837–1866

A. Primary Sources

BRITISH MUSEUM.
  DEPARTMENT OF MANUSCRIPTS.
  Bliss, Rev. Philip. *Correspondence, etc.* 1729–1857. Add. MSS. 34,567–34,582.
  Ellis, Sir Henry, *Diaries, Memoranda, etc.* 1813–1849. Add. MSS. 36,653 (1–19). *Miscellaneous correspondence, etc.* Add. MS. 42,506.
  Layard, Sir Henry. *Correspondence, official papers, etc.* 1836–1894. Add. MSS. 38,931– 39,164. [Details of letters, etc. relating specifically to the Museum are given in the notes.]
  Madden, Sir Frederic. *Correspondence, etc.* 1823–1870. Egerton MSS. 2837–2848. *Notes for a History of the British Museum.* Add. MS. 38,971. *Journal.* 1837–1866.
  Panizzi, Sir Anthony. *Correspondence, etc.,* 1797–1877. Add. MSS. 36,714–36,729.
  Peel, Sir Robert. *Official Correspondence and Papers, etc.* Add. MSS. 40,181–40,617. [Details of letters, etc. relating specifically to the Museum are given in the Notes.]

DEPARTMENT OF PRINTED BOOKS.

Collections for a history of the Department of Printed Books. [A collection of manuscript and printed material formed by W. B. Rye.]

Draft Departmental Minutes, January 12, 1861, etc.

Edwards, Edward. *Manuscript Diary, 1844–1884.*

Miscellaneous Departmental Draft Reports, etc. April 2, 1856, etc.

Panizzi, Sir Anthony. *Official correspondence and papers.* 1837–1855. Together with a few additional papers, 1856–1866.

Register of persons employed each day in the removal of the Library and operations connected therewith. [From January 1, 1838.]

PARLIAMENTARY PAPERS, HOUSE OF COMMONS.

Report from the Select Committee appointed to inquire into the Plans and Estimates for the completion of the Buildings of the British Museum. [1838, vol. XXIII, p. 1.]

Representation from the Trustees of the British Museum . . . on the subject of an enlarged Scale of Expenditure for the Supply of Printed Books, etc. [1846, vol. XXV, p. 229.]

Memorial to the First Lord of the Treasury presented on 10 March 1847 by Members of the British Association for the Advancement of Science . . . regarding the Management of the British Museum. [1847, vol. XXXIV, p. 25.]

Report of the Commissioners appointed to inquire into the Constitution and Government of the British Museum. [1850, vol. XXIV, p. 1.]

Appendix to the Report, etc. [Not issued as a Parliamentary Paper.]

Communications . . . with reference to the Report of the Commissioners, etc. [1850, vol. XXXIII, p. 247.]

Communications . . . respecting the enlargement of the Building, etc. [1852, vol. XXVIII, p. 201.]

Report of the Keeper of Antiquities . . . on want of accommodation, etc. [1857–58, vol. XXXIV, p. 195.]

Communications as to Salaries, etc. [1860, vol. XXXIX, p. 209.]

Lighting by Gas, etc. [1861, vol. XXXIV, p. 225.]

[*Communications . . . respecting the want of space, etc.*] [1859, vol. XIV, p. 51; 1860, vol. XXXIXA, p. 265.]

[*Further communications.*] [1862, vol. XXIX, p. 169; 1864, vol. XXXII, p. 167.]

Report of the Select Committee on the British Museum, etc. [1860, vol. XVI, p. 173.]

Correspondence . . . respecting Examination of Candidates, etc. [1866, vol. XXXIX, p. 241.]

Details of other papers on the affairs of the Museum during this period will be found in *General Index to the Reports of the Select Committees, 1801–1852,* in *General Index to Accounts and Papers . . . 1801–1852* and in *General Alphabetical Index to the Bills . . . Accounts and Papers, etc. 1852–1899.*

B. Secondary Sources

BENTLEY'S MISCELLANY. 'The Reading Room of the British Museum'. Vol. 32, p. 527. London, 1852.

BRITISH MUSEUM. *Catalogue of the materials of the west end of the centre building of the old British Museum . . . which will be sold by auction . . . August 29th, 1843, etc.*

The Print Room of the British Museum. An enquiry by the ghost of a departed collector. [On the want of a proper catalogue of prints and drawings, together with a short history of the Department.] *Waterlow & Sons, London, 1876.*

Department of Western Asiatic Antiquities.
Layard and his Successors. Assyrian explorations and discovery in the XIXth century. [An exhibition catalogue.] [Lonon, 1963.]

British Quarterly Review. 'Catalogue of the Printed Books in the British Museum.' (A review of this and of other catalogues and papers referring to the Museum.) August–November 1847. vol. VI, no. XI. Art. III.

BUDGE, SIR ERNEST A. W. *Memoir of the late Samuel Birch . . . Remarks and Observations on Dr. Birch's Chinese Labours by Professor R. K. Douglas.* Harrison & Sons, London, 1887.

BUDGE, SIR ERNEST A. W. *Rise and Progress of Assyriology.* Martin Hopkinson & Co., London, 1925.

CLARKE, HENRY G. *The British Museum: its Antiquities and Natural History. A handbook for visitors.* H. G. Clarke & Co., London, 1848.

COLLIER, JOHN P. *A Letter to the Earl of Ellesmere on the subject of a new alphabetical catalogue of the printed books in the British Museum.* London, 1849.

COLLIER, JOHN P. *A supplementary letter . . . occasioned by certain interrogations of the Keeper of Printed Books, etc.* London, 1849.

COWTAN, ROBERT. *A Biographical Sketch of Sir Anthony Panizzi, etc.* Asher & Co., London, 1873.

COWTAN, ROBERT. *Memories of the British Museum.* R. Bentley & Son, London, 1872 [1871].

DALE, ANTHONY. *Fashionable Brighton. 1820–1860.* Country Life, London, 1947.

DANIEL, GLYN E. *A Hundred Years of Archaeology.* Duckworth, London, 1950.

FAGAN, LOUIS. *The Life of Sir Anthony Panizzi, KCB, etc.* Remington & Co., London, 1880.

FELLOWS, SIR CHARLES. *The Xanthian Marbles. Their Acquisition and Transmission to England.* Murray, London, 1843.

GARNETT, RICHARD. *Essays in Librarianship and Bibliography.* G. Allen, London, 1899.

GARNETT, RICHARD. *The late Sir Edward A. Bond.* In *Essays in Librarianship.* p. 335.

GARNETT, RICHARD. *The late Henry Stevens.* In *Essays in Librarianship.* p. 325.

GARNETT, RICHARD. *Sir Anthony Panizzi, KCB.* In *Essays in Librarianship.* p. 288.

GARNETT, RICHARD. *The late John Winter Jones, Principal Librarian of the British Museum.* Chiswick Press, London, 1884.

GLANVILLE, STEPHEN R. K. *The Growth and Nature of Egyptology, etc.* Cambridge University Press, Cambridge, 1947.

GRAY, JOHN E. *A Letter to the Earl of Ellesmere on the management of Printed Books in the British Museum.* London, 1849.

GRAY, JOHN E. *A Second Letter, etc.* London, 1849.

GREVILLE, CHARLES C. F. *The Greville Diary. . . .* Edited by P. W. Wilson, 2 vol. Heinemann, London, 1927.

HALEVY, ELIE. *The Age of Peel and Cobden. A History of the English People, 1841–1852.* Benn, London, 1947.

JONES, JOHN W. *A List of Books of Reference in the Reading Room of the British Museum.* [Edited, with a preface, by J. W. Jones.] London, 1859.

KUBIE, NORA B. *Road to Nineveh. The Adventures and Excavations of Sir Austen Henry Layard.* Cassel, London, 1965.

LAYARD, SIR HENRY A. *Nineveh and its Remains, etc.* 2 vol. Murray, London, 1849.

LLOYD, SETON. *Foundations in the Dust. A Story of Mesopotamian Exploration.* Oxford University Press, London, 1947.

MALOT, HECTOR. *La vie moderne en Angleterre.* Paris, 1862. [Compares the Reading Room of the British Museum with the Bibliothèque Impériale.]

MASSON, DAVID. *The British Museum: historical and descriptive.* W. & R. Chambers, Edinburgh, 1850.

MILLER, EDWARD J. *Prince of Librarians. The Life and Times of Antonio Panizzi, etc.* Deutsch, London, 1967.

MITCHELL, SIR PETER C. *Centenary History of the Zoological Society of London.* Zoological Society, London, 1929.

Museums Journal. 'The British Museum and British Antiquities.' [By Sir Thomas Kendrick] Vol. 51, no. 6, September 1951.

NICOLAS, SIR NICHOLAS H. *Animadversions on the Library and Catalogues of the British Museum. A reply to Mr. Panizzi's Statement, etc.* R. Bentley, London, 1846.

OWEN, SIR RICHARD. *On the Extent and Aims of a national museum of Natural History, etc.* Saunders, Otley & Co., London, 1862.

PANIZZI, SIR ANTHONY. *On the Supply of Printed Books from the Library to the Reading Room of the British Museum.* [Correspondence between Panizzi and Sir N. H. Nicolas.]

PANIZZI, SIR ANTHONY. *Passages in my Official Life.* [London, 1871.] A privately printed pamphlet not distributed until after Panizzi's death in 1879.

Quarterly Review. 'Report from the Select Committee, 1835.' (A review of this and subsequent Parliamentary Committees and Commissions and related documents.) Vol. 88, no. CLXXV. December 1850. Art. VI.

Quarterly Review. 'Observations on the British Museum' etc. (A review of various proposals for the rebuilding of the Museum.) Vol. 92, no. CLXXXIII. December 1852–March 1853. Art. VII.

SIMS, RICHARD. *Handbook to the Library of the British Museum, etc.* London 1854 [1853.]

VAUX, WILLIAM S. W. *Handbook to the Antiquities in the British Museum, etc.* John Murray, London, 1851.

WATERFIELD, GORDON. *Layard of Nineveh.* John Murray, London, 1963.

RETRENCHMENT AND REFORM

1866–1914

A. Primary Sources

BARWICK, GEORGE F. *Miscellaneous letters, etc. to G. F. Barwick relating to the British Museum from Sir Frederice Kenyon, Sir Edward Maude Thompson and others, 1891–1919.*

BRITISH MUSEUM. DEPARTMENT OF PRINTED BOOKS.
Draft Departmental Minutes, etc. January 12, 1861, etc.
Miscellaneous Departmental Drafts, Reports, etc. April 2, 1856, etc.

PARLIAMENTARY PAPERS, HOUSE OF COMMONS. *Bill intituled an Act to author-*

ize the Trustees of the British Museum to deposit copies of local newspapers with local auth-orities and to dispose of valueless printed matter. [1900, vol. 1, p. 195.]

Bill intituled an Act to enable the Trustees of the British Museum to remove certain newspapers . . . from the present British Museum Buildings. [1902, vol. 1, p. 115.]

B.   Secondary Sources

BRITISH MUSEUM. *The British Museum Reading Room, 1857–1957.* [An exhibition catalogue.] [London, 1957.]

The Print Room of the British Museum. An enquiry by the ghost of a departed collector. Waterlow, London, 1876. [On the want of a proper catalogue of prints and drawings, together with a short history of the department.]

Programme on the Opening of King Edward the Seventh's Galleries at the British Museum by His Majesty The King . . . 7th of May, 1914. [London, 1914.]

The Royal Gold Cup in the British Museum. London, 1924.

BUDGE, SIR ERNEST A. W. *Rise & Progress of Assyriology.* Martin Hopkinson & Co., London, 1925.

BUTLER, SAMUEL. *Samuel Butler's Notebooks.* Selections edited by G. Keynes and B. Hill] Cape, London, 1951.

CHAMPNEYS, BASIL. *Memoirs and correspondence of Coventry Patmore.* 2 vol. Bell, London, 1900.

CHARTERIS, EVAN. *The Life and Letters of Sir Edmund Gosse.* Heinemann, London, 1931.

DALTON, ORMONDE M. *Franks Bequest. The Treasure of the Oxus, with other objects from ancient Persia and India, etc.* Trustees of the British Museum, London, 1905.

DALTON, ORMONDE M. *Sir Hercules Read, 1857–1929.* H. Milford, London, [1930.]

GARNETT, RICHARD. [An account of his career at the British Museum.] Biographical Press Agency, [London, 1903.]

GARNETT, RICHARD. *Changes at the British Museum since 1877, etc.* Day & Son, London, 1887.

GARNETT, RICHARD. *Essays in Librarianship and Bibliography.* G. Allen, London, 1899.

GARNETT, RICHARD. *The British Museum Catalogue as the Basis of a Universal Catalogue.* In *Essays in Librarianship,* p. 109.

GARNETT, RICHARD. *On the System of Classifying Books on the Shelves followed at the British Museum.* In *Essays in Librarianship,* p. 210.

GARNETT, RICHARD. *The Late Sir Edward A. Bond.* In *Essays in Librarianship.* p. 335.

GARNETT, RICHARD. *The Late Henry Stevens.* In *Essays in Librarianship,* p. 325.

GARNETT, RICHARD. *The Past, Present and Future of the British Museum Catalogue.* In *Essays in Librarianship,* p. 87.

GARNETT, RICHARD. *The Sliding Press at the British Museum.* In *Essays in Librarianship,* p. 262.

GARNETT, RICHARD. *On the Printing of the British Museum Catalogue, etc.* [Cambridge, 1882.]

GARNETT, RICHARD. *The Late John Winter Jones.* Chiswick Press, London, 1884.

HILL, SIR GEORGE. *Ormonde Maddock Dalton, 1866–1945.* H. Milford, London, [1945.]

HILL, SIR GEORGE. *Percy Gardner, 1846–1937.* H. Milford, London, 1938.

KENYON, SIR FREDERIC G. *Arthur Hamilton Smith, 1860–1941.* H. Milford, London, 1943.

KENYON, SIR FREDERIC G. *Sir Edward Maunde Thompson, 1840–1929.* H. Milford, London, [1930.]

KENYON, SIR FREDERIC G. *Sir George Warner, 1845–1936.* H. Milford, London, [1936.]

LLOYD, SETON. *Foundations in the Dust. A Story of Mesopotamian Exploration.* Oxford University Press, London, 1947.

NESBIT, E. *The Story of the Amulet.* T. Fisher Unwin, London, 1906.

NEWBOLT, SIR HENRY. *My World as in My Time. Memoirs.* Faber, 1932.

NICHOLS, THOMAS. *A Handbook for Readers at the British Museum.* London, 1866.

PETRIE, SIR WILLIAM M. F. *Seventy Years in Archaeology.* Sampson, Low Marston & Co., London, [1931.]

READ, SIR CHARLES H. *Sir Charles Hercules Read. A tribute to his retirement, etc.* London, 1921.

TWO WORLD WARS AND AFTER

1914–1971

A. Primary Sources

PARLIAMENTARY PAPERS, HOUSE OF COMMONS.
  Royal Commission on National Museums and Art Galleries. Interim Report. [1928–29, vol. I, VIII, p. 699. Cmd. 3192.]
  Final Report. Pt. I. General Conclusions and Recommendations. [1929–30, vol. XVI, p. 341. Cmd. 3463.]
  Final Report. Pt. II. Conclusions and Recommendations relating to Individual Institutions. [1929–30, vol. XVI, p. 525. Cmd. 3463.]
  Report of the National Libraries Committee. London, 1969. [Cmd. 4028.]
  The British Library. London, 1971. [Cmd. 4572.]
ROYAL COMMISSION ON NATIONAL MUSEUMS AND ART GALLERIES.
  Oral Evidence, Memoranda and Appendices to the Interim (Final) Report. 2 pt. London, 1928, 1929.

B. Secondary Sources

BELL, SIR HAROLD I. *Sir Frederick G. Kenyon. 1863–1952.* London, 1954.

BRITISH MUSEUM. *Air Raid Precautions in Museums, Picture Galleries and Libraries.* [London,] 1939.

BRITISH MUSEUM. *A Short Guide to the Temporary War-time exhibition in the British Museum.* London, 1918.

BRITISH MUSEUM. *Statutes and Rules, etc.* London, 1932.

BRITISH MUSEUM. DEPARTMENT OF MANUSCRIPTS. *The Mount Sinai Manuscript of the Bible, etc.* London, 1934.

DEPARTMENT OF BRITISH AND MEDIEVAL ANTIQUITIES.

The Sutton Hoo Ship Burial. A provisional guide (Fifth impression). London, 1956.

The Sutton Hoo Ship Burial. A handbook. New edition, London, 1968.

KENYON, SIR FREDERIC. *The British Museum in War Time, etc.* Johnson, Wylie & Co., Glasgow, 1934.

Index